PRAISE FOR *THE LAND REMEMBERS US*

This luminous volume is filled with myth and story tied to the land and Her deepest embedded wisdom and mysteries. This vibrant, interdisciplinary weave of women's voices provides intimate and scholarly insights on how the Divine Feminine can help us heal ourselves and Mother Earth and provides the tools to do so. What does it mean to know a place? What can the land teach us about ourselves? Why is honoring wildness so essential to our well-being? How can we live more ethically, supporting diversity and social justice in these troubled times? How can we nourish our collective spirit? What can myth and bone teach us about these vital topics? And how do these conversations fit within an academic environment and within a global community? These beautiful essays will inspire, educate, and bring about much healing.

—Dr Cristina Eisenberg, *The Wolf's Tooth* and *The Carnivore Way*

Before modern mobility, many human groups were so strongly rooted that local places appeared numinous and sacred, with strong emotional ties that affected people's lives for generations. How can we, taught to depend on the unemotional methods of science, approach a topic so saturated with human emotion? Each essay here tries it differently, for different cultures, while the first essay tackles the problem itself head-on.

—Elizabeth Wayland Barber, *The Dancing Goddesses*

The Land Remembers Us is a valuable contribution to the literature of place, the earth and the sacred. Each piece is a well-researched and -documented writing on the importance of spirit and divinity, along with protection and centrality of relationships with the earth, that has been obscured by modern times and even during much of recorded history. This volume testifies to the development of the Association for the Study for Women and Mythology (ASWM) to bring these areas to the academy and bring rigor to the research and writing on the topics so that they cannot be ignored or diminished.

This was the aim of my late wife, Patricia Monaghan, in helping to found ASWM and this shows that the goal is being reached and exceeded. Each piece shows the research, insight and wisdom that ASWM intended.

—Michael McDermott, MD, co-founder with Patricia Monaghan and director of the Black Earth Institute

Throughout this anthology, essayists write of the human/more-than-human connection, especially a heart connection with places in the world landscape. The second essay, written some years ago by one of the founders of ASWM, Patricia Monaghan, tells us that this connection creates a "biodiversity of the spirit," as opposed to a "monoculture of the spirit." Just as we need a biodiversity of flora and fauna for a healthy ecosystem, so each of us needs a biodiversity of spiritual relationships in order to be in spiritual balance. And Vicki Noble beautifully describes how she found the Goddess in a wonderful modern festival of a saint in Abruzzo, Italy.

The final essay, by Judy Grahn, similarly exhorts us to interact personally with "wind and water, fire and mountain and lights in the sky," with forms in nature large and microscopic. Indeed, all forms of life are forms of the Divine.

This collection of essays contains some poignant explanations of the multifold ways our spirits can connect to the intelligences of the land, the plants, the animals, the cells, and to the spiritual energies on our wonderfully diverse planet.

—Miriam Robbins Dexter, *Whence the Goddesses: A Source Book*; *Sacred Display: Divine and Magical Female Figures of Eurasia* (with Victor H. Mair); and *Foremothers of the Women's Spirituality Movement: Elders and Visionaries* (with Vicki Noble)

From the earliest awakenings of the Women's Spirituality movement, our yearning to know about women's sacred engagements with nature through the ages was inherent. This collection of insightful articles brings so much to fruition -- with concepts such as Gaian epistemology, language of animacy, women's weaving as sacred transformations with nature, and much more. It enlarges the scholarship of cultural history by way of laying out a grand banquet.

—Charlene Spretnak, *Lost Goddesses of Early Greece*

THE LAND REMEMBERS US
Women, Myth and Nature

PROCEEDINGS OF THE ASSOCIATION
FOR THE STUDY OF WOMEN AND MYTHOLOGY
VOLUME 3

Edited by
Mary Jo Neitz and Sid Reger

Printed in the United States of America
ISBN: 978-1-7333866-2-3

Published by

Women and Myth Press
PO Box 150018, Van Brunt Station, Brooklyn, NY 11215
www.womenandmyth.org

Interior and cover designed by Rebekkah Dreskin ~ www.blameitonrebekkah.com
Front cover art "Bee Goddess of Rhodes Banner" by Lydia Ruyle
Bee goddess logo by Sid Reger

A version of "An Ancient Festival Embraces a Modern Miracle," by Vicki Noble, was previously published in the *Journal of Archaeomythology*, Vol. 10, Winter 2020.

DEDICATION

We dedicate this volume to Rachel Carson, whose clear voice first awakened a nation to the threats of environmental pollution. Her writing continues to inspire generations of scientists, writers, and students of nature. She said, "Those who contemplate the beauty of the earth find reserves of strength that will endure as long as life lasts." May all who continue the fight for a healthy planet be strengthened by her work.

CONTENTS

FOREWORD

This is the third volume of proceedings by the Association for the Study of Women and Mythology (ASWM) from ASWM's biennial conferences. One of its founders, Patricia Monaghan, was my colleague, friend and mentor. She invited me into the organization almost two decades ago, as a newly minted PhD. At that time, I was struggling to navigate the maze and hazing of academic life, tenure requirements, and a system designed to perpetuate the patriarchal, dominant Anglo-Western view of what constitutes knowledge and rigorous scholarship. This worldview, and that of the traditional academy, is in sharp contrast to my own, in that it has often devalued the feminine, intuitive, emotional and spiritual connections we have with non-human animals and the natural world. In ASWM conferences, I found an exciting, diverse, collective community of scholarship and practice with other new scholars as well as those with decades of experience. These scholars, in one way or another, have all contributed to shaping my thinking and approach to research and what constitutes wisdom and knowledge.

When considering land and place, there is an interaction between a person's inner reality and outer reality that comes into play when one lives in a place for an extended period of time. The physical makeup and the human psyche are formed in direct ways by the distinct climate, soil, geography and living beings of a place. People make a place as much as a place makes them. People who are *indigenous* to a place, or have deep, long roots, have interacted with the places in which they and their ancestors lived so intimately that the landscape has become a reflection of their souls. This mindset is particularly challenging for modern people who are highly migratory, and this in part explains the ignorance and insensitivity of governments to the world's indigenous peoples, for whom the deep sacredness of water and land is a central value and identity construct. Additionally, it explains, in part, horrific treatment of non-human animals as "things" rather than living, sentient beings.

The land and soil hold the dust of the bones of our ancestors. Author Salmon Rushdie has remarked that, as highly migratory people, we are a new type of human being rooted in ideas rather than the sacredness of place. He has noted that people tied to a local mindset of ideas may be more prone to nationalism and racism and less open to the "other."

So, what of the migratory people and scholars among them who find themselves deeply connected to a land or place *not* of their ancestry? I believe we can follow the stories and myths as pathways to the root systems of a particular place. The land, and hence nature, *holds* and remembers the events, peoples and stories, and in the right frame of mind and openness, I believe these can be accessed as a part of our collective human ecological knowledge through deep time.

The frame of mind that allows access to the knowledge and memories held in a place are in our *metaphoric* mind or "nature mind" as some Native scholars have called it. The metaphoric mind is our oldest mind and has been developing for about three million years. Its time of greatest development occurred during the Paleolithic era about 70,000 years ago. From an evolutionary perspective, the development of the human mind parallels human development and the metaphoric mind in individuals develops from birth until the development of language. As language and the rational mind develop, the holistic experience of the metaphoric mind recedes into the subconscious, but it can still be called on or accessed during dreams, dance, creative states, rituals, spiritual experiences, and through connections with non-human animals and nature.

Metaphoric mind processes are tied to creativity, perception, images, physical senses and intuition, and the metaphoric mind reveals itself through abstract symbols, sound, art, music, dance and myth. As the rational mind develops further and language becomes literacy, the metaphoric mind becomes significantly differentiated from the rational mind, particularly in our Western social and educational conditioning. The works of Bob Samples and Robert Ornstein suggest that there is clear psychological evidence that left-brain activity is distinct from right-brain activity and that Western educational systems and science have primarily focused on left-brain functioning such as linear thinking and language. Metaphoric, symbolic perception and intuitive right-brain activity have been neglected.

The ability to retain and access our more ancient metaphoric mind may provide us meaning and reconnect us to the sacredness of place, the natural world and our deeper human intellectual legacy.

The role of affective, or feeling, elements in the creation of knowledge is another key component of the work represented here. Feeling and experiencing communal relationships through artistic and mythical dimensions, ritual and ceremony, sacred ecology and psychological and spiritual orientation is the only viable way to acquire wisdom and knowledge. Unlike the *non-feeling*, rational or linear dimension of traditional Western academic approaches, these affective elements are not easily quantifiable, observable or verbalized. This explains why the type of work ASWM scholars do is often misunderstood or ignored by mainstream academia. In 2013, I had the honor of presenting a keynote address on the sacredness of place at the ASWM conference in Minnesota. One of the major points I wanted to make to my colleagues was that if the mainstream ignores or misunderstands your work it may be a positive sign! It means that, most likely, your work is connected to our metaphoric more ancient mind and traditional ecological knowledge.

This volume focuses on our *relationships* with the natural world and non-human animals. It is a collection of knowledge and wisdom that has been preserved in places, in the land structures themselves through deep time. We have never needed to remember and access this wisdom more. Particularly in the United States, there seems to be a backlash against much of the progress made over the last several decades with regard to repairing and rebalancing our relationships with the earth and the sacred feminine. These scholars represent many disciplines and approaches to the creation of knowledge—essential *human* knowledge—that has trickled down or bubbled up from deep within places despite attempts to eradicate, stomp, bulldoze, build or burn it out of existence. *The land always remembers* and through the good work here, our readers will have access to this knowledge as well.

~ Arieahn Matamonasa Bennett
Chicago, IL
2019

INTRODUCTION

The Land Remembers Us: Women, Myth and Nature
Volume 3, Proceedings of the Association for the Study of Women and Mythology

W̶e are fortunate to remember lands of our birth and family; we may have been told tales of places that were significant generations ago. But is it possible that the land also remembers us? The prevailing paradigm in Western cultures emphasizes human action and agency in our interactions with nature. What happens when we instead consider that our relationships with nature and place may be less about domination and more about reciprocity?

In this, the third volume of proceedings from the Association for the Study of Women and Mythology (ASWM) biennial conferences, we offer writings by an array of scholars whose work addresses many facets of this question. We are happy to present in this volume articles by some of the founders of our field, as well as work by new scholars publishing for the first time. Our events draw scholars from many disciplines, using a variety of methods. Many authors explicitly draw on their own personal experiences and intuitions, working their own discoveries and emotional responses into their texts. All are passionate about the work that they do.

For this volume we have selected articles that inquire into place-based traditions and other cultures' ways of interaction with the non-human environment, including landscapes, plants and animals. Local traditions and stories are fundamental to the history of women's practice and goddess scholarship. One purpose of this volume is to collect and record knowledge of these practices. Another purpose of this volume is to be self-conscious about methodology and to share not only what we know, but how we know.

This scholarly work is a facet of a bigger project of recovering alternative, non-dominating ways of living on the earth. We hope reading this book is a journey for the readers, enabling opportunities to visit places both familiar and far away. It is also a journey inward and outward.

The first three chapters address issues of methodology and epistemology. All three also exemplify, in different ways, research that is located in place. Researchers present themselves as embodied, present and engaged researchers. They are neither value-free nor neutral; rather they are interested: they care deeply about pursuing research that preserves nearly forgotten traditions and ways of seeing.

We open this book with Dawn Work-Makinne's chapter, "Seeking the Witches' Chairs: Identity and Reflexivity in Scholarship of Place," which addresses the question, "How do you include a sacred place, stories collected about that place and the people telling about the place in the research process?" Her essay introduces the concepts from feminist methodology of partial truth and reflexivity. Her research process takes into account her own role as a researcher, what some folklorists and interpretive social science traditions call using the self as an instrument in the research outcome, resulting in an account that is "true, but also partial, reflecting the person who is writing the account." Work-Makinne's research on the Schlern witches in the Tyrolean Alps incorporates her subjective experience of her encounter with the land itself. Her essay emphasizes the importance of situated embodied knowledge in which the place and the person in the place come together. The reader travels with Work-Makinne as she hikes through the forest, armed with a little history and local legends. There, as she is searching for the witches' chair, she encounters the uncanny rock with its strange barred entrance. Work-Makinne's experience of the Schlern as a holy site came at the beginning of her research project. In this essay, written at a later date, she grapples with the complicated history of the folklore, including its appropriation by the Nazis and her own quest for identity as a German American studying Germanic Europe probing her relation to her "tribe." Work-Makinne's essay is a perfect entry point for this volume as it raises so many important questions. Other essays pick up and elaborate these threads.

In her essay, "Losing Theodiversity: The Erasure of the Cannibal Hag in Ireland," Pat Monaghan continues our examination of the connection between place and the sacred, the significance of local sites, and the question of European indigenous religions in the context of globalizing Christianity. Monaghan takes us to County Clare, Ireland, where we consider a small mountain, Sliabh Echtge, and its once vast oak forests. Starting with a discussion of changing forestry practices and their connection to colonialism and capitalism, Monaghan presents a story of ecological decline. Her rich description of the once biodiverse forest evokes a powerful sense of place. She connects a story of exploitation of the land to the loss of the goddess. Monaghan finds traces of Echtge's story in ancient sources, as well as the reconstructions of Lady Gregory and Yeats, but for today's residents, Echtge has nearly vanished, existing only as "the cannibal hag of the mountain" that some of the oldest residents remember from their mothers' threats. This chapter offers the concept of *theodiversity* as a way to value these minor divinities of place. Drawing on Aldo Leopold's work on the importance of biodiversity, Monaghan argues that, likewise, something important is lost with the erasure of these place-based divinities. With the dominance of world religions and their abstract divinities, the appreciation of the local disappears. We do not even see it. We may not immediately perceive that we have lost something, but Monaghan insists that knowledge of these divinities and the lore that exists around them is world creating, fostering qualities of intimacy and uniqueness: hence, the loss is significant.

Marna Hauk's chapter, "'WWGD—What Would Gaia Do?' Gaian Methods: Researching as Earth–Planetary Qualitative Methods," offers a framework for thinking about qualitative methods in new ways, starting with the assumption that our position as part of Earth affects our research. Hauk claims that Gaian methods entail a multisensory approach, bringing to consciousness and embracing all the ways that our embodiment in a time and place is consequential for the research we do. Hauk thereby extends feminist positionality and complexity's effects on research. Hauk takes the space in her text to plant herself: we see her living in the Pacific Northwest, at the edge of a rainforest volcano where two rivers join and enter the Pacific Ocean. Gaian methods based in Gaian theory (drawing on Lynn Margolis and James Lovelock) take as the starting point the idea that Earth is a living and self-regulating system. Hauk presents the four directives of Gaian research methods: (1) connect and collaborate with humans and the more-than-human as a researcher; (2) embed and embody the researcher, including experiences of multisensory embodiment as data; (3) extend and extol with the research attending to emergent effects of Gaia as a living system; and (4) thrum and thrive, as the research is generative and life giving. Hauk unpacks these four directives for the reader and points to connections with other research traditions in qualitative methodologies. Critical place inquiry and indigenous critical place Inquiry provide examples of attending to place and relationship. Hauk also points to the "scale-jumping leap" of "attending to planetary emergence." Finally, Hauk addresses the question of quality standards for Gaian research. She suggests substituting the idea of "litheness" for the more conventional standard of "rigor."

Following these three chapters that explicitly raise epistemological issues are chapters focused on the significance of a particular site. Anne Key and Candace Kant's chapter, "Sacred Land In the Midst of Modernity: The Temple of Goddess Spirituality Dedicated to Sekhmet," takes us to the Nevada desert, an hour's drive from Las Vegas. There, next to Creech Air Force Base and bombing range, and residing on native lands is the temple where Key and Kant have served as priestesses. In their chapter they report on visitors' experiences of this sacred site. They define a sacred site as a place where the divine and human intersect. The energy of the place itself is compounded by the activities occurring there, all with their own emotional and spiritual intents. Key and Kent use two sources of written information. The first comprises unprompted comments written in guest books left on the temple grounds for visitors to record their thoughts. The second is an Internet survey posted in 2007 that resulted in 118 useable responses. Key and Kant suggest that the many ironies of the temple's location contribute to the liminality that visitors experience. Dominant strands of rationalist, secular Western thought deny the idea of sacred land, but the temple offers an opportunity for individuals to connect with the land in multiple and profound ways. Key and Kant end with a call for people to recognize the importance of sacred lands as a route to transformation. Their chapter draws strongly on a sense of place, illuminating the interactions between the visitors and the land. Key and Kant succeed in capturing the kind of embodied knowledge basic to the sort of transformations they see as central to the work of the temple.

Mara Lynn Keller's chapter, "Divine Mistress of Nature, Plants and Animals in Ancient Greece: An Ecofeminist Perspective," uses the methodology of archaeomythology to read goddess symbols created in ancient times, and draws on ecofeminist perspectives to draw connections

4

between these ancient images and the current climate crisis. Keller's hope is that people today can draw on these ancient peoples' connections with nature to inspire the wisdom we need to respond to the challenges of climate change. She traces the deterioration of the image of the Great Mother in the European record from the Bronze Age to the Classical Age as patriarchal clans gained dominance. Yet she suggests that the older images and meanings are still there for us to draw upon in our efforts to create a more just and equal society, one that celebrates ways of life that are nature embedded and embodied.

Idoia Arana-Beobide's chapter, "Mari—The Power of Feminine Immanence in the Basque Belief System," engages with a similar theme, speaking to the ways that ancient goddess traditions help people today connect to nature and a more embodied way of being. She takes us to Basque country in northern Spain and southwestern France, to introduce a goddess whose name may be less well known. Mari, the Great Basque Goddess, can be traced back to indigenous peoples of pre-Indo European culture. Arana-Beobide sketches her characteristics: Mari is multifaceted, an ever-cyclical and regenerating force of nature, and connected to the natural environment. Arana-Beobide presents Mari as a goddess of immanence, a pervasive, ever-present matriarchal force. She draws from research about animism in other indigenous cultures, especially in North America, to understand the holistic character of indigenous worldviews. She argues that the traces of beliefs and practices relating to Mari and her presence are part of a layering of animistic, Indo-European, Christian and historical/secular strata that contributes to Basque culture's continuing survival in the world today.

Mary Louise Stone's chapter, "Pachamama and Living Landscape Sites in the Andes," continues the examination of the relation between the presence of place-based mother goddesses and understandings of immanence. Stone focuses on Pachamama, a mother goddess found in the Andean regions around Cusco and Lake Titiqaqa. In this well-researched piece, Stone draws on several different kinds of data. She compares contemporary communities where she has lived and conducted research with descriptions of the same or similar sites in pre-Inka and Inka times from the records of Spanish invaders in the 1500s and 1600s. Stone's research process involves collaborating with local women, experts in their culture. Stone shows that beliefs and practices around Pachamama are parts of a vital, practiced worldview that is continuous with practice prior to the European conquest. Stone's careful writing elaborates the lived experience of particular earth forms, known to local humans as a vital presence, interacting with humans in reciprocal relationships. Stone argues that in the relationship between Pachamama, the people and the land, there is no room for a creator god; rather the emphasis is on emergence, giving birth and in death returning to the land.

Susan Moulton's chapter, "Unsaddling the Past: The Central Role of the Lead Female in Animal Herds—A Model for Paleolithic Human Culture," shifts our attention to the relationship between humans and animals in the Paleolithic past. Moulton analyzes the depictions of animals—horses, cave bears and cave lions—and their relations with humans in the cave paintings from Chauvet in Dordogne Valley in southern France, executed between 38,000 and 17,000 BCE. She argues that these very early paintings depict collaborative interactions between humans and animals, who would have at times cohabited in the caves. She reads the paintings as providing evidence that humans learned skills for survival from the animals, especially the horse herds, who, Moulton argues, are depicted in the paintings as possessing a complex consciousness. Moulton borrows the concept of animacy from the work of Robin Kimmerer, defined as a "visual communication of intentionality shared by herd animals and by humans when the human ego ceases to obscure perception." In this view, animals, including humans, practiced a multisensory awareness of their environment and communicated with each other through visual cues as well as sound and scent. She suggests that humans observed and learned from the patterns of female leadership and the division of labor among the horses in herds. Based in current scholarship, Moulton's interpretations of the paintings as executed by women, and presenting both humans and animals as living in matrifocal and gynocentric groups, differs from previously established views. Understanding the paintings has an importance beyond the scholarly; it contributes to the work of imagining alternative ways that humans can live in harmony with the Earth.

Mary Beth Moser's chapter, "Submerged Spirituality in the Italian Alps: Goddesses, Ancestresses and Women's Ritual in the Archaeological Record," takes us to Valle Camonica, Lombardy, in the Italian Alps. There, more than 300,000 engravings were carved in the rock of the mountainside over thousands of years, from the fifth millennium BCE to the Christian era. Moser examines the archaeological record for evidence of female goddess imagery and women's spiritual agency. She cites oral tradition and place names as offering significant evidence. Moser describes cup marks carved into the rock, carved standing stones (steles), and rock slides (fertility rocks). She suggests that all these artifacts are connected to the everyday spirituality of women in this region. She documents the overlaying of traditions at spiritual sites, with pagan sites rededicated to Roman goddesses, only to be covered by Christian churches. Moser argues that this demonstrates the importance and continuity of sacred places for women's spiritual agency.

Margaret Lynn Mitchell's chapter, "Seeking Sanctuary with Saint Brigid of Ireland: A Harbor of Sacred Female Divinity," takes us to Ireland to explore the legend of Brigid. Mitchell draws upon a number of feminist research tools including feminist cultural history, archaeomythology, modern matriarchal studies, women's sacred arts and mysteries, folklore, and Irish cultural and religious studies, to reconstruct a story of Brigid and her relationship to the Irish landscape with its particular ancient stones and holy wells. Mitchell presents her own journey in Ireland to recover and experience the life of Brigid. Mitchell also discusses three sets of practices honoring Brigid that have continued to this day—those of the woven-straw Brigid crosses, the protection of Brigid's girdle and the legend of Brigid's cloak. In performing this feminist reconstruction, Mitchell participates in the life and legend of Brigid.

Kristen K. Calvert's chapter, "The Symbolic Role of String," weaves together examples from many cultures to document how string and related crafts, including spinning, weaving and embroidery, have associations with women's bodies and their connections to nature. She cites the embroideries of Hmong women and the weaving of Mayan women, Navajo/Dine women and Christian women weavers. Calvert suggests that weaving may be another example of biomimicry wherein humans learned about weaving from watching spiders spinning webs. In the chapter Calvert draws many connections between the art of weaving and women's biology, bleeding during menstruation and giving birth. She suggests that in many cultures, women regard the act of creating textiles as analogous to giving birth. For Calvert, connections point to the web, through which all women are connected to each other and to nature.

In Barbara C. Daughter's chapter, "What's Place Got to Do with It? A Non-Indigenous Woman's Search for Place Wisdom," Daughter reflects on her own relationship to place and ponders the question of what makes land sacred *for her*. The essay is framed by her questions about how she can be authentic and respectful in relation to various places in her life and to the indigenous people who inhabit(ed) them. She begins with childhood memories of relation to place, and then takes the reader to places where her personal biography might suggest she would find a connection (but it is not there) and to places where the connection was unanticipated but is strong. She journeys from Massachusetts to Minnesota, and Magdalene Island in Lake Superior. There are side trips to Visby in Gotland (Denmark) and a goddess voyage to Crete. She also experienced strong feelings of connection to the Hawaiian goddess Pele and her land. In each place Daughter considers her own emotional responses to the landscape, while at the same time reflecting on the first people who live(d) there and the ethical issues of her relationship to them. She ends her reflection both honoring ancestral connections to land and also arguing that others who lack that ancestral tie can choose to honor a place and see it as sacred.

Denise Mitten's chapter, "Wild Women on the Move: Understanding an Ethic of Earth Care through an Artemis Lens," draws on Mitten's many years as a wilderness educator to show the benefits of spending time outdoors. Drawing inspiration from the legends of Artemis as well as contemporary psychological theory, Mitten crafts a model for women's outdoor adventures as healing for women and the land. She reports on studies showing that participants in such activities developed more positive body images and feelings of empowerment. Mitten suggests these outdoor trips both reflect and help to (re)produce an ethic of care, as described by philosopher Nel Noddings. Mitten extends the idea of the ethic of care beyond the human to include the more-than-human as part of the larger community. Mitten argues that many people living today do not experience attachment to nature; however, a positive relationship, such as one modeled by Artemis, can be developed through experiences of nature, enabling women to develop spiritual bonds with the more-than-human.

In another exploration of contemporary women and their relationships with nature, Noël Cox Caniglia's chapter, "Crones of Gaia: An Ecocentric Perspective of Being on the Land," is an ethnographic study of female ranchers in the American Southwest. All of these women, aged 69 to 88, had a minimum of 25 years on their land. Although they would not describe themselves as ecofeminists, Cox Caniglia sees in their words and practices an earth-centered, feminist perspective that she identifies as *Gaia consciousness*. Cox Caniglia herself is a both an insider (having lived and worked on a ranch) and an outsider (now a researcher who also works in academia) with unique access to these elders and her own perspective based on life experience and formal training. This essay explores the women ranchers' connections with the more-than-human natural environment, and the deep understandings they have developed over lifetimes of living in close connection to the land and its inhabitants. It also counters the prevailing stereotypes and marginalization of older women in American society by presenting these women as strong, engaged, and vibrant embedded in place.

Vicki Noble's chapter, "An Ancient Festival Embraces a Modern Miracle," takes us to Abruzzo in Italy, near the Adriatic Sea. She documents the contemporary, local celebration of the Feast of Santa Gemma. Using the methods of archaeomythology, she traces motifs that are found throughout the Mediterranean region in ancient and Classical times, going back as far as the Neolithic period. There are several slightly different accounts of the 14th-century saint in whose honor the women of the village gather to bake bread, which is blessed and distributed the next day. Noble connects these rituals to very early and widespread rituals around breadmaking and grain. In the work of Marija Gimbutas, such rituals were connected to the Neolithic pregnant goddess who was often split into a mother–daughter pair symbolizing the spring renewal and fall parting. Noble notes that spring renewal and the symbolic return of a daughter to her mother are enacted during the main pageant of Santa Gemma's feast day. Like Mary Beth Moser's earlier chapter from further north in the Italian Alps, Noble traces an astonishing continuity of symbols from ancient traces through classical times to the present.

Monica Mody's chapter, "Serpent, Earth, Healing, Initiation," begins in her family's compound in Bangalore, India where Mody first encounters Nagadevi, and is called to explore the sacred energies of the serpent goddess. In a subsequent visit to Mannarasala Temple in Kerala, India presided over by Nagaraja, the king of the serpents, Mody relates feeling alienated in the patriarchal Brahminic culture of the temple, but still she continued to seek out the Serpent Path. Mody connects with Gloria Anzuldua's term, "spiritual mestizaje," as she joins with Anzaldua in "the quickening serpent movement" of transformation involved in bringing two cultures together. The last place Mody takes us in her chapter is San Francisco's Golden Gate Park where, shortly after the emergence of the

"MeToo" movement, she made an offering and asked the serpent spirits for knowledge about healing the traumas of living in the patriarchy. Mody closes with Daniel Siegel's research on interpersonal neurobiology to suggest how remembering can change the past and the future. Her chapter uses an innovative combination of personal reflection, poetry, and critical scholarship, each expressing different kinds of knowledge in a border-crossing presentation. For Mody the energy of the serpent offers an initiation, a different way of knowing and thinking about ourselves and our relation to the earth, the past and the future.

The closing chapter departs from these place-based studies with a call for a basic epistemological shift in the Goddess movement. Judy Grahn's chapter, "Goddess Is Alive! But How Do We Know?," asks for a rapprochement between the Goddess movement and science. While acknowledging the history of the long-standing rift between science and religion, she challenges readers to rethink our relationship to science in new ways. She responds to feminist science scholar Donna Harraway's quip that she would "rather be a cyborg than a goddess" with a claim that the goddess has always been a cyborg, incorporating the science of the time, through metaphors, stories and practices. She asks us to see how we can connect better with the science of our time, ending with her own exploration of new scientific work on microbiota, and a serious and playful discussion of this interconnected matrix of life as goddess.

Each chapter contributes to our understandings of myth, place and nature. Taken together these chapters stand as a testament to the robust scholarship in the field. We also celebrate the passion of the scholars and their bravery and perseverance in pursuing this work, which often challenges established knowledge and ways of knowing. We hope that readers will find enrichment here for their minds and spirits, and tools for living on the Earth in these perilous times.

SEEKING THE WITCHES' CHAIRS: IDENTITY AND REFLEXIVITY IN SCHOLARSHIP OF PLACE

DAWN E. WORK-MAKINNE

I conducted one of my first research trips without having any idea that I was *on* a research trip. I was spending a couple of weeks in the Italian Alps, in a stunningly beautiful location under a mountain known as the Schlern Massif. I barely understood the history of the area. I didn't know that the land had been part of Austria until World War I. Locals spoke both German and Italian, although the elders spoke mostly German. Tyrolean customs abounded and they were tied to the fabulous landscape. Stories told of *die Schlernhexen*, the Schlern witches, riding around the mountaintop by the thousands, making good and bad weather—mostly bad—lighting fires and dancing wildly under the full moon. I was newly embarked on my Ph.D., studying the Germanic goddesses. And though I arrived on Air Lufthansa and not on a broom, I accidentally arrived in an area full of Germanic witches and the memory of the goddesses. Perhaps some scholars become accustomed to wanton and lavish synchronicities as part of the research process, but I must confess that I never have.

The stories of the *Schlernhexen* are rooted in the landscape, especially the Schlern herself. Stories of witches flying around a sacred mountain are known throughout German lands. My quest was more confined and local: after starting to immerse myself in the lore of the area, I set out to find the *Hexenstühle*, the Witches' Chairs, giant and ancient stone seats hidden deep in the forest. I got some directions at the local tourist office and took off up the path that I could see outside my window. I was blissfully unaware that I was on the wrong mountainside. I hiked about a mile, and came to a pretty little lake, the Völser Weiher. I took pictures, and bravely asked

11

other hikers if they knew the way to the *Hexenstühle*. No one did. I finally got an idea from some passersby and took one of the trails on past the lake. It was not too far down the trail that I ran into the stone.

I did not think the giant stone I was looking at was actually the *Hexenstühle*, and I had no other notion of what it was. It had to have been twice my height, and at least that wide, and had a doorway that was barred closed with sticks (Fig. 1). It didn't look like the sticks were put there by any official agency. Part of me wanted to crawl in and see if the stone's interior felt as womblike as it looked. But I was all alone in the woods at the stone. I didn't end up violating the barrier of the sticks. The place felt uncanny, even in the bright sunlight of 2003. Two years later, I found the legend belonging to the stone, called, "The Witches' Revenge."

Not far from Völs, in the midst of the wood, is a beautiful place the witches had made their own. One summer evening, the priest from Völs took a walk in this wood, trying to find cool relief; he lay down in the soft grass and fell asleep. When he awoke, it was pitch-black night, and he couldn't find his way out of the wood. He decided to spend the night in the forest, and concealed himself in the bushes near a large stone. The woods were not reputed to be haunted, but he was still afraid. Though he didn't know it, he was very close to the *Hexenplatz*, the witches' meeting place. He hadn't been there long when he heard loud laughter in the distance. The voices came nearer. Finally the voices came right where the clergyman lay. He saw how they kindled a fire and danced in celebration. Suddenly the witches sprang into the bushes where the clergyman lay and abused him cruelly to his death. Not long after nightfall, the alarm bells of Völs rang out; the priest had not come home. The people sought him, taking torches and lanterns into the wood; they searched far and wide but could not find him. Then as day dawned, they reached the place in the bushes where he had rested. They found him lying dead on the ground, his hair pulled out and his entire body cut into pieces. His clothes lay in shreds, ragged and strewn about. This priest had, from time to time, spoiled the witches' weather-making with his holiness. The witches had taken their revenge.[1]

Between 1506 and 1510, the people in this idyllic village killed nine women as witches. At the trial, the women reported participating in ecstatic rituals during their nocturnal gatherings. One of the women, Anna Jobstin, experienced herself as "Queen of the Angels" and the other women in the group agreed. Frau Jobstin was a beautifully crowned and robed Queen,

Fig. 1. Sticks barring the doorway to the stone at Völser Lake. Photograph by author, 2003.

while the figure noted in the trial records as "the Devil" was sensed by the women as a "King of the Angels." Such ecstatic ritual experience is described by Ginzburg in his book *Ecstasies: Deciphering the Witches' Sabbath.*[2] Many historical Italian documents describe folk beliefs such as night flying, especially on Thursdays; the use of brooms, herbs or ointments; and following a goddess, to guarantee, appease and draw upon the forces of life. The women of Völs, on their sacred Schlern Mountain, found such ecstasies long ago.

What is the scholar to do with the evidence of landscape in research? How can a place be a partner in ecstasy? How is a hike to be theorized? How does one manage the strong pull to landscape and legend that a scholar can feel if she is, rightly or wrongly, seeking her own identity in the search? We are all, as Arieahn Matamanosa has said, tribal people.[3] As a German-American studying Germanic Europe, the issue of my own tribe looms large. Landscape is a partner in this type of research, and a living one (Fig. 2). The parameters of research become *experiential* and *embodied.*

American Academy of Religion president Vasudha Narayanan announced it loudly in her presidential address: embodiment is the site of our cosmology and our power.[4]

Fig. 2. The author seated on the Hexenstühle. Drawing by Rita Hillman, 2019.

A scholar's embodied experience smacks of the hopelessly subjective. It is difficult to take the insights of one's learning from the land and translate them into text. Folklorist David Hufford explores the concept of scholarly reflexivity, especially as it applies to scholarship of belief.[5] Reflexivity is a metaphor from grammar, indicating a verb that has the same thing as both subject and direct object. For example, "I introduce myself." When we study beliefs, we are humans studying humans. Hufford forces us to acknowledge the subjectivity of *all* knowledge. But that leaves many scholars in an academic no-man's-land. We have been accustomed to considering the subjective as "imaginary, illusory and unverifiable."

Do the current residents of Völs am Schlern, Italy, believe in the *Schlernhexen*? Possibly not, although maybe. Did the residents from generations back? Very possibly so. With objectivity, Hufford asserts that "impartiality in spiritual matters is an impossibility." This is especially true with folk religion, or what Hufford calls "unofficial beliefs."[6] I believe this also reflects information received and perceived from experience with the land, which may in fact be at the base of much folk belief. It certainly is so in the area of the Schlern Massif. To study these beliefs, scholars like Hufford, Nikki Bado, Rita Gross and many others call for scholarly reflexivity. This is a critical self-reflection and inclusion of the self in the scholarship, as opposed to an attempt to remove the self from the scholarship in the name of a false, unachievable objectivity. Reflexivity should honor the importance of the scholar's deeply held viewpoints and perspectives. Patricia Monaghan suggests two voices in scholarship: the scholarly voice and the personal voice. The first-person, personal voice in scholarship allows a site for reflexivity and alerts the reader to the situated embodied knowledge of the scholar. The scholarly third-person voice alerts the reader to the scholar's attempt at unbiased objectivity, always keeping the reflexive self in mind. Even combined, the voices together only offer partial truth. The reflexive scholar offers a viewpoint that exists among multiple voices, not the one final truth, the only voice for all time.[7]

Feminist theologian Laurel Schneider, although working on a theology of divinity, draws some additional helpful conclusions. A robust feminist theology, she says, would hold two poles in tension. One is the understanding that no one text, image, or idea can express all of ultimate truth. The other is that this same truth is revealing itself through a multiplicity of real, lived experiences to real people, all of the time. It is these multiple, real, lived experiences that are so impossible to theorize, according to Schneider. This tension creates a passion to deconstruct outdated structures in the first place, and in the second, robustly create new experiences. And neither is confused with anything fully and finally real.[8]

So the scholar is courageous enough to embody the radically subjective, attempt unbiased objectivity, deconstruct the old structure and be open to the radical play of the new. I want to add one last stone to the cairn, and that is the question of identity. Many scholars of goddess studies or women and mythology are also seeking a sense of identity, especially if they are scholars of the past. At the beginning of my doctoral studies, I took on this role somewhat uncritically. Seeking Germanic identity, especially through folklore, has a grim history. In the twentieth century, the drive of a desperate people for a positive German identity found its expression in the Third Reich, in National Socialism and in genocide. What is less well-known is that those in power meant folklore to play a critical role in supporting and justifying their actions. Their scholarship was designed to trace and discover a German "essence"; examining folk and fairy tales and ancient symbols; they were to reach back into the Germanic past, before Christianity, for an unbroken German continuity. Everything was done for The Fatherland. Land can be used as a political pawn far too easily. But German folklorist Deitrich Kramer doesn't want us to retreat into any supposedly safe and unpolitical realm of pure science, just because of our history. He says, this "is an alibi for the status quo, and it neutralizes potentially critical iconoclastic intelligence and knowledge."[9]

Let's be iconoclastic and ask, what did I learn from the land? Without references to books, legends, folklore and the ever-helpful tourist office down the hill? I knew, beyond a doubt, that the Schlern was a holy site, ancient and huge. And I knew the Witches' Stone was uncanny and numinous, almost spell-bound to keep passersby at a respectful distance. My spouse got to know the Schlern in another intimate way; he climbed to the peak, a very difficult climb. On the way up, he met an elderly Tyrolean man, hiking that ancient rock, if you can believe, barefoot. My spouse dug into his German vocabulary and commented to the man that he had "feet like iron." The old man grinned and stepped off the path into a field of thistles.

Long years afterward, I stumbled across the Witches' Stone again. Checking a few facts in my book on Tyrolean witch trials, I saw some tiny, familiar, black and white pictures: the pretty little lake and that strange-looking stone that I found in the woods. The author wrote:

> The Völser Lake and Summit Above. In times long ago, Witches' Gatherings often took place there, and beneath the summit an especially huge assembly took place in the year 1496. At this particular gathering, Anna Jobstin from Obervöls was chosen as the Queen of the Angels' Land. The lake-water of the moor was ever after entwined in legends and ghost-stories with this event. Proof positive is that the water deposited the Witches' Stone at the Völser Lake.[10]

Legend then tells that the water of the lake carried this mammoth stone from the summit peak down by the lakeside, from the place where the historical women met and ecstatically worshipped, down to the place where I historically walked and felt the magic of the stone. The landscape has come to meet both myth and history and I am trying to keep my head. I feel a powerful and inarticulate connection with the mysterious landscape of this corner of Germanic Europe, and the stories people tell there. People, whether Christian or those of "unofficial beliefs" have worshipped here for millennia, and if I go looking, I may just find more than what I seek.

It's a story for another day, but I did find the Witches' Chairs.

References

Benedikter, Hans. *Hexen Und Zauberer in Tirol.* Bozen: Athesia, 2000.

Dissertori, A. Otto. "Schlernhexen: Geschicte Und Sage." In *Die Schönsten Wanderwege Im Schlerngebiet: Kastelruth, Seis, Seiser Alm, Völs*, 15–40. Kastelruth: Verlag S. Trocker, 2002.

Ginzburg, Carlo. *Ecstasies: Deciphering the Witches' Sabbath.* New York: Pantheon Books, 1991.

Hufford, David. "Beings without Bodies: An Experience-Centered Theory of the Belief in Spirits." In *Out of the Ordinary: Folklore of the Supernatural*, edited by Barbara Walker, 11–45. Logan: Utah State University Press, 1996.

———. "The Scholarly Voice and the Personal Voice: Reflexivity in Belief Studies." *Western Folklore* 54, no. 1 (1995): 57–76.

Kramer, Deitrick. "Who Benefits from Folklore?" In *German Volkskunde: A Decade of Theoretical Confrontation, Debate, and Reorientation (1967–1977)*, edited by James R. Dow and Hannjost Lixfeld, 41–53. Bloomington: Indiana University Press, 1986.

Matamonasa-Bennett, Arieahn. "Honoring the Web: Indigenous Wisdom and the Power of Place." Paper presented at the annual Association for the Study of Women and Mythology symposium, St. Paul, Minnesota, April 20, 2013.

Monaghan, Patricia. "Partial Truth: Scholarly Narrative and Personal Voice." Paper presented at the October Symposium: Margins, Boundaries and Thresholds—Creativity across the Disciplines, Vermont College, Montpelier, VT, October 10, 2003.

Narayanan, Vasudha. "Embodied Cosmologies: Sights of Piety, Sites of Power."

Journal of the American Academy of Religion 71, no. 3 (September 2003): 495–520.

Endnotes

1 A. Otto Dissertori, "Schlernhexen: Geschicte Und Sage," in *Die Schönsten Wanderwege Im Schlerngebiet: Kastelruth, Seis, Seiser Alm, Völs* (Kastelruth: Verlag S. Trocker, 2002), 36-37, translation mine.

2 Carlo Ginzburg, *Ecstasies: Deciphering the Witches' Sabbath*, 1st American ed. (New York: Pantheon Books, 1991), 73.

3 Arieahn Matamonasa-Bennett, "Honoring the Web: Indigenous Wisdom and the Power of Place" (paper presented at the annual Association for the Study of Women and Mythology symposium, St. Paul, Minnesota, April 20, 2013).

4 Vasudha Narayanan, "Embodied Cosmologies: Sights of Piety, Sites of Power," *Journal of the American Academy of Religion* 71, no. 3 (2003), 495.

5 David Hufford, "The Scholarly Voice and the Personal Voice: Reflexivity in Belief Studies," *Western Folklore* 54, no. 1 (1995), 61.

6 David Hufford, "Beings without Bodies: An Experience-Centered Theory of the Belief in Spirits," in *Out of the Ordinary: Folklore of the Supernatural*, ed. Barbara Walker (Logan: Utah State University Press, 1996), 11.

7 Patricia Monaghan, "Partial Truth: Scholarly Narrative and Personal Voice" (paper presented at the October Symposium: Margins, Boundaries and Thresholds—Creativity across the Disciplines, Vermont College, Montpelier, VT, October 10, 2003).

8 Laurel C. Schneider, *Re-Imagining the Divine: Confronting the Backlash against Feminist Theology* (Cleveland: Pilgrim Press, 1998).

9 Deitrick Kramer, "Who Benefits from Folklore?" in *German Volkskunde: A Decade of Theoretical Confrontation, Debate, and Reorientation (1967–1977)*, ed. James R. Dow and Hannjost Lixfeld (Bloomington: Indiana University Press, 1986), 51–53.

10 Hans Benedikter, *Hexen und Zauberer in Tirol* (Bozen: Athesia, 2000), 174, translation mine.

LOSING THEODIVERSITY: THE ERASURE OF THE CANNIBAL HAG IN IRELAND

PATRICIA MONAGHAN

In the west of Ireland, a low range of hills straddles the border of counties Clare and Galway. Travelers rarely notice Sliabh Echtge (anglicized as the Aughty Hills) as they pass through to more scenic locations. To the west stretches the world-famous Burren, several hundred square miles of bare limestone cut by deep grooves called "grykes," within which rich grass and orchids grow. To the south, the Silvermines Mountains rise above Tipperary's rich pasturelands with their fabulously wealthy stud farms. In the north is Galway City, one of Ireland's cultural capitals and gateway to the scenic jewel called Connemara. East of Sliabh Echtge, the island's center opens out, with charming historic towns, castles, and ecclesiastical ruins. With such tempting places to visit, few even notice the inconsequential Aughty Hills.

Yet such has not always been the case. In the thirteenth century, Sliabh Echtge was sufficiently important that the *Agallamh na Senórach* (Colloquy with the Ancients) imagined Saint Patrick visiting a millennium earlier during his hero's progress through the land. Around the same time, the place-poems called the *Dinshenchas* recorded several myths about the mountains and the goddess* after whom they are named. As recently as 1839, John O'Donovan of the Ordinance Survey spoke of "the celebrated mountain of Sliabh Echtghe"[1]—celebrated because it was the home of poet Brian Merriman, whose renowned "Cúirt Á Meodlham-Oidhche" (The Midnight Court) describes the goddess Aeval adjudicating claims about whether Irish men or women were worse lovers. Merriman praised the

---

* The name of this regional goddess is spelled Echtga, Echtai, Eachtga, Eachtai, Achta, Eachtghe, Echtgha, Echtghe, Aughty and Boughty in various sources.

19

"Mountains in ranks with crimson borders/Peering above their neighbor's shoulders,"[2] still a vivid description of the piled-on-each-other quality of Aughty's hills. But a century later, when Robert Lloyd Praeger wrote his definitive work on Irish natural history, Sliabh Echtge had so dropped from consciousness that he found it unworthy of mention.

Today, the name of Sliabh Echtge is rarely recognized outside the immediate region. Without what Walter and Mary Brenneman call a "loric sense"[3] of the mountains' mythic dimensions, outsiders who glance up from the Limerick-Galway road see only low hills shadowed by a vast dark forest of Sitka spruce, planted nearly a half-century ago in a vain attempt at economic self-sufficiency through forest farming. The spruce plantations changed Sliabh Echtge utterly, for this was once one of Ireland's most biodiverse regions. For the Irish speaker, that lost biodiversity shouts from townland and village names. Along the slopes of Sliabh Echtge we find dozens of names incorporating the Irish word *doire*, typically anglicized into "Derry" and meaning "oak forest."[4] According to Augustine Henry,[5] "the ancient forest around the slopes of Sliabh Aughty ... is clearly defined by the place-names": Derrybrien ("oak wood of the O'Briens"), Derrymore ("big oak wood"), Derrykeel ("narrow oak wood"), Derrywee ("woodland of yellow oaks"), Derryfada ("long oak wood"), Derreendooagh ("little hilly oak forest"), and Derrycrag ("rocky oak wood").

Until just three hundred years ago, the slopes of Sliabh Echtge were covered with the largest native oak forest in Munster, the southwestern province of which County Clare is part.[6] Except for its size, Aughty's woodland would not have been unusual, for such biodiverse forests once covered more than two-thirds of Ireland. But the acreage under forest cover today is only 10 percent, and of that, a mere 2 percent is native woodland. On Sliabh Echtge, the climax forests of stately old-growth oaks—mostly *Quercus robur*, the common oak, and the sessile oak or *Quercus petraea*—supported beneath their canopies a teeming biotic community. The trees must have been enormous, because 50-foot-long boats made from native Irish wood have been found, although in the historical record, we find no witness to such giants. Whether such trees once grew on Echtge's slopes is impossible to say, but pollen records as well as human documents describe a majestic hardwood forest. Interspersed with ash and elm, the oaks sheltered understory trees such as holly, crabapple, elder and cherry, with carpets of ferns and violets below.[7] Not only was the flora diverse; so was the fauna. Wild

boars lived off the mast that fell from the oaks, as did squirrels and bad-
gers, while bands of deer grazed the vegetative cover. Predators, including
wolves as well as foxes, eagles and hawks, thrived on such rich prey. Down
to the level of the soil, rich with fungi, aprotozoa and nematodes, the Irish
forest teemed with life.

Oak trees were not only central to the biotic community. They were also
central to the spirituality of the human community, for oaks were sacred in
Celtic lands, sought after for the mistletoe that grew parasitically on their
branches, as Pliny famously claimed in his *Natural History*.[8] Throughout
the Celtic world, oak groves were sites of sacred power and ritual activity;
the term that described them, *nemeton*, was personified as the powerful
goddess Nemetona.[9] In Ireland, the same spiritual prominence was given
to the oak. The Brehon Laws, the land's ancient legal code, lists the oak as
chief among the seven "noble trees" (the others being hazel, holly, yew, ash,
pine and apple). Anyone who cut down an oak tree faced the severe fine
of a milch-cow (*bó*); even cutting a branch brought a penalty of a yearling
heifer.[10] The reason for the oak's primary position among trees was the
importance of its mast, or annual acorn crop, and "its dignity," according
to the eighth-century *Bretha Comaithchesa* or Laws of Neighborhood.[11]

Oak woods were held in common by the *tuath*—a word that means both
the people of the area and the land they inhabit—and were never considered private property.[12] Whereas many cultures have a concept of an *axis
mundi* or world tree, Irish culture saw trees as expressing the power of a
specific place. Each region's Bile Buadha (Tree of Power), usually an oak,
was associated with the ritual marriage of the local king with the goddess
of sovereignty, the divinity who controlled the land's fertility and thus the
wealth and health of its human inhabitants.[13]

The oak woods of Sliabh Echtge held historic as well as mythic importance. The forests around Derrybrien hid the armies of the DalCassians
under Brian Boru, who later drove the Danes from Ireland at the Battle
of Clontarf near Dublin. Historical documents emphasize the wildness of
Echtge's forested slopes and the ease with which people could hide therein.
The Burren archaeologist T.J. Westropp summarized some of the historical
records thus:

> In 1277 the McNamaras fled into "Echtge's dense forest
> and leafy foliage"; it afforded them safety in 1280, and

again in the severe winter of 1350, "by Echtge's shortest tracks, in the fast woods they made their close-set camp; in this stress and jeopardy, they passed the cold-winded, dark-visaged winter." At last fortune changed, and their enemies in their turn sought the friendly shelter in their wild and harrassed retreat under Brian Bawn from Burren to the fords of Killaloe in 1316, "until in Echtge's blue ridges, wind-tormented, cold, and with buttressed sides they found a resting place." To Echtge's forests Prince Murchad O'Brien and his adherents carried the cattle spoil of the Normans, and from them they made their forced march a few days later In May 1318, to complete the destruction of the army of Sir Richard De Clare, at Dysert O'Dea.[14]

Westropp later describes the Echtge forests as "dense woods of lofty foliage pleasant and sweet" and "woody deep-valed fastnesses,"[15] while observing that a lack of Stone Age forts suggests that the land was uninhabited until medieval times, the oakwoods providing a resource for gathering and hunting rather than a site for homesteads.[16]

But these sheltering forests threatened the colonizing British, who from the seventeenth through the early twentieth centuries relentlessly cut oaks in an attempt to remove cover for rebels. Capitalism also powered timber destruction: "Hardwood was in keen demand everywhere in Europe," writes Irish historian Nicholas Canny, "which acted as a wonderful stimulus for the British settlers, who set out to strip the country of its trees without any thought for domestic needs in the future or for conservation of the environment. In doing so, however, they could claim to be advancing a civilizing mission because the Irish woods had always been used to advantage by the native forces.... The promoters of timber processing could also claim to be promoting manufacturing employment."[17] By 1798, the Chevalier de la Latocnaye described Ireland as having "not left wood enough to make a toothpick."[18]

In the mid-1800s, British visitor Arthur Young witnessed this wanton destruction of woodlands, lamenting that "throughout every part of Ireland, in which I have been, one hundred contiguous acres are not to be found without evident signs that they were once wood, or at least very well wooded. . . . The greatest part of the kingdom exhibits a naked, bleak, dreary view for want of wood, which has been destroyed for a century past, with the most thoughtless prodigality."[19] On Sliabh Echtge, the forests were cut and the oakwood burned into charcoal for now-defunct ironworks in the towns of Feakle, Tuamgraney, Whitegate and Woodford.[20] Today only a single oak, reputed to be over 1000 years old and the oldest living being in Ireland, remains of Echtge's forest.

After the destruction of its oakwoods, the land on Sliabh Echtge was for several centuries minimally productive farmland and pasturage. In the 1960s, a period of economic depression, the Irish state bought up the hillsides from farmers all too willing to sell cheaply, then planted mile after mile of fast-growing Sitka spruce (*Picea sitchensis*), a species not native to Ireland that is useful only for pulpwood. The spruce grew quickly and thickly, forming what are now dense forests with little undergrowth—a monoculture of the sort that Ireland should dread, having suffered only 150 years ago through An Gorta Mór, the Great Hunger, when millions of Irish farmers starved after a blight wiped out the year's potatoes, their sole source of food in a landlord-controlled economy where wheat and beef were exported by the ton before the eyes of the needy. If any nation should be aware of the limits of monoculture, it surely must be Ireland.

Sliabh Eghtge's spruce have now reached the end of their lifespan, as determined by their commercial value. "In their natural, old-growth forests in the American north-west, Sitkas have lived more than 750 years and can top 75 metres," explains Michael Viney, "but in the short rotations of Irish forestry, governed by 'discounted cash flow', they are usually clear-felled from their mid-forties onwards."[21] For too many years, the semi-state agency Coillte stripped Sliabh Echtge of its spruce cover, and the trees sold to pay bills left by bankers who cashed in during the Celtic Tiger years. What will replace them? Mostly, more Sitka spruce and other non-native conifers, although a few mixed plantings are planned. Where once a thriving biotic community lived, the spruce monoculture supports little life. Merlins and hoodie crows no longer soar on Sliabh Echtge's breezes, the trees do not provide cover for herds of deer and their predators, and the soil is depleted of its rich microscopic life.

Sliabh Echtge presents not only an economic and ecological problem but a spiritual one, because the despoiled mountains were once sacred to a goddess now almost forgotten. In Ireland as elsewhere, such obscure divinities of place are in the process of being erased in the face of what Dara Molloy calls "the one-god project."[22] In the same way that monoculture threatens biodiversity, monotheism threatens theodiversity. And like biodiversity, theodiversity is more than simply the sum of many parts, for the complex totality exceeds a mere addition of local gods and goddesses.

Environmentalists for some decades have heard the call of environmentalist Aldo Leopold to "think like a mountain": to be aware of the interconnections of nature's many parts, each of which has a purpose that might not be readily recognized. The many parts of nature, Leopold argued, cannot be substituted for each other, and the same is true of the world's innumerable divinities of place, each of which expresses something unique and valuable. "The biotic mechanism is so complex that its working may never be fully understood," Leopold pointed out in *A Sand County Almanac*.[23] Specifically addressing the question of forest trees, Leopold wrote:

> Some species of trees have been "read out of the party" by economics-minded foresters because they grow too slowly, or have too low a sale value to pay as timber crops: white cedar, tamarack, cypress, beech and hemlock are examples. In Europe, where forestry is ecologically more advanced, the un-commerical tree species are recognized as members of the native forest community, to be preserved as such, within reason. Moreover some (like beech) have been found to have a valuable function in building up soil fertility. The interdependence of the forest and its constituent tree species, ground flora, and fauna is taken for granted.[24]

By "Europe," Leopold meant Germany, where the Dauerwald or "permanent woods" principle had been put into practice to create sustainable forestry. In the 1880s, German foresters made the same economically driven choice as Irish government officials 80 years later; they "discovered that pure plantations of spruce and pine outyielded the naturally-occurring, less-intensively managed forest of mixed conifers and hardwoods."[25] The resulting "spruce mania" resulted in a few "crops" of profitable wood, then quality began to decline as soils became exhausted. As Leopold described it,

> Litter failed to decay, piling upon the forest floor as a dry, sterile blanket which smothered all natural undergrowth, even moss. Roots ceased to penetrate the soil, lying in a tangled mat between the soil and the litter, with so many root grafts that cut stumps formed healing calluses by reason of their connection with nearby uncut trees. The topsoil developed excessive acidity, became bleached, and was separated from the subsoil by a dark band.... In short, pure spruce, the precocious child of timber famine and "wood factory" economics, grew up into an unlovely and unproductive maturity.[26]

By 1910, the situation was so dire that German foresters turned to the Dauerwald concept, and legislation was soon implemented to establish mixed woodlands of beech and oak within the spruce forests. Wildlife immediately began to return to the woodlands, a process that was soon enhanced by the Naturschutz ("nature conservation") movement that reintroduced threatened birds and mammals, including predators,[27] into the forests.

Leopold was deeply impressed with the changes that restoration brought forth. Writing on a scrap of hotel stationery in Berlin, Leopold exulted that "the new science of ecology ... is daily uncovering a web of interdependence so intricate as to amaze—were he here—even Darwin himself."[28] Leopold was optimistic about the "European" forests. But he did not visit Ireland and did not know that some European land had been entirely stripped of its native forests. The managed forests of Germany were not as ecologically dense as the ancient oakwoods of Sliabh Echtge, but the "permanent woods" were significantly more biodiverse than the empty, quickly eroding Aughty Hills of 1935.

"Biodiversity," a contraction of biological diversity, was coined only recently, in 1986, when the U.S. National Academy of Sciences and the Smithsonian Institution co-sponsored a "Forum on BioDiversity," using a term coined by one of the organizers, Walt Rosen. Two years later, the book *Biodiversity* was published under the editorship of E.O. Wilson, and the term attained common useage thereafter.[29] The word may be new, but the concept is not, as Leopold's biographer Curt Meine points out, citing the long history of "knowledge of biological diversity, appreciation of its role in nature and in human affairs, alarm over its loss, and attention to the challenges of conserving it.[30]

If biodiversity is essential for a healthy planet, is it not possible that theodiversity similarly important? Theodiversity, in this context, does not mean acknowledging a larger number of "important" divinities—putting Shiva or Kali on a level with Jehovah and Allah. Many scholars of religion focus primarily on divinities who hold a "higher," more abstract, position in an organized pantheon rather than on "minor divinities" rooted in a specific place. Yet as Ananda Coomaraswamy demonstrated, important myths and deities were often originally linked to specific places. Coomarasawamy coined the term "land-nam" after an "Icelandic tradition of claiming ownership of a place through weaving together a mythic metaphor of plants, animals, and geography of a place into a unique mythic story."[31] Through a process of abstraction, gods once tied to a specific setting developed a pan-local appeal. For example, JWHW was originally a land-god of Palestine honored locally as Yahweh of Samaria, Yahweh of Teman, and so forth.[32] But JWHW's local, land-based nature remains faintly discernable within the disembodied sky-god, for Israel is still considered a sacred homeland of His people.[33]

Many divinities, however, were never transformed into abstract entities—that vast number of figures too closely connected with landscape features such as rocks, old trees, streams and hills. Even among scholars interested in polytheism and henotheism, such deities are often ignored, dismissed as "minor divinities of place." But such "minor divinities of place" formed an important part of the spiritual lives of the people who lived in their "places." Loss of such divinities can be likened to the loss of the fertility of biodiverse landscapes. To consider the consequences of the loss of theodiversity, let us examine one of Ireland's most obscure deities, the goddess after whom Sliabh Echtge is named.

The region's only sizeable settlement is usually called simply "Gort," a short harsh syllable suited to a rather drab market town. But Gort has an illustrious history. The town's full name is Gort Inse Guaire, "Island Garden of King Guaire," referring to the famously generous seventh-century king Guaire Aidne mac Colmáin. Gort was then part of the ecclesiastical and intellectual center at nearby Kilmacdugh; it later became the home of the famous O'Shaughnessy clan and, most recently, was the heart of the Celtic Twilight, a nationalistic literary and artistic movement. An important force in that movement was Lady Augusta Gregory, a brilliant woman of the Anglo-Irish ascendancy who devoted herself to learning the lore of her immediate region. In doing so, Lady Gregory helped preserve the memory of an ancient goddess, a member of the Tuatha de Danann ("people of the goddess Danu"), the daughter of Nuada Silver-arm.[34] Nuada was king of his magical tribe, so Echtge's position as his daughter signals her importance, parallel to the Greek Athena (who derives status from being the daughter of Zeus) or Roman Minerva (Jove's daughter). Yet today, Echtge rarely appears in collections of Irish folklore and myth. Why has she disappeared?

The ancient texts that mention Echtge are significant ones: the Book of Leinster, the *Agallamh na Senórach* (Colloquy with the Ancients) and the collection of medieval place-poems called the *Dindshenchas*. In the Book of Leinster, she is credited as the owner of two magical cows, "remarkable for their milk-bearing fruitfulness."[35] This symbolic detail connects Echtge with the fabulous cow, the Glas Ghaibhleann or Gaibhle (anglicized as Glas Gavlen), who typically accompanies goddesses of abundance and transformation. Her myths show her to be of impossible fertility. Even if years had passed since her last calving, the Glas's milk flowed without cease. She was astonishingly strong as well. She could wander through three of Ireland's four provinces in a single day; she was "the wonderful 'glaucous cow' ... whose footprints mark the rocks in every direction"[36] in County Clare. As she traveled, she gave milk to anyone who milked her, filling any vessel, no matter how large or small. Ireland never suffered from famine so long as the great cow freely roamed.

But human greed threatened this force of abundance. Legends describe people who tried to pen the Glas for their exclusive enrichment. Sometimes she escaped or was freed, bringing abundance back to all the people.[37] Unfortunately, not all stories ended so happily; many times, the Glas abandoned humanity out of disgust. Since that time, there has been no free milk in Ireland, although you can see the Glas's rich milk spread across the sky as Bothar bó Finne, "the Grazing-Path of the White Cow"—the Milky Way. The connection of Echtge with not only one but two of these fabulous beings emphasizes the munificent fertility of her oak-rimmed mountains.

In the *Agallamh na Senorach,* a thirteenth-century text that imagines St. Patrick journeying across Ireland accompanied by two heroes of the heroic band called the Fianna, we find reference to Echtge and her eponymous mountain: "Patrick with his people set out, and away they came from the southward: through mid-Munster, past *luimnech uladh*, into *fidh na gcuan* which is called 'Cratlow'; into *sliabh aidhrid in righ*, into *sliabh Echtge* or 'the mountain of Echtge,' daughter of Nuada Silver-arm."[38] The text is interesting in this context because the inclusion of Sliabh Echtge among the most notable sights of Ireland suggests its mythic importance—sufficient that St. Patrick had to be told about it.

Two poems in the *Dindshenchas* center on Echtge (here spelled Echtga). In the first, "noble Echtga" of "mighty fame and ardour" was a "fresh girl ... dear to the Tuatha De[,]... an offspring winsome of mein." Because she had no land of her own, she wed Fergus Mac Ruide. In this text, Fergus is described as residing in Sid Nenta, otherwise known as the palace of the fairy king Midir,[39] which connects Echtge with legends about the royal center at Tara.[40] By marrying Fergus, she gained "the mountain that ye visit/with oak woods and strong places.../ hence it is called Echtga, a great-swelling plough-land;/ name it without constraint among all/ who can taste poetic lore."[41]

Another poem describes Echtge (spelled thus) as daughter of the otherwise obscure Dedad. She contested rulership of the mountains with the similarly named Echtach, also not attested elsewhere but described as the sister of Sinann, the goddess of the Shannon River that flows to the southeast of Sliabh Echtge.[42] The hills of "noble, rugged Echtga"[43] bear Echtge's name because her lover, "the cup-bearer of Gann and Sengann",[44] gave them to her as her bride-gift. Fragmentary as they are, these myths connect now-obscure Echtge with significant figures and motifs in Irish mythology.

Because ancient Irish culture was not literate, these early writings recorded older, orally transmitted tales, of which there were doubtless others about this goddess. But until recently, only a tiny fraction of Sliabh Echtge's residents could read stories about the goddess of their hills. As Lady Gregory put it, "Lonely Echtge still keeps old prophecies and old songs and some of the old speech, and but few newspapers are seen there."[45] Archaeologist T.J. Westropp, in the early part of the twentieth century, noted that Echtge's name was well remembered, as well as her identity as a member of the Danann race, and that stories were told about her as "the Awful One." Her legends were sufficiently vivid to attract the attention of William Butler Yeats, who lived near Gort from 1919 to 1929. In "The Withering of the Boughs," he sang of how he "fell asleep upon lonely Echtge of streams", which he described as filled with "leafy paths that the witches take/Who come with their crowns of pearl and their spindles of wool,/And their secret smile, out of the depths of the lake" and where (referring to the old goddess and goddesses), he claims to have seen "the Danaan kind/Wind and unwind their dances when the light grows cool/On the island lawns, their feet where the pale foam gleams."[46] He provided a footnote to the poem, identifying Echtge as the goddess of the mountain range near where he lived.

Echtge appeared not only in Yeats' poetry but also in his prose. In *Stories of Red Hanrahan,* Yeats described his fictional hero as singing about "a queen-woman dressed in silver," whom he saw sleeping on the hillside and who later haunted him. This was Echtge, a "woman of the *sidhe*" (the fairy people), and the hills were an entrance to fairyland, "a world out of sight and misty, that has for its meaning the colours that are beyond all other colours and the silences that are beyond all silences of this world."[47] That Yeats knew the land of his fairy lover can be attested by the way, in *The Celtic Twilight*, Yeats describes the Aughty Hills as a "vast desolate place, which has changed little since the old poem says, [the time when] 'the stag upon the cold summit of Echtge hears the cry of the wolves,' but still mindful of many poems and of the dignity of ancient speech."[48] Yet Yeats, the Anglo-Irishman, did not fully understand the specificity of goddesses and their places. In the 1897 version of the Hanrahan stories, he named the fairy woman as "Cleena of the Waves," although Cleena (Cliodna) was a goddess from the coast off Cork,[49] many miles from Echtge's home.

Yeats rectified this error with Lady Gregory's help and in the definitive 1927 version placed his Red Hanrahan stories firmly on the slopes of Sliabh Echtge. In the first story, Hanrahan meets four ancient women who have among them a pot, a stone, a spear and a sword, each representing one of the mythic Treasures of Ireland: the Cauldron of the Dagda, the Stone of Destiny, the Spear of Lugh and the Sword of Echtge's father Nuada.[50] But like Parsifal in the Grail legends, Hanrahan fails to ask the women about their magical objects, and the four crones bemoan the fact that because of Hanrahan's failure of nerve, "Echtge, daughter of the Silver Hand, must stay in her sleep. It is a great pity."[51]

Hanrahan meets the mountain goddess again, in a later story, when he hears a haunting voice singing,

I am beautiful, I am beautiful. The birds in the air, the moths under the leaves, the flies over the water look at me, for they never saw anyone so beautiful as myself. I am young; I am young: look upon me, mountains; look upon me, perishing woods, for my body will shine like the white waters when you have been hurried away.[52]

When the invisible singer appeared, Hanrahan did not see the beautiful fairy woman he expected. Instead, he recognized "Winny Byrne of the Cross Roads," an old woman who had been stolen by the fairies and had met "the servants of Echtge of the hills."[53] Her appearance spelled his doom, for the weather turned cold and Hanrahan, looking for shelter, went to Winny's house where he saw the same four crones, playing at cards. He hid outside the house for a time, but Winny found him and brought him in, tending him as he faded from life. Just before he died, Hanrahan met the goddess, who spoke through Winny to reveal her essence: "I am one of the lasting people, of the lasting unwearied voices, that make my dwelling in the broken and the dying, and those that have lost their wits; and I came looking for you, and you are mine until the whole world is burned out like a candle that is spent."[54]

Red Hanrahan was Yeats' quasi-mythic creation,[55] but Echtge was a living legend among the people. Because Yeats was not himself an Irish speaker, he most likely learned about Echtge from Lady Gregory. Lady Gregory learned sufficient Irish that she could travel easily among "the peasantry," as the Ascendency writers coyly called the native Irish, and could translate their oral tales. Gregory knew Echtge's slopes well from having traversed them in the cart pulled by her pony Shamrock. She knew of Echtge's heritage, for she described the goddess as the daughter of Nuada,[56] but did not record any specific legends about the goddess.

Over time, the mountain goddess and Danann queen, who bore the title of "the Awful One" in token of her awesome power, came to be described primarily as a hag or *cailleach*, a type of divinity found throughout Ireland. The *cailleach* is "the personification, in divine female form, of the physical landscape within which human life is lived and also of the cosmic forces at work in that landscape," according to Gearóid Ó Crualaoich,[57] who has collected dozens of Irish stories about this figure. The *cailleach* is the creatrix who formed the mountains by dropping pebbles from her apron and who gouged out the bays with her spoon. Because her name is not Indo-European, the *cailleach* is believed to emerge from the substrata of matrifocal pre-Celtic culture,[58] dating to the period prior to the presumed arrival of the Celts in approximately 400 BCE. Descriptions of Echtge as the daughter of a Danann king appear to date her to Celtic times, but her region is one in which hag-names litter the landscape. The *cailleach*, throughout Ireland and certainly in County Clare, is especially connected to high hills, so it appears likely that Echtge combines a pre-Celtic *cailleach* figure with a Danann goddess of sovereignty and abundance.

We have traced the regular appearance of Echtge in written literature, mostly derived from oral sources, through almost a millennium, noting that she may echo an earlier mountain goddess in the region. Yet few today know the source of the mountains' name. Gort historian Tom Hannon, who died in 2011 at age ninety, remembered her only as a threatening figure from his childhood. "Why, Patricia," he said, "in my childhood she was called a cannibal woman, but that's all I ever heard about her!"[59] Interviews with Gerard Madden, oral historian in Tuamgraney, support Tom's memory, for Madden says that as late as the 1950s, parents frightened their children with the boogiewoman Echtge.[60]

How did Echtge become so diminished? Westropp, writing not long after Yeats and Lady Gregory, ventures the theory[61] that children were once sacrificed to the goddess, a legend he also finds attached to another mountain goddess, Ethni.[62] Human sacrifice is difficult to prove or disprove, for it is often used as a way to disparage a culture. But Westropp's theory finds some support in the descriptions of other Irish mountain goddesses as the recipients of human, especially child, sacrifices. According to local legend, Ériu, who gives Ireland her name, was goddess of the central mountain of Uisneach and was ceremonially wed to the high king at Tara, whose object was to make the land fertile. As with other Irish goddesses, Ériu could appear as a beautiful young woman or as a frightening *cailleach* or hag. To turn the latter into the former required the sacrifice of a young man—either literally or figuratively, through having intercourse with the hag. In this sense, the description of Echtge as a *cailleach* not only makes her a frightening figure but emphasizes her awesome power as the source of earthly abundance.

Another explanation for Echtge's diminishment from queenly force of abundance to cannibal hag is found in the tendency for powerful female figures to become demonized by patriarchal cultures. The Greek Medusa, whose name means "queen," was a important pre-Hellenic solar divinity before shrinking into an "evil demon or bogey"[63] who turned to stone any humans who dared to look at her. The German Percht, now a folkloric figure who attacks sleepers on winter solstice night, was originally a powerful weather goddess.[64] Most pertinent to the consideration of Echtge is the Sumerian Lilith, once a "goddess who rules by night," who became a night-stalking vampire; she specialized in eating children and described in Jewish folklore as a figure "created in order to weaken the babes."[65] Even the familiar "evil stepmother" of European legend has been traced to a goddess original.[66]

But even Echtge's identity as cannibal hag is now in danger. Madden believes that Echtge is still recognized by long-term residents of the region that bears her name, but a survey in early 2012 of people in Bodyke, Scariff, Tuamgraney and Loughrea (all towns on the Aughty hillsides) resulted in not a single respondent recognizing the source of Sliabh Echtge's name. Folklorist Eddie Lenihan reported at the same time that he had not recorded a single legend about the goddess in more than two decades of work on Aughty's slopes.[67]

Echtge seems to be in danger of disappearing from local consciousness as more and more residents emigrate from the area, to be replaced by "blow-ins" from outside Sliabh Echtge. This is unfortunate, because the spiritual vision that encompasses Echtge and similar "divinities of place" deserves to be reclaimed. Geographer Patrick Sheeran believed that Lady Gregory's folkloristic work has fallen into obscurity because the geographic area she chose to research, far from central even in Irish studies, is entirely discounted by scholars outside Ireland. He claimed that "it is unfortunate … that Lady Gregory should try to recover a sacral view of the land in East Galway and North Clare. Had the mountain theology been that of the Black Mesa instead of Sliabh Echtge … doubtless *Poets and Dreamers* would today be a revered source book for bioregionalists, ecofeminists, deep-ecologists, technopeasants and Aquarian conspirators."[68]

Yet it is not just the deity of Sliabh Ecghtge who has been discounted in recent times, for she is just one of the many deities of place or *genius loci* who have fallen from notice. The "sacral view" to which Sheeran referred was once primarily the domain of those *genius loci*. The Latin term comes from Roman religion, where it referred to "a place's fingerprint … produced with similar ink as that of other places," as geographer Argyro Loukaki defines them.[69] The *genius loci* expresses both the natural history and the human history of a specific place, but the natural environment was dominant in determining a place's "spirit." Among natural settings, groves and forests were especially noted by the Romans for their spiritual qualities, for as Seneca said, "if you come upon a grove of old trees that have lifted their crowns up above the common height and shut out the light of the sky by the darkness of their interlacing boughs, you feel that there is a spirit in the place, so lofty is the wood, so lone the spot, so wondrous the thick unbroken shade."[70] Despite such reverent sentiments—or perhaps because of them—the Romans were methodical in destroying ancient Druidic groves. The massacre in 61 CE of Druids on the Isle of Mona (Angelsey)—that human and arboreal holocaust when priests and black-clad priestesses died trying to protect their sacred grove from Roman torches—stands as the epitome of the imperial attempt to crush the Celts by attacking their holiest places.[71]

Today, "spirit of place" appears only rarely in scholarly literature, most often as a term in regionalist literature and landscape architecture, neither of which typically recognize the spiritual foundation of the concept. Yet as Robert Thayer points out, there is always a spiritual dimension to grounding oneself in a specific place: "Immersion in bioregional culture and attachment to a naturally defined region offer a deepened sense of personal meaning, belonging, and fulfilment in life."[72] This spiritual meaning is what comparative religionist Walter Brenneman means by "loric power," which in his view is "implosive rather than explosive, and ... connected exclusively to that place ... like no other place on earth, and it was precisely because of this uniqueness that it was powerful."[73] Brenneman distinguishes majestic "sacred places" that are world-creating from intimate, loric ones that are "place-maintaining.... It is this quality of intimacy, based on uniqueness, that provides the possibility for placehood, which in turn is the ground of the loric."[74] When unique places as Sliabh Echtge are essentially loric, what happens if the lore that explains and honors them is lost?

Not far from Sliabh Echtge, on the Aran Islands, the former Roman and now Celtic Catholic priest Dara Molloy blames monotheism—specifically the Roman Catholic variety—for the loss of regional powers such as Echtge. Molloy argues that Christianity was the first globalization movement, for it began by crushing local religious rituals and local deities. He defines monotheism as "removing ourselves from the local and the particular. We leave the land that we are familiar with, that we identify with. We deliberately leave behind the sense of belonging, of local community, of communal identity. We become individuals, disconnected from our roots, floating, as it were, above the surface of the earth."[75] Thus we are spiritually limited by monotheism which "funnel(s) all the many possibilities of divine communication into one source,"[76] creating a veritable monoculture of the spirit. By contrast, ancient Irish culture connected people with place through innumerable named divinities[77] associated with specific land features, such as Echtge with her hills. In a profoundly localized worldview, Molloy argues, an individual's "place on this earth and in the universe was imbued with the immanent presence of countless male and female deities."[78]

Scholar of Native American religions Mary MacDonald similarly contrasts global faiths and those premised on relationship with a specific places, arguing that "some religions have gone global. That is, they have over the course of centuries moved beyond original incorporation in particular places to become potentially available to anyone who would chose to embrace them,"[79] while "indigenous people prefer the discourse of spirituality, a spirituality rooted in relationship to land, to that of religion."[80] In a famous statement of the power of place among Native Americans, the Apache sage Dudley Patterson told anthropologist Keith Basso that: "[W]isdom sits in places. Wisdom is water that never dries up." He articulated the connection of place and soul this way: "You need to drink water to stay alive, don't you? Well, you also need to drink from places. You must learn their names. You must remember what happened at them long ago."[81] Although it is common today to overlook or deny the "indigeniety" of European people, traditional Irish spirituality provides an example of what MacDonald describes. In reclaiming the importance of such minor divinities as Echtge, we reinforce the significance of connecting to specific places, wherever they are located.

On the north side of Sliabh Echtge runs the Owendalulleegh River, which takes its name from Echtge's two cows, traditional symbols of the land's fertility. There, three tiny remnants of Echtge's ancient woodlands may be found: Gortacarnaun Wood, Drummin Wood, and Lahardaun Wood, all exceedingly rich in flora and fauna[82] and assessed as including trees as old as three hundred years, thus antedating plantations and of likely natural origin. In 2005, scientists studying these vestigial woodlands found oak interspersed with elm, alder, blackthorn, yew, holly, willow, mountain ash, ash, and poplar. Beneath, a varied understory and forest floor flora includes anemones, violets, wild onion, sedges, horsetail, sweet woodruff, and wood ferns. A number of rare plants were identified in the woodlands as well, to a total of 119 different species—attesting to the biodiversity that has been lost elsewhere on Echtge's slopes.

These shreds of ancient forest survive despite the region's general loss of biodiversity. And despite globalization, immigration and emigration, Echtge is not yet extinct. Traces of her remain, for theodiversity can survive the way biodiversity does, in remnant patches, in folktales and scare-the-children boogiewomen. What would it matter, though, if she were to be forgotten? A great deal, if we assume that extinction of divinities is as much to be feared as extinction of snail darters and other "minor" players on the biological field. We should pay attention to threatened divinities the way biologists have learned to pay attention to signal species threatened with extinction. Curt Meine has explained the situation eloquently: "The prospect … of frequent, imminent, and prominent extinctions and extirpations … forced biologists to focus on extinction as a process, and to do so at the global scale. This in turn led field biologists back to the smaller, quieter, less gaudy members of the biological community, the vast majority of which, it was acknowledged, science had yet to even dignify with proper Linnean nomenclature."[83]

Echtge is one of those "smaller, less gaudy" members of the theological community. We cannot afford to lose her, or other figures like her. As Aldo Leopold declared, "The last word in ignorance is the man who says of an animal or plant, 'What good is it?'"[84] In the same way, every "minor divinity of place" has an importance that we might not recognize until after extinction when the place wisdom they embody is forgotten and their sacred land desecrated and its life-giving (or life-sustaining) ecological complexity disrupted. Echtge is not yet extinct in the hills that bear her name, but she represents an endangered divine species, one who might still be preserved for the future.

References

Ackerman, Cara. "Yeats' Revision of the Hanrahan Stories, 1897 and 1904." *Texas Studies in Literature and Language*, 17, no. 2 (Summer 1975), 505–24.

Alspach, Russell K. "The Use by Yeats and Other Irish Writers of the Folklore of Patrick Kennedy." *The Journal of American Folklore*, 59, no. 234 (October–December 1946), 404–12.

Basso, Keith. "Wisdom Sits in Places: Notes on a Western Apache Landscape." In *Senses of Place*, edited by Steven Feld and Keith Basso, 53–90. Santa Fe: School of American Research Press, 1996.

Berry, Thomas. *The Dream of the Earth*. San Francisco: Sierra Club Books, 1988.

Brenneman, Walter. "Holy Wells of Ireland." In *The Place of Power and Human Environments*, edited by James A. Swan, 134–53. Wheaton, IL: Theosophical Publishing House, 1991.

Brenneman, Walter, and Mary Brenneman. *Crossing the Circle at the Holy Wells of Ireland*. Charlottesville: University of Virginia Press, 1995.

Day, John. Y*ahweh and the Gods and Goddesses of Canaan*. The Library of Hebrew Bible/Old Testament Studies (Book 265). Sheffield: Sheffield Academic Press, 2000.

Dexter, Miriam Robbins. "The Hippomorphic Goddess and her Offspring." *Journal of Indo-European Studies*18, no. 3–4 (Fall–Winter 1990): 285–307.

Dexter, Miriam Robbins. *Whence the Goddesses: A Sourcebook*. New York: Teachers College Press, 1990.

Finneran, Richard J. "'Old lecher with a love on every wind': A Study of Yeats' Stories of Red Hanrahan." *Texas Studies in Literature and Language* 14, no. 2 (Summer 1972): 347–58.

Frothingham, A.L. "Medusa, Apollo, and the Great Mother." *American Journal of Archaeology* 15, no. 3 (July–September 1911), 349–77.

Gregory, Lady Augusta. *Gods and Fighting Men: The Story of the Tuatha De Danaan and of the Fianna of Ireland*. London: John Murray, 1905.

Gregory, Lady Augusta. *Poets and Dreamers*. New York: Oxford University Press, 1974.

Gwynn, Edward, trans. *The Metrical Dindshenchas*. Dublin: School of Celtic Studies, Dublin Institute for Advanced Studies, 1991.

Henry, Augustine. "Woods and Trees of Ireland." *Journal of the County Louth Archaeological Society* 3, no. 3 (December 1914): 237–45.

Kelly, Fergus. *A Guide to Early Irish Law*. Dublin: School of Celtic Studies, Dublin Institute for Advanced Studies, 1998.

Kernan, Henry, and Janine Guglielmino. "Putting the Green Back in Ireland—Reforestation in Ireland." *American Forests*, September 22, 1998.

Leopold, Aldo. *A Sand County Almanac*. Leopold Pines Edition. Baraboo, WI: Land Ethic Press, 2007.

Leopold, Aldo. *Round River: From the Journals of Aldo Leopold*. Edited by L.B. Leopold. New York: Oxford University Press, 1953.

Logan, Patrick. *The Holy Wells of Ireland*. Gerrards Cross: Colin Smythe, 1980.

Logan, Patrick. *The Old Gods: The Facts about Irish Fairies*. Belfast: Appletree Press, 1981.

Loukaki, Argyro. "Whose Genius Loci? Contrasting Interpretations of the 'Sacred Rock of the Athenial Acropolis.'" *Annals of the Association of American Geographers* 87, no. 2 (June 1997): 306–29.

MacCoitir, Niall. *Irish Trees: Myths, Legends and Folklore*. Cork: The Collins Press, 2003.

MacCullough, J.A. *The Religion of the Ancient Celts*. London: Constable, 1911.

MacDonald, Mary N. "The Primitive, the Primal, and the Indigenous in the Study of Religions." *Journal of the American Academy of Religion* 79, no. 4 (December 2011): 814–26.

Madden, Gerard. "Shameful Neglect of a Historic Place: Tuamgraney." *Sliabh Aughty* (East Clare Heritage Society, Tuamgraney, County Clare, Ireland) 5 (1994): 5–8.

Markeviciene, Jurate. "Genius Locii and Homo Faber: A Heritage-Making Dilemma." *Research Journal of Vilnius Gediminas Technical University and Lithuanian Academy of Sciences* (2012): 1–11.

Meine, Curt. *Aldo Leopold: His Life and Work*. Madison: University of Wisconsin Press, 1988.

Meine, Curt. *Correction Lines: Essays on Land, Leopold, and Conservation*. Washington, DC: Island Press, 2004.

Merriman, Brian. *The Midnight Court*. Translated by Frank O'Connor. Dublin: The O'Brien Press, 1989.

Molloy, Dara. *The Globalization of God: Celtic Christianity's Nemesis*. Inis Mór, Aran Islands: Aisling Publications, 2009.

Motz, Lotte. "The Winter Goddess: Perchta, Holda and Related Figures." *Folklore* 95, 2 (1984): 151–66.

Neeson, Eoin. "Woodland in History and Culture." In *Nature in Ireland: A Scientific and Cultural History*, edited by John Wilson Foster. Montreal: McGill-Queens University Press, 1997.

Ó Crualaoich, Gearóid. *The Book of the Cailleach: Stories of the Wise-Woman Healer.* Cork: Cork University Press, 2003.

O'Donovan, John, and Eugene Curry. *The Antiquities of County Clare: Ordnance Survey Letters, 1839.* Ennis, County Clare: CLASP Press, 2003.

O'Grady, Standish. *Agallamh na Senorach: The Colloquy with the Ancients.* Medieval Irish Series. Cambridge, Ontario: In Parentheses Publications, 1999.

Patai, Raphael. "Lilith." *The Journal of American Folklore* 77, no. 306 (October–December 1964): 295–314.

Pliny, the Elder. *Natural History.* Translated by H. Rackham, Loeb Classical Library, 10 vols. Cambridge, MA: Harvard University Press, 1942.

Powell, T.G.E. *The Celts.* London: Thames and Hudson, 1958.

Prager, Robert Lloyd. *The Way That I Went: An Irishman in Ireland.* Cork: The Collins Press, 1997.

Roden, Cilian, Micheline Sheehy Skeffington, and Gordon D'Arcy. "The Botany and Conservation Importance of Oak-Woods in the Valley of the Owendalullegh River, Sliabh Aughty, South-East Galway." *The Irish Naturalists' Journal* 28, no. 9 (May 22, 2007): 361–71.

Seneca. *Epistles.* 4.12.3.

Sheeran, Patrick. "The Idiocy of Irish Rural Life Reviewed." *The Irish Review*, no. 5 (Autumn 1988): 27–33.

Solnit, Rebecca. "The Lost Woods of Killarney: Old-Growth Oak Forest in Ireland." *Sierra*, March/April 1997, 44–51.

Swan, James, and Roberta Swan. *Dialogues with the Living Earth.* Wheaton, IL: Theosophical Publishing House, 1996.

Thayer, Robert L., Jr. *LifePlace: Bioregional Thought and Practice.* Berkeley: University of California Press, 2003.

Viney, Michael. "Native's Return: After Many Centuries of Deforestation Trees Are Now Making a Comeback." *The Irish Times*, April 4, 2012. www.irishtimes.com/timeseye/trees/.

Westropp, T.J. "The Marriages of the Gods at the Sanctuary of Tailltiu." *Folklore* 31, no. 2 (June 30, 1920): 109–41.

Westropp, T.J. "Dolmens at Ballycroum, near Feakle, County Clare." *Proceedings of the Royal Irish Academy (1889–1901)* 6 (1900–1902): 85–92.

Westropp, T.J. *Folklore of Clare: A Folklore Survey of County Clare and County Clare Folk-tales and Myths.* Ennis, County Clare: CLASP Press, [1910–1913] 2000.

Westropp, T.J. *Folklore of Clare: A Folklore Survey of County Clare and County Clare Folk-tales and Myths.* Ennis, County Clare: CLASP Press, repr. 2000, [1910–1913] 2003.

Westropp, T.J. "The Forests of the Counties of the Lower Shannon Valley." Section C: Archaeology, Celtic Studies, History, Linguistics, Literature. *Proceedings of the Royal Irish Academy* 27 (1908/1909): 270–300.

Westropp, T.J. "The 'Mound of the Fiana' at Cromwell Hill, Co. Limerick, and a Note on Temair Luachra." Section C: Archaeology, Celtic Studies, History, Linguistics, Literature. *Proceedings of the Royal Irish Academy* 36 (1921–1924): 68–85.

Yeats, William Butler. *The Celtic Twilight.* London: A.H. Bullen, 1912.

Yeats, William Butler. *The Collected Poems.* New York: MacMillan Publishing Inc., 1950.

Yeats, William Butler. *Stories of Red Hanrahan and The Secret Rose.* London: MacMillan and Sons, 1927.

Young, Arthur. *A Tour in Ireland: With General Observations on the Present State.* Vol. 2. London: Cadell, 1780.

Zipes, Jack David. *The Great Fairy Tale Tradition: From Straparola and Basile to the Brothers Grimm: Texts, Criticism.* New York: W.W. Norton, 2001.

Endnotes

* The name of this regional goddess is spelled Echtga, Echtai, Eachtga, Eachtai, Achta, Eachtghe, Echtgha, Echtghe, Aughty and Boughty in various sources.

1 John O'Donovan and Eugene Curry, *The Antiquities of County Clare: Ordnance Survey Letters, 1839* (Ennis, County Clare: CLASP Press, 2003), 182.

2 Brian Merriman, *The Midnight Court*, trans. Frank O'Connor (Dublin: The O'Brien Press, 1989), 15.

3 Walter Brenneman and Mary Brenneman, *Crossing the Circle at the Holy Wells of Ireland* (Charlottesville: University of Virginia Press, 1995), 43.

4 Eoin Neeson, "Woodland in History and Culture," in *Nature in Ireland: A Scientific and Cultural History*, ed. John Wilson Foster (Montreal: McGill-Queens University Press, 1997), 135.

5 Augustine Henry, "Woods and Trees of Ireland," *Journal of the County Louth Archaeological Society* 3, no. 3 (December 1914): 242.

6 Gerard Madden, "Shameful Neglect of a Historic Place: Tuamgraney," *Sliabh Aughty* (East Clare Heritage Society, Tuamgraney, County Clare, Ireland) 5 (1994): 6; Cilian Roden, Micheline Sheehy Skeffington and Gordon D'Arcy, "The Botany and Conservation Importance of Oak-Woods in the Valley of the Owendalullegh River, Sliabh Aughty, South-East Galway," *The Irish Naturalists' Journal* 28, no. 9 (May 22, 2007): 368.

7 Neeson, "Woodland in History and Culture," 133.

8 Pliny the Elder, *Natural History*, trans. H. Rackham, Loeb Classical Library, bk. 16, chap. 95 (Cambridge, MA: Harvard University Press, 1942).

9 J.A. MacCullough, *The Religion of the Ancient Celts* (London: Constable, 1911), 41, 71.

10 Fergus Kelly, *A Guide to Early Irish Law* (Dublin: School of Celtic Studies, Dublin Institute for Advanced Studies, 1998), 144.

11 Niall MacCoitir, *Irish Trees: Myths, Legends and Folklore* (Cork: The Collins Press, 2003), 13.

12 Neeson, "Woodland in History and Culture," 138.

13 Miriam Robbins Dexter, "The Hippomorphic Goddess and Her Offspring," *Journal of Indo-European Studies* 18, nos. 3–4 (Fall–Winter 1990): 293–94; Dexter, *Whence the Goddesses: A Sourcebook* (New York: Teachers College Press, 1990), 88, 146.

14 T.J. Westropp, "Dolmens at Ballycroum, near Feakle, County Clare," *Proceedings of the Royal Irish Academy (1889–1901)* 6 (1900–1902): 86.

15 T.J. Westropp, "The Forests of the Counties of the Lower Shannon Valley," Section C: Archaeology, Celtic Studies, History, Linguistics, Literature, *Proceedings of the Royal Irish Academy* 27 (1908/1909): 279.

16 Westropp, "The Forests of the Counties of the Lower Shannon Valley," 278.

17 Rebecca Solnit, "The Lost Woods of Killarney: Old-Growth Oak Forest in

Ireland," *Sierra* (March/April 1997): 44.

18 Neeson, "Woodland in History and Culture," 141.

19 Arthur Young, *A Tour in Ireland: With General Observations on the Present State*, vol. 2 (London: Cadell, 1780), 161.

20 Madden, "Shameful Neglect," 6.

21 Michael Viney, "Native's Return: After Many Centuries of Deforestation Trees Are Now Making a Comeback," *The Irish Times*, April 4, 2012, 2 (www.irishtimes.com/timeseye/trees/).

22 Dara Molloy, *The Globalization of God: Celtic Christianity's Nemesis* (Inis Mór, Aran Islands: Aisling Publications, 2009), 43.

23 Aldo Leopold, *A Sand County Almanac*, Leopold Pines Edition (Baraboo, WI: Land Ethic Press, 2007), 205.

24 Leopold, *A Sand County Almanac*, 212.

25 Curt Meine, *Aldo Leopold: His Life and Work* (Madison, WI: University of Wisconsin Press, 1988), 353.

26 Meine, *Aldo Leopold*, 353–54.

27 Meine, *Aldo Leopold*, 355.

28 Curt Meine, *Correction Lines: Essays on Land, Leopold, and Conservation* (Washington, DC: Island Press, 2004).

29 Meine, *Aldo Leopold*, 74–75.

30 Meine, *Aldo Leopold*, 118.

31 James Swan and Roberta Swan, *Dialogues with the Living Earth* (Wheaton, IL: Theosophical Publishing House, 1996), 1.

32 John Day, *Yahweh and the Gods and Goddesses of Canaan*, The Library of Hebrew Bible/Old Testament Studies (Book 265) (Sheffield: Sheffield Academic Press, 2000).

33 Molloy, *The Globalization of God*, 43.

34 T.J. Westropp, *Folklore of Clare: A Folklore Survey of County Clare and County Clare Folk-tales and Myths* (Ennis, County Clare: CLASP Press, [2000] 2003), 79–80.

35 Westropp, *Folklore of Clare*, 22.

36 T.J. Westropp, *Folklore of Clare: A Folklore Survey of County Clare and County Clare Folk-tales and Myths* (Ennis, County Clare: CLASP Press, 2000), 4.

37 Patrick Logan, *The Old Gods: The Facts About Irish Fairies* (Belfast: Appletree Press, 1981), 119.

38 Standish O'Grady, trans., *Agallamh na Senorach: The Colloquy with the Ancients*, Medieval Irish Series (Cambridge, Ontario: In Parentheses Publications, 1999), 29.

39 Edward Gwynn, trans., *The Metrical Dindshenchas* (Dublin: School of Celtic Studies, Dublin Institute for Advanced Studies, 1991), 530.

40 Lady Augusta Gregory, *Gods and Fighting Men: The Story of the Tuatha De Danaan and of the Fianna of Ireland* (London: John Murray, 1905), 22.

41 Gwynn, *The Metrical Dindshenchas*, 298–303.

42 Gwynn, *The Metrical Dindshenchas*, 533.

43 Gwynn, *The Metrical Dindshenchas*, 309.

44 Westropp, "Dolmens at Ballycroum," 85.

45 Gregory, *Gods and Fighting Men*, 74.

46 William Butler Yeats, *The Collected Poems* (New York: MacMillan Publishing, Inc., 1950).

47 William Butler Yeats, *Stories of Red Hanrahan and The Secret Rose* (London: MacMillan and Sons, 1927), 73–74.

48 Yeats, *Stories of Red Hanrahan*, 37–38.

49 Cara Ackerman, "Yeats' Revision of the Hanrahan Stories, 1897 and 1904," *Texas Studies in Literature and Language* 17, no. 2 (Summer 1975): 507.

50 Yeats, *Stories of Red Hanrahan*, 13.

51 Yeats, *Stories of Red Hanrahan*, 14.

52 Yeats, *Stories of Red Hanrahan*, 74.

53 Yeats, *Stories of Red Hanrahan*, 75.

54 Yeats, *Stories of Red Hanrahan*, 81.

55 Richard J. Finneran, "'Old lecher with a love on every wind': A Study of Yeats' Stories of Red Hanrahan." *Texas Studies in Literature and Language* 14, no. 2 (Summer 1972): 348.

56 Gregory, *Gods and Fighting Men*, 421.

57 Gearóid Ó Crualaoich, *The Book of the Cailleach: Stories of the Wise-Woman Healer* (Cork: Cork University Press, 2003), 10.

58 Ó Crualaoich, *The Book of the Cailleach*, 25.

59 Tom Hannon, interview by author, Roo, Gort, County Galway, August 26, 1999.

60 Gerard Madden, interviews by author, Mountshannon, County Clare, January 2012.

61 T.J. Westropp, "The Marriages of the Gods at the Sanctuary of Tailltiu," *Folklore* 31, no. 2 (June 30, 1920): 129.

62 T.J. Westropp, "The 'Mound of the Fiana' at Cromwell Hill, County Limerick, and a Note on Temair Luachra," Section C: Archaeology, Celtic Studies, History, Linguistics, Literature, *Proceedings of the Royal Irish Academy* 36 (1921–1924): 76.

63 A.L. Frothingham, "Medusa, Apollo, and the Great Mother," *American Journal of Archaeology* 15, no. 3 (July–September 1911): 349.

64 Lotte Motz, "The Winter Goddess: Perchta, Holda and Related Figures," *Folklore* 95, no. 2 (1984): 151–52.

65 Raphael Patai, "Lilith," *The Journal of American Folklore* 77, no. 306 (October–December 1964): 295.

66 Jack David Zipes, *The Great Fairy Tale Tradition: From Straparola and Basile to the Brothers Grimm: Texts, Criticism* (New York: W.W. Norton, 2001), 684.

67 Madden, interviews by author, 2012; Eddie Lenihan, Crusheen, County Galway, interview by author, January 22, 2012.

68 Patrick Sheeran, "The Idiocy of Irish Rural Life Reviewed," *The Irish Review*, no. 5 (Autumn 1988): 31.

69 Argyro Loukaki, "Whose Genius Loci? Contrasting Interpretations of the 'Sacred Rock of the Athenial Acropolis,'" *Annals of the Association of American Geographers* 87, no. 2 (June 1997): 308.

70 Seneca, *Epistles*, 4.12.3, 22.

71 For details, see T.G.E. Powell, *The Celts* (London: Thames and Hudson, 1958).

72 Robert L. Thayer, Jr., *LifePlace: Bioregional Thought and Practice* (Berkeley: University of California Press, 2003), 71.

73 Walter Brenneman, "Holy Wells of Ireland," in *The Place of Power and Human Environments*, James A. Swan, ed. (Wheaton, IL: Theosophical Publishing House, 1991), 137.

74 Brenneman, "Holy Wells of Ireland," 137–38.

75 Molloy, *The Globalization of God*, 2.

76 Molloy, *The Globalization of God*, 46.

77 Molloy, *The Globalization of God*, 10.

78 Molloy, *The Globalization of God*, 41.

79 Mary N. MacDonald, "The Primitive, the Primal, and the Indigenous in the Study of Religions," *Journal of the American Academy of Religion* 79, no. 4 (December 2011), 814.

80 MacDonald, "The Primitive, the Primal," 818.

81 Keith Basso, "Wisdom Sits in Places: Notes on a Western Apache Landscape," in *Senses of Place*, ed. Steven Feld and Keith Basso (Santa Fe: School of American Research Press, 1996), 70.

82 Roden, et al., "The Botany and Conservation Importance of Oak-Woods," 361–71.

83 Meine, *Correction Lines*, 71.

84 Aldo Leopold, *Round River: From the Journals of Aldo Leopold*, ed. L.B. Leopold (New York: Oxford University Press, 1953), 146–47.

"WWGD—WHAT WOULD GAIA DO?"
GAIAN METHODS:
RESEARCHING AS EARTH–PLANETARY
QUALITATIVE METHODS

MARNA HAUK

I hope it makes a small difference, as
I hope the drought will break and the morning
come rising out of the ocean wearing
a cloak of clean sweet mist and swirling terns.

~ Marge Piercy, from "Rising in Perilous Hope"[1]

In Piercy's poem the morning and the ocean bring renewal, even hope. It is the life of them, their verve, leaning on the life of the earth system of which they are a part, imbued and breathed by the interconnected life of the earth, that rises from the ocean cloaked in mist and terns. Some things are larger than us as individuals or collective humans: the life of the planet arising and swirling in scale upon scale of interlineated, interlocking, interloping, interconnected vibrancy and wholeness. We are a part of the Earth, the uprushing and tidal, the originary and fiery, airstreaming and continentally shifting. In a state of constantly interleaved and mutually informing/affecting flows and currents, making and unmaking and regeneration, the collective lives of the planet pulse in co-evolving wonder and cataclysm and process and life. Gaia, she/we, all this: named elsewhere by Lovelock as planetary geophysiology,[2] in Margulis's planetary self-regulation and meta-ecosystemic planetary symbiosis,[3] by Kimmerer as resident in the land itself,[4] by Capra as the living systems of the web of life.[5]

45

The planet as a supercosm activates in us, in Taylor's *Dark Green Religion*, as "a belonging to and reverence for the biosphere."[6] Researchers have been surfacing ancient and novel ways of including and exploring how the planetary life, including through the lens of our own personal as well as larger perceptions, can inform our research. This biophilia[7] finds expression in Spretnak's densely interconnected[8] ecological postmodernism.[9] Andrea Olsen's work in *Body and Earth* personalizes the planetary, noticing how even, and particularly, our personal embodiment is a window into the vivacious planetary system, through our guts, our skin, the dirt in our yard.[10] Other researchers have extended the original science of Lynn Margulis and James Lovelock's Gaia hypothesis into the full-fledged Gaia theory, demonstrating the superorganismic self-regulating qualities of geo-chemical planetary cycles and flows.[11]

Gaian methods offer a bursting, bustling, complex nexus of qualitative research methods for wondering "WWGD—What Would Gaia Do" if (and as) she were a qualitative researcher. The planetary living system, referred to as Gaia by Western scientists, is constantly experimenting and conducting research, both via mutualism and symbiotic evolution generally, and in myriad ways, including in and through us. As qualitative researchers, we can learn from the research movement that is guided by planetary presence to understand how to position our own research and design it with litheness and Gaian authenticity to research as the planet.

Scholarly Context and Herstory of Gaian Methods

Gaian methods represent a set of qualitative research methods I have been involved with articulating since 2010 (Fig. 3). Gaian methods as such were first suggested by Pramod Parajuli, whose work on methodological ecotones in 2008 describes overlapping "scapes" of sound, sense, learning, science, and embodiment generating new approaches to qualitative research that he described as "multisensory and Gaia methodologies."[12] Dr Parajuli connects[13] the shamanic work of Martin Prechtel in *Secrets of the Talking Jaguar*[14] with "Gaian participatory science" (as in Stephen Harding's *Animate Earth*[15]) and Jon Kabat-Zinn's sensory and meditation practices in *Coming to Our Senses*[16] with Andrea Olsen's embodiment research methods in *Body and Earth: An Experiential Guide*,[17] ethnobotanical research such as Nancy Turner's *Earth's Blanket*,[18] and Gregory

Cajete's traditional ecological knowledge (TEK) and indigenous science research (such as *Igniting the Sparkle*[19]).

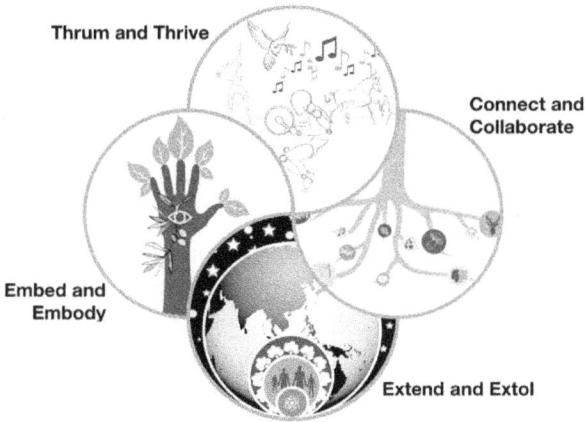

Fig. 3. The Four Characteristics of Gaian Methods, diagram by Amanda Leetch, 2019.

In May 2010, sparked by Parajuli's initial theorizing, Aimée deChambeau, Judith Landsman, and I produced a robust academic website on Gaian methods, including authoring a series of six essays, over sixty annotated resource listings and another eighty bibliographic entries categorized in over a dozen topic areas, book reviews, and interlinked multimedia resources (published at www.earthregenerative.org/gaiamethods/).[20] We also presented an interactive poster session on Gaian methods at the 2010 International Sustainability Symposium.[21] Expanding and deepening Parajuli's earlier theorizing, our work began exploring the "green and growing global research convergence" at the intersection of six fields: complexity theory, ecophilosophy (including deep ecology and ecopsychology), ecospirituality, scientific research in Gaia theory, healing and shamanism, and multisensory embodiment (the last of which includes arts-based inquiry, experiential and embodiment explorations, contemplative inquiry, and poetic inquiry).[22] For each of the six converging source areas informing Gaian methods, we identified the roots of that Gaian qualitative research method area; the extension and growth, or stem and leaves, of that research; its flowering into current applications and examples; and how that aspect of Gaian methods is seeding out to spin off new life, ideas and approaches to planetary qualitative methods.

In October 2010, in my portion of joint scholarship on "Gaian Methods: An Emergent Confluence of Sustainability Research Innovation," I articulated and developed four key directives of Gaian methods, how they allow researchers to embed and embody, connect and collaborate, extend and extol, and thrum and thrive.[23] In her portion of this joint paper, Judith Landsman deepened her findings in how Gaian methods are expressed in current ecospirituality and dance and embodiment research. Dr Jeanine Canty explored the connections between organic inquiry and Gaian methods, how both mirror natural processes guiding qualitative research. Dr Noël Cox Caniglia detailed how her depth ethnographies of Southwest women ranchers as ecojustice educators surfacing their ecocentric connection with the living systems of the land exemplified Gaian methods.

Judith Landsman helped me detail embodied soundings for a group process I had developed to enhance the experiential learning of the four key directives of Gaian methods; in October 2010, Judith Landsman and I presented these experiential teachings and introduced Gaian methods in Denver, Colorado as a peer-reviewed presentation of the Association for the Advancement of Sustainability in Higher Education.[24]

My doctoral research also informs the emergence of Gaian methods as qualitative research methodology. My research involves surfacing connections and patterns of regeneration among multiple scales of emergent human-earth collaboration, intrapersonally in earth dreaming, interpersonally in small-group creative collaboration sparked by patterns from nature, and at the scale of wisdom school design. Gaian methods empower me to pursue integrative, transdisciplinary, connective, and earth-connected research. Perhaps because of my permacultural and earth-path informed insight that earth systems are in a continual state of modeling and exemplifying regeneration, I desire to deeply understand how this regenerative modeling can guide personal, small group (or classroom) and school design and emergence to meaningfully restore empathy, creativity, and wisdom. The living earth system embodies regeneration, so research methods guided by the living planetary system promise to restore humans, our cultural and biocultural systems, in a systems-level biomimicry. I utilized Gaian methods in my doctoral research, both to include the Earth system as a research participant and to have the Earth guide my methodological design.

I strive in this article not to re-create previous scholarship regarding Gaian methods; rather, I aim to provide enough context while extending the body of thinking and theorizing and practice regarding planetary qualitative research.

Context/Gaian Research Positionality

In order to adequately situate this research, I introduce myself with an earth-based, or Gaian, positionality. Gaian methods extend feminist positionality[25] to literal earth and cultural context and position. I live a short walk sunward (south) from Mount Tabor, the only active volcano within a city limits in North America, within the southern rain shadow of a large swath of rainforest, in the bioregion of Pacific Cascadia, in the modern geographical entity of Portland, Oregon. I live in the native lands[26] of the settler-displaced Cathlacumup Band of the Multnomah peoples.[27] This is near the convergence of two rivers, currently called the Willamette and Columbia.

What does this Gaian context mean for my research? From a Gaian perspective, I imagine living near a geologically active volcano might lend a kind of fiery generativity and creativity to my scholarship, thriving here downland from where previous fire in the earth rising to the surface had forged a small mountain, near where the fire in the earth still burbles deep below. If rock lends grounding and magma brings new growth (of earth), it is not surprising that living with/in this place of earth making more of itself has birthed an interest in earth and earth regeneration in me, sparking the question, how can I interview the earth directly as qualitative research data? I walk and garden near the caldera where the earth is still making and re-making herself, here near the lively convergence of the large river that flows from the ocean to the continental plate where it meets the river that travels through a fertile valley to meet her.[28] In terms of the fact that I live in a clearcut amidst settlers whose ancestors decimated the native peoples, it might mean both that the land itself suffers from and learns to heal from many losses: the loss of its native plant guilds, the attack and pollution of modern industrial culture, and the loss of indigenous human–ecological bioculture. It might whisper instead of shout. I might need to undertake extra-respectful methods to earn the trust of this part of Gaia, if such a project is possible. There might also be some ethical implications from my positionality in terms of nurturing and restoring human-cultural biocultural matrix and relations. In terms of modern bioculture, I live in the settler grid matrix of inner Portland suburbia, on SE 58th Avenue, near the #9 bus line. In permacultural terms, I tend and thrive with/in extensive edible-medicinal-wildlife-feeding food forests in the shapes of sprawling snakes and dragons. I bring these multiple layers and scales of place and Earth relation to my research.

Gaian research positionality extends feminism and complexity's effects on research methods, such that the researcher is complicit and embedded in the research and that the researcher's standpoint must be made explicit as it is certainly informing and affecting the research.

Similar to place theorist Grueneweld (now Greenwood)'s call[29] to twin decolonization and reinhabitation to produce research that is "the best of both worlds"—catalyzing Freire's pedagogies of liberation while honoring Bowers' elder education—I align my Gaian earth and biocultural positionality within a critical place inquiry, honoring the layers of geology, bioculture, and personal history that intertwine to generate me and this particular scholarship. So in addition to being a mixed-class, middle-aged, queer doctoral researcher in sustainability education, I am generating research with the *terroir* of this rainforest volcano land at the convergence of rivers at the left edge of the continent. The flavor of Gaian methods described in this paper is birthed from this place and also partly embodied by this brief expanded researcher positionality description.

Earth Goddesses and Gaian Methods

In the imaginal intersection of the study of women and mythology and research methods, researchers can imagine that each goddess has her own research methods. Gaian methods are named after the Gaia theory, innovated by Lynn Margulis and James Lovelock, which demonstrates that the Earth is a living and self-regulating, emergent, complex system. The Gaia theory (and its earlier form, the Gaia hypothesis) was named on the suggestion of William Golding.[30]

The living Earth system is a many-faced goddess. Monaghan points out Greek Gaia's fertility was first and last parthenogenetic: "She gave birth to mountains, seas, rivers, and living beings."[31] Gimbutas notes the tripartite power of life, death, and regeneration of the ancient goddesses of Old Europe.[32] Gaian methods are generative (and we shall come to see, regenerative), inclusive, fertile, embodied, sensory and sensual, integrative, holistic. These methods might be not only those of the Greek Gaia (or Ge), a recognizable name for Westerners, but also those of Erda, Aje (African), Zemyna (Slavic), Tellus (Roman), Fjörgynn (Scandinavia), Mou-Njami (Siberian), Ponniyamman (Southeast Asia), Annapurna (Hindu), along with earth and mountain goddesses of many cultures.[33]

Four Characteristics of Gaian Methods

There are certain hallmarks of the research methods of these many Earth goddesses, and the planetary system across its multiple dimensions. The four directives of Gaian methods (first articulated in Hauk, 2010[34]) help ensure that we are not re-enacting reductionism, acting upon the Earth as a passive object, but rather infusing Gaian insights deeply in the framework, design, and conduct of our research. The emphasis on relationships is reflected in the directive "to *connect and collaborate*"[35] with the human and more than human as a researcher. *"Embed and embody"* reminds the researcher to include experiences of multisensory embodiment as research data and to embed the researchers and participants in the research system and within the Earth as a living system.[36] Gaian methods evidence the characteristics of emergence in complex adaptive systems, so part of "*extend and extol*" involves becoming aware of situating the research inside of the larger scales of emergence within (and even beyond) the emergent properties of the Earth/Gaia as a living system.[37] Gaian methods suggest that this will often result in aspects of praise for the particular aspects of the miracle of emergent properties of life and creation to imbue the research. Note that this characteristic is an invitation; researchers must learn to recognize emergent properties and emergent effects in complex systems, across scales. Finally, the research will *"thrum and thrive."*[38] Using Gaian methods means the researcher includes the Earth as a living system in the field of research as co-researcher and data and participant, and indicates how the research itself usually catalyzes more life and conditions for generativity. As Gaian methods "thrum and thrive," the research is designed to produce planetary, life-giving effects (this is related to extending meaning of catalytic validity as a research authenticity criterion). I have elsewhere described this emergence as regenerative authenticity.[39] These four characteristics of Gaian methods influence aspects of the research as summarized in Table 1.

Table 1. Researcher Directives in Gaian Methods[40]

Gaian Method Directive *(from Hauk, 2010, p. 10)*	Research Design Aspect[41]	Gaian Method Research Approach *(from Hauk, 2010, pp. 10–14)*[42]
Connect and Collaborate Relationships (especially between and among complex emergents) are primary	Expansive Collaboration	Instead of reducing things down, our research expands and spans across. The point is collaboration: how to look for similarity; in effect, the convergent evolution of insights flourishes across disciplines, similar to symbiogenesis: evolutionary advancement through the interaction and collaboration of living forms to create novel, more complex life. How can our research build on and interrelate with other research? How can the active thriving and creativity of participants and co-researchers generate greater wisdom? How can we design research so that it can be highly useful and designed to work across disciplines? With who else on campus and in our communities could we foster greater connection in order to generate novel approaches? Are there other schools or movements, ecosystems, across the entire planet, with whom we could collaborate? Our focus, instead of reduction, is on connection.
	Researcher Relationships	"Connect and Collaborate" also relates to ecological approaches; ecology largely understood is the science of relationships. How can our research and its fruits connect learners with planetary process and the appreciation and restoration of the living systems of our selves, campus, neighborhood, bioregion, biome, and planet? How can the research increase connection and generate listening to the wisdom the Earth has to share with us? How can we connect with our co-researchers, include the living systems of the planet as co-researchers? What are forms of validation for our research that we can glean from living systems?

Gaian Method Directive	Research Design Aspect	Gaian Method Research Approach
Embed and Embody Participants and relationships are embedded and embodied. Most Gaian methods involve the researcher embedded in the research rather than separated from the research in a construct of Cartesian objectivity	Researcher-Participant-System	Aware of how we are embedded in multivalent connection with the vitalizing presences and processes that generate our lively planet: home/body/Earth. We express honesty by noticing how our research is embedded in multivalent contexts. We strive neither to separate ourselves as distant observers nor to separate the focus of research phenomena from surrounding systems and interacting complex and emergent factors. Embedment in systems informs our research, can itself be the subject of our attention, and elucidates larger, even planetary patterns.
	Situatedness, Embodiment, and Experientialness	From our perspective as researchers in our human bodies, we cultivate and notice our multisensory experience, favoring movement and action. We design and participate in research that notices, honors, and privileges sensory experience and the internal phenomenological interplay of oceans in our hands, cloudscapes in velvet, and the taste of peaches. Researchers are in bodies that relate to the Earth's body, using all senses as data: gaze, sniff, savor, listen, touch.

Gaian Method Directive	Research Design Aspect	Gaian Method Research Approach
Extend and Extol Research places importance on whole-ness, life, and living systems (at whatever level of complexity)	Within and Across Emergents	The researcher must be able to go beyond our own limited perceptual capacities and look across, through, and beyond. As Gaian researchers, we notice how things function and interrelate, how they are mutually nourishing, taking a systems view, focusing on solutions-based research. How can we extend our research into the increasingly complex life of the planet? This relates to emergent properties.
	Honoring Wholeness	If we think to focus on a campus, how could this research also harvest wisdom that could be extended to other campuses? How can we situate ourselves on the edges and the ecotones, and design our solutions to cultivate resilience and diversity? How can our research be a form of praise, extolling the vibrant life of the planet? How can we research and produce research that increases awe and wonder? How can our research notice and increase wholeness and coherence, holonic truths and holistic approaches? How can our research be satisfying and life-giving to the co-researchers and resilience-building for life systems? Build transdisciplinary approaches.

Gaian Method Directive	Research Design Aspect	Gaian Method Research Approach
Thrum and Thrive Earth as a living planetary system is important/present to the field of inquiry and (re) generates the planetary living systems.	Earth as Living System	Notice and follow models of the organic and living Earth processes. Aim for flourishing and delight. Increase vitality. Go for what feels life-giving, extend the senses to include the imaginal and larger realms of information as research data, as in Romanyshyn's *Wounded Researcher* and by organic inquiry's breadth of permission. By wholeness, the Earth comes alive.
	Research Heals/ Generates/ Catalyzes	Researchers follow their bliss, their passion, what excites them in research. And dancing radiates out from the performer. Researchers and Gaian sustainability educators inspire and spark further studies and adventures, projects of hope and planetary life affirmation. Follow mystery and mysticism. Not being able to get our hands around it is understandable. We are dealing with systems that, if we limit our understanding of ourselves to the bounds of our small human skins, extends multifold complexities beyond us to emergents of emergents beyond our own embodiment and brain horsepower. How can we design research to nurture and increase Earth aliveness?

Gaian Methods Relationship with Other Inquiry Approaches

Gaian methods attend to the planetary supersystem as a point of view or lens for research, as an exemplar of processes for research, and as a researcher. Gaian methods can be considered a meta-method or lens, connecting with other ways of inquiring. One of the dynamic tensions with Gaian methods is the risk of erasure or blurring depending on the level of abstraction. Western research methods have often been critiqued for the ways that universalization and abstraction can obscure power relations and power differentials, erasing the particular, including the particular lived experiences of the oppressed and colonized.[43] Several recent movements in qualitative research attend to particularity and place and can ground Gaian methods. Ingold focuses on the experience of being alive and how movement informs the researcher who is embedded in the meshwork of embodied and animating living systems.[44] Medin and Bang, Haraway, and Martinez all emphasize the importance of relationality and kinship in research, whether through relational epistemologies (in Medin and Bang),[45] reconceptualizing other species as family members (in Haraway),[46] or through perception of kincentric ecologies (in Martinez).[47] Keating argues that this radical interconnectedness can strengthen postoppositional understandings with transformative potential.[48] Kimmerer also emphasizes the research ethics that arise through embedment in the particularizing and relational dimensions of earth-informed research. She proposes that the Earth can be the common ground for mutualistic, dynamic relations between scientific and indigenous ecological knowledge systems: "Our goal should be to learn *from* the earth, not only *about* the earth. The 'truth' about the complex relationships among elements of the natural world is resident in the land itself, so it is fitting that the earth represents the common ground from which both of these venerable knowledge systems arise."[49]

This emphasis on the land as the source of wisdom and insight processes is echoed in movements toward centering place and land in research. Critical place inquiry is relevant in a discussion of Gaian methods because of this recentering.[50] In particular, Indigenous critical place inquiry nurtures Indigenous survival and even thriving with shared commitments to refusal, non-abstractions of land, and Indigenous sovereignty. This inquiry is accomplished through approaches such as storywork, mapping placeworlds, (re)mapping to defy colonial geographic overlays to assert spatial sovereignty, community-based design work and forms of decolonial participatory action research.[51] Gaian methods have a place in this dilating attention to place and relationship in research methods.

Another gain from engaging in researching as the planetary system, without losing the power of the particular and place, is the scale-jumping leap of also attending to planetary emergence. By the researcher situating themselves within the exquisitely particular, they can also design conditions for belonging, reciprocity, and engagement with the kinds of sweep of time and place that phenomena such as climate crisis require. Speaking of the power of Gaia theory, ecopsychologists Macy and Johnstone argue that the perceptual shift about "the Earth function[ing] as a self-regulating living system" opens "a deeper collective identity" that can help Western researchers: "By refreshing our sense of belonging in the world, we widen the web of relationships that nourishes us and protects us from burnout."[52] It gives the ecopsychological boon of "see[ing] ourselves as part of a larger flow of giving and receiving," generating the gratitude that fuels our stamina and motivation for countering life-destroying patterns.[53] "Recognizing ourselves as part of the living body of the Earth opens us to a great source of strength."[54] This generous gift of Gaia can unblock our pain for the world, helping us find connectedness that is more nuanced than merging, reperceiving ourselves "as a flow of becoming."[55] Gaia feels through us and our pain becomes also our strength.[56] This shift toward our interconnectedness as a source of strength is important. Researchers and activists, "whose allegiance to wider circles of life impelled them to act in ways that brought discomfort to, and even persecution from, their peers," sustain their strength and take action.[57] Macy and Johnstone imagine that Gaia and planetary-scaled approaches, so deeply embedded in Indigenous traditions, might help heal industrial growth society, powering "a shift in identification, in which [the West] shed[s] the story of battling for supremacy and move[s] instead to playing our role as part of the larger team of life on Earth ... guided by the intention to act for the well-being of all life."[58]

Litheness Instead of Rigor in Gaian Methods

In addition to the four characteristics of Gaian methods, other quality considerations arise. I wanted to develop a form of quality in this inquiry approach that likewise embodied the signature of Gaia, and encountered litheness as a relevant consideration. The etymology of rigor relates to numbness, stiffness, and rigidity. Rather than rigor as a quality aspiration in research, I would suggest Gaian methods could aspire to *litheness* in quality. Some have suggested vigor instead of rigor, however vigor still weights growth, and in a culture where runaway hypergrowth models cause species extinction, litheness offers a more cyclic and resilient research-quality aspirational frame. Litheness carries the meaning of being easily flexible, pliant; it is also etymologically related to gentleness and slowness. This flexibility and springiness as well as life-giving qualities better convey a living systems/complexivist meaning of complicity, interconnectedness, and the flexibility of aliveness. Similar to the embedded, embodying, and extending qualities of the methods, litheness qualifies Gaian methods as matrixial,[50] which indicates the interpenetrating and mutually life-birthing qualities of mother and child as an interconnected co-becoming womb-body; perhaps even suggesting that the womb of planetary Gaia is incubating we daughter researchers within the matrix of her life-being.

Litheness also has other beneficial resonances as an aspiration for quality in research. Lithe is a homonym with Litha/Lithia, marking the fullness, abundance, and glory of the summer festival (summer solstice). Litheness is also a close homonym to Eileithyia, Cretan goddess of childbirth, used here metaphorically, for world-birthing research. It is also evocative of Lillithness and would likewise convey the cyclic birth-death-rebirth qualities of the research. Thus lithe (rather than vigorous or rigorous) Gaian methods research would be world-birthing, world-renewing, as well as reflecting the qualities described of connecting and inviting collaboration, embedding and embodying, extending the research into the planetary system, extolling and enhancing the life of earth.

Summary

In this article, I have explored the question, "What would Gaia do (WWGD) if She were (and as the planetary system is) a qualitative researcher?" What litheness in research and Gaian methods makes clear is that the living planetary system can guide and inform qualitative research approaches. The life of the planet is converging from across fields such as ecophilosophy, complex adaptive systems, Gaia theory, and the living wisdom traditions. The planet in self-metacognizing folds and blossoms of query and delight have surfaced several characteristics of Gaian qualitative research methods. Gaian methods are connective, collaborative, embedding, embodying, immersive, honoring, planetary, and life-giving. They produce research collaborations across species and ecosystems, honor the deeply earth-embedded positionality of researchers both human and more than human. Gaian methods bring renewal to personal and planetary systems. Connected with embodiment, critical place inquiry, and relationality, they aim for litheness rather than the stiff rigidity of rigor, thereby promoting life and resilience. Gaian methods are, as with Eileithyia, Cretan goddess of childbirth, world-birthing. Future research directions include exploring validity and authenticity criteria for Gaian methods[60] as well as how Gaian methods relate to earth regeneration. Gaian methods include and extend specific place-based methods, an ecofeminist lens, and terrapsychology to foster research that is life-giving and renewing. Marge Piercy affirms the expansive nature of Gaian methods and their invitation to include what human researchers sometimes otherwise forget, when she suggests, "I feel the earth, /rolling beneath as we face out /into the endlessness we usually /ignore."[61]

References

Cajete, Gregory. *Igniting the Sparkle: An Indigenous Science Education Model.* Skyand, NC: Kivaki Press, 1999.

Capra, Fritjof. *The Web of Life: A New Scientific Understanding of Living Systems.* New York: Anchor Books, 1996.

Chalquist, Craig. *RebEarths: Conversations with a World Ensouled.* Walnut Creek, CA: World Soul Books, 2010.

———. *Terrapsychology: Re-Engaging the Soul of Place.* New Orleans: Spring Journal Books, 2007.

deChambeau, Aimée, Marna Hauk, and Judith Landsman. "Gaian Methodologies," on Gaian Methods official website, May 2010. www.earthregenerative.org/gaiamethods/.

———. "Gaian Methodologies Overview: Research Resources," on Gaian Methods website, May 2010. www.earthregenerative.org/gaiamethods/.

———. "Gaian Methods: Qualitative Research with Earth." Poster session of the International Sustainability Symposium, Prescott, AZ. May 19–21, 2010.

Ettinger, Bracha L. *The Matrixial Borderspace*. Theory Out of Bounds, bk. 28. Minneapolis: University of Minnesota Press, 2006.

Gimbutas, Marija. *The Language of the Goddess*. HarperSanFrancisco, 1989.

Graves, Bill. "Portland-Area Native Americans Burdened by Health Hurdles Generation after Generation." *The Oregonian*, May 2, 2012. www.oregonlive.com/health/index.ssf/2012/05/portlands_native_americans_wag.html.

Gruenewald [Greenwood], David. "Best of Both Worlds: Critical Pedagogy of Place." *Educational Researcher* 32, no. 4 (2003): 3–12.

Harding, Sandra. *The Feminist Standpoint Reader: Intellectual and Political Controversies*. New York: Routledge, 2004.

―――. *Animate Earth: Science, Intuition, and Gaia*. White River Junction, VT: Chelsea Green, 2006.

Haraway, Donna J. *Staying with the Trouble: Making Kin in the Chthulucene*. Durham, NC: Duke University Press, 2016.

Hauk, Marna. "Four Characteristics of Gaian Methods." In Marna Hauk, Judith Landsman, Jeanine Canty, and Noël Cox Caniglia. "Gaian Methodologies—An Emergent Confluence of Sustainability Research Innovation." Paper presented at annual conference of the Association for the Advancement of Sustainability in Higher Education, Denver, CO, October 10–12, 2010.

―――. "Gaia E/mergent: Earth Regenerative Education Catalyzing Empathy, Creativity, and Wisdom." PhD diss., Prescott College, 2014.

Hauk, Marna, and Judith Landsman. "Gaian Methodologies—An Emergent Confluence of Sustainability Research Innovation." Lecture at the Association for the Advancement of Sustainability in Higher Education. Denver, Colorado, October 10–12, 2010. earthregenerative.org/pdf/AASHE-2010-HAUK-LANDSMANN-GAIAN-METHODOLOGIES-PRESENTATION-FINAL.pdf.

Hauk, Marna, Judith Landsman, Jeanine Canty, and Noël Cox Caniglia. "Gaian Methodologies—An Emergent Confluence of Sustainability Research Innovation." Paper presented at the annual Association for the Advancement of Sustainability in Higher Education Conference, Denver, CO, October 10–12, 2010. earthregenerative.org/pdf/GAIAN-METHODS-FINAL-HAUK-LANDSMAN-CANTY-COX-CANIGLIA-AASHE-2010.pdf.

Ingold, Tim. *Being Alive: Essays on Movement, Knowledge, and Description*. New York: Routledge, Taylor, and Francis, 2011.

"Invisible Nations: Native American Population" (Interactive web map). *The Oregonian*. Accessed May 3, 2012, projects.oregonlive.com/maps/native.php.

Kabat-Zinn, Jon. *Coming to Our Senses: Healing Ourselves and the World through Mindfulness.* New York: Hyperion, 2005.

Keating, AnaLouise. *Transformation Now: Toward a Postoppositional Politics of Change.* Champaign: University of Illinois Press, 2013.

Kellert, Stephen, and E. O. Wilson. *The Biophilia Hypothesis.* Washington, DC: Island Press, 1993.

Kimmerer, Robin Wall. "The Fortress, the River and the Garden: A New Metaphor for Cultivating Mutualistic Relationship between Scientific and Traditional Ecological Knowledge." In *Contemporary Studies in Environmental and Indigenous Pedagogies: A Curricula of Stories and Place*, edited by Andrejs Kulnieks, Dan Roronhiakewen Longboat, and Kelly Young, 49–76. New York: Sense Publishers, 2013.

Lovelock, James. *Gaia: The Practical Science of Planetary Medicine.* New York: Oxford, 2000.

Macy, Joanna, and Chris Johnstone. *Active Hope: How to Face the Mess We're in without Going Crazy.* Novato, CA: New World Library, 2012.

Margulis, Lynn. "Gaia by Any Other Name." In *Scientists Debate Gaia: The Next Century,* edited by Stephen H. Schneider, James. R. Miller, Eileen Crist, and Penelope J. Boston, 7–12. Cambridge, MA: MIT Press, 2004.

———. *Symbiotic Planet: A New Look at Evolution.* New York: Basic Books, 1998.

Martinez, Dennis. "Redefining Sustainability through Kincentric Ecology: Reclaiming Indigenous Lands, Knowledge, and Ethics." In *Traditional Ecological Knowledge: Learning from Indigenous Practices for Environmental Sustainability*, edited by Melissa K. Nelson and Daniel Shilling, 139–74. Cambridge University Press, 2018.

Medin, Douglas L., and Megan Bang, *Who's Asking: Native Science, Western Science, and Science Education.* Cambridge, MA: MIT Press, 2014.

Monaghan, Patricia. Volumes I and II of the *Encyclopedia of Goddesses and Heroines.* Santa Barbara, CA: Greenwood/ABC-CLIO, 2010.

Olsen, Andrea. *Body and Earth: An Experiential Guide.* Hanover, NH: Middlebury College Press, 2002.

Parajuli, Pramod. "Notes on Research Design and Methodological Ecotones." Unpublished manuscript. Prescott College, Prescott, AZ, 2008.

Piercy, Marge. *Colors Passing through Us.* New York: Alfred A. Knopf, 2004.

Prechtel, Martin. *Secrets of the Talking Jaguar: A Mayan Shaman's Journey to the Heart of the Indigenous Soul.* New York: Jeremy P. Tarcher, 1998.

Spretnak, Charlene. *Relational Reality: New Directions of Interrelatedness That Are Transforming the Modern World.* Topsham, ME: Green Horizon Books, 2011.

———. *The Resurgence of the Real: Body, Nature, and Place in a Hypermodern World.* New York: Routledge, 1999.

Swanton, John R. *The Indian Tribes of North America.* Bulletin 115, Bureau of American Ethnology. Washington, DC: US Government Printing Office, 1953. Reproduced in *AccessGeneaology* (website), Multnomah Indian tribe location, 2011. Accessed May 3, 2012, www.accessgenealogy.com/native/oregon/mult-nomah_indian_tribe_location.htm.

Taylor, Bron. *Dark Green Religion: Nature Spirituality and the Planetary Future.* Berkeley: University of California Press, 2010.

Turner, Nancy J. (2005). *The Earth's Blanket: Traditional Teachings for Sustainable Living.* Seattle: University of Washington Press.

Wilson, E. O. *Biophilia.* Cambridge, MA: Harvard University Press, 1984.

Endnotes

1   Marge Piercy, "Rising in Perilous Hope," in *Colors Passing Through Us* (New York: Alfred A. Knopf, 2004).

2   James Lovelock, *Gaia: The Practical Science of Planetary Medicine* (New York: Oxford, 2000), 24–31.

3   Lynn Margulis, *Symbiotic Planet: A New Look at Evolution* (New York: Basic Books, 1998).

4   Robin Wall Kimmerer, "The Fortress, the River and the Garden: A New Metaphor for Cultivating Mutualistic Relationship between Scientific and Traditional Ecological Knowledge," in *Contemporary Studies in Environmental and Indigenous Pedagogies: A Curricula of Stories and Place*, ed. Andrejs Kulnieks, Dan Roronhiakewen Longboat, and Kelly Young, 49–76 (New York: Sense Publishers, 2013).

5   Fritjof Capra, *The Web of Life: A New Scientific Understanding of Living Systems* (New York: Anchor Books, 1996).

6   Bron Taylor, *Dark Green Religion: Nature Spirituality and the Planetary Future* (Berkeley: University of California Press, 2010).

7   See Stephen Kellert and E. O. Wilson, *The Biophilia Hypothesis* (Washington, DC: Island Press, 1993), and E. O. Wilson, *Biophilia* (Cambridge, MA: Harvard University Press, 1984).

8   See, for example, Charlene Spretnak, *Relational Reality: New Directions of Interrelatedness That Are Transforming the Modern World* (Topsham, ME: Green Horizon Books, 2011).

9   Charlene Spretnak, *The Resurgence of the Real: Body, Nature, and Place in a Hypermodern World* (New York: Routledge, 1999).

10   Andrea Olsen, *Body and Earth: An Experiential Guide* (Hanover, NH: Middlebury College Press, 2002).

11   For example, one of its founders: Lynn Margulis, "Gaia by Any Other Name," in *Scientists Debate Gaia: The Next Century*, ed. Stephen H. Schneider, et al. (Cambridge, MA: MIT Press, 2004), 7-12.

12   Pramod Parajuli, "Notes on Research Design and Methodological Ecotones" (unpublished manuscript, Prescott College, Prescott, AZ, 2008).

13   Ibid., 4–7.

14   Martin Prechtel, *Secrets of the Talking Jaguar: A Mayan Shaman's Journey to the Heart of the Indigenous Soul* (New York: Jeremy P. Tarcher, 1998).

15   Stephen Harding, *Animate Earth: Science, Intuition, and Gaia* (White River Junction, VT: Chelsea Green, 2006).

16   Jon Kabat-Zinn, *Coming to Our Senses: Healing Ourselves and the World through Mindfulness* (New York: Hyperion, 2005).

17   Olsen, *Body and Earth.*

18   Nancy Turner, *The Earth's Blanket: Traditional Teachings for Sustainable Living* (Seattle: University of Washington Press, 2005).

19   Gregory Cajete, *Igniting the Sparkle: An Indigenous Science Education Model* (Skyand, NC: Kivaki Press, 1999).

20   Aimée deChambeau, Marna Hauk, and Judith Landsman, "Gaian Methodologies" [website], May 2010, retrieved from www.earthregenerative. org/gaiamethods/

21   Aimée deChambeau, Marna Hauk, and Judith Landsman. "Gaian Methods: Qualitative Research with Earth" (poster presented at the International Sustainability Symposium, Prescott, AZ, May 19–21, 2010).

22   Aimée deChambeau, Marna Hauk, and Judith Landsman, "Gaian Methodologies Overview: Research Resources" [web page], *Gaian Methodologies* [Website], May 2010, retrieved from www.earthregenerative.org/gaiamethods/

23   Marna Hauk, Judith Landsman, Jeanine Canty, and Noël Cox Caniglia, "Gaian Methodologies—An Emergent Confluence of Sustainability Research Innovation" (paper presented at annual conference of Association for the Advancement of Sustainability in Higher Education Conference, Denver, CO, October 10–12, 2010); retrieved June 27, 2019 from earthregenerative. org/pdf/GAIAN-METHODS-FINAL-HAUK-LANDSMAN-CANTY-COX-CANIGLIA-AASHE-2010.pdf

24   Marna Hauk and Judith Landsman, "Gaian Methodologies—An Emergent Confluence of Sustainability Research Innovation" [peer-reviewed presentation] (lecture at Association for the Advancement of Sustainability in Higher Education, Denver, Colorado, October 10–12, 2010); retrieved June 27, 2019 from earthregenerative.org/pdf/AASHE-2010-HAUK-LANDSMANN-GAIAN-METHODOLOGIES-PRESENTATION-FINAL.pdf

25   For more on feminist positionality, see, for example, Sandra Harding, *The Feminist Standpoint Reader: Intellectual and Political Controversies* (New York: Routledge, 2004).

26   "Invisible Nations: Native American Population" [interactive web map], *The Oregonian*; retrieved May 3, 2012 from http://projects.oregonlive.com/maps/native.php. See also Bill Graves, "Portland-Area Native Americans Burdened by Health Hurdles Generation after Generation," *The Oregonian*, May 2, 2012; retrieved May 3, 2012 from www.oregonlive.com/health/index.ssf/2012/05/port-lands_native_americans_wag.html

27   John R. Swanton, *The Indian Tribes of North America*, Bulletin 115, Bureau of American Ethnology (Washington, DC: US Government Printing Office, 1953); reproduced in AccessGeneaology (2011), Multnomah Indian tribe location [web page], and retrieved May 3, 2012 from www.accessgenealogy.com/native/oregon/multnomah_indian_tribe_location.htm

28   This place-informed approach to positionality could qualify as terrapsychological. See Craig Chalquist, *Terrapsychology: Re-Engaging the Soul of Place* (New Orleans: Spring Journal Books, 2007); and Craig Chalquist, *RebEarths: Conversations with a World Ensouled* (Walnut Creek, CA: World Soul Books, 2010).

29   David Gruenewald [Greenwood], "Best of Both Worlds: Critical Pedagogy of Place," *Educational Researcher* 32, no. 4 (2003): 3–12.

30   Lovelock, *Gaia*, 22–24.

31 Patricia Monaghan, "Gaia," in "Greece," *Encyclopedia of Goddesses and Heroines*, Vol. 2, *Europe and the Americas* (Santa Barbara, CA: ABC-CLIO/Greenwood, 2010), 404.

32 Marija Gimbutas, *The Language of the Goddess* (HarperSanFrancisco, 1989), 316–17.

33 See extensive discussion of "Earth goddesses" in Monaghan, Vol. I, *Encyclopedia*, xxviiii–xxxi.

34 Marna Hauk, "Four Characteristics of Gaian Methods," in Marna Hauk, Judith Landsman, Jeanine Canty, and Noël Cox Caniglia, "Gaian Methodologies—An Emergent Confluence of Sustainability Research Innovation" (paper presented at annual conference of the Association for the Advancement of Sustainability in Higher Education, Denver, CO, October 10–12, 2010), 10–14.

35 Ibid., 12.

36 Ibid., 11–12.

37 Ibid., 12–13.

38 Ibid., 13–14.

39 Marna Hauk, "Gaia E/mergent: Earth Regenerative Education Catalyzing Empathy, Creativity, and Wisdom" (PhD diss., Prescott College, 2014), 153–55.

40 Adapted from Hauk, "Four Characteristics," 10–14.

41 Ibid., 10.

42 Ibid.

43 43 Kimmerer, "The Fortress, the River, and the Garden," 2013. See also Eve Tuck and Marcia McKenzie, *Place in Research: Theory, Methodology, and Methods* (New York: Routledge, 2015).

44 Tim Ingold, *Being Alive: Essays on Movement, Knowledge, and Description* (New York: Routledge, Taylor, and Francis, 2011).

45 Douglas L. Medin and Megan Bang, *Who's Asking: Native Science, Western Science, and Science Education* (Cambridge, MA: MIT Press, 2014).

46 Donna J. Haraway, *Staying with the Trouble: Making Kin in the Chthulucene* (Durham, NC: Duke University Press, 2016).

47 Dennis Martinez, "Redefining Sustainability through Kincentric Ecology: Reclaiming Indigenous Lands, Knowledge, and Ethics," in *Traditional Ecological Knowledge: Learning from Indigenous Practices for Environmental Sustainability*, ed. Melissa K. Nelson and Daniel Shilling (Cambridge University Press, 2018), 139–74.

48   AnaLouise Keating, *Transformation Now: Toward a Postoppositional Politics of Change* (Champaign: University of Illinois Press, 2013).

49   Kimmerer, "The Fortress, the River, and the Garden," 61.

50   Tuck and McKenzie, *Place in Research.*

51   Ibid., 130–49.

52   Joanna Macy and Chris Johnstone, *Active Hope: How to Face the Mess We're in Without Going Crazy* (Novato, CA: New World Library, 2012), 31–32.

53   Ibid., 56.

54   Ibid., 94.

55   Ibid., 93.

56   Ibid., 97–98.

57   Ibid., 95.

58   Ibid., 100.

59   Brache Ettinger, *The Matrixial Borderspace*, Theory Out of Bounds, bk. 28 (Minneapolis: University of Minnesota Press, 2006).

60   See Marna Hauk, "Gaia E/mergent," 153–55, for a discussion of regenerative or autopoietic validity. Note: The manuscript for this paper was presented and submitted for proceedings in 2012 and makes up an acknowledged portion of my doctoral scholarship. See Hauk, "Gaia E/mergent," 91–100 and 652. The scholarship on regenerative validity mentioned in this note was written after the paper was presented.

61   Piercy, "Leonids Over Us," 88.

SACRED LAND IN THE MIDST OF MODERNITY: THE TEMPLE OF GODDESS SPIRITUALITY DEDICATED TO SEKHMET

ANNE KEY AND CANDACE KANT

Introduction*

In the tiny village of Cactus Springs, Nevada, lies a pagan temple. On twenty acres surrounded by hundreds of acres of BLM (Bureau of Land Management) land on Highway 95, less than an hour north of Las Vegas, it is a refuge of peace. The desert teems with wildlife—jack rabbits, owls, kangaroo rats, lizards, spiders, snakes, coyotes, and bobcats wander about. Hawks, ravens, buzzards, bluebirds and goldfinches flutter about. Groves of fragrant creosote, mesquite trees and salt cedars are nourished by the aquifer. To the east of the Temple is a true oasis, the shaded Cactus Spring, local animal watering hole and home to frogs and turtles. At night, in the dark velvet of the sky, the Milky Way sweeps across, and shooting stars punctuate viewers' thoughts. The celestial heavens whisper. Visitors to the temple can watch the sunlight play upon the mountains' craggy face as shadows dance across them. To the east is the Sheep Range, over which the sun and moon rise, and the Spring Mountain range is to the south; these mountains enfold the temple in its valley. This is a perfect place for a modern Pagan temple dedicated to an Egyptian goddess: In the desert but atop an aquifer, secluded, but with easy highway access.

With all the markings of modern goddess-oriented paganism, the temple is decidedly feminist-activist with a goddess and peace focus rooted in the spiritual activism of Starhawk and Z. Budapest. The temple was conceived, designed, and funded by women. Actual construction was accomplished by a group of young peace activists, mostly women and a few men, who called themselves CHAOS: which stood for cooking, housework, and other stuff. The eco-friendly straw-bale structure has four doorways open to the directions and the roof is open to the sky, embellished with a yantra formed by a copper seven-petalled lotus filled with crystals. The statue of Sekhmet in the temple was made by Marsha Gomez, a Mexican/Indian artist. With the head of a lion and a woman's body, Sekhmet fittingly embodies all that is animal, human, and divine; Gomez captured her very human and female nature in her bare breasts, one slightly larger than the other.

The temple not only has an exclusive goddess focus but also has socio-political ties with the peace and justice activist communities. In light of these ties, attendees at temple rituals cut a wide swath, including the usual suspects: pagans, wiccans, and goddess followers, not necessarily exclusive to one another. There is also the feminist contingent, most of whom identify with the philosophical stance of the temple but do not necessarily adhere to a pagan spiritual practice. And then there are the activists of all faiths. The temple has especially close ties with the Catholic Worker peace move-ment as well as a variety of a-religious grassroots groups. Added to this mix is the odd UFO chaser hanging out in the desert who joins the rituals for something to do. Rituals tend to have fifteen to thirty in attendance for the full moons and thirty to sixty for the wheel-of-the-year celebrations; participants are generally 60 percent female and 40 percent male.

The Temple of Goddess Spirituality Dedicated to Sekhmet was built through the benefaction of Genevieve Vaughan, a philanthropist, feminist, peace activist and author of the theory of the gift economy. The temple was built in 1993 to honor Sekhmet, and the funding for the temple, retreat center, and priestess continue under her sponsorship. Her philosophies of feminism, peace activism and goddess spirituality are guiding principles.[1]

Sacred Land

A sacred site is thought of as one where the divine issues forth into the human realm, a place where the mundane and the sacred intersect, a rupture in the ordinary domain through which the divine penetrates.[2] Jean Shinoda Bolen believes that sacred sites are where "worlds overlap or interpenetrate and life is imbued with depth and meaning."[3] They are thought to be an axis mundi, where Earth and Divine meet.

Locations such as these have drawn people to them over a period of time in awareness or reverence of the sacred and are used over and over for rituals. It is thought that the site itself takes on a collective energy from the emotional and spiritual intent focused there, coupled with the natural energy of the place itself. Carol Christ writes, "The earth holds the energies of the beings who have lived upon it. Sacred places hold the dreams, visions, and hopes of all the people who have visited them."[4] These sentiments are echoed by those who visit the temple.

We have developed two sources of information that provide a glimpse into the ideas of those who come to the temple about the concept of sacred land. The first is very informal—a small guest book and a pen. A series of these blank guest books have been inside the temple since 1997. People often leave written messages, of both the sacred and profane types (sometimes very profane!), when they visit the temple. As the temple is often empty during the day, visitors write unprompted in the guest book; many comments reflect their feelings as they are inside the temple.

> *4/97: I thank God for this sacred place where I find a deep peace. This place is full of spiritual presence.*
>
> *8/98: Thank you for sharing the peace, tranquility, and force of the desert and sky with us today.*
>
> *8/04: This place rocks!*
>
> *5/05: Yo no creo ni en una ni en otra cosa pero lo único que puedo decir es que hay muy buena energía.*
>
> *9/06: Thank you for this beautiful place, so charged, so tangibly close to deity.*

A profound sense of gratitude that this sacred space exists pervades the messages in the books. We do not try to determine whether those who enter the temple experience this sense of the sacred because of some concrete physical reason or because they "feel" as if they should feel different. In fact, we are not really sure that can be quantified. What we do know is that many people, for whatever reason, report feelings associated with sacred space, most notably peace and a connection to the Divine.

The second source of written information is an Internet survey we created and vetted by a series of professionals from different disciplines. The survey was made available from June through August 2007 to a wide variety of people connected to the temple through individual emails and postings on various Internet group sites. It resulted in 118 respondents who submitted answers to a variety of questions. Those we focus on in this paper are the questions regarding ideas of sacrality and the temple, and how individuals define the term "sacred land."

When responding to the question—"Do you consider the Temple to be sacred land? Why or why not?"—a few of the respondents made the connection between the Native American ancestral heritage of the land and its present use:

> *The Temple ground and hence the temple is sacred land for two reasons. First, I believe it belonged to the Indian reservation and secondly it was developed as the Temple for a specific purpose by women for women and others seeking it.*

Some replied that all land is sacred—"Simply because it is part of the Earth Mother." Others wrote that the land at the temple has special qualities:

> *The plants talk to me. I walk with presence there. All of nature is alive and can be interacted with. It is clean and there is mutual respect by all life there.*

Overwhelmingly, respondents wrote that it was the connection between the activities on the land and its status that made it sacred:

> *The work done on the land, the intention of the temple, the temple itself and the way it is served by the people who activate it.*

When asked "What does the term 'sacred land' mean to you?" respondents replied with some rather eloquent pieces. Some responded with the idea that sacred land is land that has been dedicated by persons for use in a sacred way, set aside for ritual. Some responded with remarks on the inherent sacred nature of all land. But, then, many wrestled with the idea that some land is more sacred than others:

All land is sacred to me, and yet some land has been enhanced by protection and spiritual work done on it, and some land has natural qualities that enhance its ability to connect humans to source.

Sacred land ... all land is sacred ... but some seems to be more sacred somehow.

Land where we can easily connect with the divine ... in ourselves and others.

Land that builds and holds power.

Others commented on the connection between the land's inherent qualities and human action:

I understand that it is commonly thought that we sanctify and purify sacred spaces by spiritually practicing and performing rituals upon it. I suppose that all land begins as sacred, but we change the spirituality of it through our uses and the way we treat it.

The musings of visitors to the temple, whether in the guest book or on an Internet survey, seem to bear out Christ's and Bolen's ideas about the sacred. The temple is a place where people sense a connection with the Divine. The fact that others consider the temple sacred is important, giving it that sense of collective energy.

Irony of Place

That the temple is held by so many as sacred land is one of its deepest ironies, for its placement is at the crux of the overlapping of the sacred and profane, the spiritual and the earthly, the environment and human, good and evil. The temple lies on liminal space, space that demarcates an edge, a threshold. In many cultures, liminal spaces needed to be protected, and often an apotropaic deity was revered at these places for protection, such as Hecate's veneration at the crossroads in Ancient Greece. Such is the threshold bespeaking the temple, where our modern demons confront the modern sacred.

Less than forty miles south of one of the most established goddess temples in the United States solely dedicated to feminist values and goddess spirituality, is Las Vegas, that monument to materialism, America's largest opium den, and arguably the leader in the commodification of women's bodies.

Due east of the temple lies another front in the interminable war of human versus human, a large prison complex with two state prisons and various "boot camps." These prisons house almost 3,500 male "guests of the state."[5]

To the north of the temple is a bombing range covering over 4,000 square miles. This range is in constant use to test the effectiveness of bombs and accuracy of delivery systems, resulting in ground-shaking, window-rattling deep booms. Predator and Reaper UAVs (unmanned aerial vehicles) are being maneuvered daily, monitoring the accuracy of bomb strikes.

Immediately across the street from the temple on the north side of Highway 95 is Creech Air Force Base. F-15s, F-16s, and A-10s regularly fly over, disrupting the silence with their bone-jarring roars. The planes actually line up with the temple on their approach.

The land near the temple is strikingly similar to that of Afghanistan and northern Iraq, so this area is used as a training ground before troops deploy. After dark, the air is lit by flares, sometimes tracing the path of bullets and sometimes lighting the battlefield so those engaged in war games can see each other. Black Hawk helicopters fly low over the terrain, often in groups, seemingly searching for something or someone. The Thunderbirds practice their maneuvers in the skies. As one respondent to the Internet survey said upon reflecting about his first visit to the Temple:

> *How can you think straight with what I saw going on across the freeway! The air force was shooting at something and it was quite scary. From a logistics standpoint, it seems challenging to plant a Temple next to a firing range or whatever Creech is. LOL.*

The Temple dedicated to peace is in a place where one can never forget war.

As if that were not enough, to the northwest of the temple is the Nevada Test Site, truly a monument to "man's" disregard and destruction of each other and the Earth. It is here, of course, that mushroom clouds from atomic testing were celebrated and the effects of radiation repeatedly ignored. Yucca Mountain, proposed site to dump nuclear waste, lies just a bit farther north.

Another irony of place is the temple's location on land sacred to the indigenous inhabitants, illustrating that the naming of what is sacred and the demarcation of the sacred is definitely the purview of "who's in charge." Prior to the arrival of European colonists, the area comprising Yucca Mountain, Creech Air Force Base, the bombing range, and the temple had long been considered sacred land to the Shoshone and Paiute.[6] Ancestors of the Shoshone are buried on Yucca Mountain, and the water in the surrounding area, including the water from Cactus Spring near the temple, is considered sacred. The Shoshone refer to Yucca Mountain as Snake Mountain, and the rock prayer rings are places to communicate with the Great Spirit. It is a place where one's prayers are heard, and messages received. As told by the late Corbin Harney, Western Shoshone spiritual leader, the legend of Snake Mountain is that one day the mountain will awaken and break open, and poisons will spew through the gash. Many see that as a prophecy for Yucca Mountain, a prophecy of the bad omen ilk.

After her purchase of the land and the construction of the Temple, Genevieve Vaughn ceded the twenty acres back to the Newe people, the native word for the Western Shoshone. She wrote: "I gave the land back to the Shoshone to whom it originally belonged, in a ceremony for the commemoration of the 500 years of oppression and colonization of the Americas in 1992."[7] The temple land has been used at times by the Newe, especially when there is a peace action at the Nevada Test Site. The temple serves as a "home base" for activities.

But the Newe people do not use the temple land for ceremonial grounds. Nor do they wholeheartedly agree with the principles of a goddess-oriented, neo-pagan wiccan spiritual practice. While some view the temple with benign amusement, others view the practitioners as akin to devil worshippers.[8] This irony raises yet more questions. Is this temple yet another stage of colonization? Is its presence a source of recognition, of re-sacralization? Or is it desecration? The temple land, as well as all land in the United States, is literally terrain filled with complex histories of subjugation, rights, conquest, domination, and destruction. Nevertheless, it is the intent and hope of those who honor and worship on the temple land that it, somehow, bridges the disconnect between those that live on the land and the land itself.

It is within these deep ironies of place that the Temple derives its liminality, its power as a sacred space. By placing a temple in an area considered "desert," bringing to mind the words "lifeless" and "worthless," Vaughan has unwittingly carried out a grand experiment. What happens when land considered worthless and lifeless suddenly becomes a global site for goddess worshippers, pagans, and peace activists? In twenty-eight short years, this land has gone from completely ignored, forgettable, to sacred, powerful, healing, and alive. Has the land changed? Or has the relationship between the people and the land changed? Or both?

The Land and the Sacred:
The Great American Disconnect

The ideas of "land" and "sacred" in the context of the United States are truly disconnected. A quick look at American cyberspace psyche (i.e., Google) shows that a search for the terms "sacred," "land" and "America" results in multiple sites for saving land considered sacred by Native American tribes, further demonstrating the disconnect between the current dominant culture and the land that sustains it. The underlying assumption seems to be: certain land was sacred to Native Americans, but this is relevant to the dominant (Euro-American/Christian) culture *only* as a political issue. There appears to be a complete disconnect between the land and spiritual heritage.

It is this lack of the recognition for the sacred nature of the land of the United States that reveals what Clifford Geertz terms "misworkings": "The questions that anthropologists have pursued among exotic religions have arisen from the working—or the misworkings—of Modern Western Society, and particularly from its restless quest for self-discovery."[9] The discovery of "self" seems completely disconnected to the land that "self" lives on, that land that supports the very life of "self." This is most evident in regards to the relationship between land and spirituality.

The basis for the separation of the ideas of land, sacred, and America might be seen as an outgrowth of the predominant Abrahamic spiritual heritage. In the early twenty-first century, 52 percent of Americans identified themselves as Protestant, 24 percent Catholic, 1.3 percent Jewish, 0.5 percent Muslim, and 14 percent as having no religion.[10] With the majority of Americans claiming Christianity as their religion (76 percent in 2010) the Holy Land is indeed Israel and Palestine, not North America.

While the dominant American culture recognizes the term "Holy Land" as referring to Jerusalem and Israel, and certainly many Americans travel to sites considered holy and sacred by other cultures, the mainstream culture does not recognize the land its people are currently living on as sacred. In what can be seen as the pinnacle of postmodernism in terms of separation of perception and reality, the most powerful religion in arguably the most powerful country has the highest stakes for sacred land in another country, unknown and un-experienced by the vast majority of people identifying as co-religionists.[11]

Winona LaDuke, a Native American activist and theorist, discusses the dominant culture's views of sacred land: "While Judeo-Christian sacred sites such as the 'Holy Land' are recognized, the existence of other Holy Lands [our capitalizations] has been denied.... The concept of 'Holy Land' cannot be exclusive in a multi-cultural and multi-spiritual society, yet indeed it has been treated as such."[12] Herein lies the Great Disconnect. In the eyes of the dominant culture, the land of America is not viewed as having inherent value in and of itself. The land is not sacred, not worthy. This is quite likely the biggest difference between immigrant/conqueror and indigenous societies regarding the land. For the latter, the land is sacred, holy. For the former, the land is a place to live and live off of until a possible return, later in life, to a distant sacred land.

Additionally, Euro-American philosophy is not disposed to viewing land as sacred or perceiving the relationship between spiritual practice and land. Two well-known scholars of Western European cultural life in the early twentieth century suggested not only that land is lifeless matter but also that what is sacred and what is profane are two different spheres of existence that do not meet. Sociologist Max Weber observed that the "fate of our times" was characterized by rationalization, intellectualization and, above all, the disenchantment of the world. In this statement he referred to the idea that rationalization had displaced magical elements in modern Western societies. Emile Durkheim purported that a separation of the sacred and profane was a "distinctive trait of religious thought."[13]

Carrying this theme a bit further, theologian Paul Tillich views the concept of land as sacred to occur early in the development of culture, meaning that more developed cultures do not have sacred ties to their land.

Tillich states: "The conception of nature that we find earliest in history, so far as we have knowledge of it, is the magical-sacramental conception.... At this phase of cultural development, the distinction between the sacred and profane is not a fundamental one."[14] This view implies that a connection to the sacredness of land is almost infantile, certainly not that of an educated modern American.

Vine Deloria Jr., one of the most prominent indigenous voices explaining Native American history and culture, replies to Tillich: "If the early religious view is sacramental, it is an attitude that requires a specific approach to the world and its beings. It recognizes that they have values in and of themselves."[15] According to many indigenous people, sacred does not signify something of religious significance and therefore believed in with emotional fervor, that is, something "venerable, consecrated, or sacrosanct." It is not something that is built by humans. Nor is it necessary for it to commemorate some historic event. Rather, sacred indicates something that is filled with an intangible but very real power or force.[16] Many indigenous cultures feel that everything in the cosmos is understood as participating in the sacred: everything is imbued with consciousness and spirit and partakes in the greater power of being: "If the Great Spirit or Great Mystery holds everything in its thought, then everything is sacred."[17] Although the sacred is omnipresent, it lodges most intensely in particular places, like the sun, trees, and animals.[18]

The Effect of Sacred Land: The Disconnected Connected

One way to view the particular tenets of a spiritual practice is to study its images and metaphors. As Geertz so aptly states, religion, or spiritual practice, is "embodied in the images and metaphors its adherents use to characterize reality."[19] For pagans and other indigenous religions, the images and metaphors are the land. The prominent pagan theorist Michael York says that "[t]he earth and nature constitute the seminal and unifying sacred text" for pagan spiritual expression.[20] It is this idea of earth as sacred text that moves pagans and indigenous peoples to see land as Holy ... Sacred.

In the world surrounding the temple, humans are separated from nature, from the land. Jane Caputi observes that, "At work, in our religions, our entertainments, and in our living places—there is little occasion for sensual interactions with nature, with organic matter and living organisms."[21] Instead, people interact mostly with machines—factory tools and devices, cars, computers, televisions, cell phones."[22] This separation becomes disorienting, altering our values, encouraging us to gauge our success by the number of our material possessions. "In the rationalist world view, a great chasm exists between the sacred and the mundane. The elemental world, nature, and animals are desacralized, said to be lacking in soul, consciousness, and purpose—and, hence, can be exploited at will."[23] Separation of this sort puts us out of balance, and leads us to think that we, as living organisms, are indeed separate from the context that gives and sustains life.

The temple reverses this, compelling those who are on temple land to become conscious and connected with the land. In this context, the concept of "sacred" signifies a reconnection of humans to the Earth. But those who come to the temple assert that the meaning of such particular land is more than simply becoming conscious of and enjoying nature. On freezing nights in midwinter, the enjoyment of nature is not what draws people out of their warm homes to celebrate the turning of the seasons in the open, and very cold, air. And, in August, what draws hundreds to subject themselves to the almost unbearable and dangerous heat to give honor to an Egyptian goddess? Most will say that this land has a special energy, or, if not special, then an energy which is more easily felt on that site than in our asphalt-covered wilderness.

The concept of the sacred is complex.Callois writes that the sacred is "the inexhaustible source that creates, sustains, and renews."[24] Caputi describes the sacred as "the cosmic potency to make things happen, the endlessly fruitful energy that creates life. At the same time, life is always in a process of growth, transformation, death, and rebirth. Thus, the sacred is a two-faced power--one that not only advances but also retreats, one that creates and sustains, but also destroys and transforms."[25]

Perhaps the notion of transformation is most important with regard to the temple. Those who come to the temple look for a transformation in their lives, from the very mundane of hoping to find a job, to the sublime of looking for deep meaning and purpose in existence. In addition, the presence of the temple is a visible symbol of transformation. As Sekhmet gazes toward the test site, one wonders if this Egyptian goddess, whose story involves the punishment of humans who disregarded the gods, is pondering the wounding of the Earth with atomic blasts, bunker busters, and "Divine Strake." The very existence of this monument to peace, and the rituals performed on this land, are engaged in transformation. According to Jane Caputi:

> Ritual is organized activity that strives to manipulate or direct nonmaterial energies toward some larger goal. Ritual consists of actions organized to produce power in order to effect transformations, to influence direction, to reconceptualize and hence reconfigure reality. Like prayer, ritual intends to tap into cosmic sources of power to effect some end.[26]

Perhaps, as well, we do not just "read" the text at that supposed distance. Rather we enter into it and feed it energetically. Perhaps as a result of our participation in these "small ceremonies," certain powers or potentialities are bolstered and thereby realized (literally, made real); concomitantly others are banished, neglected, degraded, starved, undone.[27] Ritual is intended to achieve some end, and in the process those who participate in the ritual are in turn transformed by it.

The pagan rituals, performed at the turning of the seasons and the solstices and equinoxes, engage the participants with the land. It is this connection that recognizes land once considered "just desert," or worse, a site that could be bombed or used to house nuclear waste, and re-sacralizes it, recognizing it as Holy Land. And it is the recognition of our sacred lands that will alter our lives. If indeed the twentieth century was an experiment to see what would happen if the dominant culture of a country never recognized the sacred in its own home, we are hopeful that the twenty-first century will be an experiment of what happens when those who came as conquerors begin to be indigenous and connect to the sacred, holy land upon which they live.

References

Caillois, Roger. *Man and the Sacred*, trans. Meyer Barash. Glencoe, IL: Free Press, 1959.

Caputi, Jane. *Goddesses and Monsters: Women, Myth, Power, and Popular Culture*. Madison: University of Wisconsin Press, 2004.

Christ, Carol. *Rebirth of the Goddess*. New York: Routledge, 1997.

Durkheim, Emile. *The Elementary Forms of Religious Life*. London: Allen and Unwin [1912; English trans. 1915], 1976.

Geertz, Clifford. *Islam Observed: Religious Development in Morocco and Indonesia*. New Haven, CT: Yale University Press, 1968.

_____. "Two Types of Ecosystems," in *Environment and Cultural Behavior*, ed. A. Vayda. Austin: University of Texas Press, 1969.

Lago, Luis. "The Decline of Institutional Religion." Paper presented at Faith Angle Forum, South Beach, Florida, March 2013.

Mies, Maria. *Patriarchy and Accumulation on a World Scale: Women in the International Division of Labor*. New York: Zed Books, 1998.

Sanchez, Carol Lee. "Animal, Vegetable, and Mineral: The Sacred Connection," in *Ecofeminism and the Sacred*, ed. Carol J. Adams, 207–28. New York: Continuum, 1993.

Tate, Karen. *Sacred Places of Goddess*. San Francisco: CCC Publishing, 2006.

Vaughan, Genevieve. "Introduction." In *Women and the Gift Economy: A Radically Different Worldview Is Possible*, edited by Genevieve Vaughan. Toronto: Inanna Publications and Education Inc., 2004.

York, Michael. *Pagan Theology: Paganism as a World Religion*. New York: New York University Press, 2003.

Endnotes

* This paper was first drafted in 2006 and has been revised many times. We delivered earlier versions of the work at various conferences, including the American Association of Religion (2007), Far West Popular Culture Conference (2008) and Association for the Study of Women and Mythology (2018).

1 Genevieve's story is iconic. On a tour in Egypt with her husband in 1965, her guide took her to a Sekhmet temple in Karnak. He advised her that if she wanted something, she should ask Sekhmet, and that she should offer Sekhmet a promise. She knew nothing of Sekhmet or goddess spirituality, but as she had been unable to conceive, Genevieve asked Sekhmet for a child. She promised Sekhmet that she would build Her a temple. Genevieve conceived her first child only days later, and over the course of years had three daughters. She built the temple to Sekhmet. For almost fifteen years, the temple has stood as a beacon

and a refuge of international status for those in the goddess communities as well as the peace and social justice activist communities. The temple is held by many as sacred land.

2   Karen Tate, *Sacred Places of Goddess* (CCC Publishing, 2006), 17, quoting Kathryn Rountree, "Goddess Pilgrimages and the Politics of Performance" (lecture, Social Anthropology Department, School of Social and Cultural Studies, Massey University, Auckland, New Zealand, [2005]).

3   Quoted in Tate, *Sacred Places of Goddess*, 17.

4   Carol Christ, *Rebirth of the Goddess* (New York: Routledge, 1997), 28.

5   Resident totals as of October 15, 2007: Indian Springs Boot Camp, 60; Indian Springs Conservation Camp, 228; Southern Desert Correctional Center, 1,354; High Desert State Prison, 1,816.

6   According to the Ruby Valley Treaty of 1863, the Shoshone have rights to 60 million acres in Nevada, Idaho, Utah, and California, which includes Yucca Mountain. The land was never deeded to the US, though the treaty states that there are certain activities that the US can engage in on this land. The US now claims over 80 percent of that land as solely belonging to the federal government due to "encroachment." The federal government has tried to persuade the Shoshone to accept financial compensation for their land, but they refuse. The Shoshone are adamantly opposed to nuclear testing on their native lands. For more information, see www.sacredland.org/endangered_sites_pages/yucca_mountain.html and www.wsdp.org/. For a video about the fight of two Shoshone grandmothers against the federal government for grazing rights, see act.oxfamamerica.org/oxfamamerica/ourland_ourlife.html.

7   Genevieve Vaughan, "Introduction," in *Women and the Gift Economy: A Radically Different Worldview Is Possible*, ed. Vaughan (Toronto: Inanna Publications and Education Inc., 2004). See n. 1.

8   From personal communications with various Newe people in the region, 2004–2007.

9   Clifford Geertz, *Islam Observed: Religious Development in Morocco and Indonesia* (New Haven, CT: Yale University Press, 1968), 398.

10   Data from General Social Surveys, 1972–2010, The Pew Forum on Religion and Public Life, Pew Research Center, Washington, DC, in Luis Lago, "The Decline of Institutional Religion" (paper presented at Faith Angle Forum, South Beach, Florida, March 2013, available at www.washingtonpost.com/r/2010-2019/WashingtonPost/2013/03/25/Editorial-Opinion/Graphics/Pew-Decline-of-Institutional-Religion.pdf).

11   The most extreme version of this separation could be the Christian Zionism movement that hopes to hasten the arrival of massive war in the Holy Land, from which they are comfortably removed. Israeli journalist and author Gershom Gorenborg, in a 2008 radio-broadcast interview, spoke on this issue: "The people who promote the idea of Christian Zionism are looking at Israel in mythological terms. They are seeing the Jews as actors in a Christian drama leading toward the end of days. Real Zionism as a Jewish movement is a movement aimed at taking Jews out of the mythological realm, and making them into normal actors in history, controlling their fate and acting for pragmatic reasons in the here and now." (From "Fresh Air," WHYY-FM, Philadelphia, broadcast nationally by National Public Radio, September 18, 2008.) All religion needs a Holy Land, and we are seeing the effects of a powerful and displaced community that mythologizes a land far removed. The disconnect between Americans and this land has ramifications reaching far beyond our borders.

12   Winona LaDuke, *Recovering the Sacred: The Power of Naming and Claiming* (Boston: South End Press, 2005), vi.

13   Emile Durkheim, *The Elementary Forms of Religious Life* (London: Allen and Unwin [1912; English trans. 1915], 1976), 37: "The division of the world into two domains, the one containing all that is sacred, the other all that is pro-fane, is the distinctive trait of religious thought; the beliefs, myths, dogmas and legends are either representations or systems of representations which express the nature of sacred things, the virtues and powers which are attributed to them, or their relations with each other and with profane things."

14   Paul Tillich, *The Protestant Era*, edited by James Luther Adams (Chicago: University of Chicago Press, 1948), 99–100.

15   Vine Deloria Jr., *Evolution, Creationism, and Other Modern Myths: A Critical Inquiry* (Golden, CO: Fulcrum Publishing, 2004), 143.

16   Paula Gunn Allen, quoted in Caputi, *Goddesses and Monsters*, 164.

17   Carol Lee Sanchez, "Animal, Vegetable, and Mineral: The Sacred Connection," in *Ecofeminism and the Sacred*, ed. Carol J. Adams (New York: Continuum, 1993), 22.

18   Caputi, *Goddesses and Monsters*, 244.

19   Clifford Geertz, "Two Types of Ecosystems," in *Environment and Cultural Behavior*, ed. A. Vayda (Austin: University of Texas Press, 1969), 3.

20   Michael York, *Pagan Theology: Paganism as a World Religion* (New York: New York University Press, 2003), 16.

81

21 Maria Mies, *Patriarchy and Accumulation on a World Scale: Women in the International Division of Labor* (New York: Zed Books, 1998), 218.

22 Jane Caputi, *Goddesses and Monsters: Women, Myth, Power, and Popular Culture* (Madison: University of Wisconsin Press, 2004), 249.

23 Ibid., 244.

24 Roger Caillois, *Man and the Sacred*, trans. Meyer Barash (Glencoe, IL: Free Press, 1959), 22.

25 Caputi, *Goddesses and Monsters*, 243–44.

26 Ibid., 164.

27 Ibid., 163.

DIVINE MISTRESSES OF NATURE, PLANTS AND ANIMALS IN ANCIENT GREECE: AN ECOFEMINIST PERSPECTIVE

MARA LYNN KELLER

Great Goddesses of Nature

Scholars speak of primal religions as animistic, that our earliest human ancestors believed divine powers animated all life on earth. Sometimes primal religions are referred to as shamanism, because certain members of the social group—female and male shamans, and sometimes the entire social group—would call upon specific animal, plant, or cosmic powers to aid individuals and communities, for procreation, healing, and flourishing.

From the ancient Mediterranean world we find shamanistic images of magical beings who are part human and part animal, or part plant, or part insect. This demonstrates humans' abilities to identify with the lives of other creatures and their distinct powers—including the bee, bird, snake, cat, cow, horse, lioness, dolphin, and more. For example, in Egypt, the Neolithic bird goddess from the Nile Delta, dated to circa 7000 BCE,[1] combines the powers of woman and the great winged bird; she was the symbol of the soul's resurrection. Hathor was a Great Mother Goddess depicted as a horned cow; she was the source of life and nourishment. Cow goddesses also appear in Crete and Anatolia; and in Greece, where she was called Hera. Isis, also a Great Mother Goddess in Egypt, was a great winged goddess of fertility, healing, laws, and resurrection. Bast or Bastet, the cat goddess, was worshiped, as were all cats in Egypt. Bast was the goddess of the home, cats, fertility, childbirth, and women's secrets; she "protected the home from evil spirits and disease, especially diseases associated with women and children."[2] We find goddesses who are part feline or accompanied by felines not only in Egypt, but also in Anatolia, Greece, and later in Rome.[3]

Ancient Greeks perceived the whole of Earth to be a living goddess, whom they named Ge or Gaia. She created heaven and then, after consorting with heaven, gave birth to all the deities and all creatures on Earth. According to Hesiod, who during the Archaic Age recorded various oral traditions or folklore about goddesses and gods: when Gaia birthed starry heaven, Uranos, she created him as her equal.

And Earth first bare starry Heaven, equal to herself.[4]

This earliest expression of a sacred marriage in the mythologies of Greek deities was one of equals, as designed by the Great Goddess, Gaia. And perhaps for millennia, this was the kinship model followed by the earliest peoples in the region that later became known as Greece. This partnership model was also expressed in the relationship of Greek male farmers with Mother Earth, who saw themselves working together in harmony with her to bring forth her powers of fertility.[5]

Gaia was fruitful, and all the plants and animals issued forth from the womb of Gaia. She was revered as the source of abundance and well-being, holding the beginning and ending of life. One poet wrote:

Yea, summon Earth, who brings all things to life,

and rears, and takes again into her womb.[6]

The Greeks felt great gratitude to the Earth for all She provided. Women and men found healing in attuning to the rhythms of the Earth. Another poet from the Archaic Age wrote a praise-hymn to "Earth, Mother of All."

Gaia, Mother of all, I sing, oldest of gods

Firm of foundation, who feeds all creatures living on earth,

As many as move on the radiant land and swim in the sea

And fly through the air–all these does she feed with her bounty.

Mistress, from you come our fine children and bountiful harvests,

Yours is the power to give mortals life and to take it away…

Hail to you, mother of gods, wife of starry Uranos! [7]

In ancient Greece, goddesses and gods were probably first seen as an-iconic; that is to say, they had no specific image or icon, but were experienced directly, as manifest powers of nature. Gaia was the Earth. Uranos was the starry sky above. The Titan goddess Phoebe, a daughter of Earth and heaven, was the moon. Hestia was the hearth-fire that drew families together for warmth, hot drinks, and cooked food. Divine powers eventually came to be personified in humanized icons. An anthropomorphic or human-like image of a mistress of plants from Pylos in southern Greece, shows her taking great pleasure in the fragrance of the lilies that bloomed every spring; lilies were one of the symbols of the goddess of nature, in Crete as well as Greece.

A beautiful image of the goddess of abundance comes from the Women's Grave Circle of Mycenae, also in southern Greece, 16th century BCE. We see papyrus plants emerging from her body, pouring forth as the profusion of the life force, becoming a headdress for the goddess. This lovely image adorns a gold and silver pin that is inscribed with the blessing,

Countless Joyful Years![8]

At Thebes, in northern Greece, a Greek goddess was depicted in the shape of a female sphinx, combining into one body the powers of divine woman, lioness, and great winged bird. In Greece there are many such sphinxes, all of them female (in contrast to the more famous sphinxes of Egypt). In a Theban legend about Oedipus, this female sphinx is guarding the path the young man wants to take, posing a riddle for him to solve before she will allow him to pass. The riddle is as follows: what walks on four legs in the morning, on two legs at noon, and on three legs in the evening? The answer is: this is the life cycle of every human, who crawls on all fours as an infant, then walks upright on two legs in the middle of life, and then in their waning years, walks with a cane.

How I interpret this myth is that the female sphinx as ancient guardian goddess asks us to remember that each human life is one of dependence in infancy and limitation in old age, and thus humans have always depended for life on the succor of others—a fact that many androcentric men seem to disregard. Moreover, we can recognize that our life is like that of other beings, and our fate is bounded by nature, as surely as the life of every other creature on Earth. This knowledge is crucial for understanding our species as part of nature, providing the humility that allows us to tap into the wisdom of our human ancestors and of other creatures as well, and not be carried away with hubris, with overbearing pride and rapacious imbalances of psyche and soul, politics and economics. This is the riddle we must be able to answer in order to move forward, individually and as a community, into our own greener and healthier futures.

A nature-embedded image of the goddess Demeter as Earth Mother comes from Boeotia in northern Greece, from the 5th century BCE; it depicts her as mistress of plants and animals. She is seated on a throne shaped like a bird. A bird flies up to visit her. She holds wheat and pomegranates, and a scythe for harvesting wheat. Her dress and the throne are decorated with triangles with a dot inside—interpreted by archaeologist Marija Gimbutas as symbolizing a seeded and fertile field[9]—the same symbols found incised on goddesses in Crete and Old Europe, and also on a votive offering dedicated by the woman Ninnion to Demeter at Eleusis, during the first part of the 4th century BCE.[10] Another striking image of Demeter comes from Phigalia in the Arcadian highlands of southern Greece. She has the body of a woman and the head and hair of a horse, serpents and other creatures surround her, and she holds a dolphin in one hand and a dove in the other.[11] As a Great Goddess of nature, Demeter was the bringer of seasons and giver of rich gifts.[12]

The Homeric hymn to Demeter from the Archaic Age also asserts that Demeter was the greatest source of help and joy to mortals and immortals.[13] We see Demeter depicted on a ceramic disc from Eleusis, from the Roman era, as a great cosmic mother of nature.[14] Sun rays are streaming from around her head, and her headdress displays wheat stalks and a pomegranate. A waxing or waning moon crescent sits at each of her shoulders, implying that she, as central figure, is the full moon, as the mother moon in the maiden-mother-crone triad of the moon cycle and female life cycle. A dual serpent caduceus of healing floats to her left side, an eight-pointed star to her right, above the ritual sistrum rattle of Isis. She holds a scepter in one hand, and a rooster, symbol of resurrection, in the other. Her skirt is reminiscent of the costume of the goddess of Crete and her priestesses. In front of her are four galloping horses. The whole disk is surrounded by laurel leaves, a sign of peace, honor and reverence.

In ancient Crete, the goddess or goddesses of nature were also some-times represented in anthro-therio-morphic sculptures or human–animal forms, combining the body of the divine woman with an animal figure into a single being. Archaeologist Marina Moss argues for the identification of some of the bovine sculptures as a cow goddess, reminiscent of the cow goddess Hathor in Egypt.[15] One also finds shamanic combinations of the divine female with other creatures, such as the snake or bee. A snake goddess from Hierapetra, dated to the Neolithic Age, circa 6000 BCE, is part woman, part snake. The bare-breasted snake goddesses from the tem-ple-palace of Knossos, dated to the Middle Bronze Age, circa 1600 BCE, hold snakes in their hands and snakes wrap around their arms and waist; a cat sits on the head of one. On the apron of one of the three snake goddesses are dotted triangles, symbolizing a seeded and fertile field. On a gold signet ring from Isopata, dated to 1600–1450 BCE, the bee goddess, part woman, part bee, is depicted sharing a ritual dance with her priestesses, among the lilies of spring. Her priestesses were called Melissai, honeybees, as they also were named in Ephesus, Rhodes, Eleusis and Delphi. The Melissai priestesses of the goddess were producers of sweetness.

Artemis as Great Mother,
Mistress of Animals and Huntress

Artemis at Ephesus (Fig. 4) in Anatolia was worshipped as a Great Mother Goddess, well into the historical era. She was a cosmological mother of nature, adorned from head to toe with images of bees, roses, acorns, eggs, goats, rams, bulls, griffins, and sphinxes; and wearing a necklace with con-stellations of the zodiac. One of her names was Artemis Polymastos, the many-breasted Artemis. Turkish archaeologist Resit Ergener writes of this goddess's extraordinary powers:

> In the hundreds of inscriptions referring to the Ephesus Artemis, she is described as a founder, a savior, a com-mander, a guide, an advisor, a legislator, a queen, a spreader of light, a controller of fate, as victorious, invincible, pow-erful; great, magnificent, inviolate, one who listens to and accepts prayers, ready at all times and all places.[16]

Fig. 4. Artemis of Ephesus. Photograph by Blcksprt / CC BY-S
(https://creativecommons.org/licenses/by-sa/4.0)

The city of Ephesus was founded by Amazons and named for the queen bee. The name Ephesus is related to the Hittite term, *aspasa*, or "bee."[17] The first priestesses of Artemis were Amazons, and (as noted above) they were called Melissai, honeybees. The Ephesians built for their goddess the greatest temple of the ancient world, even larger than the Parthenon built for Athena on the Acropolis of Athens. The temple of Artemis of Ephesus was one of the Seven Wonders of the ancient world.

Three statues of Artemis of Ephesus escaped the destructions of the early Christian emperors. Two are now in the Selchuk Museum near Ephesus, including the one described above. A third, a black Artemis, was taken to Italy and now resides in the National Archaeological Museum of Naples. The black stone of this black Artemis connects her to Kubabe/Kybele/Cybele, who represented the black meteorite stone that fell from the heavens.[18]

In Greece, Artemis was worshipped as a maiden Goddess, daughter of Leto and Zeus. Artemis was born on the Aegean island of Delos. First-born of twins, she helped her mother give birth to Apollo, and thus was gifted with the skills of a midwife. And so pregnant women would call upon Artemis for aid in giving birth. Leto was the daughter of Phoebe, goddess of the moon; and Artemis also was a moon goddess, connected to its first quarter, the youthful and waxing aspect.

That Artemis in Greece has Leto and Zeus as parents, indicates that this persona of Artemis as a daughter was established during the patriarchal epoch brought by the Indo-European warrior clans who worshipped Zeus as their chief deity. Yet at Eleusis, where Demeter was the presiding deity, Artemis was worshiped as the daughter of Demeter, born from Demeter's union with Poseidon, god of the sea. A small temple was built to Artemis of the Portals and to Poseidon, at the entranceway to the precinct of Demeter's great temple, where initiates came annually to be initiated into the greater mysteries of Demeter and Persephone. Here, Artemis and Persephone were sisters.

Unlike Artemis of Ephesus, presiding deity of that great city, the Greek Artemis was said to shun the cities, choosing instead to dwell with her companion nymphs in the wooded forests on the mountains. In Crete, her closest friend was Britomartis, whom she loved dearly.[19]

In both Crete and Greece, as also in Anatolia, Artemis was called Potnia Theron, mistress of animals, who cared for animals and also hunted them. She was often depicted in art with a friendly deer. She was associated also with the bear, and thus with the Big Bear constellation. Her young girl priestesses-in-training dressed up as bear cubs.

The mythology of Artemis in Greece sometimes emphasized the killing of animals. A hymn "To Artemis" from the Archaic Age draws a picture of her as sending forth her arrows of anguish ... slaying the race of wild beasts.[20]

Artemis's image deteriorated from great mother, to maiden mistress of animals with beloved women companions, to ruthless goddess of the hunt. This type of diminishment of goddesses intensified from the Bronze Age to the Classical Age. However, many people continued to revere a pre-eminent goddess as primary to their society, as in Crete, Eleusis, and at Athens, where Athena with her serpents and owls reigned supreme.

Relevance of Divine Mistresses of Nature, Plants and Animals for Today's Ecological Crises

Joan Marler, scholar and biographer of archaeomythologist Marija Gimbutas, organized a conference in 1999 on the beautiful Greek island of Madouri, on the subject of "Archaeomythology: Taking the Disciplines Deeper." The archaeologists and scholars of mythology and religion from different countries in Europe and the United States presented papers on how to use archaeomythology to unearth more of the buried connections in the ancient world between religion (mythology) and daily life. I believe we can deepen the contemporary academic field of ecofeminism by drawing upon the ancient images of empowered and empowering nature goddesses, in conjunction with the mythic wisdoms of the more nature-embedded, embodied, and egalitarian ways of life, before the rise of patriarchal warrior clans, whose reign by now has become like the polluted water in which we swim.

Carolyn Merchant, professor emerita of environmental history, philosophy and ethics at the University of California at Berkeley, published her groundbreaking ecofeminist book, *The Death of Nature: Women, Ecology, and the Scientific Revolution*, in 1980. The first chapter, "Nature as Female," explains that for most of human history, people lived in an "organic relationship with the natural order for their sustenance."[21] The prevailing worldview was that of an abundant and nurturing Mother Nature, "a kindly beneficent female who provided for the needs of mankind in an orderly way."[22]

But with the beginning of the modern era, this changed drastically with the rise of expansionary capitalism and the scientific revolution. Nature was now seen as disorderly and random and in need of control by men, and women were viewed by men as virgin, mother, or witch, also in need of control. In her latest research, Merchant focuses on how the Industrial Age has produced what is being called the Anthropocene Age, where the impact of humans has been rapidly overwhelming all the other organic systems of nature. Men's androcratic efforts to control women and nature have, among other factors, brought us face-to-face with human-made environmental disasters; and according to a recent United Nations report, climate change is killing at least 9 million persons every year.[23] Humanity is on the verge of massive ecocide.

Spiritual ecofeminist philosopher and Green activist Charlene Spretnak relates her own terrifying experience of climate crisis caused by fossil fuel emissions. She and her family and hometown very narrowly escaped the Thomas Fire in southern California, in 2017.

> Recently I was hurled across the existential divide that separates the millions of people around the world who have experienced a life-threatening extreme weather event from those who have not. In December 2017 unseasonal Santa Ana winds roared off a California desert across two drought-parched counties, not for the usual 48 hours but for more than a week, blowing a brush fire across 440 square miles. It was named the Thomas fire, the largest in California history…
>
> The two mountain ranges forming the walls of the Ojai Valley were incinerated as the town on the valley floor was evacuated but, in the end, was saved. A month later 23 people were killed in nearby Montecito by mudslides that brought boulders and debris crashing down from the burned out mountainside after only one hour of an unusually intense rainstorm. The ground shook as a thunderous roar arose. The impact of the fast-moving debris flow obliterated many houses, splintering them instantly and sweeping the remains into the growing torrent that ran to the sea…
>
> Such unprecedented weather events now occur frequently, driven by ever more powerful forces. Hurricanes carry

more rain and at higher speeds than before climate change; megafires have become common; and coastal flooding surges relentlessly as sea levels rise. Tornados strike where they never have before, and the fast-warming Arctic has led to a weakening polar vortex that causes the winter dipolar effect in North America, resulting in extremely cold winters in the east and abnormally high temperatures in the west.... The long-standing patterns of weather and climate on which life depends are unraveling.[24]

Since the Thomas Fire of 2017, California has seen even more ferocious and lethal fires, such as the one that completely destroyed the town of Paradise in northern California in November 2018, killing 85 people and turning to ash over a thousand structures. In October 2018, the United Nations reported that there might only be twelve more years until climate change becomes irreversible. In spring 2019, the banks of the great Mississippi and Missouri Rivers were overwhelmed by torrential rains, causing massive flooding of the fertile heartland of the US. And in summer 2019, India was scorched by an extreme heatwave with temperatures over 120 °F (50 °C).

What must we do to meet the climate crisis? Spretnak provides us with a more in-depth understanding of the problem of global warming and then underscores what she thinks is needed for change.

What natural system can function well if it's overheated? Since the heat shield is made of the carbon emissions and methane gas releases we send into the air, it doesn't make sense that we continue to send more of those fossil-fuel emissions up there. That makes the heat-trapping even worse and the weather events even more catastrophic. But luckily for us it's easier than ever before to stop producing emissions by switching to renewable sources of energy... *We really need elected officials and business leaders who will act immediately on this because the extreme weather events are going to keep coming, killing lots more people in lots more places* [emphasis added].[25]

Spretnak also argues for the inclusion of more women in policy deci-sion-making positions. "It's been widely noticed that most women tend to think holistically and to grasp the many implications of a particular situa-tion or a proposed solution. Ergo, women should constitute at least half of every governing body from the neighborhood to the international level."[26]

Peggy Shepard, a co-founder of the ecosocial justice movement in the United States, explains that environmental harm primarily afflicts peo-ple of color, as in the water crisis in Flint, Michigan. Kendyl Crawford, another Black woman environmental leader in the United States, believes that these problems require "a more intersectional view of environmental justice [connected] with economic justice, social justice and racial jus-tice."[27] Crawford's leadership is about "mobiliz[ing] a religious response to climate change through energy conservation, energy efficiency, and renew-able energy."[28]

Many thousands of schoolchildren from some 100 countries, led by the teenager Greta Thunberg of Sweden, have been organizing school strikes; they are calling for a global climate strike, beginning September 20, 2019, in conjunction with the UN Climate Action Summit 2019.[29] These young people want adults to wake up and realize that, as Thunberg states, "our house is on fire!"[30]

I want to draw this essay to a close by focusing on just one Earth eco-system that is devastatingly impacted by climate change: the sea. The priestess of Artemis at Tauris once prayed to

"The Sea, who can wash clean all the foulness of mankind."[31]

But today, instead of the oceans diluting and dispersing much of human-ity's waste, we find that the oceans are being filled with human garbage and toxins while sea-life is being decimated by the acidification caused by carbon dioxide. Gyres of plastic and fishing nets, hundreds of miles wide and larger than the state of Texas, keep growing in the Pacific and Atlantic and Indian Oceans; ocean liners and freighters discharge sewage into the waters; and there are increasing levels of mercury in fish, which in turn are poisoning humans.

Women's spirituality author Mary Mackey's prophetic poem, "Cytherea," written in 1987, speaks powerfully about the devastations of the seas, personified here as the Greek goddess Cytherea.

Cytherea is angry
that we have poisoned her oceans
at night she climbs the waves
straddles the white foam
and calls to her whales
"are you catfood yet?"
She howls
"have the Japanese turned you all
into soup and lipstick?"

She has picked the brains
of all the philosophers who ever drowned
looking for the causes of human folly
she has mastered the concept of original sin
and thinks there may be something to it
she is acquainted with the theory of eternal forms
that holds that if the oceans of earth die
the idea of oceans will persist unchanged
in some godly sphere of boredom and perfection
but the only oceans Cytherea cares about
are these
bitter and dirty
salty and dying
these small mortal oceans
it makes her weep to see them...

Cytherea
the flowers we throw to you
come back oil-soaked
and dying
we stand on your beaches
calling you up
but you no longer appear
at our feet you scatter
pieces of styrofoam cups
tin cans, beer bottles, hunks of insulation
stinking fish and dead birds

> *and sometimes a jelly fish*
> *pulsing and dying*
> *like a punctured soap bubble*
> *like a human heart*
> *gone bad.*[32]

Now, what more can we do to make the water clean and clear, beautiful and healthful for sea-life and for humans? How can we solve the riddle of human nature we must solve in order to move forward to a more ecologically sane and socially secure future? What will motivate people to genuinely respect ourselves and other creatures; to see how inter-related we all are; and how much we depend on the health and well-being of one another?

My prayer is, if we can recall clearly an earlier way of life, when our ancestors were more nature embedded and nature loving, when nature itself was seen as sacred, then we might feel called to do whatever we can to save the earth, air, and water from ongoing pollution, to take little and then big steps—cleaning up the oceans, leaving a smaller carbon footprint, becoming more vegetarian, recycling and reusing, voting for pro-environmental political candidates, and developing a more compassionate and loving relationship with self and others, including other species.

I hope these mythic images and sacred stories of divine mistresses of nature, plants and animals of Ancient Greece will remind us of our deep bonds with nature, and that we will find new ways for these dynamic energies and sacred powers to inspire the wisdom we need to make the urgent changes our threatened lives require.

References

Aeschylus, "Libation Bearers." In *Aeschylus, II, Oresteia: Agamemnon. Libation-Bearers. Eumenides*. Loeb Classical Library. Cambridge, MA: Harvard University Press, 2009.

Dexter, Miriam Robbins. "Ancient Felines and the Great-Goddess in Anatolia: Kubaba and Cybele." In *Proceedings of the 20th Annual UCLA Indo-European Conference: Los Angeles, October 31–November 1, 2008*, edited by Stephanie W. Jamison, H. Craig Melchert, and Brent Vine, 53–67. Bremen: Hempen Verlag, 2009.

Elawar, May. "The Black Stone." In *She Is Everywhere: An Anthology of Writing in Womanist/Feminist Spirituality*, edited by Lucia Chiavola Birnbaum, 60–71. New York: iUniverse, Inc., 2005.

Elkins, Paul, Joyeeta Gupta, and Pierre Boileau, eds. *Global Environment Outlook: GEO 6: Healthy Planet, Healthy People*, 6th rev. ed. Cambridge University Press, 2019.

Ergener, Resit. *Anatolia: Land of the Mother Goddess*. Ankara, Turkey: Hitit, 1988.

Euripides, *Iphigenia in Tauris*. In *Euripides, Three Plays: Alcestis: Hippolytus: Iphigenia in Tauris*, translated by Philip Vellacott. New York: Penguin Books, [1953] 1980.

Foley, Helene P., ed. *The Homeric Hymn to Demeter: Translation and Interpretive Essays*. Princeton, NJ: Princeton University Press, 1994.

Gold-ivory pin with Goddess of Nature. Grave Circle A, Shaft Grave III, "Grave of the Women." In Athens National Archaeological Museum, Athens, #75.

Gimbutas, Marija. *The Language of the Goddess.* San Francisco: Harper & Row, 1989.

Harrison, Jane Ellen. *Prolegomena to the Study of Greek Religion*. London: Merlin Press, [1903] 1960.

Hesiod. *Theogony of Hesiod*. In Hesiod, *The Homeric Hymns, and Homerica*, translated by Hugh G. Evelyn-White, 78–153. Cambridge, MA: Harvard University Press, 1950.

Homer, *The Odyssey*. Translated by A. T. Murray. Vols. I, II. Cambridge, MA: Harvard University Press, [1919] 1980.

Kanta, Katherine G. *Eleusis: Myth, Mysteries, History, Museum*. Translated by W. W. Phelps. Athens: K. Kanta, 1979.

Mackey, Mary. "Cytherea." In *The Jaguars That Prowl Our Dreams: New and Selected Poems, 1974–2018*. East Rockaway, NY: Marsh Hawk Press, 2018.

Mark, Joshua J. "Bastet." In *Ancient History Encyclopedia*, July 24, 2016. www.ancient.eu/Bastet/. Accessed June 6, 2019.

Merchant, Carolyn. *Death of Nature: Women, Ecology, and the Scientific Revolution*. New York: Harper Collins, 1980.

Moss, Marina L. *The Minoan Pantheon: Towards an Understanding of Its Nature and Extent*. BAR International Series 1343. Oxford: John and Erica Hedges, Ltd. British Archaeological Reports, 2005.

Nilsson, Martin P. *Minoan–Mycenaean Religion and Its Survival in Greek Religion.* 2nd rev. ed. New York: Biblo and Tannen, 1949.

Pausanias, "Book VIII: Arcadia." In Pausanias, *Description of Greece*, Vol. III, Books VI–VIII. Translated by W. H. S. Jones. Cambridge, MA: Harvard University Press, [1933] 1977.

Preka-Alexandri, Kalliope. "Ninnion Tablet," *Eleusis.* 2nd ed. Athens: Ministry of Culture, Archaeological Receipts Fund, 1997.

Seval, Mehlika. *Step by Step Ephesus.* Istanbul: Minyatur Publications, 1988.

Spretnak, Charlene. "Field-Dependent or Field-Astute?" *Feminism and Religion* (blog), July 8, 2011. feminismandreligion.com/2011/07/08/field-dependent-or-field-astute-by-charlene-spretnak/. Accessed June 11, 2019.

_____. *Relational Reality: New Discoveries of Interrelatedness That Are Transforming the Modern World.* Topsham, ME: Green Horizon Books, 2011.

_____. "A View from the Chute." *Feminism and Religion* (blog), February 21, 2018. feminismandreligion.com/?s=Charlene+Spretnak&x=17&y=16. Accessed June 11, 2019.

Thunberg, Greta. "Full Speech at UN Climate Change COP24 Conference." December 15, 2018. www.youtube.com/watch?v=VFkQSGyeCWg; accessed June 10, 2019.

"To Artemis." In *The Homeric Hymns: A Verse Translation*, trans. Thelma Sargent, 76. New York: W. W. Norton & Co., 1973.

"To Earth, Mother of All." In *The Homeric Hymns: A Verse Translation*, trans. Thelma Sargent, 79. New York: W. W. Norton & Co., 1973.

"The Homeric Hymn to Demeter," trans. Helene P. Foley. In *The Homeric Hymn to Demeter: Translation, Commentary, and Interpretive Essays.* Edited by Helene P. Foley. Princeton, NJ: Princeton University Press, 1993.

"UN Climate Action Summit 2019." www.un.org/en/climatechange/un-climate-summit-2019.shtml. Accessed June 13, 2019.

Willis, Samantha. "Black Women Are Leading the Way in Environmental Justice," *Essence*, January 11, 2019.

Endnotes

1 I use the dating system of the American Academy of Religion where BCE = before the Common Era, and has the same year-numbering system as the Christian dating system, BC = before Christ.

2 Joshua J. Mark, "Bastet," in *Ancient History Encyclopedia*, July 24, 2016. www.ancient.eu/Bastet/, accessed June 6, 2019.

3 See Miriam Robbins Dexter, "Ancient Felines and the Great-Goddess in Anatolia: Kubaba and Cybele," in *Proceedings of the 20th Annual UCLA Indo-European Conference: Los Angeles, October 31–November 1, 2008*, ed. Stephanie W. Jamison, H. Craig Melchert, Brent Vine, 53–67 (Bremen: Hempen Verlag, 2009).

4 Hesiod, *Theogyny of Hesiod*, trans. Evelyn-White, lines 116–122, in Hesiod, *The Homeric Hymns*, and *Homerica*, trans. Evelyn-White (Cambridge, MA: Harvard University Press, 1950), 10.

5 Hesiod, *Theogony*, lines 969–974. See also Homer, *The Odyssey*, trans. A. T. Murray (Cambridge, MA: Harvard University Press, [1919] 1980), I:5.125.

6 Aeschylus, *Choephori* [Libation Bearers], line 127, trans. Jane Ellen Harrison, as cited in Jane Ellen Harrison, in *Prolegomena to the Study of Greek Religion*, (London: Merlin Press [1903] 1960), 267.

7 Homeric Hymn #30, "To Earth, Mother of All," trans. Thelma Sargent, lines 1–6, 17, in *Homeric Hymns: A Verse Translation by Thelma Sargent*. trans. Thelma Sargent (New York: W.W. Norton & Company, [1973] 1975).

8 Gold-silver Pin with Goddess of Nature, Grave Circle A, Shaft Grave III, "Grave of the Women," Athens National Archaeological Museum, Athens, #75.

9 Marija Gimbutas, *The Language of the Goddess* (San Francisco: Harper & Row, 1989), 144–45.

10 "Demeter-Isis Disc," in Katherine Kanta, *Eleusis*, fig. 82, 149.

11 Pausanias, "Arcadia," in Pausanias, *Description of Greece*, Vol. III, Books VI–VIII, trans. W. H. S. Jones (Cambridge, MA: Harvard University Press, [1933] 1977), bk. VIII: lines XLII.4, 111.

12 Homeric Hymn to Demeter, line 192, trans. Foley, in Foley, ed., *Homeric Hymn to Demeter: Translation and Interpretive Essays* (Princeton, NJ: Princeton University Press, 1994), 12.

13 Homeric Hymn to Demeter, lines 268–269, trans. Foley, in Foley, ed., *Homeric Hymn to Demeter*, 16.

14 Kalliope Preka-Alexandri, "Ninnion Tablet," in Preka-Alexandri, *Eleusis*, 2nd ed. (Athens: Ministry of Culture, Archaeological Receipts Fund, 1997), fig. 9, 9.

15 Marina L. Moss, *The Minoan Pantheon: Towards an Understanding of Its Nature and Extent*, BAR International Series 1343 (Oxford: John and Erica Hedges, Ltd. British Archaeological Reports, 2005), 196.

16 Resit Ergener, *Anatolia: Land of the Mother Goddess* (Ankara, Turkey: Hitit, 1988), 49.

17 Mehlika Seval, *Step by Step Ephesus* (Istanbul: Minyatur Publications, 1988), 13.

18 May Elawar, "The Black Stone," in *She Is Everywhere: An Anthology of Writing in Womanist/Feminist Spirituality*, ed. Lucia Chiavola Birnbaum (New York: iUniverse, Inc., 2005, 60–71.

19 Martin P. Nilsson, *Minoan-Mycenaean Religion and Its Survival in Greek Religion*, 2nd rev. ed. (New York: Biblo and Tannen, 1949), 510.

20 "To Artemis," lines 6, 9, in *The Homeric Hymns*, trans. Thelma Sargent, 76.

21 Carolyn Merchant, *Death of Nature: Women, Ecology, and the Scientific Revolution* (New York: Harper Collins, 1980), 1.

22 Ibid., 2.

23 Paul Elkins, Joyeeta Gupta, and Pierre Boileau, eds., *Global Environment Outlook: GEO 6: Healthy Planet, Healthy People*, 6th ed. (Cambridge University Press, 2019), 1. See also content.yudu.com/web/2y3n2/0A2y3n3/GEO6/html/index.html?page=4&origin=reader; Susan Matthews, "It's Finally Sinking In," *Slate*, May 7, 2019, slate.com/technology/2019/05/climate-change-our-planet-un-report-species-humanity-doom.html; and Associated Press, "Dire UN Climate Change Report Reveals It's Not Too Late to Save Planet," *New York Post*, March 13, 2019, nypost.com/2019/03/13/dire-un-climate-change-report-reveals-its-not-too-late-to-save-planet/, accessed June 13, 2019.

24 Charlene Spretnak, "A View from the Chute," *Feminism and Religion* (blog), February 21, 2018, available at https://feminismandreligion.com/?s=Charlene+Spretnak&x=17&y=16.

25 Ibid.

26 Charlene Spretnak, "Field-Dependent or Field-Astute?" *Feminism and Religion* (blog), July 8, 2011, accessed June 11, 2019, feminismandreligion.com/2011/07/08/field-dependent-or-field-astute-by-charlene-spretnak.. See also Spretnak, *Relational Reality: New Discoveries of Interrelatedness That Are Transforming the Modern World* (Topsham, ME: Green Horizon Books, 2011), ch. 6.

27 Kendyl Crawford is quoted in Samantha Willis, "Black Women Are Leading the Way in Environmental Justice," *Essence*, January 11, 2019, www.essence.com/news/black-women-are-leading-the-way-in-environmental-justice/.

28 Ibid.

29 UN Climate Action Summit 2019, accessed June 13, 2019, www.un.org/en/climatechange/un-climate-summit-2019.shtml.

30 Greta Thunberg, Full Speech at UN Climate Change COP24 Conference, accessed June 10, 2019, https://www.youtube.com/watch?v=VFkQSGyeCWg.

31 Euripides, *Iphigenia in Tauris*, line 1193, in *Euripides, Three Plays: Alcestis: Hippolytus: Iphigenia in Tauris*, trans. Philip Vellacott (New York: Penguin Books, [1953] 1980), 168.

32 Mary Mackey, "Cytherea," in Mackey, *Jaguars That Prowl Our Dreams: New and Selected Poems, 1974–2018* (East Rockaway, NY: Marsh Hawk Press, 2018), 112.

MARI—THE POWER OF FEMININE
IMMANENCE IN THE BASQUE BELIEF SYSTEM

IDOIA ARANA-BEOBIDE

Humans have been traveling and exchanging the fruits of their devel-opment across the globe for millennia. It is said that the Basque are a great mystery; they are considered a unique people speaking an isolate lan-guage.[1] Yet, new research connects the Basque with North America during the Paleolithic Solutrean and Clovis eras around 21,000 BCE.[2] Could this ancient link help us understand the Basque uniqueness in any way?

The Basques are the only living European indigenous peoples that sur-vived the Indo-European invasions from which most present-day Europeans descend (from 2500 BCE), and also survived Romanization (from 300 BCE–100 CE). Roger Collins states that "the Basque ... [are] a people who have successfully resisted absorption by a succession of conquering or neighbouring cultures, and ... despite the loss of their political independence have preserved not only a unique language and material culture but also a distinctive physical identity that marks them off from the rest of man-kind."[3] Indeed, the Basque claim to be descendants of the Upper Paleolithic Cro-Magnon, and there are plenty of archaeological remains in the caves of northern Spain and southern France to validate this theory.[4] Relevant sites expanding from the Paleolithic period include: Altxerri from the Aurignacian (35,000 BCE), Isturitz from the Solutrean (20,000–15,000 BCE), and Ekain and Santimamiñe from the Magdalenian (15,000–7500 BCE).

The Romans who identified the Basque-speaking peoples documented tribes encroached by the Pyrenes Mountains and the Atlantic Sea including the Aquitaine (people from Gascoyne) in France. In 178 BCE, the Romans described how these people who speak a strange non–Indo-European language were fighting the earlier invading Indo-European Celtic tribes and paternalistic culture from 500 to 100 BCE. By the era of the Roman Emperor Augustus (27 BCE–14 CE), his Greek geographer Strabo, and later, Ptolemy, described these groups in Gallia (France), the Aquitani, and in Hispania (Spain) the Vascones, Varduli, Caristii and Autrigones.[5] The Basque and their language survived in the harsh mountainous terrain of the region, but the fertile flatlands were heavily Romanized. The great wines of Rioja in Spain and Bordeaux in France are a legacy of that Romanization period. The loss of the language and distinct identity was another more debatable legacy.

What was the identity the Romans encountered? What worldview was lost or altered with Romanization? In order to best analyze this world-view, we need to address those who kept a closer relationship with the land itself and its rhythms—the peoples of the countryside and rural com-munities. Like Julio Caro Baroja says, if we want to understand what the ancient Basque believed, we need to address the layering of animistic, Indo-European, Christian, and historical/secular strata in the people's rural culture.[6] It is acknowledged that the Basque, Euskaldunak, were originally a sedentary matrilineal culture based on the *etxea*, the home, where the *etxekoandre*, the lady of the house, was the respected and honored cen-tral figure of the household and usually the inheritor.[7] It is interesting to note that many indigenous North-American societies like the Blackfoot, or Siksikaitsitapi, were also originally matrilineal cultures and that the tipi, the home, was the woman's property.

Marija Gimbutas studied the matriarchal focus of the indigenous Neolithic communities in Europe and made a direct connection with the Basque traditional organizational system. In *The Language of the Goddess*, she explains that in Old Europe, the core of that matriarchal or motherhood principle, the image of that being-ness was a goddess, and that "[t]he same goddess still plays a prominent role in beliefs of the European as the ... Basque *Mari*. This powerful goddess was not wiped out from the mythical world."[8] Gimbutas went on to assert that Mari is an inspiration for the revival of the feminine principle in present-day societies, inasmuch as any images of goddesses strengthen women's self-confidence and courage. Mari, the great Basque goddess, appears as the supreme manifestation from whom all other creatures and forces emanate. She is a shape-shifter and multi-faceted being, the ever cyclical and regenerating life force found indigenous pre–Indo-European cultures.

She is the force of nature that rural people, who are connected with the natural environment, have always respected.

Joxe Migel Barandiaran (1889–1991), the father of contemporary Basque anthropology, insisted that in order to understand Mari and Basque mythology, one needs to understand the concepts of magic and animism.[9] Animism is a rather controversial term originating with E. B. Tylor (1832–1917), who founded the first seat of anthropology at Cambridge University and developed the theory of "animism" in his book *Primitive Culture*. His description of animism as early primitive belief systems preceding Greek and Roman civilizations, was applied by association to all indigenous religions, as superstitious beliefs in ghosts and spirits.[10] This unfortunate misconception of the indigenous worldview and experienced reality has led to a new philosophical epistemology called "new animism." Graham Harvey challenges Tylor's definition of animism as "belief in spirits," theorizing that instead animism is the understanding "that the world is full of persons, only some of whom are human, and that life is always lived in relationship with others." Harvey's description of animism as a "relational epistemology" distances it, therefore, from "spiritualism" as the basis of its ontology.[11]

Yet, indigenous peoples insist on talking about the sacred, as the sacred is infused in everything. As Betty Bastien states in *Blackfoot Ways of Knowing*, everything is sacred, *aatsimapi*. Nature, as living energy, is the foremost assumption and understanding of any indigenous epistemology. She continues explaining that "[b]eing *Niitsitapi* [of the Blackfoot Confederacy people] means living life with the sacred; now 'knowing' comes through living up to the responsibilities of maintaining and renewing the sacred balance of our natural alliances."[12] Indigenous peoples have no challenges in understanding matter and spirit simultaneously, because they are infused, they are one and the same. Blair Stonechild elaborates: "[Indigenous] [p]eoples believe that spirit beings are not only real, but that it is possible to develop relationships with them. The quest for spirit knowledge and interaction is a central feature of Indigenous life."[13] In this worldview, humans are responsible for finding their own place in creation through ceremonies where they realize that "humans are Spirits clothed in flesh," and that this world is a quantum, a magical realm, an illusion of sorts in which humans are to learn to be in proper relationships with the universe and each other.[14] In his article, "Magick and

Quantum Physics," Dave Lee explains that "reality" is truly a "probability wave," a "potentia," meaning that possible states of a physical system exist in a kind of metaphysical Platonic realm.[15] For indigenous peoples, this quantum reality is precisely the world of the shaman, and the world where the shaman, if properly trained, can alter reality itself. According to Stonechild, "This is why practitioners of spirit medicine are reluctant to perform in the presence of sceptics, including scientists, as non-belief militates against the success of efforts."[16]

It is likely that the ancient Basque saw themselves in these terms. Originally the Basque world was seen as a single holistic expression based on Mari, the divinized manifestation of natural forces. It is important to understand that Mari is not an objectified divinity (as is typical in patriarchy-grounded religious belief systems), but rather she is an entity in the sacred liminal sense of indigenous belief systems. Mari is not a force or goddess separate from the act of creation, which is transcendence, but she herself is constant creation, the nature of immanence.[17] Thus, the Basque understood the world as engendered with and through an all-powerful feminine force, Mari, the Goddess of All.[18] She is the manifestation of divinized natural forces. Mari could well be the ancient Paleolithic Great Mother Goddess, because in Basque "Mari" refers to *ama* (the mother) and *-ri* (to), which translates as "To the All Mother." As the force of nature, she represents ever-cyclical and regenerating life, where life and death are but existence, and thus she is the source of the good and the bad, generous and cruel like Nature herself.[19] Since Mari is all, she is a shapeshifter and she manifests in many forms. She takes zoomorphic shapes like the horse, cow, ram, goat, serpent, and vulture in her subterranean dwellings. She is also represented as a beech tree in the shape of a woman engulfed in flames. When she flies in the sky and moves her residence from mountain top to mountain top with great thunder, she takes the form of a sickle or circle on fire.[20]

Mari takes the shape of a majestic and radiant woman when walking on the earth, her undulating hair also in flames. She is seen richly dressed, many times in red and holding a golden *etxea*, the symbol of the sacredness of the Basque home and the hearth, where she is ever-present. Mari is incredibly wealthy; in her underground dwellings, her throne and utensils are made of gold since her domain is rich with gold and precious metals.[21] Mari appears in many caves in the mountains where she resides, of which

Gorbea, Oiz, Mugarra, Aizkorri, Txindoki, Aralar, Ayako Arria and Ory Mendi are the most important. Because she is seen in all these places, she is called the Lady, the Dame of each of them.

Mari is understood as the principal divinity, the "ruler" and "queen" of all living and earthly divine forces, (the "telluric numen" of the Romans). All creatures, phenomena, and natural cycles are but different manifestations of all creation, of Mother Nature, of Mari.[22] Some of the most important and main identified numen would be Sugaar (Maju), Iraunsuge, Laminak (Maideak), Ireltxo, Gaueko, Praka gorri, Mikolasa, Basajauna (Basaandere), Jentillak, Olentzero and Tartalo.[23] Sugaar (Maju) is Mari's partner and his name means *suge-* snake, and *arr-* male, but also, *su-* fire, and *gar-* strength because he flies on fire like a dragon. In the regenerating cycle of life, Sugaar as a snake represents the perishable male impregnating aspect of Mari's eternal engendering ability. Even if all these creatures have different forms and characteristics, they are not to be understood as independent personages. The process of anthropomorphizing Mari and the forces of nature that occurs later is probably driven by Indo-European influences.[24] Following the tradition that survived to the present, all these numen should be understood as parts of Mari's being, since they are linked and subject to her will, and are essentially aspects of the natural environment that she herself embodies.

For the traditional Basque, nature is cyclical and seeks to always balance itself. That is why Mari is a teacher of honesty, accountability, and reciprocity. Ever watchful and pragmatic, Mari lives by natural law and ends up enriching herself with the *Ezezkoak*, human denial. She lives by "*Ezari emana, ezak eraman.*" This expression is not easy to translate in an Indo-European language, but it basically means "that which is given to denial, the thing denied will be lost and taken away." It is how she teaches people to be real, to tell the truth, be honest, reliable, and ultimately, accountable. What she takes away is that which was precisely lied about or hidden. It is her punishment to the false ones and pretenders.[25] Far from being a capricious deity "acting out," Mari teaches a rigorous practice that is ancient and vital. Being trustworthy and accountable is absolutely necessary for a tribal society where people depend on another.

The Basque have practiced *Auzolan* (literally, "work in neighborhood") for millennia as an economic model of communitarian sharing of major workloads.[26] The communitarian roots of the Basque people are truly apparent when Mari proclaims that the people need to, above all, fulfill the "Given Word," *Euskal Itza* (the Basque given word). She demands that people avoid deceit, stealing or acting arrogantly. This premise or "rule" is inherently animistic and relates to a tribal society in which the shared understanding is that everything is connected, and all are affected by each other's actions. In contemporary terms we might understand it as "karma" or more recently as the "law of reciprocity."[27] One manifests one's truest intentions for him/herself and those around her/him. This is why the spoken word is so important, and in Basque the Given Word is sacred. It is an old wise saying that, *"Izena badu, bada."*[28] In Basque to *"Izen,"* to name something, and *"Izan,"* to be/become reality, are the same concept. Words manifest and become reality, which is also something Bastien's own *Siksikaitsitapi* (Blackfoot) grandmother insisted upon. The issue is not simply that deceit is morally wrong; for indigenous peoples the world is sacred because it is in a constant state of emanation and actualization, "a world that is called into being by the people's words."[29]

Mari is generous to those who address her. To honor and find her favor, one can conjure the fire, particularly the fire of the heart where she is ever-present. The primary teeth of children, for example, are thrown into the fire with a prayer to ensure the growth and vitality of new teeth. Since she knows and affects everything, Mari also offers counsel as an oracle.[30] When addressing Mari in her caves, one needs to use *Ika*, the direct Basque manner of speech, deferentially, while always standing, and one needs to leave exactly as one entered, that is, facing her, walking backwards.[31] It is indeed how one needs to address the force of nature, never idle, without false bravado, in respect, always giving face to reality. Honesty, honoring, accountability—all these are the ancient recurring expression of Basque values because all is reciprocal, and ultimately, all seeks balance. This philosophy and understanding are clear in *arreman*, the Basque word for "relationship." *Arreman* is composed of *ar* (take) and *eman* (give), but also *ar* (male), and *ema* (female). The language itself shows that, in Basque, opposites comprise the one, the relationship, the whole.[32] In this belief system, opposites are complementary, which is what makes life responsive, compensating, and ultimately, cyclical. In Basque, relationship literally implies *"artzeko eman"*: to take (one) has to give. Life is a give-and-take, the cyclical relationship of harmonious evolution.

Matriarchalism for the Basque is thus a manifestation of the feminine indigenous worldview—motherhood values of Mari—that understands the world as the Whole, as One, All, *Dana*.[33] It is said that "*Dana (ari) dana (bat) da*" ("All that is happening is one"). In this holistic worldview the complementarities of opposites, day/night, sun/moon, warm/cold, good/evil, are the polarities that create the continuum of space and energy in which one can experience, honor and celebrate the All that is Mari.[34] This is the ancient Paleolithic- and Neolithic-based worldview that the patriarchal Indo-Europeans and Christianity altered. Whether the Solutrean and Clovis hypothesis can be proven or not, contemporary understanding of North American indigenous spirituality and animism is very helpful in appreciating the ancient uniqueness of the Basque people—particularly their deep identity and cultural roots based on the indigenous–non-European Palaeolithic original substratum. Indeed, the Basques' deep-rooted, animistic worldview has endured for millennia in the face of countless historical and contemporary challenges. Consciously or unconsciously some traditions have been syncretized with newer imposed structures. Yet, the manifestation of the immanence of Mari—the creatrix, the begetter, the mother of all, is still present since prehistoric times. Her immanent omnipresence assures the preservation of all that is Basque for future generations.

References

Arrinda, Donato. *EuskalErri Zaarra*. Barcelona: Editorial R. M., 1969.

———. *Jainko Txikiak.* Bilbao: Kardaberz, 1973.

Barandiaran, José Miguel. *Mitología vasca*, 18th ed. Donostia: Editorial Txertoa, 2014.

Bastien, Betty. *Blackfoot Ways of Knowing: The Worldview of the Siksikaitsitapi.* Calgary, Alberta: University of Calgary Press, 2004.

Basterretxea, M. Carmen. *Euskal Herria, Kultura Matrilineala*. Madrid: Potlatch Editorial, 2016.

Bergara, Aritza. *Mitologika—Euskal Herriko Izaki Magikoak Gaur Egungo Ikuspuntuatik.* Bilbao: Astiberri Ediciones S.L., 2002.

Bradley, Bruce, and Dennis Stanford. "The North Atlantic Ice-Edge Corridor: A Possible Palaeolithic Route to the New World." *World Archaeology* 36, no. 4 (2004). doi: 10.1080/0043824042000303656.

Byrne, Rhonda. *The Secret*. New York: Atria Books/Beyond Words, 2006.

Caro Baroja, Julio. *Los Vascos*. Madrid: Ediciones Istmo, S.A., 2000.

———. *Estudios vascos*. San Sebastian: Editorial Txertoa, 1973.

Collis, Roger. *The Basques*, 2nd ed. Oxford: Basil Blackwell Ltd., [1986] 1990.

Estornes Lasa, B. *Orígenes de los Vascos*. Vol. IV. San Sebastian: Editorial Aunamendi, 1966.

Gimbutas, Marija. *The Language of the Goddess*. New York: Thames & Hudson, 2006.

Harvey, Graham. *Animism: Respecting the Living World*. New York: Columbia University Press, 2006.

Historical Atlas of the World. Boulder, CO: Rand McNally, 1993.

Larrañaga Elorza, Koldo. "El periodo colonial romano." In *Gran atlas histórico del mundo vasco*. Bilbao: El Mundo, 2009.

Naberan, Josu. *La vuelta de Sugaar: Un proyecto de futuro, para un pueblo con pasado*. Donostia: Basandere Argitaletxea, 2001.

Ortiz-Osés, Andrés. *La diosa madre: Interpretación desde la mitología vasca*. Madrid: Editorial Trotta, S.A., 1996.

——— and Franz-Karl Mayr. *El matriarcalismo vasco*, 3rd ed. Bilbao: Universidad de Deusto, 1988.

Piquero, Guillermo. *Mitología Salvaje: Reconstruyendo la Cosmovisión Indígena Europea*. Author, 2013. ISBN: 978-84-942152-4-7.

Stonechild, Blair. *The Knowledge Seeker: Embracing Indigenous Spirituality*. Regina: University of Regina Press, 2016.

Tylor, E. B. "Primitive Culture." In *A Reader in the Anthropology of Religion*, edited by M. Lambek. Oxford: Wiley-Blackwell, 2002.

Endnotes

1 "Languages of Europe," in *Historical Atlas of the World*, 4th rep. (Boulder, CO: Rand McNally, 1993), 30.

2 Bruce Bradley and Dennis Stanford, "The North Atlantic Ice-Edge Corridor: A Possible Palaeolithic Route to the New World," *World Archaeology* 36, no. 4 (2004): 459–78.

3 Roger Collis, *The Basques*, 2nd ed. (Oxford: Basil Blackwell Ltd., [1986], 1990), 4.

4 Donato Arrinda, *EuskalErri Zaarra* (Barcelona: Editorial R. M., 1969), 37–38.

5 Koldo Larrañaga Elorza, "El periodo colonial romano," *Gran atlas histórico del mundo vasco* (Bilbao: El Mundo, 2009), 34. Strabo (c. 64 BCE–24 CE) was a Greek geographer, philosopher, and historian in charge of documenting the new geographical boundaries with Julius Cesar's campaigns. Claudius Ptolemy (c. 100–170 CE) was a Greco-Roman mathematician, astronomer, geographer and astrologer who defined the maps for the Roman Empire.

6 Julio Caro Baroja, *Los Vascos* (Madrid: Ediciones Istmo, S.A., 2000), 290–99.

7 M. Carmen Basterretxea, *Euskal Herria, Kultura Matrilineala* (Madrid: Potlatch Editorial, 2016), 42.

8 Marija Gimbutas, *The Language of the Goddess* (New York: Thames & Hudson, 2006), 320.

9 José Miguel Barandiaran, *Mitología vasca*, 18th ed. (Donostia: Editorial Txertoa, 2014), 25.

10 Edward Burnett Tylor, "Primitive Culture," in *A Reader in the Anthropology of Religion*, ed. M. Lambek, 23–24 (Oxford: Wiley-Blackwell, 2002).

11 Graham Harvey, *Animism: Respecting the Living World* (New York: Columbia University Press, 2006), 2.

12 Betty Bastien, *Blackfoot Ways of Knowing: The Worldview of the Siksikaitsitapi* (Calgary, Alberta: University of Calgary Press, 2004), 181.

13 Blair Stonechild, *The Knowledge Seeker: Embracing Indigenous Spirituality* (Regina: University of Regina Press, 2016), 91.

14 Douglas Cardinal (architect and Anishinaabe elder, sweat lodge ceremony, Ottawa, Ontario, Canada), in discussion with the author, February 27, 2018. Cardinal's ancestry is of the Kainai (Blood) Blackfoot Confederacy of southern Alberta. He is best known for his organic approach to architecture, having created masterpieces such as the National Museum of the American Indian for the Smithsonian Institution in Washington, DC, the Canadian Museum of History in Gatineau, Quebec, and many other civic and indigenous buildings in North America.

15 Dave Lee, "Magick and Quantum Physics," in *Chaotopia: Magick and Ecstasy in the PandaemonAeon* (Attractor, 1997). cdn.preterhuman.net/texts/religion.occult.new_age/Magick/Magick%20and%20Physics.pdf.

16 Stonechild, *The Knowledge Seeker*, 106.

17 Guillermo Piquero, *Mitología Salvaje: Reconstruyendo la Cosmovisión Indígena Europea* (Author, 2013), 45. ISBN: 978-84-942152-4-7, 2013.

18 Andrés Ortiz-Osés, *La diosa madre: Interpretación desde la mitología vasca* (Madrid: Editorial Trotta, S.A., 1996), 23.

19 Josu Naberan, *La vuelta de Sugaar: Un proyecto de futuro, para un pueblo con pasado* (Donostia: Basandere Argitaletxea, 2001), 244.

20 Julio Caro Baroja, *Estudios vascos* (San Sebastián: Editorial Txertoa, 1973), 66–67.

21 Donato Arrinda, *Jainko Txikiak* (Bilbao: Kardaberz, 1973), 11.

22 Andrés Ortiz-Osés, *El matriarcalismo vasco* (Bilbao: Universidad de Deusto, 1988), 80.

23 See Barandiaran, *Mitología vasca*, 61–62, for a more comprehensive list.

24 Caro Baroja, *Estudios vascos*, 65.

25 Bernardo Estornes Lasa, *Orígenes de los Vascos*, Vol. IV (San Sebastian: Editorial Aunamendi, 1966), 35.

26 Basterretxea, *Euskal Herria, Kultura Matrilineala*, 47–48.

27 Rhonda Byrne, *The Secret* (New York: Atria Books/Beyond Words, 2006), 7.

28 Also, "Izena duen guztia, omen da," in Barandiaran, *Mitología vasca*, 24. Relating to the power of words, Barandiaran, a priest himself, explained that there was a "compromise" between ancient belief systems and the Christian faith regarding the older conceptual world and its numen, witches, and magic. It was said that: "*Direnik, ez da sinistu bear; ez direla, ez da esan bear*" ("One should not believe that they exist; but one should not say that they do not exist"), 42.

29 Bastien, *Blackfoot Ways of Knowing*, 127.

30 Arrinda, *EuskalErri Zaarra*, 107.

31 Barandiaran, *Mitología vasca*, 100.

32 Basterretxea, *Euskal Herria, Kultura*, 70.

33 Ortiz-Osés, *El matriarcalismo vasco*, 79.

34 Ortiz-Osés, *La diosa madre*, 21.

PACHAMAMA AND LIVING LANDSCAPE SITES IN THE ANDES

MARY LOUISE STONE

R egarding Andean shrines, the colonial Spaniard Blas Valera recorded
in 1590, "The old wizards seek solitude in the hills. They don't lack
statues; the hills, the river basins, and the cliffs serve as their temples
and sanctuaries."[1]

Even more jarring to the colonial mindset, evidently, Jesuit Francisco
Patiño complained in 1648 to Cuzco's archbishop about the divergent
Andean worldview:

> Seizing some small idols from a community leader in
> Guamanga, the *curaca* [village leader] brazenly told me:
> "Father, why do you tire yourself taking away these idols?
> Take this hill, if you can, for this is the god that I worship.[2]

These attitudes of regarding a landscape site, a rock outcropping, a hill,
or a river as a sanctuary challenge modern thought. How do Andeans view
these sites and how can modern people understand them?

In the substantially different Andean worldview, today's Euro-descended
understanding can be turned upside down. In the material/spiritual split,
Nature provides raw materials to sell, God created the world from the outside, and death is so feared as the end that few talk about it or prepare for it.
In contrast, many traditional Andean peoples maintain reciprocal relations
with landscapes in Nature, the Earth and the Andean Mother Pachamama
give birth to the world and to humans rather than creating them, and death,
rather than an ending, continues the journey toward another reemergence. An
integral part of Andean conversations and practices, these concepts around
landscape sites and Pachamama reach beyond the material way of thought.

Here I postulate that parallels exist between the living landscape sites, especially those that mark places of origin, and the qualities of Pachamama. These parallels heighten the fundamental significance of both the sites and the Mother in Andean worldviews. Indeed, many Andean cultures hold mothering qualities, or parenting qualities, in high esteem—for men, women, children, entire communities, and even states.[3] Thus, these world-view features may deepen understanding of contemporary practices as well as archaeological sites and their interpretations.

For data, I compare selected contemporary community sites from Cusco to the Lake Titiqaqa region, juxtapose descriptions of such sites recorded in the 1500s and 1600s, and further, compare them with beliefs about Pachamama today. From these comparisons, I conclude that both the emergence sites and Pachamama embrace non-modern concepts perhaps unfamiliar and misunderstood and I select a few to address here: both sites and Pachamama give birth to all rather than create the world, both highly respect women, both hold unseen animating force or presence that perme-ates the everyday material world, and both offer refuge at death as well as continuity beyond death. Finally, I review a few practices of reciprocity with the sites.

For twelve years while living in Quechua and Aymara communities around Lake Titiqaqa in Peru and Bolivia, I participated in small daily rituals as well as the largest religious festivals in the Andes. From 1993 to 2005 and in biennial return visits since then, I partook of kitchen talk and walks with grandpas to Condor Rock and the like, largely in the Quechua community of Taquile Island and the nearby city of Puno, Peru, on Lake Titiqaqa. I used connected knowing as a women's way of knowing that is based on personal participation and empathy and seeking others' points of view to explore rather than argue, to understand rather than judge, and to collaborate rather than debate.[4]

Primarily, I listen to American Indians as experts in their culture, as do the participants in the Smithsonian's National Museum of the American Indian, and Maori and academic Linda Tuhiwai Smith, who formulated decolonizing methodologies.[5] Ritual arts, such as offerings, weaving, and celebrations of music and dance, as well as oral narratives and histories draw forth deep beliefs not found in written texts or religious institutions. My Andean community colleagues urge me to share our findings to increase respect for their ancestral culture, a major heritage of the Americas.

While a few studies address Pachamama and another few *paqarinas*,[6] very few analyses compare the two. To expand my experiences into a wider overview, I include data from the Cusco region from archaeologist Adan Choqque, a native of Pitumarka, and ethnographer Catherine Allen on Sonqo, from anthropologist Joseph Bastien about the Kallawaya people in Charazani, Bolivia, as well as data from records of the 1500s and 1600s uncovered by various historians.[7] Amid different areas and time periods, the diverse local details point to the widespread significance of these sites.

Paqarina Sites of Dawning and Emergence

To form some links between modern views and Andean sanctuaries, I invite the reader to imagine a place in Nature that nurtures her or him with a feeling of well-being. To encourage the imagination, venerated landscape in the Andes includes placid blue lakes and earth openings into moist dark interiors, red rock cliffs and unusual stones, and pairs of features (Fig. 5). Imagine some type of relation with the place—prayer, conversation, reflection. Further, imagine leaving some sort of offerings there, perhaps as thanks, perhaps for well-being—they could be food or sweets, flowers or art, or even music and dance. Such links with Mother Nature at specific sites may support a feeling of belonging and well-being in the modern world as well as a motivation to care for the natural environment—which might ease the spiritual and ecological crises today.

In Andean worldviews, honoring and respect fill everyday activities in ways that many modern people would designate spiritual, in the philosophical split between sacred and mundane. Eminent ethnohistorian María Rostworowski pointed out that the word "sacred" in colonial documents was mistranslated from the

Fig. 5. Red rock formation, Puno, Peru. Photograph by author, 1998.

Quechua word *wak'a* that referred to the vital force that animates the world. Choqque reported the communication, affection, and reciprocal relation that his neighbors felt with a site, rather than the sense of "sacred."[8] Thus a "sacred site" in the Andean context might be described as a place of vital animating force with which Andeans cultivate a relation. As the quotes here from colonial documents and today's interviews show and as many Andeans emphasized to me, principles and practices around Pachamama and living sites are also not folkloric remnants, much less myths, but rather parts of a living, practiced worldview long held by many in Andean cultures.

What, more precisely, is a *paqarina* site? The Quechua *paqarina* (noun) and *paqariy* (verb) mean "dawn" and "to be born" both today and in Spanish colonial times.[9] *Paqarina* refers to "place of dawning," a place of origin, emergence, and birth into this world. In their physical appearance, *paqarinas* are recessed places in the earth, lakes, springs, and grottoes, often embellished with offerings of art and used to commune with unseen entities and forces (e.g., Fig. 5). Though called by various names—earth shrine, Earth Being, *wak'a,* place of emergence[10]—I use the older name of *paqarina*, common in pre-Hispanic times with the evocative meaning of dawning. Rather than Hispanicized adaptations, I employ the spelling of the official Quechua and Aymara alphabet, established by law in Bolivia (1984) and Peru (1985), which reflects native speakers' pronunciation. Delving into *paqarinas*, then, the first area of potential parallels of places of dawning and other landscape sites with understandings of Pachamama comprises birth, emergence and nurture.

Birth and Nurture

Historical documents recorded the principal venerated sites during Inka times as the village origin sites—every settlement had one. The Spanish chronicler Cristóbal de Albornoz in the 1580s led efforts to destroy Andean temples, idols and landscape sites:

> [T]he principal kind of *guacas* [*wak'as,* sacred sites] from before being Inka subjects, were called *pacarisca* [*paqarina*], which means creators of their beings. They have different forms and names according to the provinces: some have rocks, others springs and rivers, others caves, others animals and birds and others trees and plants....

> Understand that no settlement, no matter how small or
> large, was without a sacred *guaca pacarisca*.[11]

One reason the word *paqarina* is less common today emerged in Spanish colonial documents. During the persecution of Andean spirituality, the Catholic clerics erased the community origin narratives around the sites in order to copy the Bible's precepts. In extensive historical research, Rostworowski found that, "In order to explain their idea of one creator God, ... [the priests] omitted the multiple indigenous references to the *paqarinas* or emergence sites." Longstanding practices and locales of animate force—of the Mother—were replaced with the story of one father God. Despite the Spanish impositions, however, Rostworowski clarified that "in the Andean magical-religious environment, animated by a primordial vital principle, there was no room for gods who created humanity." For Andeans in colonial times and today, birth is key rather than creation.[12]

What beliefs today relate to *paqarinas*? Downhill from Lake Titiqaqa's northeast shores lies the Kallawaya region of Charazani, Bolivia. The isolated and traditional Kallawaya people have long traveled as healers and ritualists respected across the Andes, and their cosmology and healing skills were recognized by UNESCO in 2003 as an Intangible Cultural Heritage of Humanity. Kallawaya communities range from high-altitude Aymara-speaking herders living near marshes for their llamas to lower-altitude potato farmers cultivating their curved terraces on steep hills above rushing rivers. Quechua speakers in even lower and warmer valleys grow corn, peas and dahlias, and trade with still lower villages along Amazon tributary rivers. Bastien found that a central metaphor unified these varied Kallawaya peoples today, as it did for the pre-Inka people of Huarochirí, Peru, whose worldview was recorded in church archives of Andean testimonies. The hill slope residents of both areas perceived the principal mountain as a human body that united the ecologically diverse communities. The summit provided the head, the slopes formed the chest, and two lower river valleys outlined the legs—and all levels contained their own earth shrines.[13]

When Margarita Yanahuaya was born in the Kallawaya community of Kaata, her grandparents Carmen and Marcelino called a diviner to discern her earth shrine, a site that also fulfilled the function of a *paqarina* of origin. The divination process revealed that the female lake shrine of Qota claimed Margarita, a shrine low on the mountain slopes that signified fertility and abundance. Springs, lakes, and low places comprised female shrines; high unusual rocks, cliffs, and caves male sites (e.g., Fig. 5). The Kallawaya earth shrines lay in natural openings or in small holes dug into the ground covered with rocks except while ritualists opened them to place offerings to Pachamama and others. Baby Margarita would share life with her lake site and make offerings to that shrine, which, in reciprocity, would guide her with counsel.[14]

The surrounding communities understood their common origin to be from the watery mountain highlands. High on Mount Kaata, Pachaquta Lake focused the worldview as the origin point. The *ichu* bunchgrass grazed by the herds and the llamas growing woolly fiber resembled the hair on the head of the landscape metaphor of Mount Kaata.[15]

For Kallawayas, then, a *paqarina*-like earth shrine was indeed often a recessed place in the earth and used as a place of communion with earth beings. As a major function, the site accompanied the individuals it claimed throughout their lives and gave guidance in exchange for human offerings, prayers and attention.

Northwest of Lake Titiqaqa in the Quechua mountain village of Sonqo near Cusco, landscape sites also brought forth life. Sonqo farmers recounted that their first ancestors, three males, "sprang up," *phaway*, from the earth and established communities. Allen translated the places that the ancestors sprang from, *Tirakuna*, as Sacred Places and as Earth Beings that localized the vitality animating the material earth as a whole. "*Tirakuna* are not spirits, but the Places themselves," Allen observed, "who live, watch, and have ways of interacting with the human beings, plants, and animals that live around and upon them." The farmers called the places our nurturers, *uywaqninchiskuna*.[16] In Sonqo as well as among Kallawayas and despite increasing interaction with urban Cusco, humans emerged from living places of the earth and continually remembered these living places that nurtured them.

In the same Cusco region, the town of Pitumarka nestles in the foothills of the highest mountain between Cusco and Titiqaqa, Mount Ausangate (20,945 feet, 6,384 meters). Another Quechua area of farmers and higher herders, Pitumarka sits near traditional and tourist routes that circumambulate Ausangate, and the village weavers recover ancestral techniques maintained by women in the higher, more isolated settlements. The jagged lower peaks rise above the town to display the archaeological remains of villages of Inka and earlier Qanchi times as well as various cliffs. Archaeologist Adan Choqque, a native of Pitumarka, recently catalogued the land formations, or geoforms, along with community narratives of the peaks, outcroppings, and springs.

Though the word *paqarina* as a place of origin is not widely used in recent times, its functions have continued. For instance, a man was born from his mountain site, from "the place from which one emerged," *de donde ha salido* in Spanish, *lluqsimusqa* in Quechua. Again as in Sonqo, Pitumarka neighbors told Choqque that "each hill is alive." The living hill was called a *pukara*, that is, an entity who functioned in both its spiritual and its visible forms and helped humans in daily life. The landscape forms were conceived as persons with the agency to talk, act, and maintain social relations through their invisible as well as their tangible forms.[17]

A widespread *paqarina* function emerged during a ceremony at birth— often called *mink'akuy* or reciprocating mutually—to discover which of the local geoforms or *pukaras* would arrive to "collect" the child and become its godparent. From then on, the living "person" of that site would accompany the new child through life, provide for it, and offer guidance. Local Pitumarka belief held that every person had such a godparent, male or female, in a parallel to the Kallawaya earth shrines that claimed newborns. The site's protection continued as long as the human gave offerings and respect in remembrance. Reciprocity cultivated the relation. Along with guidance, the relation with the site provided cultural identity for each person of the region, Choqque explained, and a deep sense of belonging to a landscape site, to a community, and to a people.[18]

One group of nurturing sites occupies a prominent spot seen above the village of Pitumarka to form the image of a woman on the mountain side. Most visible are her two breasts, two similar prominences called in Quechua, *Ñuñuyuq*, "having breasts." Below the breasts lies a swath where the rocky ravines are likened to the folds of the bulky gathered skirt, *pollera* in Spanish, often worn by Quechua women. The large earth woman apparently forms a metaphor of Pachamama watching over the people.[19]

In summary, in these three communities, dynamic and alive landscape forms, persons really, continually communicated with humans to give care. In the landscape, ancestors were birthed in the three communities, features formed images such as the Kallawayas' mountain metaphor and Pitumarka's earth woman, places lived, spoke, and acted such as in narratives from Sonqo and Pitumarka, and the places often helped humans in their endeavors such as in the relations with the godparents of Kallawayas and Pitumarka and the nurturers of Sonqo. The large earth woman on the terrain in Pitumarka images the widespread Pachamama caring for the people of the region.

Pachamama

In 1590, the friar Martín de Murúa described the widespread veneration to Pachamama, Mother Earth according to the Spanish:

> It was a common thing among the Indians to adore the fertile earth ... which they called Pachamama, offering her *chicha* [corn beer] by spilling it on the ground, as well as coca and other things so that she would provide for them; to mark this, they placed a long stone in the midst of their fields in order to invoke the virtues of the earth from that point, so that she would protect their fields.[20]

Still today in Sonqo, Allen concluded that ongoing prayers remember Pachamama first as a basic religious duty for an Andean-identified person.[21]

Who is Pachamama today? Narratives of birth and nurture around *paqarina* sites from the three communities of the northern Titiqaqa region reflect the widespread attitudes towards Pachamama that I elaborated elsewhere.[22] Do these beliefs still hold in 2019? To confirm the stability and resilience of these principles (or not), I returned to longtime friends and colleagues on Taquile Island in northern Lake Titiqaqa. While the word *paqarina* is not used for a landscape site on the island today, certain sites receive offerings and act to help the inhabitants[23] and Pachamama is commonly greeted.

Taquile Island, near Puno, Peru, is a traditional Quechua community of around 2,000 farmers and fishers that was awarded UNESCO recognition in 2005 as an Intangible Heritage of Humanity for its strong communal organization and ancestral textile skills. Residents gained renown for rejecting outside hotels and developing locally-run community tourism.[24] Textiles fill the weaving cooperative and seasonal festivals of dance and music celebrate Pachamama.

Overlooking azure Lake Titiqaqa in April 2019, Teodosia Quispe and I welcomed her sister Paula Quispe winding her way through the purple and red quinoa heads in front of the house. From the bundle on Paula's back, yellow and orange flowers protruded as well as spiky stems and broad green leaves from the herbs she had collected to dry for the year's home remedies. While Paula selected a few fragrant flowers and leaves, Teodosia heated water for a tonic tea.

As we settled on a patch of grass, I asked the two sisters why women tend to sit on the ground (Fig. 6), while men prefer to sit on benches, handy stones, or chairs. Teodosia responded, "We like to sit on the ground, it's warmer, and women always sit like this." Paula elaborated, "We are mothers and we sit close to Pachamama. It's a custom of our grandmothers that we don't lose." This linkage between Pachamama and women for the ability to bring forth life does not, of course, limit women to *only* bearing children, but recognizes with respect women's diverse capacities to create and nourish life around them in family care, crop cultivation, resource management, and community well-being, as I have described elsewhere. Aymara Vicenta Mamani, of lake side Escoma, Bolivia, also linked women with Pachamama. "Women are in constant contact with Pachamama," Mamani explained, "[as] both are sources of life."[25] As a prominent proverb begins, "From Pachamama we emerge."

"Who is Pachamama for you, today in 2019?" I asked the sisters. Teodosia began, "Pachamama is very important for us because, it's true, we farm our fields on her, we harvest our food, we build our houses on her and from her. We do everything on the earth; we sit on the ground to weave our textiles. She is crucial for us. Without Pachamama in the air, how would we breathe and live?"

"For me," Teodosia added thoughtfully, "Pachamama is not ours to use as we wish.

Fig. 6. Woman offering coca leaf prayer, Lake Titiqaqa, Peru. Drawing for thesis by author, 2009.

Rather we are hers, for her to use as she wishes. This is what I taught my daughter Saide." She laughed self-consciously. "And it is true. We live because of Pachamama, we eat thanks to her, and we ask her for everything."

The proverb continues, "on Pachamama we live"—Pachamama accompanies humans through life endeavors from weaving to farming to providing for their needs.

Furthermore, Pachamama is all-encompassing. Amid a diversity of descriptions, on Taquile Island, Teodosia clarified, "Of course, Pachamama is Mother Earth. And Pachamama is everything else as well, the air, Mother Lake."

Paula agreed, saying, "Pachamama is Mother Earth, and she is everything."

Aymaras around Lake Titiqaqa concur. In Puno, Jorge Apaza, anthropologist of environment and society at Puno's High Plateau National University, is an Aymara of Ilave, south of Puno. "One thing I want to make clear," Apaza emphasized in our interview in Puno in April, 2019: "Pachamama is everything—earth, trees, water, air, stars, the universe. And from that everything, we are born from her as our Mother."

Aymara Vicenta Mamani and others confirmed Pachamama's all-inclusive nature: "Pachamama is energy and the source of life." On social and cultural levels, Mamani explained, "Pachamama is our identity."[26] Pachamama's presence might be compared, in modern terminology, with immanence. Many Andean views embrace the integral nature of land forms in which the divine infuses, merges, and manifests in the everyday material world on Earth.

In sum, Pachamama gives birth, brings forth life, and nurtures it, and in tandem *paqarina* earth shrines, as described, provide the landscape places to ground these beliefs, the places where humans and others emerge onto the Earth. Further, these sites accompany and guide their new offspring through life, even as the humans reciprocate with continual prayers and offerings. *Paqarinas* parallel Pachamama's birth and nurturance. As reminders and aniconic depictions, the *paqarinas* root and bond Andeans with their Mother of origin.

More than an image, the *paqarina* site is living. From colonial documents, Ernesto Vargas, a Quechua and researcher of the former National Institute of Culture in Cusco, concluded, "For the pre-Inka population . . . their deities were Pachamama and Mamaqucha [Mother Lake]...who were physically present in their *paqarina* emergence sites."[27]

Death and reemergence

Along with birth and nurturance, a second area of potential parallels between *paqarinas* and Pachamama is death and reemergence. In the 1500s, Spanish chronicler Cieza de León recorded narratives of the life cycle from the Qanchi people, Pitumarka's ancestors.[28] The *paqarinas* of emergence linked not only to individuals' origin, but also to their return after death. Distant from Church doctrine, Cieza de León noted in 1553 with incredulous disbelief, the Andean cycle of birth, return, and reemergence based on a great lake:

> [They] were convinced in past times that the souls who left their bodies went to a great lake where they inanely believed they had their beginning, and there they entered the bodies of those being born.[29]

Other chroniclers recorded similar Andean testimonies and echoed Cieza's skeptical disdain.[30]

How is the cycle of life, death, and reemergence viewed today? Does it include Pachamama and the *paqarinas*? Surprisingly perhaps to the modern view, the places of origin still serve also as places of return at death for rest. Among the traditional Kallawaya ritualists with their earth shrines, the departed was believed to swim in underground waterways back to the origin place in high Pachaquta Lake to complete its cycle. In a regenerative process, the mini person swam to the summit point to reemerge as a baby born from the highland lake of origin.[31] Of course, readers will take care not to assume that the many non-modern views around the world on continuity after death, such as India's reincarnation and others, are the same. Along with points of convergence, the ancestral Andean concepts of reemergence and the diversity of worldviews each deserve respect for their uniqueness.

Sonqo Quechuas told Allen that their ancestors also travel around in water. Sonqo's most venerable sacred place occupies a high hill along with the archaeological remains of burial towers conceived to hold the oldest local ancestors. The ancestral Sacred Places were considered to store the potential for Sonqo's future in a sort of subterranean animating substance, *sami*, of the flow of life. Evidently, Sonqo's deceased journeyed to their origin place to join the pool ready to people Sonqo's future population. In Pitumarka, Choqque summarized oral traditions and colonial records: death "is simply a re-creation or physical metamorphosis and the continuation of life as part of the flow of life. Life continues, although with time it can adopt a different material and physical form, and death as such does not exist."[32]

On Taquile Island, Teodosia Quispe affirmed, "Not only do we live from, eat from, and celebrate with Pachamama, we also return to her when we die." The widespread proverb reveals a fundamental part of the Andean worldview: "From Pachamama we emerge, on Pachamama we live, and to Pachamama we return." As one specific expression of this worldview, the film *Ajayu* graphically depicted the return of death. Written with Bolivian anthropologists, Aymara residents of the Island of the Sun in southern Lake Titiqaqa described their beliefs and acted in the film. Death was portrayed not as an end but as a journey across a lake carried out with much stamina and the collaboration of friends and loved ones. The deceased eventually arrived at an otherworldly Aymara village to continue working the soil.[33]

In sum, today in many Andean conceptions, Pachamama gives birth and nurture throughout life as well as refuge at death, and for some at least, continuity and reemergence. The life force at the *paqarinas* ushers a person through the cycle of life, death, and reemergence; the narratives around the sites illustrate the continuity of Andean life and peoples. The conceptions around *paqarina* sites of return at death and reemergence again parallel Pachamama's continual cycle of life.

As postulated, essential parallels of the Andean life cycle and world-view exist between emergence sites and Pachamama: birth is key, nurture is paramount, women are valued, death implies continuance, and the presence of vital force permeates physical landforms and everyday activities. *Paqarina* sites were present in every settlement, large or small, during Inka times and continue today. Being the most common venerated sites resonates with contemporary Pachamama as the first remembered in ever-present ritual greetings, as the base of life for traditional Andeans whether urbanites or farmers. The superlatives underscore the significance of both Pachamama and the sites of emergence, remembrance, and reflection. Future research can contribute to the overlap and diversity of Andean vocabulary for the sites, of women's outlooks and practices, and of diverse expressions of the cycle of life, death, and reemergence. Highlighting *paqarina* sites, Pachamama, and other mother deities in investigations of Andean practices today and in interpretations of archaeological remains[34] may increase understanding of an alternative value system with high regard for women, deep understanding of the life cycle, and pervasive insight into the presence of life force.

Practices of Reciprocity

To further demonstrate the ongoing relations of many Andeans with Pachamama and landscape sites, reciprocity pervades practices such as coca leaf prayers, larger offerings, and celebrations. On Taquile Island, in Teodosia Quispe's first description of Pachamama, she gracefully swept her hand above her head in a greeting with an offering of coca leaves and replied, "We always remember Pachamama." Her sister Paula expanded: "We respect our Pachamama. The first thing we do is our ritual to remember her, for weaving, for sowing, for building a house," as I repeatedly observed. Taquile farmers taught me to select three perfect leaves for a bundle or *k'intu*. Considering my intent, I was to blow my greeting to the unseen entities around onto the leaves and lift them to the surroundings (Fig. 6).

Coca leaves permeate healing remedies with their high content of vitamins and minerals, particularly vitamin A and calcium.[35] On another level, the coca leaf prayer and exchange comprises a constant reciprocity. No event seems to begin or end in the Andes without a greeting to Pachamama. A special verb, *akulliy*, indicates the ritual exchange of coca leaves: "Let us exchange and chew coca leaves in the respectful Andean way," that is, let us enter mindful consciousness and commune with Pachamama and other nurturing entities of the sites. By giving back, Andeans understand they belong to the community—and to Pachamama.

Larger offerings as well are built for Pachamama and for the shrines. Kallawaya ritualists converse with many living places through narrative prayers as they build offerings for personal healings and community well-being; larger celebrations occur seasonally. In Pitumarka, especially on the first of August, the offering is served, *haywakuy*, with coca leaves, corn, beans, flowers, fast-burning llama fat, sweets, and other desired items.[36] On Taquile Island, Paula Quispe explained: "We dance for Pachamama and are happy for her." As one example, the islanders build a community offering to Pachamama at Easter, complete with music, dance, and ceremonies.

123

A modern practice of reciprocity and respect has developed that under-scores the widespread veneration of Pachamama and landscape sites: enacting the legal rights of Pachamama and the living landscape. Along with Ecuador in 2008, Bolivia passed its own plurinational constitution in 2009 that seeks "the recovery of the right to a relation with Mother Earth," and in 2012, a law that safeguards Mother Earth and integral development. The current president in Bolivia, President Evo Morales, listed four of Pachamama's rights: the rights to life, regeneration of biocapacity, clean water, and harmony and balance among all. To the north, the Supreme Court of Colombia declared in 2018 that the Amazon rainforest has rights and ordered the Colombian government to immediately create a plan to combat deforestation. Internationally, Bolivia initiated the United Nations General Assembly's 2009 declaration to amend the name of Earth Day to *Mother* Earth Day to emphasize the human family that must live together on the planet.[37]

References

Albornoz, Cristóbal de. "Instrucción para descubrir todas las guacas del Pirú y sus camayos y haziendas." *Journal de la Société des Américanistes* 56, no. 1 ([1580s] 1967): 17–39.

Allen, Catherine. "To Be Quechua: The Symbolism of Coca Chewing in Highland Peru." *American Ethnologist* 8, no. 1 (1981): 157–71.

———. *The Hold Life Has: Coca and Cultural Identity in an Andean Community*. Washington, DC: Smithsonian Institution Press, 2002.

Barreiro, José. "Andean Journal: Along the Inka Road." National Museum of the American Indian website, December 1, 2010. blog.nmai.si.edu/main/inka-road/2010/12/page/3/.

Bastien, Joseph. *Mountain of the Condor: Metaphor and Ritual in an Andean Ayllu*. Long Grove, IL: Waveland Press, 1985.

Belenky, Mary, Blythe Clinchy, Nancy Goldberger, and Jill Tarule. *Women's Ways of Knowing: The Development of Self, Voice, and Mind*. New York: Basic Books, 1986.

Bertonio, Ludovico. *Vocabulario de la lengua aymara*. Digitized book from Oxford Library, (1612) 1984. Accessed August 7, 2019. archive.org/details/vocabulariodela00bertgoog/page/n248.

Cajías, Francisco, and Francisco Ormachea. *Ajayu*. Film. Directed by Francisco Cajías and Francisco Ormachea. La Paz: Taller Arawi, 1996.

Choqque, Adan. "Simbolismo de las geoformas en la concepción social prehispánica del paisaje en el valle del Ausangate." Thesis, Universidad Nacional de San Antonio Abad (Cusco, Peru), 2018.

Cieza de León, Pedro de. *Crónica del Perú: El señorío de los Incas*. Biblioteca Ayacucho website, (1553) 2005. Accessed September 23, 2015. www.bibliotecayacucho.gob.ve/fba/index.php?id=97&backPID=96&swords=cieza%20 de%20leon&tt_products=311.

De la Cadena, Marisol. *Earth Beings: Ecologies of Practice across Andean Worlds*. Durham, NC: Duke University Press, 2015.

Doyle, Mary Eileen. "The Ancestor Cult and Burial Ritual in Seventeenth- and Eighteenth-Century Central Peru." PhD diss., University of California, Los Angeles, 1988. ProQuest (8822310).

Duke, James A., David Aulik, and Timothy Plowman. "Nutritional Value of Coca." *Botanical Museum Leaflets* 24, no. 6 (1975): 113–19. Cambridge, MA: Peabody Museum.

Genge, Cole D. "Nurturance: An Andean Amerindian Way of Life as an Alternative Construct to Development Theory and Practice." PhD diss., University of Massachusetts-Amherst, 2003. ProQuest (3110489).

González Holguín, Diego. *Vocabulario de la lengua general de todo el Perú llamada lengua quechua, o del Inca*. Federal University of Minas Gerais, Brazil, website (1608) 2007. Accessed August 7, 2019. www.letras.ufmg.br/padrao_ cms/documentos/profs/romulo/VocabvlarioQqichuaDeHolguin1607.pdf.

Granadino, Cecilia, and Cronwell Jara. *Las ranas embajadoras de la lluvia*. Lima: Minka, 1996.

Gudynas, Eduardo. "Colombia reconoce los derechos de la Naturaleza en su Amazonia." Systemic Alternatives website, April 6, 2018. systemicalternatives.org/2018/04/09/ colombia-reconoce-los-derechos-de-la-naturaleza-en-su-amazonia/.

Huanacuni, Fernando. *Vivir bien/buen vivir: Filosofía, políticas, estrategias y experiencias regionales*. La Paz: Instituto Internacional de Integración-Convenio Andrés Bello, 2010.

Lara, Jesús. *Diccionario Qheshwa-Castellano, Castellano-Qheshwa*. La Paz: Amigos del Libro, 2001.

Mamani, Vicenta. *Identidad y espiritualidad de la mujer aymara.* La Paz: CIMA, 2000.

Mamani, Vicenta, and Calixto Quispe. *Pacha.* Cochabamba, Bolivia: Editorial Verbo Divino, 2007.

Morales, Evo. *The Earth Does Not Belong to Us, We Belong to the Earth.* La Paz: Ministry of Foreign Affairs of Bolivia, 2010.

Rösing, Ina. *Diálogos con divinidades de cerros, rayos, manantiales y lagos: Oraciones blancas Kallawayas.* La Paz: Hisbol, 1995.

Rostworowski, María. *Estructuras andinas del poder: Ideología religiosa y política.* Lima: Instituto de Estudios Peruanos, 2007.

Sherbondy, Jeanette. "El regadío, los lagos y los mitos de origen." *Allpanchis Phuturinqa* 20 (1982): 3–32.

Silverblatt, Irene. *Moon, Sun, and Witches: Gender Ideologies and Class in Inca and Colonial Peru.* Princeton, NJ: Princeton University Press, 1987.

Smith, Linda Tuhiwai. *Decolonizing Methodologies: Research and Indigenous Peoples.* London: Zed Books, 1999.

Stone, Mary Louise. "The Andean Mother: Weaving a Culture of Reciprocity." Master's thesis, California Institute of Integral Studies (San Francisco, CA), 2009. ProQuest (1466047).

———. "An Andean Paradigm of Mothering." In *An Anthropology of Mothering*, edited by Michelle Walks and Naomi McPherson, 185–95. Bradford, ON: Demeter Press, 2011.

———. "Dance for Mother Lake on the Arid Titiqaqa Plateau: Observations from Fieldwork Seasons 1993–2005." *Archaeological Review from Cambridge* 34, no. 1 (April 2019): 122–42.

United Nations General Assembly. "General Assembly Proclaims 22 April 'International Mother Earth Day' Adopting by Consensus Bolivia-Led Resolution." United Nations website, April 22, 2009. www.un.org/press/en/2009/ga10823.doc.htm.

Urton, Gary. *History of a Myth: Pacariqtambo and the Origin of the Incas.* Austin: University of Texas Press, 1990.

Van Kessel, Juan. "Tecnología aymara: Un enfoque cultural." In *La cosmovisión aymara*, edited by Hans van den Berg and Norbert Schiffers, 187–220. La Paz: Universidad Católica Boliviana/Hisbol, 1992.

Vargas, Ernesto. *Tipón: Santuario del agua de los Inkas.* Cusco: Imprenta Edmundo Pantigozo, 1999.

Zorn, Elayne. *Weaving a Future: Tourism, Cloth, and Culture on an Andean Island.* Iowa City: University of Iowa Press, 2004.

Endnotes

1 Quoted in Ernesto Vargas, *Tipón: Santuario del agua de los Inkas* (Cusco: Imprenta Edmundo Pantigozo, 1999), 199. Translations by the author.

2 Quoted in Vargas, *Tipón*, 201.

3 For example, Cole D. Genge, "Nurturance: An Andean Amerindian Way of Life as an Alternative Construct to Development Theory and Practice" (PhD diss., University of Massachusetts-Amherst, 2003, ProQuest 3110489); Mary Louise Stone, "An Andean Paradigm of Mothering," in *An Anthropology of Mothering*, ed. Michelle Walks and Naomi McPherson, 189–95 (Bradford, ON: Demeter Press, 2011); Juan van Kessel, "Tecnología aymara: Un enfoque cultural," in *La cosmovisión aymara*, eds. Hans van den Berg and Norbert Schiffers (La Paz: Universidad Católica Boliviana/Hisbol, 1992).

4 Mary Belenky, Blythe Clinchy, Nancy Goldberger, and Jill Tarule, *Women's Ways of Knowing: The Development of Self, Voice, and Mind* (New York: Basic Books, 1986), 219, 225.

5 José Barreiro, "Andean Journal: Along the Inka Road," National Museum of the American Indian blog, December 1, 2010, para. 14, accessed March 29, 2013, blog.nmai.si.edu/main/inka-road/2010/12/page/3/; Linda Tuhiwai Smith, *Decolonizing Methodologies: Research and Indigenous Peoples* (London: Zed Books, 1999).

6 For example, Pachamama: Quechua prayers, in Catherine Allen, "To Be Quechua: The Symbolism of Coca Chewing in Highland Peru," *American Ethnologist* 8, no. 1 (1981): 161–62; and Aymara women, Vicenta Mamani, *Identidad y espiritualidad de la mujer aymara* (La Paz: CIMA, 2000); in-depth studies, Vicenta Mamani and Calixto Quispe, *Pacha* (Cochabamba, Bolivia: Editorial Verbo Divino, 2007); Mary Louise Stone, "The Andean Mother: Weaving a Culture of Reciprocity" (master's thesis, California Institute of Integral Studies, San Francisco, 2009, ProQuest 1466047); Stone, "An Andean Paradigm."

For example, *paqarinas:* Mary Eileen Doyle, "The Ancestor Cult and Burial Ritual in Seventeenth- and Eighteenth-Century Central Peru" (PhD diss., University of California-Los Angeles, 1988, ProQuest 8822310); Jeanette

Sherbondy, "El regadío, los lagos y los mitos de origen," *Allpanchis Phuturinqa* 20 (1982): 3–32; Gary Urton, *History of a Myth: Pacariqtambo and the Origin of the Incas* (Austin: University of Texas, 1990).

7   Adan Choqque, "Simbolismo de la geoformas en la concepción social pre-hispánica del paisaje en el valle del Ausangate" (Thesis, Universidad Nacional de San Antonio Abad, Cusco, 2018); Catherine Allen, *The Hold Life Has: Coca and Cultural Identity in an Andean Community* (Washington, DC: Smithsonian Institution, 2002); Joseph Bastien, *Mountain of the Condor: Metaphor and Ritual in an Andean Ayllu* (Long Grove, IL: Waveland, 1985). Historians: María Rostworowski, *Estructuras andinas del poder: Ideología religiosa y política* (Lima: Instituto de Estudios Peruanos, 2007); Irene Silverblatt, *Moon, Sun, and Witches: Gender Ideologies and Class in Inca and Colonial Peru* (Princeton, NJ: Princeton University Press, 1987); Vargas, *Tipón*.

8   Rostworowski, *Estructuras andinas*, 12; Choqque, "Geoformas," relation, 219; "sacred," 24.

9   Current Quechua: Jesús Lara, *Diccionario Qheshwa-Castellano, Castellano-Qheshwa* (La Paz: Amigos del Libro, 2001), 174; colonial Quechua: Diego González Holguín, *Vocabulario de la lengua general de todo el Perú llamada lengua quechua, o del Inca*, Federal University of Minas Gerais, Brazil, website, (1608) 2007, 182, accessed August 7, 2019, www.letras.ufmg.br/padrao_cms/documentos/profs/romulo/VocabvlarioQqichuaDeHolguin1607.pdf; colonial Aymara: Ludovico Bertonio, *Vocabulario de la lengua aymara*, digitized book from Oxford Library, (1612) 1984, accessed August 7, 2019, archive.org/details/vocabulariodela00bertgoog/page/n248, 141–42.

10   Earth shrines: Bastien, *Mountain of the Condor*; Earth beings: Allen, *The Hold Life Has*, 32; Marisol de la Cadena, *Earth Beings: Ecologies of Practice across Andean Worlds* (Durham, NC: Duke University Press, 2015); *wak'a*: Rostworowski, *Estructuras andinas*, 11–12.

11   Cristóbal de Albornoz, "Instrucción para descubrir todas las guacas del Pirú," *Journal de la Société des Américanistes* 56, no. 1 ([1580s] 1967): 20.

12   Rostworowski, *Estructuras andinas*, omitted, 172; gods, 13; birth, 13; van Kessel, "Tecnología aymara," 195.

13   Bastien, *Mountain of the Condor*, healers, 215; ecology, 43–48; metaphor, 189–91.

14   Ibid., ritual, 87–91; openings, 57.

15   Ibid., Pachaquta, 86; highlands, 47.

16   Allen, *The Hold Life Has*, sprang, 76; Earth beings, 32; places, 26; vitality, 33; *uywaqninchiskuna*, 26.

17   Choqque, "Simbolismo de las geoformas," emerged, 117; hill, 181; agency, 210.

18   Ibid., ritual, 135–36; *mink'akuy*, 184; everyone, 114; reciprocity, 135; identity, 212–13.

19   Ibid., *Ñuñuyuq*, photo, 120; skirt, 88; Pachamama, 178.

20   Quoted in Silverblatt, *Moon*, 24.

21   Allen, "To Be Quechua," first, 162–63; duty, 165.

22   Stone, "Andean Mother."

23   Cecilia Granadino and Cronwell Jara, *Las ranas embajadoras de la lluvia* (Lima: Minka, 1996).

24   Elayne Zorn, *Weaving a Future: Tourism, Cloth, and Culture on an Andean Island* (Iowa City: University of Iowa Press, 2004).

25   Stone, "Andean Mother," 93–108; Mamani, *Identidad*, women, 106; sources of life, 30.

26   Mamani, *Identidad*, 107; Mamani and Quispe, *Pacha*, energy, 32, 33; source, 28; everything, 27.

27   Vargas, *Tipón*, 200.

28   Choqque, "Simbolismo de las geoformas," 51–52;

29   Pedro de Cieza de León, *Crónica del Perú: El señorío de los Incas*, Biblioteca Ayacucho website, (1553) 2005, accessed September 23, 2015, www.bibliotecayacucho.gob.ve/fba/index.php?id=97&back-PID=96&swords=cieza%20de%20leon&tt_products=311, 250.

30   Choqque, "Simbolismo de las geoformas," 146; Doyle, "Ancestor Cult."

31   Bastien, *Mountain of the Condor*, 86.

32   Allen, *The Hold Life Has*, travel, 35; ancestors, 41; future, 43; Choqque, "Simbolismo de las geoformas," 209.

33   Francisco Cajías and Francisco Ormachea, *Ajayu*, directed by Francisco Cajías and Francisco Ormachea (La Paz: Taller Arawi, 1996).

34   For example, Mary Louise Stone, "Dance for Mother Lake on the Arid Titiqaqa Plateau: Observations from Fieldwork Seasons 1993–2005," *Archaeological Review from Cambridge* 34, no. 1 (April 2019): 122–42.

35   James A. Duke, David Aulik, and Timothy Plowman, "Nutritional Value of Coca," *Botanical Museum Leaflets*, 24, no. 6 (1975): 113, Peabody Museum.

36   Kallawayas, Bastien, *Mountain of the Condor*, 57; Ina Rösing, *Diálogos con divinidades de cerros, rayos, manantiales y lagos: Oraciones blancas Kallawayas* (La Paz: Hisbol, 1995); Pitumarka, Choqque, "Simbolismo de las geoformas," 136–37.

37   Ecuador and Bolivia, Fernando Huanacuni, *Vivir bien/buen vivir: Filosofía, políticas, estrategias y experiencias regionales* (La Paz: Instituto Internacional de Integración-Convenio Andrés Bello, 2010), 22–23; rights, Evo Morales, *The Earth Does Not Belong to Us, We Belong to the Earth* (La Paz: Ministry of Foreign Affairs of Bolivia, 2010), 51–52; Colombia, Eduardo Gudynas, "Colombia reconoce los derechos de la Naturaleza en su Amazonia," Systemic Alternatives website, April 6, 2018, accessed May 12, 2018, systemicalternatives.org/2018/04/09/colombia-reconoce-los-derechos-de-la-naturaleza-en-su-amazonia/; United Nations General Assembly, "General Assembly Proclaims 22 April 'International Mother Earth Day' Adopting by Consensus Bolivia-Led Resolution," United Nations website, April 22, 2009, accessed August 21, 2015, www.un.org/press/en/2009/ga10823.doc.htm.

UNSADDLING THE PAST:
THE CENTRAL ROLE OF THE LEAD FEMALE
IN ANIMAL HERDS—A MODEL FOR
PALEOLITHIC HUMAN CULTURE

SUSAN MOULTON

[O]ur relationship with land cannot heal until we hear its
stories. . . . [I]n Native ways of knowing, human people
are often referred to as "the younger brothers of Creation."
We say that humans have the least experience with how
to live and thus the most to learn—we must look to our
teachers among the other species for guidance. Their wisdom is apparent in the way that they live. They teach us
by example. They've been on the earth far longer than we
have been, and have had time to figure things out.[1]

Stunning realistic depictions of Paleolithic animals lay hidden deep
within the Chauvet cave sanctuary in the Dordogne Valley, Pont d'Arc,
Ardèche in the south of France, palimpsests of the mind overlaid on a cave
wall, accrued across time 30,000 to 40,000 years after humans emigrated
from Africa. In the absolute quiet of the chthonic deep cave enclosure early
Aurignacian *homo sapiens* depicted these animals in a shared landscape,
extolling their beauty and wisdom, surrendering to the spiritual wonders
of the world around them. These images tell the oldest human story. They
are connections to a primordial past that speak directly to the soul from a
collective memory that extends beyond time.

Decoding the earliest extant parietal art found in these caves has
eluded scholars and scientists since their discovery in 1994. Considering

these remarkable images from the perspective of an inclusive temporal and geographic context may be key to understanding them, particularly given the exclusive subject matter of animals and the prominent, unprecedented reference to the sacred human female found at this site. These are celebrative images reflective of a quiet, nuanced co-existence of species viewed only after an arduous passage into the dark, quiet chthonic recesses of the earth. The humans who decorated these walls regularly returned to this cave across millennia as a central site of reflection and introspection on the primal aspects of all life; a cave that also meant they simultaneously co-inhabited with cave bears and cave lions that occupied the same space year round.

Progress in understanding the roots of human culture often occurs when the prevailing paradigms are challenged by an expanded scope of inquiry and the discovery of new evidence, and by recognition of the validity of direct empirical experience. New insights are frequently brought about using disciplines not traditionally considered when examining the remote pre-historical past.[2] Information or angles of perception proposed by or which focus on women and indigenous people, particularly in relation to animals, often is dismissed due to prevailing patriarchal, Eurocentric bias. In this time of dominating technology, mass species extinction and rapid global climate change, it is difficult to imagine a world in which food and animals existed in abundance and interacted with humans in a shared context of mutual respect.

Yet, ancient artworks around the world demonstrate that our human ancestors shared rich understandings and relationships with many other species. The vast and detailed artworks found in Chauvet Cave provide us with especially deep insights into such an ancestral paradigm. The Panel of Horses includes about twenty distinct animals done in a highly realistic style. The richly decorated panoramic depictions of the End Chamber is the most lavishly illustrated area of the cave. The entire cave inventory totals about 345 animals and 45 collections of signs including lines, circles, dashes, broken lines and six pubic triangles. The left side of the wall contains nine lions, one reindeer, seventeen rhinoceroses and other animals drawn in charcoal or painted. The central niche contains only one horse drawn so that it seems to be emerging from the recess. The right side of the recess includes rhinos, mammoths, a pride of lions and bison, nearly all facing left. The depictions are not randomly placed, but interact with one another and utilize the shape of the walls, niches, fissures and irregularities for visual effect.

The images from Chauvet were generated by humans with a deeply rooted sense of community in wild Nature. The interconnected external networks between flora and fauna help create subtle bonds. Such an authentic and deeply sensate, primal experience is difficult to contemplate in our hectic world informed by science and technology, but can be glimpsed if one is fortunate to have a powerful multisensory experience of herds of wild herds of animals moving in unison.

Collaborative, female-led herds existed long before the Paleolithic. In 2013 tracks from a herd of thirteen prehistoric elephants of all ages (*stegotetrabelodon*) followed by a lone larger animal, were found in what is now the Abu Dhabi desert. They date from the Miocene, some six to eight million years ago.[3] Then, like now, a thundering herd reminds us of the power of Nature and of animals. Our sense of separation, of our "superiority" or "ego," is impacted by the enormity of the sensory input of animated wildness, triggering primal instincts, expanding our sense of appreciation, and often overwhelming our modern perception of being an isolated "self" living outside or above Nature. This multisensory knowledge is fundamental to the guiding visual narrative celebrated throughout the dark quiet of this Paleolithic cave (Fig. 7).

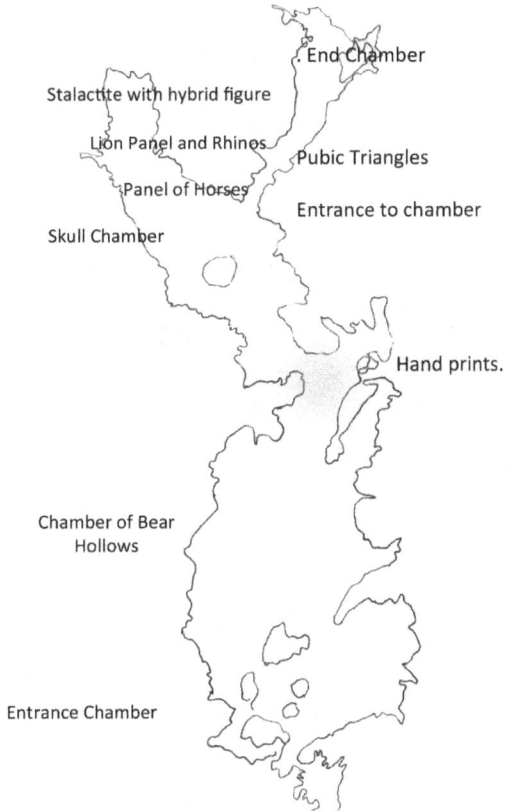

Fig. 7. Plan of Chauvet Cave. Courtesy of the author.

133

Only recently has science confirmed what were the ancient practices and wisdom of indigenous cultures living symbiotically with Nature. Paleolithic Aurignacians focused on survival, the sacred feminine and celebrating what they learned from their living surroundings, particularly their animal neighbors. Predating "writing," these awe-inspiring images at Chauvet were executed between 38,000 and 17,000 BCE. They decorate a site that required effort to access and was the year-round habitat of cave bears[4] and cave panthers. These striking images—organized, juxtaposed, and composed with an awareness of space and psychology (Fig. 8)—commemorate the first intimate human–animal recognition and interaction. The creatures depicted on the walls thrived in a fertile post-glacial landscape. The representation of both predatory and prey animals as well as frequent depictions of animal groups confirm that these images represented more than just "good fortune in hunting by dominant male *homo sapiens*."[5] Their style, location and configuration indicate they are instructive objects of reverence. There is no visual or archaeological evidence that the animals depicted were primary sources of hunting and food, even though some may have been food sources. Instead, for this imagery their beauty and prescient psychology resonate at a primal level influencing the way we see, inspiring inclusive balance and harmony in an expansive spiritual world.

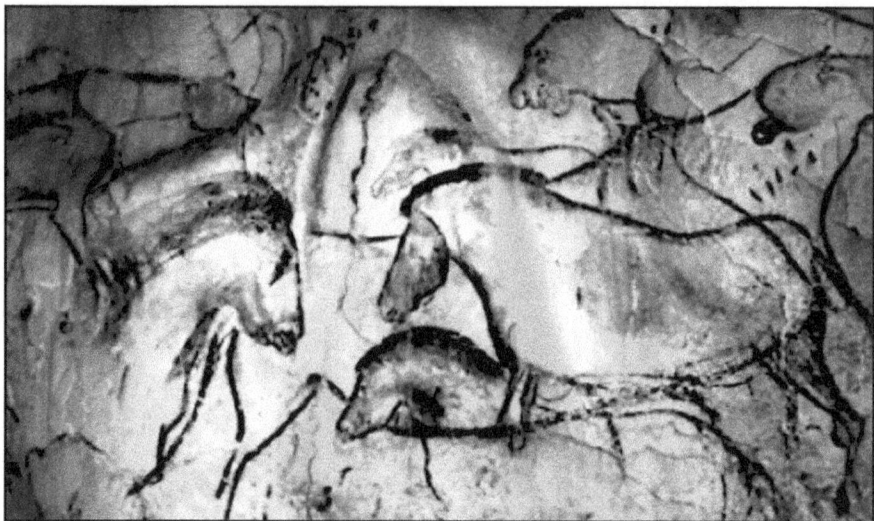

Fig. 8. "Communicating" horses with cave lion, Chauvet Cave.
Photography by Stephen Alvarez, 2015.

When frequent human reference does appear in the subsequent Neolithic era, it is usually of an older, and/or gravid female with a focus on "her" body that symbolically and metaphorically functioned as a symbol for life-death-and-regeneration in Nature.[6] This research contends that the Neolithic focus was inspired by the collaborative gynocentric/matrifocal role of Paleolithic herd animals as models of collaboration essential for collective survival. The lead female equine, for example, responsible for finding safe places for food, water, and giving birth, dominates the cave imagery. When a foal is born the other mares and siblings of both genders in a family gather around for protection and assistance as the new life begins its interaction with the external world. Even birthing is collaborative in herds. This primary leadership role of older females is similar for most herd species including deer, elephants (wooly mammoths), goats, sheep, bison and others commemorated on the Chauvet walls.

Survival, Communication and Adaptability

Though these surprisingly realistic images seem "contemporary," chronologically they are as distant from Lascaux—some 17,000 years—as Lascaux is from us today. Paleolithic artists developed a style and subject matter that has endured for tens of thousands of years, capable of communicating a vibrant message, capturing the essence, gestures and psychology of animals—a style that functions as a universal language located in an enduring, permanent place of reflection and reverence. While symbols, marks and signs require prior cultural knowledge and context, highly realistic imagery remains accessible to diverse audiences regardless of time or species as a visual language. The universally accessible, realistic pictorial style of Chauvet is not unlike the shared mental image communication used by animals and by humans.[7] Called a "language of animacy," it includes realistic images in a sacred place that visually commemorate aspects of a dynamic living world to be shared with future generations across millennia to accommodate change.

Adaptation was key to collective survival, and horses were one of the most adaptable mammals from the Pleistocene Period forward transitioning from browsers to grazers, as regions transitioned from forests to grasslands in North America, Asia and Europe. Their speed, strength and endurance have carried them into the modern era across changing landscapes, through

Ice Ages and droughts, across hard soils of grassy plains from one continent to another. Their eyes, teeth and guts changed to accommodate climate change during the Miocene epoch when harsh grasses replaced forests.[8] Their social natures, reliance on other members of a herd, innate curiosity about their surroundings and their ability to communicate with each other subtly and overtly supported their remarkable ability to evolve.

Early human culture survived and evolved in part by assimilating some of the complex social structures of the animals they knew, particularly the subtle but directive role of a herd's older "lead" female. Herd behavior, governed by a lead mare through animal cognition, gesture and vocalizations that feral horses still use today must have been understood by Paleolithic humans.

Integrated Systems Thinking: "We Are All One"
(In Lakota and Yankton Sioux, Mitàkuye Oyás'in translation: "We are all related")

Animal behaviorists, veterinarians, ecologists and others who work closely with animals and Nature understand the complex interrelationship and psychology of species influenced by the conditions of a specific a place and time as well as the overriding sense of being as oneness and harmony found in all forms of life, as an overarching spiritual balance. Contextual referencing, what scientists now term integrated "systems thinking," must have been characteristic of these early humans. However, this has been lost as indigenous peoples in the last millennium have been marginalized or exterminated. Early integrated gynocentric understanding was suppressed and overlaid by a belief in the superiority of European men with a hierarchy of values that subordinated women, non-Eurocentric people and animals, implying that our human ancestors from the remote past were also isolated from Nature and functioned within a narrow patriarchal frame of egocentric reference (e.g., "cave men"). Most "modern" anthropocentric frameworks consider animals and often women as objects, beasts and/or a dangerous "other" whose principal role was to enhance male status, or for male utility, slaughter, profit or recreation,[9] precluding awareness of the symbiotic integrative relationship of all life including humans within their biosystems. Since archaeologists and anthropologists derive their perceptions from Cartesian and Darwinian theory, they consider male-dominated humanity superior to or disaggregated from

Nature, and view animals as "beasts" to be feared, sentimentalized and/ or anthropomorphized.[10]

Theory, however, does not have the power or the multisensory thrill of actually being and living among hundreds or thousands of animals moving together through a wilderness landscape, communicating with each other, responding to the environment, to climactic or seasonal changes or interacting socially within their herds. The visceral reaction Paleolithic humans must have experienced watching their animal cohabitants run freely can only vaguely be gleaned in photographs and videos. Fortunately, many indigenous peoples today recall instructive and compelling stories in which they are an integral part of a larger coeval whole. Only now in the face of species extinction, global climate change and ecological collapse have we begun to explore and align indigenous understanding of an integrated biosphere with archaeological evidence from Nature-based cultures from the remote past.

For most tribal peoples, all of Nature, particularly animals and even plants, share divine or supernatural qualities: "They are a part of the natural order of the universe no less than man himself, whom they resemble in the possession of intelligence and emotions."[11] People living in balance with Nature experience life contextually and relationally. This requires a mindset that works through generational stories, experienced, inherited wisdom and association rather than abstract theory. Over millennia Nature-based cultures developed sophisticated encyclopedic, nuanced knowledge of life and its cycles conveyed through oral traditions, marks, signs, symbols, three-dimensional renderings and visual depictions. Traditional lore indicates communion with the powers of Nature through respect for all living beings as equally valued parts of a vibrant, dynamic whole with complex interrelationships.

Despite prevailing archaeological resistance to finding parallels with Indigenes today, Chauvet archaeologist Jean Clottes now believes: "It is a safer bet to wager that Paleolithic hunter-gatherers' ways of thinking were closer to those of early Native Americans or Australian Aborigines rather than to ours today ... An understanding of Native American ... cultures provides a kind of prism by which the ancient past can be examined and explored, beyond the heavy intellectual weight imposed by our Western worldview."[12]

The Language of Animacy

Animal images from the remote past have traditionally been viewed through the lens of modern Eurocentric imagination as the equivalent of an anthropic "zoo" or pictorial museum. The ancient relational and transcendent functions of sacred sites like Chauvet have been lost to us, their art characterized most often as the work of dominant men with special powers as "shamans," their images as "totems" with protective abilities, or depictions of prey to be magically caught with the help of visual images. Yet there is no evidence to confirm this dominant masculine view in any of the extant images at Chauvet.

Cognitive ethologists, veterinarians, natural horsemanship practitioners and scholars like primatologist Diane Fossey who spend intimate, extended time with animals in their natural contexts understand this "language." Witnesses attest to the fluid, non-verbal, nuanced energy and mental picture-based communication they experience through close observation of subtle gestures, heightened sensory perception and non-verbal indicators by animals. Effectively adapting human behavior to this new visual grammar has yielded remarkable results. Potawatomi scholar Robin Kimmerer calls this a language of "animacy,"[13] or visual communication of intentionality shared by herd animals and by humans when the human ego ceases to obscure perception.

In the wild, animals and indigenous people know drawing attention to oneself increases the chance that you will become a target or "dinner" for predators.[14] Disregard of the collective "herd mind" by independent action can be dangerous to the welfare of a herd and to individual members. In many indigenous cultures, collective survival requires egoism be actively discouraged while punishment for disrespect can be harsh, including expulsion from the tribe, which often means death.

In the absence of a dominant self-focus, herd animals have immediate access to a "social brain," or shared thoughts in the form of images, energetic fields and intention, essential when responding to threats. Like an orchestra conductor, selected, directive animals—lead mares and stallions—play their part in the collective dynamic using specialized skills and shared mind required for the protection, direction and regeneration of their herd, allowing them to move synchronously *en mass* when needed. The dominant stallion functions as a wary sentinel for the herd, but defers to the lead mare. In "un-culled" herds, satellite bachelor stallions, provide an extra layer of protection. These are often siblings who can remain for a lifetime with their family. The lead female functions as a directive "computer mother board" or repository of generational wisdom. She knows where water sources are to be found, where it is safe to give birth, where traditional pastures are. Always alert, she and the lead stallion often quietly stand apart from the herd. In this protective context the lead mare or stallion may well be the lone equine figure depicted in a niche below the "cavalcade" of animals (Fig. 9).

Fig. 9. Horse in niche, Chavet Cave. Photograph by Stephen Alvarez, 2015.

The charismatic and dramatic behavior of stallions who can be explosive and compelling as they challenge one another for mating privileges (a role not depicted at Chauvet) eclipses the less theatrical demeanor of lead mares. The composed presence of the horses depicted in the cave reflects the communicative role of the lead female instructing and controlling the daily movements of the herd. This lead female behavior observed in diverse herd species contradicts conventional understanding with its focus on a dominant stallion. However, survival and regeneration for herd animals is dependent on the wisdom of the older, lead female. This lead mare behavior provided observant Paleolithic humans with examples of an egalitarian, matrifocal, fluid and adaptable social organization.[15]

Beyond the directive role of the lead mare, each of the herd animals also has a vital part to play. Collective movement is usually highly structured and fluid; lead mare directives are supported and enforced by dominant females and stallions with subordinate bachelors located at the sides and to the rear of the herds. Consideration of feral herd behavior has been overlooked since most archaeologists experience domestic horses that are usually removed or introduced to new stables or groups with little regard for any established equine social relationships or continuity. Rarely today are stallions kept with mares or other stallions. In the wild a feral herd is dynamic. Each horse knows its function within the herd. Offspring learn their behavior from their mothers and siblings can stay with their family for a lifetime. Subordinate "bachelors" offer vital protection against predators like lions or challenges from outside males, particularly when vulnerable newborn foals are present. Eventually one or more of the bachelor stallions may have a herd of his own as dominant stallions age and move back to the periphery of the herd. This is an inclusive, protective arrangement that requires the active participation of every animal. A collective group of sub-herds called a "band," generally numbers three to five mares, some with foals, each usually with a stallion and often one satellite bachelor stallion. This is a well-organized, integrated, social group that functions to guarantee collective stability and survival. During seasonal periods sub-herds collect to graze together with some exchange of mares and stallions but always, a dominant lead mare and stallion.

This fluid organization must have been observed by nearby humans who understood and appreciated its value as a matrifocal participatory model, imitating it in their own social structures. The female lead was a vital repository of generational knowledge essential for the collective survival of the group in a changing environment impacted by seasonal, as well as more widely spread climate change.[16] This collaborative arrangement of wild herds has endured into the present day although there are few extant un-culled herds. The Chauvet image of "Conversing Horses," illustrates a dominant horse, probably a lead female, focusing her attention on younger mares grouped around her. Many of the groups of animals of diverse species are delineated in an attentive, watchful posture, much as they would be in Nature.

The more obvious gestures and movements of horses, particularly their ears, are well known. Flattened ears indicate misbehavior, danger or threat. Forward ears, seen in Fig. 9 indicate listening and awareness of the surroundings; one ear forward and one back indicate relaxed omnidirectional awareness of the thousands of peripheral noises and activities at the edge of their vision.

When the lead mare is no longer able to function, another—often her daughter—is ready to "step into" the role. Mark Rashid tells the story of an infant foal, daughter of a lead mare in the Arizona desert whose herd was led over 100 miles across a great distance to a very remote water source during a time of extreme drought. The yearling became the lead mare upon the death of her mother and fifteen years later, during another extreme drought, the young mare led her herd to the same source of water. [17] Hunters and politicians today who do not understand the value of the older lead females sanction killing them, often destroying the entire herd. They also remove or kill the protective satellite stallions, considering old mares and extra males unnecessary. We know from herd behavior of feral horses, mule deer in Montana[18] or elephant herds that the female-led, collaborative herd arrangement is ancient, developed, vital to survival of the herd and passed on to succeeding generations.

Stallions, male rhinos and other herd males seasonally fight for mating dominance, but rarely, if ever, is it a fight to the death. Young animals engage in preparatory play activities to develop needed muscles and to sharpen their defensive skills, hence "play" is an essential part of life.[19] This is one interpretation of the two rhinoceroses at Chauvet (Fig. 10). The weaker adult male rhino or horse usually ceded to the more powerful, after what was often an elaborate display of strength and dominance. Less known is that males of diverse species routinely claimed their territory and pathways before "fighting" with liberal piles of dung and urine spray.[20] Even before physical interaction, male horses and rhinos identified the stronger animal by smelling manure or urine traces, so that any actual "fighting" was usually "pro forma." Dung and urine contained important information, about estrogen and testosterone levels, mating readiness, and overall health critical to establishing mating protocols and defining male dominance in a herd. Indigenous people understood the significance of dung and avoided stepping over manure in their pathway out of respect for the animals. They often studied it to determine the identity, sex and foraging information of their animal neighbors.

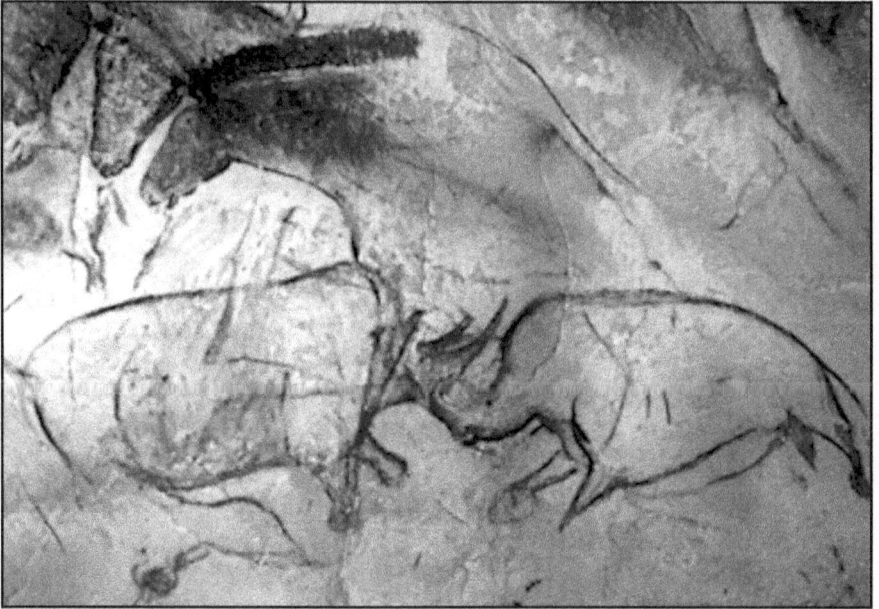

Fig. 10. Rhinoceroses at play and/or fighting, Chauvet Cave. Photograph by Stephen Alvarez, 2015.

Procreation rights were not just the result of male physical dominance. Feral equine mares and female rhinos will often fight off a male suitor for days before allowing him to mate, if they allow it at all.[21] In Chauvet details of the gender of the rhinos or horses is not indicated. This particular female role in mating behavior and the fact that young animals play in this posture as well, indicates the images, like so many others in the cave, are polysemic, rather than limited just to one interpretation, like rival males vying for mating privileges.[22] Multiple interpretations for all the images were important, particularly if they were keys to inherited stories or myths that guided social behavior and built a sense of community for humans with animals.

Each of the many different animals depicted on the walls was honored for its special contribution to the bioregion. The recurring drawings of rhinos, known for their ability to find the closest water sources, indicates that they may have been included for this uncanny ability, functioning as "bulldozers" through dense underbrush opening up more direct access for other animals and humans.

Gynocentric Mytho-Poetic Fusions

Closely observing the flora and fauna of local ecosystems with particular focus on animals, early Aurignacians learned to live in community, share food and shelter and guide future generations in collaborative behavior, or what we term "culture." This included stories, rituals and aesthetic expressions in response to a bioregion to create an enduring common identity and sacred exchange, visually encoded on the walls of caves or on objects, as they were embodied as rituals or in dance. Supporting the role of painted images, certain music and "folk" dances have ancient roots celebrating animal behavior and movement, such as the "crane dance" in central Europe, which is a fusion of animal and human behavior, analogous as a movement-based language.[23] Rituals like this were undoubtedly associated with the earliest depictions in the caves.

The preponderance of archaeological evidence from later Paleolithic and Neolithic sites indicates that artistic human forms most often display female characteristics with a focus on the reproductive parts of the body. These are metaphors for life-death-regeneration, most notable in the later Neolithic, in "goddess" figures. The close human–animal relationship also continues into the Neolithic in human female forms frequently combined with animal masks or conflated with bodies of animals.[24] While common in the Neolithic, Jean Clottes notes the depiction of humans is extremely rare in Paleolithic art.[25] At Chauvet it consists of negative red hands in the entrance chambers and five detailed human-female pubic triangles with engraved vulvas. The human hand "markers" are located at the entrance and various places inside the cave. Most assume these indicate the presence of the artist. It could be argued also that they are similar to the cave bear claw markings used to mark territory (Fig. 11).[26] A logarithmic study of the finger

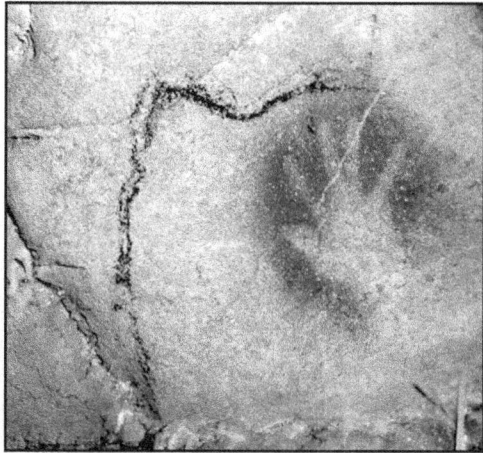

Fig. 11. Red hand, Chauvet Cave.
Photograph by Stephen Alvarez, 2015.

143

measurements of the 32 handprints in the cave done in 2013 found that 75 percent of them were female suggesting a significant role for women as creators of this Paleolithic cave imagery.[27]

The early merging of animal and human forms at Chauvet is unprecedented. A centralized depiction of a human female lower torso with genitalia in chalk and red paint on a hanging stalactite, outside and opposite the Lion Panel "with two black felines and a horse on one side, and, on the other side, a black creature, upright and leaning slightly forward: the top of its body is that of a bison, and the bottom that of a human, with the two legs well indicated. . . . It is this figure that one sees when one arrives in the chamber."[28] (See Fig. 12.) This hybrid image is strategically placed at the end of the cave system deep in the gallery farthest and lowest from the entrance on an isolated hanging pendant. Visually "directing" the "cavalcade" of animals (frequently referred to as "chaos"),[29] the depiction of human vulva and the lower part of her body merges with animal imagery, facing the animals on the opposite wall.[30] The profile figure of a bison on one side is juxtaposed with a lion on the other side. Despite efforts to identify a male bison called the "Sorcerer," no distinct gender references appear for the bison or lion.[31] Male and female bison and lions at this time had similar features: bison had thick, dark coats, broad chests and horns, while the male and female cave lions both lacked the shaggy mane we associate with male African lions today.

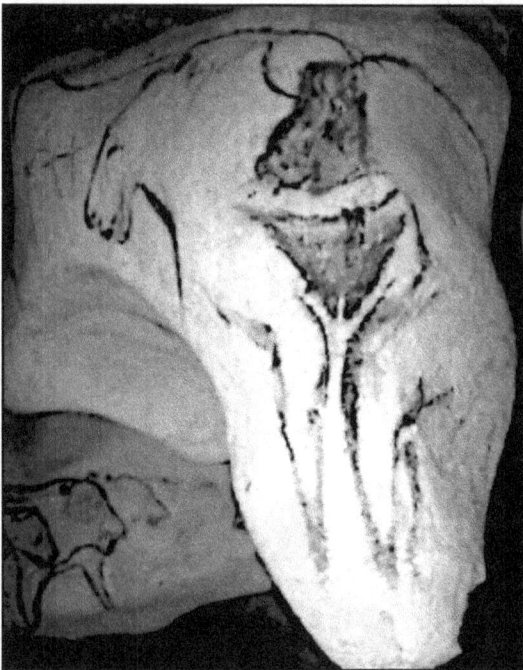

Fig. 12. Hybrid female/bison/cave lion figure on stalactite, Chauvet Cave. Photograph by Stephen Alvarez, 2015.

The conflation of the human female genitalia with the bison is visually commanding. The "bison's" eye looks outward, creating a direct and inclusive implied "bridge" to the observer. Its location and actions are similar to those of a "lead female" whose presence functions both as a sentinel and director. While physically isolated, it is visually connected to the "cavalcade" of animals on the opposite wall when viewed from the deeper cave interior. The bison head is positioned above the genitalia with its front legs becoming part of the lower torso while the figure of a lion emerges from the other side. This is the earliest known hybrid image of animals merged with human features. Millennia later in the Neolithic the conflating of humans and female reproductive elements with animals is a frequent metaphor for life-death-regeneration and spiritual transformation.[32] Strategically located, this Chauvet image and other incised and drawn "V"s or symbolic vulvas in the cave affirm the primal function of the sacred female in Nature and the isolated central position of the stalactite imagery indicates that it is at the very heart of the overall meaning of the cave.

Intimate Human–Animal Relationships and Cohabitation Behavior

Paleolithic ecologies in diverse regions of what is now southern France and northern Spain saw *Homo sapiens* evolve as distinct species in different habitats, like the *Neanderthals* in Southern Europe, Africa and Asia.[33] Grave evidence, however, indicates both *Homo sapiens* and *Neanderthals* were buried with animal bones more than 100,000 to 60,000 years ago, documentation of a special relationship and respect for animals integral to spiritual beliefs long before these cave decorations.[34]

Consideration of coeval human–animal relationship is comparatively recent. As noted earlier, it is not uncommon to find animal species denigrated as wild "beasts," primarily a source of food or material prestige for male human "exceptionalism."[35] Cognitive ethologists study consciousness and adaptation, including moral and ethical questions relating to animals,[36] in contrast to traditional studies that view animals as "resources" for human development and domination. With dramatic species extinction and the loss of natural habitats, few animals today are able to function as "wild" creatures, making it difficult for us to witness their natural interactions and understand how they might have served as models for human cultural development in the remote past as they do here.

Chauvet can be viewed as an inclusive "social landscape" in which all living beings were considered "relations," similar to Nature-based indigenous practices.[37] By 40,000–35,000 BCE, *Homo sapiens* predominated in Europe[38] so they most likely decorated the walls and ceilings of caves and useful objects with revered animal images. The aesthetic sensitivity, perceptive ability and advanced artistic skill found in animal images on rough, irregular cave walls, particularly the numerous images of horses, has challenged our traditional "cave man" view of Paleolithic humans. Rarely mentioned are practical issues involved with animals, like the year-round habitation of the caves by *Ursus spelaeus*, the cave bear, and the cave lion, *Panther leo spelaea*. The distilled essences of these co-inhabiting animals are masterfully captured in simple, expressive line drawings and profile images in a style that reflects significant skill and a profound understanding of the creatures depicted by people who managed to actively share their space.

Equally unprecedented is the representation of complex, nuanced consciousness by animals, particularly horses.[39] Dr Robert Miller, DVM, has found in a lifetime of working with horses and zoo animals that whatever a young animal experiences within the first few hours of birth will be familiar to it and the animal will imprint on it and have no fear of it.[40] Modern experience proves that a young foal whose mother might have died giving birth may well have imprinted on a Paleolithic rescuer to form a close human–animal relationship. This intimacy is not a function of dominance, utility or domestication, but compassion, respect and shared consciousness. Moreover, there is much contemporary and historical evidence of humans riding horses without bits, reins, saddles or controlling devices, indicating that humans deeply respected and must have been companions to animals or possibly even ridden horses or other animals thousands of years before "bit wear" and formal domestication occurred.[41]

While human–animal communication remains a topic of controversy today, early humans living amid dense herds of wild animals likely communicated with them, and certainly relied on their acute sight, hearing and sense of smell for survival. The thrall of this reality must have been true for Paleolithic humans who daily experienced the coordinated, intertwined energy of wild herds quietly grazing, interacting and responding to the thousands of warning calls and actions of other animals or birds of their bioregion and thereby developing an encyclopedic knowledge of its flora and fauna.[42]

Equus caballus

Most numerous in the cave depictions are horses. A very early model of adaptability, *Equus caballus* evolved over fifty million years from the early Eocene as a dog-size animal of about fifty pounds with four hoofed toes on its front legs and three on the rear, and related to the other odd-toed ungulate mammals, the rhinos and tapirs.[43] Remains of this early "dawn horse," *eohippus*, have been found on almost every continent, their global distribution occurring during the Cenozoic era when travel across continents was facilitated by the connected land masses of North America, Greenland and the British Isles. *Eohippus* transitioned from browsers to grazers with the changing flora and fauna of the European continent and thrived over thirty million years in North America. They evolved into the larger, stronger, smarter animals of the Paleolithic era, developing in size, strength and agility up to the present.[44] Horses accommodated Miocene changes from forests to grasslands. Abundant grazing fodder led to diverse species of horses in North America and Europe with more complex digestive systems, stronger teeth and longer jaws that allowed them to grind the prairie grasses more efficiently, and thus grow in size and weight like the *tarpan* from the Russian steppes, which are similar to those at Chauvet. However, recent science has proven they are genetically unique and the Paleolithic *equus caballus* is extinct.[45]

Horses migrated westward into Eurasia across the Bering Strait before global warming at the end of the last Ice Age. Extinct in North America for an unknown reason about 10,000 years ago,[46] the horse, notably, found its way to the lush prairies of the Russian steppes where most scholars believe they were eventually "domesticated" around 4000 to 3500 BCE, based on evidence of "bit wear."[47] This, however, is belied by evidence of human–animal interaction in which bits and restraints are not necessary.[48] Questions regarding the first horse–human contact and intentional interaction remain open, but some of the oldest visual images from Chauvet help us reconstruct and confirm a horse–human interrelationship that predated by millennia human "control and dominance."

The creatures most traditional scholars considered "beasts," work-horses, household companions, or sources of food are deeply sentient creatures who feel sorrow and bliss, experience anxiety, build relationships, develop languages among themselves that can be translated into human understanding, and are capable of complex, often reasoned thought and many are able to develop and use tools.[49] Natural horsemanship practitioners and Native Americans have shown that intimate bonding, special affection and multi-modal communication and intentionality[50] can develop between animals and humans and that meaningful interaction occurs through patience and compassion. Aimeé Brimhall McCord explains that horses communicate by projecting pictures and intention that humans can experience and use themselves when ongoing mutual respect and ethical treatment characterize their horse–human relationship.[51] The earliest communication between horses or other animals and humans may have followed this pattern of visual and intentional projection, thus accounting for the highly developed "realism" of the imagery at Chauvet, using a universal "language of animacy" independent of time or species.

Conclusion

Most of us no longer know what it is to live intimately within Nature or to closely observe its integrated web of life. Paleolithic humans with a deep understanding and awareness of Nature experienced mutual respect and interaction with the animals around them without domination. The foundational matrifocal "integrated systems," view may best describe Paleolithic and later Neolithic life, but it has been obscured by a singular focus on human exceptionalism and male privilege. From approximately 40,000 BCE to 20,000 BCE when the Chauvet cave was accessible to humans, Aurignacians lived embedded in Nature, adapting to change, protecting, respecting and nurturing those things upon which they depended for survival, using aural and visual languages consisting of verbs "to describe vital beingness," rather than objectified nouns to indicate subordination.[52] The paintings in Chauvet may well be mnemonic, expressing these basic values directed by a wise metaphoric female, anticipating the matrifocal Neolithic. This Paleolithic imagery and its messages take on new urgency as we reflect on our modern restrictive ethnocentric view that has contributed to the slow global destruction of our "web of life," leading to human-caused global climate change if not inevitable collapse as we face the Sixth Mass Extinction.[53] By recognizing animal and human connection in this universal "language of animacy" at the core of ecological sustainability for millennia, we can begin to "unsaddle" our understanding of the remote past to recognize the images at Chauvet as vital vessels of meaning that celebrate a sacred coequal relationship of living earth and its creatures essential for our survival today.

References

Anthony, David W. *The Horse, the Wheel, and Language: How Bronze-Age Riders from the Eurasian Steppes Shaped the Modern World*. Princeton, NJ: Princeton University Press, 2010.

Anthony, David W., Dorcas R. Brown, and Christian George. "Early Horseback Riding and Warfare: The Importance of the Magpie around the Neck." In *Horses and Humans: The Evolution of the Equine–Human Relationship*, British Archaeological Reports International Series 1560, ed. Sandra L. Olsen, Susan Grant, Alice Choyke, and Laszlo Bartosiewicz, 137–56. Oxford: Archaeopress, 2006.

Anthony, David, Dimitri Y. Telegin, and Dorcas Brown. "The Origin of Horseback Riding," *Scientific American* (December 1991), 94–100.

Bahn, Paul, Michel Lorblanchet, and Pierre Soulages. *The First Artists: In Search of the World's Oldest Art*. London: Thames and Hudson, 2017.

Barón Birchenall, Leonardo. "Animal Communication and Human Language: An Overview." *International Journal of Comparative Psychology* 29 (2016). escholarship.org/uc/item/3b7977qr.

Berger, Joel. *Wild Horses of the Great Basin: Social Competition and Population Size*. Chicago: University of Chicago Press, 1986.

Bibi, Faisal, Brian Kraatz, Nathan Craig, Mark Beech, M. Schuster, and A. Hill. "Early Evidence for Complex Social Structure in Proboscidea from a Late Miocene Trackway Site in the United Arab Emirates." *Biology Letters* 8, no. 4 (2012): 670–73. doi: 10.1098/rsbl.2011.1185.

Capra, Fritjof, and Pier Luigi Luisi. *The Systems View of Life: A Unifying Vision*. Cambridge: Cambridge University Press, 2014, 78–83.

Chauvet, Jean-Marie, Eliette Brunel Deschamps, and Christian Hillaire. *Dawn of Art: The Chauvet Cave*. London: Henry Abrams and Thames of Hudson, 1996.

Clottes, Jean. Epilogue to *Dawn of Art: The Chauvet Cave*, by Jean-Marie Chauvet, Eliette Brunel Deschamps, and Christian Hillaire. London: Henry Abrams and Thames of Hudson, 1996.

————. "The Salle du Fond Chamber: Venus and The Sorcerer." *International Newsletter on Rock Art* (2001): 29. bradshawfoundation.com/chauvet/venus_sorcerer.php.

————. *Chauvet Cave: The Art of Earliest Times*. Salt Lake City: University of Utah Press, 2003.

————. Foreword to *Cave Paintings and the Spirit: The Origin of Creativity and Belief*, by David Whitley. Amherst, NY: Prometheus Books, 2009.

De Steiguer, Edward. *Wild Horses of the West: History and Politics of America's Mustangs*. Tuscon: University of Arizona Press, 2011.

Fagan, Brian. *The Intimate Bond: How Animals Shaped Human History*. New York: Bloomsbury Press, 2015).

Franzen, J. *The Rise of Horses: 55 Million Years of Evolution*. Baltimore: The Johns Hopkins University Press, 2010.

Gimbutas, Marija. *The Goddesses and Gods of Old Europe: Myths and Cult Images*, rev. ed. Berkeley, Los Angeles, and New York: University of California Press, 1982.

————. *Civilization of the Goddess: The World of Old Europe*. San Francisco: HarperCollins, 1991.

Held, Suzanne, and Marek Spinka. "Animal Play and Animal Welfare." *Animal Behaviour* 81 (2011): 891–99.

Higgs, William, Anthony Kirkham, Graham Evans, and Don Hull. "A Late Miocene Proboscidean Trackway from Western Abu Dhabi," *Tribulus* 13, no. 2 (2003): 3–8.

Hutto, Joe. *Touching the Wild: Living with the Mule Deer of Deadman Gulch*. New York: Skyhorse Press, 2014.

Ilieva, Anna, and Anna Shturbanova. "Zoomorphic Images in Bulgarian Women's Ritual Dances in the Context of Old European Symbolism." In *From the Realm of the Ancestors: An Anthology in Honor of Marija Gimbutas*, ed. Joan Marler, 309–12. Manchester, CT: Knowledge, Ideas and Trends, Inc., 1997.

Ingold, Tim. "The Animal in the Study of Humanity." In *What Is an Animal?*, ed. Ingold, 84–99. London: Routledge Press, 1988.

————. *The Perception of the Environment: Essays in Livelihood, Dwelling, and Skill*. London: Routledge Press, 2000.

Jenness, D. "The Ojibwa Indians of Parry Island: Their Social and Religious Life." *Bulletins of the Canada Department of Mines, National Museum of Canada* (Ottawa), no. 78 (1930).

Kimmerer, Robin Wall. *Braiding Sweetgrass*. Canada: Milkweed Editions, 2013.

Kluger, Jeffrey. "The Animal Mind: How They Think, How They Feel, How to Understand Them." *Time Magazine*, special summer edition, June 9, 2017, 96 pp.

Kolbert, Elizabeth. *The Sixth Extinction: An Unnatural History*. New York: Henry Holt and Company, 2014.

Kuhn, Thomas. *The Structure of Scientific Revolutions*. Chicago: University of Chicago Press, 1962.

Levine, Marsha. "Domestication of the Horse." In *The Oxford Companion to Archaeology*, edited by Neil Asher Silberman, 15–19. Oxford: Oxford University Press, 2012.

Maroukis, Thomas Constantine. *Peyote and the Yankton Sioux: The Life and Times of Sam Necklace*. Norman: University of Oklahoma Press, 2005.

McCarthy, Susan. *Becoming a Tiger: How Baby Animals Learn to Live in the Wild*. New York: HarperCollins, 2004.

Miller, Robert M. *Imprint Training of the Newborn Foal: A Swift Effective Method for Permanently Shaping a Horse's Lifetime Behavior*. Fort Worth, TX: Western Horseman, [1991] 2008.

Moffett, Mark. *The Human Swarm: How Our Societies Arise, Thrive and Fall*. Lebanon, IN: Hachette Book Group, 2019.

O'Connell, Caitlin. *The Elephant's Secret Sense: The Hidden Life of the Wild Herds of Africa*. New York: Free Press, 2007.

Owen, Richard. "Description of the Fossil Remains of a Mammal *(Hyracotherium leporinum)* and of a Bird *(Lithornis vulturinis)* from the London Clay." *Transactions of the Geological Society of London*, ser. 2, VI (1841): 203–208.

Owen-Smith, Norman. In *The Encyclopedia of Mammals*, 1st ed. hardback, ed. D. MacDonald. New York: Facts on File, 1984.

Papagianni, Dimitra, and Michael Morse. *The Neanderthals Rediscovered: How Modern Science Is Rewriting their Story*. London: Thames & Hudson, Inc., 2015, 20–21.

Pastoureau, Michel. *The Bear: History of a Fallen King*. Cambridge, MA: Belknap Press, 2011.

Penny, Malcolm. *Rhinos: Endangered Species*. New York and Oxford: Facts On File, Inc., 1988.

Price, Steve. *America's Wild Horses: The History of the Western Mustang*. New York: Skyhorse Publishing, 2017.

Safina, Carl. *Beyond Words: What Animals Think and Feel*. New York: Henry Holt and Company, 2015.

Scientific American. "Secret Lives of Animals: Strange True Tales from the Wild Kingdom," *Scientific American*, special collector's edition, 26, no. 2s, May 2017.

Straus, Lawrence Guy. *Iberia Before the Iberians: The Stone Age Prehistory of Cantabrian Spain*. Albuquerque: University of New Mexico Press, [1992] 2011.

Westfall, Stacy. "Bareback riding WITHOUT Reins." February 29, 2008. www.youtube.com/watch?v=-Pg1EbXbZO4.

Wohlleben, Peter. *The Inner Life of Animals: Love, Grief, and Compassion— Surprising Observations of a Hidden World*. Munich: Ludwig Verlag/Random House, 2017.

Wolfe, Cary, ed. *Zoontologies: The Question of the Animal*. Minneapolis and London: University of Minnesota Press, 2003.

Endnotes

1   Robin Wall Kimmerer, *Braiding Sweetgrass* (Canada: Milkweed Editions, 2013), x, 7–9.

2   See Thomas Kuhn, *The Structure of Scientific Revolutions* (Chicago: University of Chicago Press, 1962).

3   Faisal Bibi, Brian Kraatz, Nathan Craig, Mark Beech, Mathieu Schuster, and Andrew Hill, "Early Evidence for Complex Social Structure in Proboscidea from a Late Miocene Trackway Site in the United Arab Emirates," *Biology Letters* 8, no. 4 (2012), doi: 10.1098/rsbl.2011.1185. Kraatz noted, "We know that the two elephant species today show female-led family groups, and this study shows that such behavior extends beyond their last common ancestor, if indeed, the track maker was *Stegotetrabelodon*." See also William Higgs, Andrew Kirkham, Graham Evans, and Don Hull, "A Late Miocene Proboscidean Trackway from Western Abu Dhabi," *Tribulus* 13, no. 2 (2003): 3–8.

4   Michel Pastoureau, in *The Bear: History of a Fallen King* (Cambridge, MA: Belknap Press, 2011), 12–21, discusses the cave bear, *Ursus spelaeus*, which was abundant during the Upper Paleolithic. The cave bear was larger than the brown bear (11.5 feet for a standing male) and it had a vegetarian diet. It hibernated every winter and disappeared between 15,000 and 12,000 BCE. The Chauvet cave had the most depictions of *Ursus spelaeus* (at least twelve). The numerous bear skulls that appear to be ritually arranged suggests the existence of a bear cult or that the bear was one of the earliest deities. The bear is the only

mammal capable of standing upright and the female bear nurses her young much like a human. At Chauvet the horse is most frequently depicted followed by the mammoth indicating special reverence.

5   Prevailing assumptions corrected by scientific evidence include the discovery that Paleolithic women were stronger than many male athletes today, because they engaged in heavy lifting, running, and other load-bearing work identifying them as central to human culture and survival at the time.

6   See Marija Gimbutas, *The Goddesses and Gods of Old Europe: Myths and Cult Images*, rev. ed. (Berkeley, Los Angeles, and New York: University of California Press, 1982), and her *Civilization of the Goddess: The World of Old Europe* (San Francisco: HarperCollins, 1991).

7   Mark Moffett, *The Human Swarm: How Our Societies Arise, Thrive and Fall* (Lebanon, IN: Hachette Book Group, 2019).

8   J. Edward de Steiguer, *Wild Horses of the West: History and Politics of America's Mustangs* (Tuscon: University of Arizona Press, 2011), 36.

9   Fritjof Capra and Pier Luigi Luisi, *The Systems View of Life: A Unifying Vision* (Cambridge: Cambridge University Press, 2014), 78–83. See also Carl Safina, *Beyond Words: What Animals Think and Feel* (New York: Henry Holt and Company, 2015), 26–27. Safina describes the institutional repudiation of any notion of animal sentience: "My own initiation into formal training included the classic directive: Do not attribute human mental experiences—thoughts or emotions—to other animals. (Doing so is called 'anthropomorphism.').... [T]he whole subject became verboten.... Description—and only description—became 'the' science of animal behavior.... Suggesting that other animals can feel *anything* wasn't just a conversation stopper; it was a career killer." Susan McCarthy, in *Becoming a Tiger: How Baby Animals Learn to Live in the Wild* (New York: HarperCollins, 2004), x, noted: "In researching *When Elephants Weep*, my coauthor Jeffrey Moussaieff Masson and I had to wrestle with a widespread scientific reluctance to write of emotion. That animals feel emotion is still anathema in some circles; that animals learn is not. *How* animals learn is often the controversial part."

10   Brian Fagan, in *The Intimate Bond: How Animals Shaped Human History* (New York: Bloomsbury Press, 2015), attempts to outline the complex, dynamic relationship between animals and humans, but claims in the Preface (p. xi) that: "The endless debate over the humanity of animals is, however, irrelevant to these pages." Throughout the book he refers to both predatory animals and their prey as "beasts." His frame of reference, perhaps unwittingly, denigrates animal sentience as "anthropomorphizing" because we "attribute human emotions and feelings to them." Moreover, he avoids any discussion of Chauvet Cave's

remarkable depictions of animals and the absence of human images, except for female pudenda as part of a hybrid bison/lion creature.

11   D. Jenness, "The Ojibwa Indians of Parry Island: Their Social and Religious Life," *Bulletins of the Canada Department of Mines, National Museum of Canada* (Ottawa), no. 78 (1930): 29.

12   Jean Clottes, foreword to David Whitley, *Cave Paintings and the Spirit: The Origin of Creativity and Belief* (Amherst, NY: Prometheus Books, 2009), 15, 19.

13   Kimmerer, *Braiding Sweetgrass*, 7–9.

14   Gary Snyder (Pulitzer Prize–winning poet and anthropologist, Sitka Writer's Symposium, Sitka, Alaska), in discussion with the author, June 1987.

15   For similar behavior and extraordinary sensitivity in elephants, models for mammoth behavior, see Caitlin O'Connell, *The Elephant's Secret Sense: The Hidden Life of the Wild Herds of Africa* (New York: Free Press, 2007).

16   Moffett, *The Human Swarm*, discusses social cohesion and the advantages of collaborative societies for mammals, but still focuses on male dominance without recognizing the role of the lead females in herd cultures.

17   Cary Wolfe, Introduction, and "In the Shadow of Wittgenstein's Lion: Language, Ethics, and the Question of the Animal," chap. 1 in *Zoontologies: The Question of the Animal*, ed. Wolfe (Minneapolis and London: University of Minnesota Press, 2003). Joel Berger, a biologist, published the following important study based on his research in the Granite Range horse herds of northwestern Nevada from 1979 to 1983: *Wild Horses of the Great Basin: Social Competition and Population Size* (Chicago: University of Chicago Press, 1986).

18   Joe Hutto, *Touching the Wild: Living with the Mule Deer of Deadman Gulch* (New York: Skyhorse Press, 2014).

19   Suzanne Held and Marek Spinka, "Animal Play and Animal Welfare," *Animal Behaviour*, 81 (2011): 891–99. This article discusses aspects of play for domestic animals, who benefit from it in terms of fitness, an absence of physical threats, and enhanced social welfare.

20   Northwest Inuit and Tlingit peoples believed that scat should be avoided, stepping around it rather than over it out of respect when they found it on the trail. Inuit elders, Sitka Nature Writer's Symposium, Sitka Alaska, discussion with author, June 1987.

21   Malcolm Penny, *Rhinos: Endangered Species* (New York and Oxford: Facts On File, Inc., 1988). This behavior in feral horses was also witnessed and reported by Mackenzie Davis and Craig London during the June 2017 University

of California-Davis "Mustangs: Living Legacy" experience, a week of following wild herds of horses on horseback near Montgomery Pass, California.

22 Penny, *Rhinos*, 19, 25. "The tracks which black rhinoceroses use as they travel through the bush are followed by many other species, either to go to and from the same watering hole, or just as convenient passages. There is often a groove in the ground about 20 in wide, and as much as 14 in deep, beneath a tunnel through the bushes 6 feet high. Following an already cleared track saves them effort, but it also enables them to move quietly and less conspicuously...." The word "rhinoceros" is derived through Latin from the Ancient Greek, ῥῑνόκερως, which is composed of ῥῑνο- (*rhino-*, "nose") and κέρας (*keras*, "horn"). The plural in English is *rhinoceros* or *rhinoceroses*. The collective noun for a group of rhinoceroses is *crash* or *herd*. The name has been in use since the fourteenth century. Rhinos have no natural predators, except for humans, and they are exclusively herbivores. The rhinos depicted at Chauvet probably weighed between 5,000 and 6,000 pounds and were of the African "white rhino" species. For more specific information, see Norman Owen-Smith, in *The Encyclopedia of Mammals*, ed. D. MacDonald, 490–95 (New York: Facts on File, 1984). See also www.livescience.com/27439-rhinos.html. It is difficult to study the behavior of the wild rhinoceros today to extrapolate aspects of their behavior. All rhinoceros species are near extinction, their populations decimated because of the Asian belief that their horn is an aphrodisiac. The last living male white rhino died in 2018.

23 See Anna Ilieva and Anna Shturbanova, "Zoomorphic Images in Bulgarian Women's Ritual Dances in the Context of Old European Symbolism," in *From the Realm of the Ancestors: An Anthology in Honor of Marija Gimbutas*, ed. Joan Marler (Manchester, CT: Knowledge, Ideas and Trends, Inc., 1997), 309–21.

24 See Gimbutas, *Goddesses and Gods*.

25 See Jean Clottes, epilogue to Jean-Marie Chauvet, Eliette Brunel Deschamps, and Christian Hillaire, *Dawn of Art: The Chauvet Cave* (London: Henry Abrams and Thames of Hudson, 1996), 110.

26 Paul Bahn, Michel Lorblanchet, and Pierre Soulages, in *The First Artists: In Search of the World's Oldest Art* (London: Thames and Hudson, 2017), 16, note a "constant rapport between the animal engravings and the bear clawmarks...."

27 In *Smithsonian Magazine*, October 9, 2013, Rachel Nuwer wrote: "Women artists may be responsible for most cave art." She noted that "women tend to have ring and index fingers of about the same length, whereas men's ring fingers tend to be longer than their index fingers." Using a logarithm designed to evaluate the 32 handprints found in the Chauvet

Cave, 75 percent were female. See www.smithsonainmagcom/smart-news/ancient-women-artists-may-be-responsible-for-most-cave-art-1094929/?no-ist.

28 Chauvet, et al., *Dawn of Art: The Chauvet Cave* (London: Henry Abrams and Thames of Hudson, 1996), 110.

29 Jean Clottes, *Chauvet Cave: The Art of Earliest Times* (Salt Lake City: University of Utah Press, 2003), *passim*.

30 Four other references to female genitalia exist in the form of the pubic triangle are located at the entrances of adjacent niches and cavities. See Jean Clottes, "The Salle du Fond Chamber: Venus and The Sorcerer," *International Newsletter on Rock Art* (2001), 29, bradshawfoundation.com/chauvet/venus_sorcerer.php.

31 Clottes, *Chauvet Cave* (2003), 140. The pendant also has a lion's head and engraved horse head on the internal surface, barely visible from the chamber.

32 See Gimbutas, *Goddesses and Gods* and *Civilization of the Goddess*.

33 Dimitra Papagianni and Michael Morse, *The Neanderthals Rediscovered: How Modern Science Is Rewriting Their Story* (London: Thames & Hudson, Inc., 2015), 20–21.

34 Ibid., 115–19.

35 Fagan, *The Intimate Bond*, xi.

36 Tim Ingold, "The Animal in the Study of Humanity," in *What Is an Animal?* ed. Ingold, 84–99 (London: Routledge Press, 1988). See also his *The Perception of the Environment: Essays in Livelihood, Dwelling, and Skill* (London: Routledge Press, 2000).

37 Mitákuye Oyás'in is a Lakota phrase that translates as "we all are related" in a worldview of interconnectedness. This concept and phrase is notably found in many Yankton Sioux prayers as well as in ceremonies in other Lakota communities. The prayer describes the oneness and harmony of all forms of life, including people, animals, birds, insects, trees and plants, and even rocks, rivers, mountains and valleys. See Thomas Constantine Maroukis, *Peyote and the Yankton Sioux: The Life and Times of Sam Necklace* (Norman: University of Oklahoma Press, 2005), 160.

38 Chauvet, et al., *Dawn of Art*.

39 David W. Anthony, Dorcas R. Brown, and Christian George, "Early Horseback Riding and Warfare: The Importance of the Magpie around the Neck," in *Horses and Humans: The Evolution of the Equine–Human Relationship*, British Archaeological Reports International Series 1560, ed.

Sandra L. Olsen, Susan Grant, Alice Choyke, and Laszlo Bartosiewicz (Oxford: Archaeopress, 2006), 6; and Levine, Marsha. "Domestication of the Horse." In *The Oxford Companion to Archaeology*, edited by Neil Asher Silberman, 15–19. (Oxford: Oxford University Press), 2012.

40 Robert M. Miller, DVM, *Imprint Training of the Newborn Foal: A Swift Effective Method for Permanently Shaping a Horse's Lifetime Behavior* (Fort Worth, TX: Western Horseman, [1991] 2008). Robert M. Miller (Horse Expo, Sacramento, CA), in discussion with the author, June 9, 2015; and Miller and Pat Parelli (Horse Expo, Sacramento, CA), in discussion with the author, June 10, 2016. Precocial or prey animals can see and walk within hours of being born. In contrast, predators and humans are born helpless, and in some cases, like cats, blind until six weeks old. Humans and predators require the care and protection of parents for the first year or so of their lives.

41 David W. Anthony, Dorcas R. Brown, and Christian George, "Early Horseback Riding and Warfare: The Importance of the Magpie around the Neck," in *Horses and Humans: The Evolution of the Equine–Human Relationship*, ed. Sandra L. Olsen, Susan Grant, Alice Choyke, and Laszlo Bartosiewicz, British Archaeological Reports International Series 1560, 137–56 (Oxford: Archaeopress, 2006). They acknowledge that a hackamore does not affect the bones or teeth of a horse and may have been used much earlier. For early horseback riding around 6,000 years ago and its impact on culture, see David Anthony, Dimitri Y. Telegin, and Dorcas Brown, "The Origin of Horseback Riding," *Scientific American* (December 1991), 94–100.

42 Clottes, in foreword to *Cave Paintings and the Spirit* (pp. 15, 19): "It is a safer bet to wager that Paleolithic hunter-gatherers' ways of thinking were closer to those of early Native Americans or Australian Aborigines rather than to ours today. . . . An understanding of Native American (and other traditional non-Western) cultures provides a kind of prism by which the ancient past can be examined and explored, beyond the heavy intellectual weight imposed by our Western worldview."

43 Richard Owen, "Description of the Fossil Remains of a Mammal *(Hyracotherium leporinum)* and of a Bird *(Lithornis vulturinis)* from the London Clay," in *Transactions of the Geological Society of London* series 2, VI (1841): 203–208. See also Lawrence Guy Straus, *Iberia Before the Iberians: The Stone Age Prehistory of Cantabrian Spain* (Albuquerque: University of New Mexico Press, [1992] 2011), 146.

44 Recent examination of physical evidence indicates the horses depicted on the walls of Chauvet derived not from the tarpan or Prezwalski horse, but

the *Equus antunesi*, now extinct, a horse well suited for fast running across open spaces. J. Franzen, *The Rise of Horses: 55 Million Years of Evolution* (Baltimore: The Johns Hopkins University Press, 2010), 170–71.

45 Ibid., 104–106. See also Steve Price, *America's Wild Horses: The History of the Western Mustang* (New York: Skyhorse Publishing, 2017), 2–4.

46 Ross McPhee, curator of the division of vertebrate zoology and of the international exhibit, The Horse, "The Archaeology and Paleontology of the Horse" (lecture, Museum of Natural History, New York City, sponsored by the Bentley Foundation, San Francisco, CA, May 2016).

47 Anthony, et al., "Early Horseback Riding."

48 Ibid. See also Stacy Westfall, "Bareback riding WITHOUT reins," February 29, 2008, www.youtube.com/watch?v=-Pg1EbXbZO4.

49 Peter Wohlleben, *The Inner Life of Animals: Love, Grief, and Compassion—Surprising Observations of a Hidden World* (Munich: Ludwig Verlag/Random House, 2017). Evidence that attitudes toward animals and their improving status in the human world today is found in Jeffrey Kluger, "The Animal Mind: How They Think, How They Feel, How to Understand Them," *Time Magazine*, special summer edition, June 9, 2017, 96 pp., and in "Secret Lives of Animals: Strange True Tales from the Wild Kingdom," *Scientific American*, special collector's edition, 26, no. 2s (May 2017). The *Cambridge Declaration on Consciousness*, written by Philip Low and edited by Jaak Panksepp, et al., was publicly proclaimed in Cambridge, UK, on July 7, 2012, at the Francis Crick Memorial Conference on Consciousness in Human and Non-Human Animals, signed by the conference participants with Stephen Hawking, and memorialized by CBS 60 Minutes.

50 Wohlleben, *The Inner Life of Animals*; Leonardo Barón Birchenall, "Animal Communication and Human Language: An Overview," in *International Journal of Comparative Psychology* 29 (2016): 6, escholarship.org/uc/item/3b7977qr.

51 Aimeé Brimhall McCord, conversation with author at Inspirational Horse Clinic, Gilroy, California, January 2015. See also inspirationalhorse.com.

52 Kimmerer, *Braiding Sweetgrass*, 17.

53 Elizabeth Kolbert, *The Sixth Extinction: An Unnatural History* (New York: Henry Holt and Company, 2014).

SUBMERGED SPIRITUALITY IN THE ITALIAN ALPS: GODDESSES, ANCESTRESSES AND WOMEN'S RITUAL IN THE ARCHAEOLOGICAL RECORD

MARY BETH MOSER

The mountains and valleys of the northern Italy are steeped in spiritual mysteries. The snowy Alps are marked by the striking presence of the even older Dolomites, once the reefs of an ancient sea. Glaciers shaped the fertile river valleys. High mountain meadows offer lush seasonal wildflowers and herbs. Forests of larch, pine and fir shelter wild animals. Alpine lakes and thermal pools beckon from deep within the mountainous terrain. The long history of the mountain people is held in the land itself, upon which they depended, a relationship infused with reverence and influenced by the moon, sun and stars. Women's spiritual history is present although it has been submerged by layers of time, overlooked by the recorders of history, dismissed, negated and at times suppressed. Yet the evidence is there.

The long story of women's spirituality is carved in stone and bone, marked with ochre red and crafted into metal; it is held by the magical powers of the female characters in the folk stories once told in nightly gatherings; it is manifest in the everyday spiritual acts of folk women that honor the sources and cycles of life; it is spun, stitched and washed; it is cooked, celebrated and shared; it is gathered, boiled and distilled; it is defended by maidens and voiced by Old Wives. It is transmitted in the values that have been passed down over the ages and carried by immigrants across the sea.

This essay focuses on the archaeological record, providing evidence of goddesses, ancestresses and women's sacred ritual. This sampling spans a considerable length of time from the fifth millennium BCE into the Christian era. It includes a female figure carved on bone from the fifth millennium BCE, known as the Venus of Gaban, who wears a crescent pendant and bears a conifer tree from her prominent red vulva; petroglyphs of female figures in ritual and cupmarks from nearby Valle Camonica; monolithic carved stones known as *stele*, possibly ancestors or deities, from the Bronze Age; Reitia, the goddess for whom the Retic culture may have been named, whose people crafted amulets of metal and made inscribed offerings at outdoor sanctuaries in high places; an indigenous water goddess, whose sacred site was overlaid by a Roman temple to the Goddess Minerva; and Diana, midwife and moon goddess of the Romans whose temples were overlaid by Christian churches.

The examples presented here illustrate themes that appear in folk culture which are sources of spiritual agency, including women's bodies, menstrual blood, the moon and sun, plants, trees, animals, water, stone, jewelry and cloth. There is evidence of the persistence of sacred place and a thread of veneration of and by females that can be perceived, even with successive waves of cultural and institutional influences. The presence of veneration to women and sacred ritual by women in the archaeological record offers evidence of women's spiritual agency, which is closely aligned with nature and with the sources and cycles of life.

Gaban "Venus"

Outside of what is now the city of Trento, in a narrow valley bordered by a hill, a rich source of archaeological evidence was discovered in 1970 in a natural rock shelter or *riparo*. Known now as the Gaban site by archaeologists, it was used almost uninterruptedly for nearly six thousand years, from the Mesolithic to the Middle Bronze Age.[1]

Among the artifacts uncovered is a carefully-incised female figure from the fifth millennium BCE (Fig. 13).[2] The Gaban figure, carved on the bone of a red deer,[3] measures five cm (about two inches) in size.[4] Her form has several attributes of note including a downward-pointing crescent moon pendant that hangs from a necklace-like collar, a belt with parallel vertical notches, and a large and prominent vulva, below which is an incised reticular design. A tree form emerges from the top of the opening of the vulva. The front and back of the figure are marked with red ochre, considered a symbol of blood, life and regeneration since the Paleolithic, states Trentino archaeologist Annaluisa Pedrotti in her chapter on the Neolithic in the detailed volume *Storia del Trentino: La preistoria e la protostoria*. The Gaban female is interpreted as a "representation of the rebirth and growth of the vegetal world through the earth mother, here symbolized by a female divinity."[5]

As a source of life, menstrual blood and erotic mystery, the vulva is a potent sign of female agency. Vulva symbols have been present in the archaeological record from the Upper Paleolithic through succeeding ages into historical times, and represent the powerful, generative powers of the Goddess, according to Marija Gimbutas.[6] In European folk traditions, women sought to influence the growth of flax through their exposed genitals.[7] Lotte Motz presents cross-cultural evidence in archaeology, folk customs, folk tales and mythology of the power attributed to a woman exposing her vulva, whose impact, she concludes, acts to "shock, shatter, and dispel danger and aggression."[8]

Fig. 13. Gaban figure, Trento, Italy. From commons. wikimedia.org/wiki/File:Figura_ femminile_-_Gaban_-_MUSE.jpg.

The tree form is paired with vulva symbols in Paleolithic caves and sometimes takes the place of the vulva on figurines from the Neolithic in Europe.[9] A conifer-like form similar to that sculpted on the Gaban female dating from the upper Paleolithic was engraved fourteen times in flint found on the Plain of Marcesina in Trentino.[10] Fred Hageneder, who has researched and documented the deep cultural significance of trees in Europe, presents the symbol on the Gaban image in context of the birth and rebirth aspects of the Tree of Life.[11]

Indeed, the trees that established themselves after the receding of the glaciers, eventually becoming conifer and deciduous forests, have been vital to the life of the mountain people as a source of shelter, food, clothing, and medicine.[12] Images of trees appear on the *stemma* or coat of arms for the municipalities of my grandparents' birthplaces: three fir trees for Dimaro, a single large pine with ten branches for Baselga di Pinè, and three pine cones along with a birch tree, shown with its roots, for Bedollo.[13] During a nature hike, Maurizio Bontempelli, a Trentino storyteller who also works with trees and wood, explained that birch acts as a kind of mother tree that grows first in the field if everything has been cut; it helps the forest expand by fixing nitrogen in the soil so other types of trees and plants can grow.[14] He characterized this action by referring to the birch as Dea Madre, an Italian title meaning God the Mother, and said it is considered a sacred tree, not used casually. Later that day, in an act of transformation, he crafted a *scodella* (bowl) from pine wood, as a gift for me and my husband to take home.[15]

In Nordic mythology, first woman and first man were made from the wood of two different trees, elm and ash.[16] In explaining the possible origins of a Trentino folk story, Giovanni Borzaga notes the presence and influence of the Etruscans, whose Goddess Velthe/Urcla creates humans from one of the most beautiful forests on Mt. Cimini in Tuscany.[17]

The Gaban figure is sometimes referred to as the "Gaban Venus,"[18] a misnomer in the sense that Venus is the Roman goddess of beauty who arrived thousands of years later. The name does, however, acknowledge her importance with its bestowal of divine status and implicitly links her with veneration of the female across the ages, specifically with the other so-called "Venuses" found throughout Eurasia from thousands of years earlier made from bone, stone, ivory or clay. Venus is the "morning star," the name given to the bright planet that shines in the morning and evening, a cosmic entity connected to the divine female in antiquity, notably the Sumerian Goddess Inanna whose written sign from the fourth millennium BCE includes a star, a designation of divinity.[19]

Venus is retained in popular culture in Trentino. The poem by Simone Dapra (1872–1965) from Val di Sole refers to "*la stela de la di*" in dialect, which is translated in the English version both as Venus and "the morning star."[20] Venus is portrayed as a nude figure with a dolphin on the *stemma* for the municipality of Ziano di Fiemme.[21] Friday, *Venerdi* in Italian, is named for Venus, *Venere*.[22] In German, *Freitag* (Friday) is related to the Goddess Frigg and the older Goddess Freyja.[23] Freyina, "little Freya" is said to be the oldest village in Ampezzo Valley in Wolff's folk story, "The Artist of Faloria."[24]

Another artifact from the Gaban site includes a handle carved of an animal bone on which is inscribed a figure with arms upraised in orans position and legs spread downward, whose form is similar to the petroglyphs in Valle Camonica discussed in the next section; the figure is standing above a zigzag motif, which appears to represent a course of water.[25] Although the gender of the figure is unknown, it evokes a ritual act in connection to water, a subject that also emerges in folk stories.[26]

Valle Camonica Petroglyphs—Women, Rocks and Ritual

In Valle Camonica, Lombardy, adjacent to Trentino and accessible via Tonale Pass from Val di Sole, numerous petroglyphs have been carved into the mountain-side rocks over the millennia. Deemed so important that it has been designated as a UNESCO "World Heritage Site," this record of history includes figures of interest to this study, including women in ritual, vulva symbols and cupped indentations, which are addressed in the following sections. Additional relevant examples of engraved symbols are cited throughout the study.

Overview of the Valley

Like other Alpine and pre-Alpine river valleys, Valle Camonica was covered with glacial ice several times during the major ice ages. During the last ice age, the glaciers covering the plains and valleys of northern Italy receded, smoothing and sculpting large dark surfaces of Permian sandstone along the slopes of the valley. After the glaciers finally withdrew, around 8000 BCE, and continuing over the ages until the Romans arrived and beyond, these rock surfaces have been engraved with figures.[27]

Numbering over 300,000, the engravings shed light on the history of the Alpine zone.[28] Archaeologist Emmanuel Anati, who has conducted significant research since 1956 and founded the Centro Camuno di Studi Preistorici where research continues today, refers to the rock engravings as "primary documents."[29] He challenges the division between history and prehistory, arguing that engravings, like written texts, are meaningful. Recognizing that the written records of the Romans are limited and from their point of view, Anati observes that the record of Valle Camonica:

> ... adds eight thousand years to the last two thousand, full of emperors and generals, of "wars won" and "glorious anniversaries," which separate us from the day Augustus' monument at La Turbie was erected, when the Camunians

> [the people of Valle Camonica] become merely an histor-
> ical footnote, dismissed with the dry definition of *Gentes
> alpinae devictae* (conquered Alpine peoples).[30]

While Anati rightfully argues for inclusion of the archaeological record as history, a rich oral legacy also exists in the folk stories and living people of the Italian Alps.

Moss and vegetation have naturally covered the rocks over the years. This can happen in a relatively short period of time: during my field research in 2009, for example, one guide commented that the rock with engraved symbols in front of us, which he had discovered a few years earlier, was already becoming hidden with natural growth. Although large-scale explo-ration, documentation and research of the rock art in Valle Camonica have taken place in the last fifty years, it is an emerging story since it is unknown how many petroglyphs are still hidden.

The magnitude of the number of carvings seems to signify their impor-tance. Engravings have been found on more than 2,500 rock surfaces.[31] Several parks or reserves have been created as viewing areas. Areas of rock art are named and the rocks are numbered within each section. Most of the rocks have been carved with stones implemented using a pecking technique. Some engraved surfaces are more than 150 feet long and have more than a thousand figures.[32] At Luine, a sacred hill near the town of Darfo Boario Terme, a great, inclined surface known as Rock 34, bears the most inscriptions of any rock in the valley with thousands of signs spanning more than 8,000 years.[33] Figures include humans and animals, shields, deer, solar symbols, lobed figures with nine dots known as Camunian Roses, and labyrinths.[34] In Foppe di Nadro, there are several engravings in "Reto-Etruscan" characters.[35]

Females in Ritual

Early anthropomorphic figures from the Neolithic time period are simple engravings, like stick figures, characterized by arched downward legs and mirrored by a similar shape of the arms reaching upward, creating a kind of symmetry, with a single straight line for the torso and a dot for the head. Some of the figures have identifying anatomy, indicated by a dot for a vulva and/or sometimes two dots for breasts, or male anatomy, and others do not.[36] Often called a "worshipping" figure because of the raised arms, Anati characterizes their appearance in Valle Camonica as "rather frequent." [37]

Among the carvings of this type is a figure with raised arms and spread legs dating from the fifth millennium BCE, near a circle or "disk" with a dot in the center, which has been interpreted both as sun and as "female symbol." [38] The volunteer guide from the museum during my visit in 2004 said that at that time, scholars considered it to be the "sex" of the figure, thus identifying her as female.

An important interpretation of the figure with upraised arms, sometimes described as *orans*, Latin for praying, comes from the work of Mary B. Kelly, who found repeated images of "strong female images" in her analysis of international textiles. The *orans* figure is widespread in folk women's textile art in Europe and Central Asia, according to Kelly, who calls them goddesses. Sometimes they were named as a local goddess or more likely in recent times as queens, ladies or mistresses. [39] In Romania, "one of the most enduring motifs is the figure of the goddess with upraised hands," a figure also common throughout Bulgaria. [40]

Large Female with Necklace, Breasts and Vulva

A well-known engraving possibly dating from around 3300 BCE is the so-called "Sellero Idol" whose name comes from its location in Sellero Park, and whose designation as "idol" apparently results from its large size and specific portrayal. [41] This figure stretches over a large rock engraved with over 700 figures. [42] Two circles in the breast area of a body and a circle with a dot in the center at her vulva area (also referred to as a cupped disk) identify her as a female—and would seem to support the interpretation of this symbol as a vulva. In an illustration that highlights her image, she appears to wear necklaces. The figure is flanked by additional circles with dots in the center. [43]

Vulva Symbols—Female as Source

Circular, almond-shaped, or V-shaped figures are among the shapes categorized as "vulva symbols" by Ausilio Priuli, director of the Didactic Museum of Prehistoric Art and Life, and an archaeologist who has made significant discoveries in Valle Camonica. He groups the "figurative culture and traditions in Italy and in the alpine arch" into a hundred categories in his publication, *Valcamonica: Valley of Prehistory*, including symbols of interest to this study: stars, trees, numerous types of animals, "decorations" (which appear to include necklaces), looms and cupmarks.[44] Priuli notes three vulva symbols on a rock in Sellero that likely served as an altar, a term that seems to indicate its sacred ritual use.[45] A rock at Seradina incised with figures is itself in the form of a vulva.[46]

Groups of Females in Ritual

Other carvings include a line of females with arms raised and legs spread at Naquane on Rock 32 (Fig. 14). Scholars cite the possibility of initiation, healing or funerary rites. In *Valcamonica Rock Art*, this scene is summarized as

> ... a clear composition referable to the Neolithic Age which describes either a funerary ceremony or one of heal- ing: female figures are next to an elongated being who is positioned near a figure with arms raised, defined as a praying or shaman figure.[47]

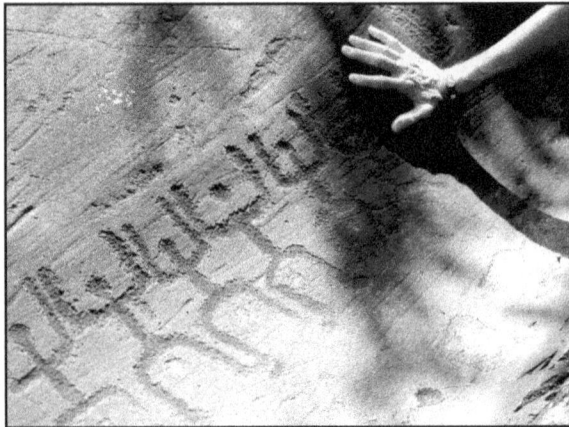

Fig. 14. Rock carving of women in ritual, Val Camonica, Italy.
Photograph by author, 2014.

Priuli describes this as a "probable scene of initiation: female figures seem to dance alongside a woman lying down, not far from a place of worship."[48] Naquane, the name of the region, is similar to Anguane, female water dei- ties that have continued in the local oral tradition as protagonists of the folk stories.[49] In a similar scene carved on Rock 1 at Naquane at least three females are in a line with raised arms, with a horizontal female figure below, which Priuli also describes as women's initiatory rites.[50]

To these possible interpretations, I propose the addition of birth, menstruation, and fertility rites. When I presented a photo of this image to a group of female graduate students in the United States, one of them immediately connected it with women giving birth. Also significant to the interpretation, according to Franco Gaudiano, is a water groove or hollow underneath the figure.[51] In the next sections, I present ways in which women ritually engage, or may have engaged, with the rock as a life-giving source, via water and directly. They attest to a worldview in which nature is directly experienced and valued as a source of life, a theme that recurs in folk stories and in folk women's lives.[52]

Cupmarks—Signs of Women's Ritual

Cupmarks, or *coppelle* in Italian, small carved indentations that form depressions or cups in the rock, are a very common figure. According to Priuli, they belong to a classification into which falls an "enormous" disproportionate number of all the rock art; they are so commonly found and easily made that they were probably made by "common folk" rather than specialists, whom he postulates may have done the more elaborate engravings.[53] Perhaps it is this reason that they have received less attention; however it is precisely because of their relationship to everyday people, and as we shall see, to women, that they are of particular interest to this inquiry.

Blessed Water from Rocks

The presence of cupmarks in Europe is extremely ancient. They were engraved into stones before 40,000 BCE in Europe, according to Gimbutas.[54] The water from cupmarks is considered sacred, healing, and a source of life that even today is considered efficacious.[55] Women in the Baltics and Scandinavia use water from cupmarks for offerings, according to Kelly. A contemporary photo from Estonia shows water-filled indentations in a rock with a sacred cloth draped nearby.[56]

Italian archaeologists Umberto Sansoni, Silvana Gavaldo, and Cristina Gastaldi present important evidence on the apparent relationship of water, cupmarks, women, and sacred sites in Valtellina, a mountainous region in

Lombardy.[57] Their documentation includes a tally of the number and types of figures on rocks, photos of the rocks, and the local traditions in the surrounding areas. In the 1800s, before the rock was moved, they report that in the small village of Ca' Bianchi, at a small chapel to the Virgin of the Rosary, women would meet near a round rock slab with cupmarks to recite the rosary, using the blessed water in the cavity of the rock to sign themselves.[58] Centuries earlier, in Vione in Valle Camonica, women processed to a rock with cupmarks where they poured water into the cavity from the baptismal font in order to obtain the gift of rain from Santa Paola; the rock was destroyed in 1624 by order of San Carlo Borromeo.[59] In other localities, cupped rocks were used as baptismal fonts and basins for holy water inside the church. Also mentioned is the rock altar at Naquane and the cupped rock in the narthex of Sant'Ambrogio in Milano.[60] In Trentino, cupmarks appear on a smooth curved boulder at Lago d'Ezza in Val di Mocheni.[61]

Cupmarks and Menstruation

Not mentioned among these interpretations are specific women's rituals of menstruation and menarche rites.[62] The "dot" under the legs of some female figures could be a record of menstrual rituals. The cupmarks, prolific in number, may have been places in the rock where menstrual blood was offered during puberty rites or monthly menstruation. Puberty rituals and rock art are linked in the US Southwest and elsewhere.[63] The girls of the Nez Perce reportedly made pictographs of objects that they saw or dreamt about during their puberty ceremonies. Painting of the rocks is part of the puberty rites of the girls of the Thompson River Indians and Luiseno.[64] Illustrations of the "cupholes and incisions" at Lago Nero in Valle Camonica appear similar to the "pit and groove" markings of the Pomo in California associated with fertility and weather rituals.[65]

If women believed, perceived or experienced that the rocks held the fertilizing life force, then offering life-giving menstrual blood, and perhaps also birth blood, back to the rocks as replenishment would have seemed reasonable—as well as seeking this generative force of the rocks for fertility. This could have been viewed as a mutually fertilizing relationship with the rocks giving and receiving life energy. In Hawaii, there are numerous rocks with *puka* or cupmarks into which the umbilical cord stump, or *piko*, of a newborn is placed to give it strength and spiritual health.[66] These brief observations introduce some possibilities and point to future investigation, especially when considering the strong relationship of rocks and fertility in the following discussion.

Rocks of Fertility

A further intimate association of rocks as a source of women's agency is manifested in women's rituals in the past regarding fertility. Sansoni documents the presence of so-called "rocks of fertility," already well-known in the popular culture.[67] Sansoni further asserts that

> ... many rocks with cupmarks of the alpine arch were utilized also as *scivoli* (slides) in pagan rites of fertility: the women were utilizing the cupmarks for spilling out oily substances or water, and then, they were sliding from the summit of the mass for propitiating the birth of children.[68]

A photo of a large rock at San Giovanni di Teglio engraved with cupmarks shows a clearly visible shiny band on the rock from its use as a slide.[69]

Priuli has identified numerous carved rocks in the area of Edolo and records the presence of a fertility slide at Mu, above the town of Edolo, and another at Fobia on a rock covered with cupped indentations. At Mu there are boulders and rocks "profusely carved with cupholes."[70] At Corteno Golgi, in Valli di Sant'Antonio, a boulder with over three hundred cupmarks, often joined by channels, is pictured.[71] Rocks with cupmarks and fertility slides lend support to the idea that they may have been used in sacred rites not only for women to receive fertility but also for women to make offerings of their fertility.

A study by Fabio Copiatti and Alberto De Giuli on the practice of using rocks as fertility slides presents specific evidence that supports the connection of rock and women's sacred rites.[72] Although the authors say that these practices were suppressed, there is still a "roc de vita" or rock of life at sanctuaries in Oropa, in Varallo, and in Boca.[73] Numerous examples are cited of fertility practices in Europe by the authors. In Trentino, there were particular rocks used by women more than a century ago to *sdrucciolo*, presumably meaning to slide in dialect, if they wanted to become pregnant.[74] The rocks that were used until recent times in Borzoli, near Genova, were made of green serpentine.[75] Rock of the color green was also prized as amulets for childbirth, *parto*.[76] A saying still exists in the town of Mergozzo, Piedmont, that if a girl is pregnant without being married, *è scivolata,* she has slid.[77]

The archaic cults to "Dôn, Dana, or Ana" became Diana, according to Copiatti and De Giuli, and then substituted by Saint Anne mother of Mary, whose cult is "most diffuse" in the valleys, with many chapels dedicated to her where women go to pray for having children.[78] Roberto Gremmo has also collected evidence of the popular perception of what he calls "magic rocks," which includes standing stones, boulders, pyramidal stones, natural caves, and rocks imbued with fertilizing, healing power in the Alps, especially in Piedmont, stating that "the main centers of devotional pagan stones have become the most important Christian sanctuaries in the Alps."[79]

Sacred rocks, although too vast of a subject to be treated adequately in this essay, are closely linked to women and sacred ritual. Rocks become places of both shelter for the wild women in the folk characters, and a place of banishment for the witches.[80]

Stele

Carved standing stones of human effigies from the fourth to the second millennium BCE, known in Italian as *stele* have been found throughout the Alpine Arch, notably in Northern Italy, Switzerland, and Liguria.[81] Having been submerged, forgotten and hidden, they have resurfaced in people's fields, gardens, building foundations, and chapels. In 1942, in Valtellina a woman discovered three stele covered with carvings in her vineyard.[82] Six came to light in Trentino during excavation in Arco of the new hospital in 1989 and 1990. In Laces, Bolzano, a stone of white marble, carved with engravings and dating from at least 5,000 years ago, was discovered under the altar of the Church of Our Lady in 1992 during the restoration of the church.[83]

Although gender representation can be difficult to assign, some stele are carved to have breasts, as does "Arco IV" which measures a little less than three feet.[84] Cloth mantles or shawls with a striped or checked pattern are engraved on some of the stones of both females and males. Anati describes the stones as "the body of the 'supernatural' being," noting their carved displays of breasts, necklaces, weapons, pubic triangles, or snakes.[85] Gimbutas names the stele with carved owl-like faces as "goddesses," calling attention to the change in symbolic carvings after the arrival of the Indo-Europeans from the second half of the fourth millennium BCE to include male gods, weapons, and solar symbols.[86] Max Dashu, a "herstorian of suppressed histories," refers to them as the "ancestral mothers" part of a foundational matrilineal culture across Europe and Africa.

> These early monumental women are omitted by nearly all histories and minimized even in many archaeological surveys. The cultural focus on ancestral mothers suggests matrilineage, while the communal burials in the megalithic womb tombs ("passage graves") reflect a collective clan-oriented society.[87]

Anthropologist Michela Zucca cites the enduring presence of the female form in the Alpine region across time, beginning with the numerous stele from Neolithic times and continuing with the iconography of the Celtic mothers, and the Black Madonnas in Christianity in historic times, as evidence that the Mother has always been honored in the stone of the mountains. [88] Megaliths mark the prehistoric migration paths of Africans, according to Birnbaum, calling attention to the sanctuary of Har Karkom, known as Mt. Sinai, dating to 40,000 BCE, which features arrangements of upright stones, incised to resemble humans.[89]

Goddess Reitia

From 3000 BCE, the alpine region experienced the development of metals: copper, bronze, and then iron. After the Hallstadt culture of the first Iron Age, a new identifiable culture group emerged in the fifth century BCE in the central Alpine area of Trentino and Alto Adige, named by archeologists as the Fritzens-Sanzeno culture,[90] which was characterized by "cultural and tribal unity."[91] The writers of antiquity named the people of the Alps as Reti (Raeti, Rhaeti, Raetians or Rhaetians),[92] various tribes or groups of people whom the Romans subdued.[93] While these writings are valuable, they must be read with the understanding that they are from the conqueror's point of view, rather than the Alpine people's description of themselves.

"The most plausible explanation of the name Raetians is that the Alpine tribes were given the name by outsiders because they worshipped the goddess Reitia," according to the website for the South Tyrol Museum of

Archaeology.[94] My cousin Angelo, upon learning of my interest in female deities, first alerted me to the Goddess Reitia, stating that the area was once named after her. In Sanzeno, the Museo Retico, a new museum about the Retic culture seems to symbolize an emerging identity as studies of the archaeological artifacts reveal more details.

The Reti were characterized by their religious ritual—specifically by their outdoor shrines, near the larger farming communities, where they made sacrifices which were burned and offered votive objects.[95] A written text used for religious purposes emerges in the archaeological evidence around 500 BCE.[96] Inscriptions on bone, stone, horn, ceramics, and metals have been found, along with representations of divinities in human form.[97] Like Etruscan and other non-Indo-European languages, the Retic alphabet does not contain the letter "o."[98] The Etruscans and the Celts, who were present in the Alpine region, both preserved traits indicative of matrilineal society, according to Gimbutas, a social structure that she proposes is highly likely to have existed throughout Europe during the Neolithic, based upon the religious symbolism.[99] Folk stories also present evidence of lineage being traced through the mother.

The locations of several sanctuaries where offerings were made have been identified. The museum of Reti culture e in Sanzeno, which gave its name to the Fritzens-Sanzeno culture by which the Reti are also known, is built on the high cultivated terrain near where a sanctuary once was.

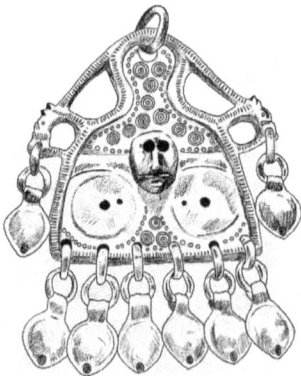

Fig. 15. "Goddess of the Horses," Sanzeno, Italy. Drawing by Rita Hillman, 2019.

A bronze ornament of an "anthropomorphic female" or "Lady of the Animals" was found in Sanzeno (Fig. 15), dating from the fifth to the second century BCE, and may represent the Goddess Reitia.[100] This "Goddess of the Horses," as she is also called,[101] stylistically holds two horse heads, a motif also found in pendants from Greece. In another pendant, her head appears sun-like and the horses' heads are more prominent. Other pendant/amulets have a triangular body and outstretched or upraised arms.[102] Mary Kelly, in her comparison of symbols on textiles throughout Europe and Asia, documents similar motifs on Russian amulets, which she calls "riding goddesses."[103] The Goddess Epona, a horse-riding goddess, was prevalent in Celtic Europe.[104]

In Val d'Ultimo in South Tyrol, an outdoor Retic shrine was located at S. Valburga, consisting of a series of stone altars and clay sacrificial platforms, where there were fires. A large gravel mound ringed by stones in the center of the shrine likely had a cult image at the top, which is portrayed as dark and female in the reconstruction of the shrine in the South Tyrol Museum of Archaeology.[105] The sanctuary site bears the name of a female saint, Saint Valburga, implying the recognition of this place as dedicated to the sacred.

A sanctuary to the Goddess Reitia near a branch of the Adige River in Este, Veneto, is considered to be "the most important Retic sanctuary" by archaeologists.[106] Originally under Etruscan influence in the seventh century BCE, it remained in use until the second or third century CE.[107] Numerous ex-voto offerings have been found, including more than a hundred figures in bronze, hundreds of figures made from thin sheets of metal, numerous anatomic figures, items related to cloth and weaving, and tablets with written dedications to Reitia.[108] Andrea Zanzotto refers to Reitia as "straightener of the world, weaver, and healer at the head of a pantheon almost entirely female."[109] In Swiss Alpine regions, the name of the Goddess Reitia became Risa, Madrisa, or Mother Risa, reflected in similar place names.[110]

On a round votive disk from Montebelluna, a figure described as a goddess carries a large key; she is flanked by an animal and a bird; other bronze disks with women bearing keys are interpreted as "priestesses of a divinity tied to birth and to fertility."[111] Numerous actual iron keys which are large, curved, and elaborate have been found as part of the Reti culture.[112] According to Hilda Ellis Davidson in *Roles of the Northern Goddess*, keys held by a sacred female in iconography symbolize the power to control wild animals, guardianship during the transition after death to the Otherworld, and help to mothers during childbirth for releasing the child from the womb.[113] Gimbutas seems to substantiate the latter role in her reference to the Venetic Goddess Retia as "the Birthgiver," whom she also relates to Artemis.[114] Language analysts Alfred Toth and Linus Brunner propose that the Veneti assumed the name and veneration of the Reti Goddess from the adjacent region of Reitia.[115]

Indigenous Water Goddess and Goddess Minerva of Valle Camonica

In 1986, a sanctuary to the Goddess Minerva, described as "one of the most interesting modern archaeological discoveries in Northern Italy" in the archaeological brochure, was discovered by chance during a construction project in Breno in Valle Camonica.[116] It provides a case study for the presence of female deity associated with natural water, the continuity of sacred place, and the long memory of oral tradition.

Described as "a site of great mystery and sacredness," the sanctuary was built on the bank of the Oglio River, at a place with natural caves and water gushing from the rocks. Water was "at the core of the open air cult of a female deity established by the local alpine population in the fifth century BCE," according to the sanctuary guide.[117]

> The outcropping of water from the earth was felt in fact as the epiphany, the manifestation of the deity, whom men could be brought into contact with through ceremonies and purification rites. During the Iron Age, the dwellers of Camonica valley had associated a female deity to the springs in the caves, personification of the immanence of Nature in the life of men.[118]

In 2003, an amulet of a water goddess was found at an outdoor shrine located near a sacred spring that gushed out of the rock nearby. The votive pendant, cut and worked from a sheet of bronze, from the fifth century BCE was found in a sacrifice area which had a place for burned offerings. The pendant is described as "a stylized goddess on a solar boat."[119] The upper body is of a stylized orans figure, that is, with raised arms extending upward. In this stylized representation, the head and two upraised arms form a trident of three equal shapes, each squared on top. Below the waist is a crescent shaped "boat" with the head of a water bird at each end. The pendant is decorated with four disks of concentric circles on the body, five triangles opening downward from below the belt, evoking a kind of flow or fringe, and numerous dots outlining the figure.

Filli Rossi, who has documented the iconographical connections of this figure with others in Europe in the book *Unknown Goddess*, includes for comparison bronze votives from Alpine shrines; artifacts of female divinity of central Europe, the Mediterranean, the Balkans and Adriatic; and the bronze icon known as Sequana found in Dijon, France, protective deity of the Seine River, which is a standing figure of a goddess in a curved boat with the head and tail of a duck.[120]

A larger-than-life statue of Minerva was also discovered in-situ in 1986, the central figure of the temple, in view of a large stone altar for offering rites and sacrifices. Minerva's healing attributes are reflected in her form. She wears an aegis with a "gorgonian" head necklace centered between her breasts, modeled after the Greek Goddess Athena Hygeia, Athena the Healer, of the fifth century BCE in Athens. The Gorgon breastplate of Athena was considered apotropaic, that is having the ability to turn away harmful spirits, like an amulet. Minerva's right hand once held an offering plate to receive offerings. The statue, which is headless, was deliberately defaced in ancient times.[121] Minerva is a virgin goddess.[122]

The sanctuary to Minerva represented "the fulfillment of the Roman conquest of Camonica Valley," while maintaining the more ancient water cult. [123] Similar practices may have occurred elsewhere, as there is a folk story about the Lago di Lagole, which tells of Anguane whose sacred spring was taken over with a temple built nearby to Hecate.[124]

Although the sanctuary to Minerva was destroyed by fire in the fourth century, and buried in the mud from floodwaters in 1200, the memory was retained by the people in the oral tradition. Near the sanctuary, south of Breno, is a small sixteenth century church to the Virgin Mary known as the "church of the Minerva," with a dedication inside to Minerva from the eighteenth century.[125] The common name of the medieval bridge not far from where the Minerva statue was found is the Ponte della Minerva.[126] Even though the existence of the temple was submerged and forgotten, the memory of the sacredness of the place and of the Goddess Minerva was retained in the oral tradition, *before* any artifact or temple was found. This serves as an important example of the oral tradition and its value in cultural history.

Goddess Diana in Trentino

The presence of the Goddess Diana at two churches near Lake Caldonazzo in Trentino points to the importance and continuity of sacred place and to Diana's attributes which are strongly tied to women and nature. Just as the Romans apparently overlaid indigenous sacred sites, Christianity overlaid the sites of Roman religion.

The church of San Ermete on a rocky relief above the lake in the town of Calceranica al Lago, about ten miles from Trento, is described as *antichissima*, most ancient, by Trentino historical journalist Aldo Gorfer.[127] At the back of the church, there is a votive altar to Diana and another Roman stone pillar.[128] On the stone brick wall at the gated entrance to the church, a sign in three languages says: "Church S. Ermete. Church from 4th century A.D. built in an ancient place of pagan faith dedicated to the goddess Diana."[129] In the town, popular *giochi* or games still endure on the traditional *sagra* festival day, one of which is *l'albero della cuccagna*, literally, the tree of abundance, likely a greased log or pole with a prize affixed at the top.[130]

According to tradition, the church of San Cristoforo near Pergine in the tourist hamlet of San Cristoforo al Lago, about seven miles from Trento, was erected on in the same place as a sacred temple to Diana and Neptune.[131] Perched on Permian metamorphic rock in a serene location above the lake, with a large rock in front, this is the church where my cousin Angelo, a skilled hunter, was married; he informed me that it had been a temple to the Goddess Diana. At one time there were fresco paintings portraying the hunt with Neptune, Diana and the Nymphs, which were deleted in a reconstruction commissioned by Domenico Prada of Pinè in 1703, along with the Romanesque-gothic structure.[132]

In addition to being the Roman goddess of the hunt, Diana is the goddess of wilderness and the moon, and protector of women and childbirth, all elements that are still important in the folk culture of the region today. Frances Bernstein, an archaeologist in the US specialized in documenting Roman goddess traditions, calls attention to her roles of Moon Goddess, Aid Bringer, Huntress and Mistress of the Wild Animals and Virgin Goddess; in her most ancient guise, Diana was an "Italic Goddess of the Earth, Woods, and Groves."[133] She was especially revered by women, and her special day was the Ides, or full moon of August. Women of Rome processed to a sacred grove and sanctuary at Nemi, Bernstein says, an event that slave women were able to attend. During the ritual, women washed their hair and made votive offerings, including hand-sculpted models of uteri.[134]

Italian historian Carlo Ginzburg has documented widespread cults, myths and rituals in Europe that involved nocturnal gatherings to a female deity, sometimes called Diana.[135] Randy Conner's research presents extensive evidence of Diana's presence in literature.[136]

Diana was one of several names for female divinity across Europe, according to Pinuccia Di Gesaro who identifies in her and others "traces of a most ancient pre-Christian religion" dating back to the Neolithic and centered on a beneficent female divinity, Dea Madre. She was the Signora del Gioco (Lady of the Game) in Tyrol, Venus in other zones and Diana for the church of Rome. In Germany she was Holda, Perchta, or Abonde.[137]

Summary

The presence of goddesses, ancestresses and women in ritual in the archaeological record offers evidence of women's spiritual agency especially through their affinity with nature and their portrayal as the source of life. While only selected examples have been included here, they illustrate themes that I propose are sources of spiritual agency, including women's bodies, menstrual blood, the moon, plants, trees, animals, water, stone, jewelry and cloth. I address the presence of these themes in folk stories, folk traditions and everyday practices in my dissertation, "The Everyday Spirituality of Women in the Italian Alps." Fertility rocks and cupmarks indicate a close relationship between women and rock. The discovery of a statue of the Goddess Minerva near a church and bridge bearing her name affirms that the oral tradition and place names hold valuable information.

References

Anati, Emmanuel. *Studi Camuni*. Vol. 13, *Valcamonica Rock Art: A New History for Europe*. Translated by Thomas King and Jason Claiborne. Capo di Ponte, Italy: Edizioni del Centro, 1994.

———. "The Way of Life Recorded in the Rock Art of Valcamonica." *Adoranten* (2008): 13–35. www.rockartscandinavia.com/images/articles/a8anati.pdf.

Autonomous Province of Trento Department of Emigration. *Voices of Trentino Poetry*. "The Homeland" Monograph Series. Trento: Casa Editrice Panorama, 1988.

———. *800 Years of the Principality of Trento*. "The Homeland" Monograph Series. Trento: Casa Editrice Panorama, 1990.

Arosio, Paola, and Diego Meozzi. "Stone Pages, Glossary," 2010. www.stonepages.com/glossary.html.

Bernstein, Frances. *Classical Living: Reconnecting with the Rituals of Ancient Rome: Myths, Gods, Goddesses, Celebrations, and Rites for Every Month of the Year*. San Francisco: HarperSanFrancisco, 2000.

Birnbaum, Lucia Chiavola. *dark mother: african origins and godmothers*. Lincoln, NE: iUniverse, 2001.

Bonomi, Francesco. Dizionario Etimologico Online, 2008. "Search: Venerdi." www.etimo.it/?term=venerdi.

Borzaga, Giovanna. *Leggende dei Castelli del Trentino*. Calliano: Manfrini Editori, 1998.

Bjarnadóttir, Valgerður Hjördís. *The Saga of Vanadís, Völva and Valkyrja: Images of the Divine from the Memory of an Icelandic Woman*. Cologne: Lambert, 2008.

Busk, Rachel Harriet. *The Valleys of Tirol*. New York: AMS Press, [1874] 1983.

Comuni-Italiani.it. "Stemma Comune di Ziano di Fiemme." 2012. www.comuni-italiani.it/022/226/stemma.html.

———. "Stemmi Comuni Prov. di Trento." 2012. www.comuni-italiani.it/022/stemmi.html.

Conner, Randy P. "Of Diana, Witches, and Fairies: An Excerpt from 'The Pagan Heart of the West.'" In *She Is Everywhere! An Anthology of Womanist/Feminist Spirituality*. Vol. 3, edited by Mary Saracino and Mary Beth Moser, 179–208. Bloomington, IN: iUniverse, 2012.

Copiatti, Fabio, and Alberto De Giuli. "'Sfregarsi sulle Pietre Miracolose Cercando Grazie. . .' Gli Scivoli della Fecondità: Usanza Femminile di Origine Preistorica." In *Domina et Madonna: la figura femminile tra Ossola e Lago Maggiore, dall'antichità all'Ottocento*, 21–36. Mergozzo: Antiquarium Mergozzo, 1997.

Cordier, Umberto. *Guida ai Luoghi Misteriosi d'Italia*. Cassale Monferrato: Edizione Piemme Spa, 1997.

Cristiani, Emanuela, Annaluisa Pedrotti, and Stefano Gialanella. "Tradition and Innovation between the Mesolithic and Early Neolithic in the Adige Valley (Northeast Italy): New Data from a Functional and Residue Analyses of Trapezes from Gabin Rockshelter." *Documenta Praehistorica* (Department of Archaeology, Faculty of Arts, University of Ljubljana, Slovenia) 36 (2009): 191–204. arheologija.ff.uni-lj.si/documenta/pdf36/36_12.pdf.

Dashu, Max. "Grandmother Stones," 2011. www.suppressedhistories.net/catalog/granmastones.html.

Davidson, Hilda Ellis. *Roles of the Northern Goddess*. London: Routledge, 1998.

Demetz, Stefan. *South Tyrol Museum of Archaeology: The Guide*. Bolzano: Folio Verlag, 1998.

Di Gesaro, Pinuccia. *I Giochi delle Streghe*. Bolzano: Praxis 3, 1995.

Fabbro, Claudio. *I Mòcheni: Ritorno nella velle incantata*. Trento: Pubilux, 2003.

French, Claire. "Danu, Raetia, Marisa: Mountain Goddess of the Alps." In *Goddesses in World Culture*, Vol. 2, edited by Patricia Monaghan, 281–93. Santa Barbara, CA: Praeger, 2011.

Gimbutas, Marija. *The Civilization of the Goddess: The World of Old Europe*. New York: Harper Collins, 1991.

———. *The Language of the Goddess: Unearthing the Hidden Symbols of Western Civilization*. London: Thames & Hudson, 2001.

———. *The Living Goddesses*. Edited by Miriam Robbins Dexter. Berkeley: University of California Press, 2001.

Ginzburg, Carlo. *Ecstasies: Deciphering the Witches' Sabbath*. Translated by Raymond Rosenthal. New York: Penguin Books, 1991.

Gorfer, Aldo. *Le Valli del Trentino: Trentino Orientale*. Calliano: Manfrini, 1986.

Gremmo, Roberto. *Le Grandi Pietre Magiche: Residui di paganesimo nella religiosita popolare alpina*. Biella: Storia Ribelle, 2009.

Hageneder, Fred. *Yew: A History*. Gloucestershire: Sutton Publishing Limited, 2007.

Hartungen, Christoph. "Rhaetians and Romans." In *Insight Guides: South Tyrol*, edited by Joachim Chwaszeza, 31–38. London: APA Publications, 1992.

Hays-Gilpin, Kelley A. *Ambiguous Images: Gender and Rock Art*. Walnut Creek, CA: AltaMira Press, 2004.

Höck, Anton, and Wolfgang Sölder. *Culti nella preistoria delle Alpi: Le offerte, i santuari, i riti*. Bolzano: Folio Editore and Museo Archeologico dell'Alto Adige, 1999.

James, Van. *Ancient Sites of Hawai'i: Archaeological Places of Interest on the Big Island*. Honolulu: Mutual Publishing, 2005.

Kelly, Mary B. *Goddess Embroideries of the Balkan Lands and the Greek Islands*. McLean, NY: StudioBooks, 1999.

———. *Goddess Embroideries of the Northlands*. Hilton Head Island, SC: StudioBooks, 2007.

Kenny, Erin. *A Naturalist's Journal*. Vashon Island, WA: KotaPress, 2003.

Lanzinger, Michele, Franco Marzatico, and Annaluisa Pedrotti, eds. *Storia del Trentino*. Vol. I, *La preistoria e la protostoria*. Bologna: Il Mulino, 2001.

McGowan, Charlotte. *Ceremonial Fertility Sites in Southern California*. San Diego, CA: San Diego Museum of Man, 1982.

Meador, Betty De Shong, ed. *Inanna, Lady of Largest Heart: Poems of the Sumerian High Priestess Enheduanna*. Austin: University of Texas Press, 2000.

Metzner, Ralph. *The Well of Remembrance: Rediscovering the Earth Wisdom Myths of Northern Europe*. Boston: Shambhala, 2001.

Monfosco, Gari. *Dolomiti: Storie e Leggende* [Dolomites: stories and legends]. Bassano del Grappa: Ghedina & Tassotti Editori, 1987.

Moser, Mary Beth. "The Everyday Spirituality of Women in the Italian Alps: A Trentino American Woman's Search for Spiritual Agency, Folk Wisdom, and Ancestral Values." PhD diss., California Institute of Integral Studies, 2013. ProQuest (3560748).

Motz, Lotte. "The Winter Goddess: Percht, Holda, and Related Figures." *Folklore*, 95, no. 2 (1984): 151–66.

———. *The Beauty and the Hag: Female Figures of Germanic Faith and Myth*. Vienna: Fassbaender, 1993.

Priuli, Ausilio. *Preistoria: l'arte e la sua evoluzione*. Brescia: Museo d'Arte e Vita Preistorica, 1982.

———. "La Donna nella Preistoria: ruolo ed immagini." In *Domina et Madonna: la figura femminile tra Ossola e Lago Maggiore, dall'antichità all'Ottocento*, 11–18. Mergozzo: Oca Blu, 1997.

———. *Valcamonica: Valley of Prehistory*. Capo di Ponte: Museo Didattico d'Arte e Vita Preistorica, 2002.

Rossi, Filli, and Lucia Miazzo. *La dea sconosciuta e la barca solare: Una placchetta votiva dal santuario protostorico di Breno in Valle Camonica*. Milano: Edizione ET, 2005.

Sansoni, Umberto, Silvana Gavaldo, and Cristina Gastaldi. *Simboli sulla Roccia: L'arte Rupestre della Valtellina Centrale dale Armi del Bronzo ai Segni Cristiani*. Archivi Vol. 12. Capo di Ponte: Edizione del Centro, 1999.

Superintendent of Archaeological Goods of Lombardy. *The Sanctuary of Minerva Archaeological Park: Valle Camonica, Breno (Brescia)*. Breno: Ministero per i bene e le attività culturali, 2007. (Pamphlet from author's private collection.)

Toth, Alfred, and Linus Brunner. "Raetic: An Extinct Semitic language in Central Europe," 2007. The Association for Hungarian Art, Literature, and Science in The Netherlands, *Mike's International* (website). www.federatio.org/mi_bibl/Toth_Brunner_Raetic.pdf.

Wolff, Carl Felix. *The Pale Mountains: Folk Tales from the Dolomites.* Translated by Francesca la Monte. New York: Minton, Balch, 1927.

Zanzotto, Andrea. "The Euganean Hills." *Interdisciplinary Studies in Literature and Environment*, 12, no. 1 (2005): 139–45.

Zucca, Michela, ed. *Matriarchy and the Mountains 3, Convention Proceedings—December 1999.* Report 23. Trento: Centro di Ecologia Alpina, 2000.

Endnotes

1   Emanuela Cristiani, Annaluisa Pedrotti, and Stefano Gialanella, "Tradition and Innovation between the Mesolithic and Early Neolithic in the Adige Valley (Northeast Italy): New Data from a Functional and Residue Analyses of Trapezes from Gabin Rockshelter," *Documenta Praehistorica* (Department of Archaeology, Faculty of Arts, University of Ljubljana, Slovenia) 36 (2009): 192, arheologija.ff.uni-lj.si/documenta/pdf36/36_12.pdf. Specific dates cited are from the Mesolithic (7500 calibrated BCE) throughout the Neolithic and Middle Bronze Age (1600 calibrated BCE).

2   Michele Lanzinger, Franco Marzatico, and Annaluisa Pedrotti, eds., *Storia del Trentino*, vol. I, *La preistoria e la protostoria* (Bologna: Il Mulino, 2001), 140.

3   Cristiani, Pedrotti, and Gialanella, "Tradition and Innovation," 193.

4   Marija Gimbutas, *The Language of the Goddess: Unearthing the Hidden Symbols of Western Civilization* (London: Thames & Hudson, 2001), 103.

5   Lanzinger, Marzatico, and Pedrotti, , *La preistoria*, 138 (my translation).

6   Marija Gimbutas, *The Civilization of the Goddess: The World of Old Europe* (New York: Harper Collins, 1991), 223.

7   Gimbutas, *Language*, 102.

8   Lotte Motz, *The Beauty and the Hag: Female Figures of Germanic Faith and Myth* (Vienna: Fassbaender, 1993), 22.

9   Gimbutas, *Language*, 102–103.

10   Lanzinger, Marzatico, and Pedrotti, *La preistoria*, 60.

11   Fred Hageneder, *Yew: A History* (Gloucestershire: Sutton Publishing Limited, 2007), 167–70.

12   See Ausilio Priuli, *Valcamonica: Valley of Prehistory* (Capo di Ponte, Italy: Museo Didattico d'Arte e Vita Preistorica, 2002), 16, for progression of flora and fauna over time.

13   Comuni-Italiani.it, "Stemmi Comuni Prov. di Trento," 2012, www.comuni-italiani.it/022/stemmi.html.

14   Erin Kenny notes the nitrogen-fixing attribute of red alder, *Alnus rubra*, in the northwest United States. See Kenny, *A Naturalist's Journal* (Vashon Island, WA: KotaPress, 2003), 24.

15   In dialect this word is *la scudela*. After he crafted the bowl, he applied bee's wax and rubbed it with a wool cloth to protect it.

16   Valgerður Hjördís Bjarnadóttir, *The Saga of Vanadís, Völva and Valkyrja: Images of the Divine from the Memory of an Icelandic Woman* (Cologne, Germany: Lambert, 2008), 211.

17   Giovanna Borzaga, *Leggende dei Castelli del Trentino* (Calliano, Italy: Manfrini Editori, 1998), 145–46.

18   Cristiani, Pedrotti, and Gialanella, "Tradition and Innovation," 193.

19   Betty De Shong Meador, ed., *Inanna, Lady of Largest Heart: Poems of the Sumerian High Priestess Enheduanna* (Austin: University of Texas Press, 2000), 12–13.

20   Autonomous Province of Trento Department of Emigration, *Voices of Trentino Poetry*, "The Homeland" Monograph Series (Trento, Italy: Casa Editrice Panorama, 1988), 126–27.

21   Comuni-Italiani.it, "Stemma Comune di Ziano di Fiemme," 2012, www.comuni-italiani.it/022/226/stemma.html.

22   Francesco Bonomi, *Dizionario Etimologico Online*, 2008, "Search: Venerdi," lines 3–5, www.etimo.it/?term=venerdi.

23   Ralph Metzner, *Well of Remembrance: Rediscovering the Earth Wisdom Myths of Northern Europe* (Boston: Shambhala, 2001), 154.

24   Carl Felix Wolff, *The Pale Mountains: Folk Tales from the Dolomites*, trans. Francesca la Monte (New York: Minton, Balch, 1927), 83.

25   Lanzinger, Marzatico, and Pedrotti, *La preistoria*, 137.

26   Folk stories are discussed in detail in my dissertation: Mary Beth Moser, "The Everyday Spirituality of Women in the Italian Alps: A Trentino American

Woman's Search for Spiritual Agency, Folk Wisdom, and Ancestral Values" (PhD diss., California Institute of Integral Studies, 2013; ProQuest 3560748).

27 Emmanuel Anati, *Studi Camuni*, vol. 13, *Valcamonica Rock Art: A New History for Europe*, trans. Thomas King and Jason Claiborne (Capo di Ponte: Edizioni del Centro, 1994), 47–50, 54.

28 Ibid., 27.

29 Ibid., 11.

30 Ibid., 167–68.

31 Ibid., 27.

32 Ibid., 78.

33 Ibid., 196.

34 Priuli, *Valcamonica: Valley of Prehistory*, 66.

35 Ibid., 38. See Lanzinger, Marzatico, and Pedrotti, *La preistoria*, 547, for a map of the distribution of inscriptions in the north-Etruscan alphabet in the Alps, including the alphabet of Sanzeno, the alphabet of Magré, and the alphabet of Sondrio-Valcamonica.

36 Franco Gaudiano, Valcamonica resident tour guide and author of novels about the region, lecture at Vashon Island King County Library, Vashon, WA, August 2010.

37 Anati, *Valcamonica Rock Art*, 103.

38 Anati notes other interpretations that have been proposed, such as a psychological symbol of "self" as well as interpretations in other cultures of the disc symbol as a place, water hole, hut, egg, sun, moon, star, island, or all-seeing eye of God. Ibid., 103.

39 Mary B. Kelly, *Goddess Embroideries of the Balkan Lands and the Greek Islands* (McLean, NY: Studio Books, 1999), xiii.

40 Ibid., 27, 54.

41 Anati, *Valcamonica Rock Art*, 112–13.

42 Ibid., 206.

43 Ibid., 112, fig. 81.

44 Priuli, *Valcamonica: Valley of Prehistory*, 8–9. Priuli uses the word "cupholes."

45 Ibid., 4. They are portrayed in Ausilio Priuli, *Preistoria: l'arte e la sua evoluzione* (Brescia: Museo d'Arte e Vita Preistorica, 1982), 20, fig. 15.

46 Emmanuel Anati, "The Way of Life Recorded in the Rock Art of Valcamonica," *Adoranten*, 2008, Scandinavian Society for Prehistoric Art website, www.ssfpa.se/pdf/2008/anati_adorant08.pdf, 14.

47 Anati, *Valcamonica Rock Art*, 204. This description appears in Anati's Appendix III, "Itinerary for Viewing Camunian Rock Art," compiled by Tiziana Cittadini Gualeni, 195–207.

48 Ausilio Priuli, "La Donna nella Preistoria," in *Domina et Madonna: la figura femminile tra Ossola e Lago Maggiore, dall'antichità all'Ottocento* (Mergozzo: Oca Blu, 1997), 18, fig. 5.

49 See Moser, "The Everyday Spirituality of Women in the Italian Alps." The similarity of the name Naquane to Aquane was pointed out to me by a local guide and author, Franco Gaudiano. Gaudiano, email to author, January 20, 2010.

50 Priuli, *Valcamonica: Valley of Prehistory*, 28.

51 Gaudiano, email to author, January 20, 2010.

52 See Moser, "The Everyday Spirituality of Women in the Italian Alps."

53 Priuli, *Valcamonica: Valley of Prehistory*, 13.

54 Gimbutas, *Civilization of the Goddess*, 222.

55 Gimbutas, *Language*, 322; also Gimbutas, *Civilization of the Goddess*, 432.

56 Mary B. Kelly, *Goddess Embroideries of the Northlands* (Hilton Head Island, SC: StudioBooks, 2007), plate 32.

57 Umberto Sansoni, Silvana Gavaldo, and Cristina Gastaldi, *Simboli sulla Roccia: L'arte Rupestre della Valtellina Centrale dale Armi del Bronzo ai Segni Cristiani*, Archivi vol. 12 (Capo di Ponte: Edizione del Centro, 1999).

58 Ibid., 132; see also 148.

59 Ibid., 132.

60 Ibid., 149.

61 Claudio Fabbro, *I Mòcheni: Ritorno nella velle incantata* (Trento: Pubilux, 2003), 180.

62 In a query regarding the possibility of rock engravings in Valle Camonica made as part of female menstruation rites, Emmanuel Anati, noting the presence of female initiation in the Neolithic, responded that the subject had never been adequately considered, and that further research would be welcome. Emmanuel Anati, in email to author, March 30, 2010.

63 Kelley A. Hays-Gilpin, *Ambiguous Images: Gender and Rock Art* (Walnut Creek, CA: AltaMira Press, 2004), 107–26.

64 Charlotte McGowan, *Ceremonial Fertility Sites in Southern California* (San Diego, CA: San Diego Museum of Man, 1982), 15.

65 Hays-Gilpin, *Ambiguous Images*, 80–81. See Priuli, *Valcamonica: Valley of Prehistory*, 61.

66 Petroglyphs illustrating round piko points are said to represent the navel, the genitals, a woman's birth canal and blood relatives. Van James, *Ancient Sites of Hawai'i: Archaeological Places of Interest on the Big Island* (Honolulu: Mutual Publishing, 2005), 66, 114, 132, 166.

67 Popular knowledge of fertility rocks was confirmed in my presence. At Foppe di Nadro, near the autumnal equinox in September 2009, one of the local women in the group, in response to a question from the guide, knew that the shininess of the rock in a certain place—visibly evident—was from being used as a fertility slide. This was at Rock 1 in Foppe di Nadro on the same rock surface and not far from the Neolithic figure with raised hands and spread legs next to a vulva or solar disk described earlier in this section.

68 Sansoni, Gavaldo, and Gastaldi, *Simboli sulla Roccia*, 132.

69 Ibid., see 163, fig. III.74.

70 Priuli, *Valcamonica: Valley of Prehistory*, 58.

71 Ibid., 59.

72 Fabio Copiatti and Alberto De Giuli, "'Sfregarsi sulle Pietre Miracolose Cercando Grazie...' Gli Scivoli della Fecondità: Usanza Femminile di Origine Preistorica." In *Domina et Madonna: la figura femminile tra Ossola e Lago Maggiore, dall'antichità all'Ottocento*, 21–36 (Mergozzo: Antiquarium Mergozzo, 1997).

73 Ibid., 28–29.

74 Ibid., 34.

75 Ibid., 34.

76 Anton Höck and Wolfgang Sölder, *Culti nella preistoria delle Alpi: Le offerte, i santuari, i riti* (Bolzano: Folio Editore and Museo Archeologico dell'Alto Adige, 1999), 144.

77 Copiatti and De Giuli, "Sfregarsi," 36.

78 Ibid., 26.

79 Roberto Gremmo, *Le Grandi Pietre Magiche: Residui di paganesimo nella religiosita popolare alpina* (Biella: Storia Ribelle, 2009), 130.

80 For discussion of links among women, sacred rocks and ritual, as well as rocks becoming shelter and places of banishment, see Moser, "The Everyday Spirituality of Women in the Italian Alps."

81 Authors of the *Stone Pages* website define "stele" as monoliths of less than 75 centimeters high, with one face only decorated with a cut-away carving or low-relief sculpture. See Paola Arosio and Diego Meozzi, 2010, *Stone Pages*, Glossary, "Stele," www.stonepages.com/glossary.html.

82 Anati, *Valcamonica Rock Art*, 27.

83 Umberto Cordier, *Guida ai Luoghi Misteriosi d'Italia* (Cassale Monferrato: Edizione Piemme Spa, 1997), 131.

84 Lanzinger, Marzatico, and Pedrotti, *La preistoria*, 218.

85 Anati, "Way of Life," 22.

86 Gimbutas, *Civilization of the Goddess*, 396.

87 Max Dashu, "Grandmother Stones," 2011, www.suppressedhistories.net/catalog/granmastones.html, para. 2.

88 Michela Zucca, ed., *Matriarchy and the Mountains* 3, Convention Proceedings, December 1999, Report 23 (Trento: Centro di Ecologia Alpina, 2000).

89 Lucia Chiavola Birnbaum, *dark mother: african origins and godmothers*. (Lincoln, NE: iUniverse, 2001), 44–47.

90 Christoph Hartungen, "Rhaetians and Romans," in *Insight Guides: South Tyrol*, ed. Joachim Chwaszeza, 31–38 (London: APA Publications, 1992), 31.

91 Stefan Demetz, *South Tyrol Museum of Archaeology: The Guide* (Bolzano: Folio Verlag, 1998), 27.

92 Various spellings in English are used in the literature: Raeti, in Demetz, *South Tyrol Museum*; Rhaeti in Hartungen, "Rhaetians and Romans"; Raetians, on the South Tyrol Museum of Archaeology website, "The Celtic Helmet from Pfatten: The Raetians"; and Rhaetians in the Museo Retico Museum Guide by the Center for Archaeology and Ancient History of Val di Non. In this study, I use "Reti" following the spelling in Lanzinger, Marzatico, and Pedrotti, *La preistoria*, as on p. 484, for example.

93 See Lanzinger, Marzatico, and Pedrotti, *La preistoria*, 486–92, for excerpts of these ancient texts about the Reti. See also I:485 for references to them as wild.

94 South Tyrol Museum of Archaeology, "The Celtic Helmet from Pfatten: The Raetians." The spelling of the name of the goddess, like the area, can include Rhetia, Raetia, Rehtia, and Reitia, the name I have used in this study.

95 Demetz, *South Tyrol Museum*, 27, 28.

96 Ibid., 29.

97 Ibid., 29–31.

98 Lanzinger, Marzatico, and Pedrotti, *La preistoria*, 546.

99 Gimbutas, *Living Goddesses*, 122, 113.

100 This representation, however, differs from the Venetic Goddess Reitia. Lanzinger, Marzatico, and Pedrotti, *La preistoria*, 524, 538.

101 Autonomous Province of Trento Department of Emigration, *800 Years of the Principality of Trento*, "The Homeland" Monograph Series (Trento: Casa Editrice Panorama, 1990), 10.

102 Lanzinger, Marzatico, and Pedrotti, *La preistoria*, 538–39.

103 Kelly, *Goddess Embroideries of the Northlands*, 216.

104 Carlo Ginzburg, *Ecstasies: Deciphering the Witches' Sabbath*, trans. Raymond Rosenthal (New York: Penguin Books, 1991), 104.

105 Demetz, *South Tyrol Museum*, 32.

106 Höck and Sölder, *Culti*, 42.

107 Ibid., 42.

108 Ibid., 42–43.

109 Andrea Zanzotto, "The Euganean Hills." *Interdisciplinary Studies in Literature and Environment* 12, no. 1 (2005): 140.

110 Claire French, "Danu, Raetia, Marisa: Mountain Goddess of the Alps," in *Goddesses in World Culture*, ed. Patricia Monaghan (Santa Barbara, CA: Praeger, 2011), 2:284.

111 Höck and Sölder, *Culti*, 141. The female is portrayed in profile, with a large nose and a large eye. She wears a long gown covered with spirals and a veil on her head that falls below waist level.

112 Lanzinger, Marzatico, and Pedrotti, *La preistoria*, 526. See portrayal of key opening a door in Demetz, *South Tyrol Museum*, 31.

113 Davidson, *Roles of the Northern Goddess*, 34–35, 43, 149.

114   Gimbutas uses the spelling "Rehtia." Gimbutas, *Civilization of the Goddess*, 314.

115   Alfred Toth and Linus Brunner, "Raetic: An Extinct Semitic Language in Central Europe," 2017, The Association for Hungarian Art, Literature, and Science in The Netherlands, *Mike's International* (website), accessed February 13, 2013, www.federatio.org/mi_bibl/Toth_Brunner_Raetic.pdf, 28–29.

116   Superintendent of Archaeological Goods in Lombardy, *The Sanctuary of Minerva Archaeological Park: Valle Camonica, Breno (Brescia)*, "The Archaeological Excavations," Valle Camonica, Breno (Brescia) (Breno: Ministero per i bene e le attività culturali, 2007), pamphlet.

117   Superintendent of Archaeological Goods in Lombardy, *The Sanctuary of Minerva Archaeological Park*, untitled summary section on last, unnumbered page.

118   Superintendent of Archaeological Goods in Lombardy, *The Sanctuary of Minerva Archaeological Park*, "The Site."

119   Superintendent of Archaeological Goods in Lombardy, *The Sanctuary of Minerva Archaeological Park*, "The Archaeological Excavations."

120   Filli Rossi and Lucia Miazzo, *La dea sconosciuta e la barca solare: Una placchetta votiva dal santuario protostorico di Breno in Valle Camonica* (Milano: Edizione ET, 2005), 15–40.

121   Superintendent of Archaeological Goods in Lombardy, *The Sanctuary of Minerva Archaeological Park*, "The Rites," "The Statue of Minerva" and "The Archaeological Excavations."

122   Frances Bernstein, *Classical Living: Reconnecting with the Rituals of Ancient Rome: Myths, Gods, Goddesses, Celebrations, and Rites for Every Month of the Year* (San Francisco: HarperSanFrancisco, 2000), 56.

123   Superintendent of Archaeological Goods in Lombardy, *The Sanctuary of Minerva Archaeological Park*, "The Rites."

124   Gari Monfosco, "Le Anguane del Lago di Lagole," in *Dolomiti: Storie e Leggende* (Bassano del Grappa: Ghedina & Tassotti Editori, 1987), 65–72.

125   Superintendent of Archaeological Goods in Lombardy, *The Sanctuary of Minerva Archaeological Park*, untitled summary section on last, unnumbered page.

126   Ibid.

127   Aldo Gorfer, *Le Valli del Trentino: Trentino Orientale* (Calliano: Manfrini, 1986), 849.

128   Ibid.

129   Busk notes that it was Diana of Antioch. Rachel Harriet Busk, *The Valleys of Tirol* (New York: AMS Press, [1874] 1983), 388.

130   Gorfer, *Le Valli del Trentino*, 850.

131   Ibid., 846.

132   Ibid., 847.

133   Bernstein, *Classical Living,* 151–52.

134   Ibid., 152, 154.

135   Ginzburg, *Ecstasies*, 98.

136   Randy P. Conner, "Of Diana, Witches and Fairies: An Excerpt from 'The Pagan Heart of the West,'" in *She Is Everywhere! An Anthology of Womanist/ Feminist Spirituality*, vol. 3, ed. Mary Saracino and Mary Beth Moser, 179–208 (Bloomington, IN: iUniverse, 2012), 179–208.

137   Pinuccia Di Gesaro, *I Giochi delle Streghe* (Bolzano: Praxis 3, 1995), 8–9.

SEEKING SANCTUARY WITH SAINT BRIGID OF IRELAND: A HARBOR OF SACRED FEMALE DIVINITY

MARGARET LYNN MITCHELL

H onoring the spirit of place of the Boston conference site chosen in 2016 by the Association for the Study of Women and Mythology where I was to present my recent doctoral research on the legacy of Saint Brigid of Ireland, I began with an Internet search of Saint Brigid and Boston and 940,000 entries appeared. Many of these were related to the numerous churches, schools, and charitable organizations named in tribute to her. Honoring the theme of the conference, "Seeking Harbor in our Histories," I proposed a plausible assumption that many within the large immigrant Irish Catholic population of Boston carried a personal connection to Brigid in their hearts as they journeyed from Ireland to America, and that this connection continues to serve as harbor, sanctuary and welcoming beacon of light.

Why is this remarkable woman so beloved? To answer that question, I chose her as the subject of my dissertation several years ago and began my research with what was known about the historic woman/saint. She was born in 453 AD, daughter of a slave mother and tribal chieftain father in rural Ireland. She broke free of the life planned for her and rose to prominence and religious sovereignty as the abbess of a monastery for women and men that she established in 470 AD at a critical crossroads in time that included the melding of indigenous pagan and Celtic beliefs with emerging Christianity. This monastery of learning in Kildare (or Cill Dara, Church of the Oak) became renowned as a sanctuary that fostered hospitality for pilgrims of diverse cultural and spiritual beliefs and promoted gender equality in education. Brigid's leadership style embodied the essence of a welcoming harbor, with guiding principles of safety, acceptance and inclusion.

What are the phenomena associated with Brigid as a symbol of sacred female divinity, whose flame has been rekindled many times throughout history and whose legacy continues to inspire devotion and veneration in modern times? In order to study her life and legacy from both a scholarly and embodied research level, I utilized women's spirituality methodologies of feminist cultural history, archaeomythology, modern matriarchal studies, women's sacred arts and mysteries, folklore and Irish cultural and religious studies.

I journeyed back to Ireland on my own, started at her birthplace site and mapped out a plausible path where Brigid would have walked. I went to her shrines, knelt in her kneeling stones, placed "clooties" (strips of woven cloth with pilgrim supplications) in sacred groves, drank from her holy wells and began to tell her story. My path of investigation and exploration ultimately led to a feminist cultural reconstruction of her life in fifth and sixth century Ireland. I also decided to emphasize the significance of place and geography in the shaping of Brigid's unifying character, and as a factor that I posited had contributed to her remarkable rise to religious authority. Thus, I widened the geographical net to include a discussion of the ancient monuments that lay within reach of her path, and the plausible impact of these prehistoric community sites on her spiritual development. I realized that Brigid's story and lineage were part of a much larger story of ancient African and Indo-European migrations into what is now known as Western Europe.

Near Brigid's birthplace in Faughart, County Louth, a remarkable prehistoric structure still stands (in the middle of a golf course!) known as the Proleek Dolmen. Irish archaeologists state that these dolmens, also known as "cromlechs," are single-chambered portal tombs for the dead, built during the Neolithic period 4000 to 2000 BCE and ending with the start of the Bronze Age.[1] In mythology and local legends, they are also known as Giants' graves, Druids' altars or the beds of Diarmuid and Grainne, fugitive lovers of ancient lore. However, what I theorize is more relevant in Brigid's story is the research of Lucia Chiavola Birnbaum, a feminist cultural historian, who posits that dolmens are indications of a sacred site constructed by migrating cultures of the peoples of ancient Africa worshipping the sacred divine feminine in the form of a dark mother goddess.[2] Birnbaum's research indicates that the roots of these dolmens may reach back to the Paleolithic age when women were the symbol of birth, death and regeneration, and that dolmens, such as those in Sardinia, suggest the birth canal and funeral rituals where the corpse may have been covered in red ochre—symbol of birth, menstruation, and new life.[3] Birnbaum's theories are provocative and controversial, yet I resonated with her feminist cultural perspective as I felt a strong sense of a birth canal or portal as I walked through the Proleek Dolmen on a balmy spring evening with my pregnant niece.

We also noted the hundreds of stones thrown on top of the dolmen, result of an ongoing local legend that promises marriage if you throw a stone up to the top and it remains there instead of rolling off. I later met several local women on my research journey who remembered visiting the dolmen and Brigid's birthplace shrine as a routine stop on their family outings to the beach in the summertime. Brigid was known as a walker, often walking by herself across Ireland to aid the needy and help settle intertribal disputes in her peacemaker role. Is it plausible that Brigid also walked here? At the very least, one can surmise that, based on the fact of her birth near the land in which this ancient and sacred site is situated, the people of her community knew it and the site remained as part of the local community psyche to the present.

Brigid's birthplace shrine in Faughart contains some interesting ancient stones worth exploring for their possible connection to earlier times associated with a culture that honored sacred female divinity. The setting is splendid with a cascading stream down a prominent mountainside amid a grove of sheltering trees, reminiscent of descriptions about Celtic worship sites. A modern-day chapel has been built here, along with many statues of Brigid resembling Mary, the mother of Jesus; faucets for gathering holy water; and a large hedge filled with pilgrim's prayers left for Brigid such as tied ribbons, holy cards, family pictures, baby booties and coins. It is a moving and welcoming site, filled with hopes and dreams, and a palpable sense of devotion to Brigid. When I arrived at the site, I was both startled and welcomed by the loud chiming electronic bells emanating from the chapel for the daily Angelese, the six o'clock evening call to prayer in Ireland.

The stones of Brigid's Faughart shrine are still included in specific ritual instruction in contemporary pilgrim manuals, such as instructions to say the Our Father, Hail Mary and Creed at the Hoof-Marked, Knee, and Waist Stones, respectively, followed by ten circuits around the Eye Stone (Cloch na Suile) while reciting one decade of the rosary.[4] I find this present-day blending of native local tradition, perhaps of ancient origin or Celtic tribal origins, with modern ecclesiastical traditions to be quite remarkable.

The Eye Stone riveted my attention the most for its remarkable similarity to inscriptions and ancient art still visible on so many other prehistoric structures surrounding Brigid's path in Ireland, most notably those of Newgrange, Knowth and Dowth in the Boyne Valley. The archaeomythologist Marija Gimbutas posits the following:

> [T]he large eyes with which the Goddess is portrayed strongly suggest the epithet "all-seeing" for her. However, the symbolism which surrounds the eyes speaks to an even more fundamental attribute, namely that the eyes, like the goddess's mouth or breasts, are a divine source.[5]

Gimbutas also provides archaeomythological evidence for a further delineation of the goddess's eyes into associations with the owl, the snake and the sun. Gimbutas theorizes that the compound rendering of the occuli motif with a radiating sun motif was first composed of eyes and vulva, as an abstract rendering of the goddess. She states that "suns as radiant divine eyes are also encountered on the megaliths of the tomb-shrines in Ireland usually associated with dot-in-circles, concentric circles, and brush marks,"[6] with the brush/comb symbol signifying regenerative power.

The symbolism of the snake and the sun are most certainly associated with Brigid as Goddess and historical figure, and in the reenactment of contemporary rituals in her honor. Her February 1 Feast Day marks the return of the sun for spring planting and the following chant is noted in several sources to be spoken on this day, often while beating the ground with an effigy of a serpent or a cloth bag filled with burning coals: "Today is the day of Bride, The serpent shall come from the hole, I will not molest the serpent, Nor will the serpent molest me."[7]

The abundance of the Eye Goddess motif, whether representative of snake or sun or both, among the prehistoric monuments on Brigid's path is striking. I have walked among the prehistoric megaliths of Newgrange, Knowth, and Dowth, in the sacred Boyne Valley several times in the past thirty years with these ancient eyes staring at me. I used the coiled-snake triple spiral of the inner chamber at Newgrange, still illuminated yearly by the winter solstice sunrise, on my business cards for my first acupuncture practice in the 1980s as a symbol of healing and regeneration. Now I envision Brigid gathering strength for her life of service and healing as she journeyed through and past the watchful gaze of these ancient stones.

Another extremely significant element emerges from the actual construction of these ancient structures from circa 3200 BCE, in that they all appear to be in the shape of a woman. The large mounds themselves are certainly reflective of a woman's breast or symbolic of the regenerative and life-giving force inherent in a women's pregnant belly. Gimbutas and others claim that they were built to reflect the shape of the Mother Goddess herself as actual representations of the standing or seated goddess.

> The interior structures of many Irish Neolithic "court tombs" of the 4th millennium BCE are outlined in a clearly anthropomorphic form. In addition to the large oval abdomen (pregnant belly?) and head, some have legs and even eyes... [T]he court marks the inner contour of the anthropomorphic figure's open legs; the chambers or a corridor-like structure next to it leading into the very center of the mound is the vagina and uterus.[8]

The artist and scholar Cristina Biaggi also comments extensively on the female body shape evident in the Neolithic temples of Malta and Gozo in the Mediterranean, whose ancient peoples were connected, by sea or land migration, to the same culture that built the Neolithic structures on the Orkney and Shetland islands of Scotland, and then possibly in Ireland.[9] As we journey southwest away from the Boyne Valley toward Kildare, the site of Brigid's monastic center, we discover several Bronze and Iron Age fortresses that appear to have been built on top of ancient Neolithic sites. The archaeologist Michael Dames refers to one such site, Almu, which has been excavated, and he alludes to the possibility of the structure itself as a representative of a Mother Goddess, or at the very least, an honoring of the life-giving force of the sacred divine female shape.[10]

Almu is also referred to as Dun Ailinne or the Hill of Allen, subject of the poem written in the tenth century to honor Brigid's Christianized conquering of the ancient ways (and Celtic intertribal strife). When I journeyed from the Boyne Valley to the site of her original monastery in

Kildare, I climbed a seventh-century Viking round tower on the grounds of St. Brigid's Cathedral, and was able to see the Hill of Allen from the top window. While in Kildare I visited the Brigidine Sisters of the Solas Bhride[11] community on the occasion of a visit to Brigid's sacred sites by the Dalai Lama, who was also there to receive an award from the sisters for his work toward peace and justice in our world. One of the items given to him was a freshly woven Brigid's Cross (Cros Brighe), which I was also blessed to receive from the sisters a few days earlier.

I was delighted to see a picture of the Dalai Lama holding up this cross splashed across the front page of the *Irish Times* the next day in the Dublin airport as I prepared for my flight home. At that sacred moment, I felt this startling front-page picture symbolized a unique blending of Eastern and Western religious beliefs, perhaps a hopeful portent of a more unified world for the future. Personally, this moment was reflective of my own spiritual journey, as I recover the promise of my childhood Irish Catholic heritage through my scholarly research and personal experiences with Brigid as both goddess and saint, and merge this resurrection with my adult life immersed in healing and studying Eastern medicine and philosophy. Brigid herself was credited with serving an important role in the merging of Christian and pagan Celtic beliefs in the fifth century, and helping to forge a more unified Ireland. The far reaches of her dynamic spinning cross continue to symbolize unity and renewal across centuries of time.

This participation in ritual and connection with groups and individuals dedicated to honoring Brigid's legacy as part of their mission in life, such as the abovementioned Brigidine Sisters of Solas Bhride, formed the core of my embodied research. I interviewed individuals utilizing Brigid's symbols as contemporary spiritual touchstones in rituals of healing, personal connection, and empowerment. I discovered three primary symbols most associated with these rituals: the Cros Brighe (Brigid's Cross); the Crios Brighe (Brigid's Sacred Belt/Girdle); and the Bhrat Bhride (Brigid's Sacred Cloak). I then explored possible vestiges within these symbols indicative of ancient cultures expressing worship of sacred female divinity.

The Cros Brighe is perhaps the most frequently seen symbol associated with Brigid today. The cross appears in many forms, the most common of which is plaited from fresh springtime rushes around a solid central core that ultimately emerges as a square with four radiating spokes tied off by string or another piece of rush. It is generally displayed on its side and thus resembles a spinning or turning movement, which has been associated with the spinning wheel, the turning and honoring of the seasons in the Celtic calendar, the harvesting of grain for community sustenance, and as a plausible symbolic connection with an ancient lineage of rituals honoring the grain and sun goddesses brought to Ireland by indigenous Indo-European and Old European civilizations.

In my research, Brigid's Cross is the most frequently cited symbol associated with an individual's connection to Brigid, especially for those born in Ireland who learned to weave the cross in grammar school on St. Brigid's Feast Day. I have seen this symbol worn as a necklace by Irish and Irish-American women, in both silver and gold, as a type of talisman of protection and as a symbol of devotion to Brigid. I have most frequently seen this symbol hanging next to or above the front door of an Irish home, shop or barn, or an Irish American household, often renewed or replaced every year on her feast day. I associate this placement of her cross as possibly related to one of her birth legends, in which her mother gave birth on a door threshold. Over time this legend has evolved to symbolize Brigid's capacity to be the guardian of the threshold and one to call upon for comfort and aid in times of transition.

Another important, though less common, ritual associated with Brigid involves the weaving of a type of straw belt or girdle, the Crios Brighe, which is brought to the household on Brigid's Feast Day. Then family members are encouraged to walk through the plaited circle of straw and thus guaranteed protection by Brigid for the coming year. From the western shores of Ireland, Barbara Callan speaks eloquently of her first experience with Brigid's Girdle while participating in a government-sponsored heritage project in Connemara in 1990. Callan exclaims, "So it was for me that my first sight of the Crios Bride ritual by a Renvyle hearth was an unexpected, heart-stopping moment, and in stepping through that circle of straw I began a journey to my spiritual homeland."[12]

In 1995, Irish poet Seamus Heaney received the Nobel Prize in Literature and in the following year a collection of his poems to date was published in *The Spirit Level*.[13] One of the poems is simply titled, "St. Brigid's Girdle," and the ode appears to be written to a friend in distress as Heaney weaves his words of comfort and support using the memory and tradition of the protective plaited circle evoked by Brigid's Girdle. Heaney was born in 1939 in Northern Ireland at Mossbawn, which is situated about thirty miles northwest of Belfast and directly due north of Brigid's birthplace at Faughart. I believe that the depth of his knowledge of the tradition of Brigid's Girdle, and the healing power evoked by the use of this ritual, imply understanding and reverence. I also feel the poem speaks eloquently by itself to validate the importance of Brigid's continuing presence in the Irish psyche, even across the war-torn and politically imposed north and south borders of Ireland that Heaney would have lived with during his lifetime.

In my search for ancient vestiges of this ritual in goddess-worshipping cultures of Old Europe, I also focused on the importance of the weaving itself and the protective aspects of the ritual. Spinning and weaving, connecting and creating, gathering and strengthening fibers and threads and creating community in the process—all of these are attributes credited to women's sacred work in the world for thousands of years, whose evidence we see incised and displayed on goddess figurines throughout Old Europe since Paleolithic times. Elizabeth Wayland Barber speaks of a bone carving of a goddess figurine found at Lespugue, France, circa 20,000 BCE that displays a woman wearing "a skirt made of twisted strings suspended from a hip band, possibly associated with childbirth."[14]

Gimbutas displays numerous photographs and drawings of goddess figurine relics indicating the importance of what she refers to as "hip-belts," which she categorizes as a reflection of ritual costume and ornamentation that may have fringe or incisions with net or ladder motifs such as those seen on figurines from western Ukraine and a Vinca mound in Yugoslavia, circa 5000 BCE.[15] These net motifs, associated with chevrons in Gimbutas's other writings, are believed to be indicative of weaving and symbolic of the expressed language of the goddess in those ancient times. It is interesting to note that these net motifs also appear on several kerbstones of Newgrange. Gimbutas further elaborates on the chevron motif as reflective of the art of spinning and weaving as evidenced by its inscriptions on Neolithic and Copper Age spindle whorls and comments on the following specific reference to Brigid.

> Twisting, spinning, weaving, and sewing are common to the Greek Athena, Roman Minerva, and the goddesses still alive in European folk beliefs: the Basque Andrea Mari, Irish St. Brigit, Baltic Laima, East Slavic Mokosh/

Paraskeva-Pyatnitsa ("Friday"), and Romania Sfinta
Vineri ("St. Friday"). People would perform no work
which involved turning, twisting, or spinning on Friday,
the special day of the Goddess. Any twisting was tabu on
that day in honor of St. Brigit in Ireland.[16]

The scholar Pamela Berger offers us another important insight into
the ancient vestiges associated with this girdle ritual contained within the
actual linguistics of Imbolc, the feast day on February 1 associated with
St. Brigid and with the start of spring in the Celtic calendar. She states that
in Old Irish the prefix *im-* means around or about and *bolc* or *bolg* means
belly. Berger questions whether this word also reflects an ancient ritual
of going around an arable field (as symbolic belly of the mother goddess)
before tilling and sowing.[17]

The third major ritual symbol associated with Brigid is the Bhrat Bride
(Brigid's Cloak). We first encounter the importance of this symbol in the
legends and supernatural mythology that arose during the centuries after
her death. There are several versions of this story, but the unifying principle
is that Brigid asked the territorial leader for land upon which to build her
monastery of education and religious training for women and men, and the
response was that she would be given as much land as the cloak that she
was wearing could cover. Upon hearing this, she removed her cloak, laid
it upon the ground and it miraculously grew to cover the entire *curragh*
(plains) of midland Ireland, an area still renowned for its rich pastureland.

Some legends speak of four other women (priestesses or nuns?) stretch-
ing the cloak in the four directions, which appears to have contributed to its
magical properties. Was this in fact indicative of co-opting Celtic beliefs
into the Christian domain at the time to lend further credence to Brigid's
religious power? I believe that the inclusion of the four other women in this
legend is symbolic of the power of women working together for a common
goal to provide abundance for all. I feel this legend represents the very
best of women's spiritual leadership—we see a need and we stretch our
resources to manifest the solution!

Many components of this legend live on today and the Bhrat Bhride
remains symbolic of protection, nourishment, abundance and manifestation. It is used in contemporary rituals honoring Brigid on February 1
when a cloth is placed outside the threshold on the eve of the holiday after

sundown and retrieved before sunrise when it is wet with dew or frost. The cloth is considered to have been visited by Brigid herself during the night and it becomes a cloth of healing for use throughout the year. In another form of the ritual, the cloth is cut into strips that are then placed in key positions in the home or barn, or carried on one's person for protection.[18]

Patricia Monaghan referred to her participation in this ritual and a blue cloth that she carried with her as follows:

> I have never felt more Irish than I did that night. I felt an atavistic sense of blood connection, an awareness that I was celebrating in ways that had been part of my heritage for generations and generations. I felt as though my body were temporary, almost illusory, existing only to trace ancient sunwise paths around a holy place.[19]

Mary Condren has been leading rituals and celebrations honoring Brigid in Ireland and abroad for the past two decades. In a 2015 posting on a Goddess Scholars mailing list, she states:

> Very suggestive connections exist between the cloak of creation and the regenerative fluids of the earth, specifically, the early morning dew. In fact, throughout world religions, the "dew of mercy" is one of the most ancient metaphors associated with female divinities. In Scotland, the druids considered dew to be the most precious of all forms of water.[20]

Condren specifically refers to a legend of Brigid healing a disabled sister and blind brother by pouring the morning dew upon them as indicated in a hagiography of saints. Condren further states that in many cultures, female divinities shelter humankind under their mantles, and in ancient texts mantles were used to hide enemies from one another, and that wearing the cloak signified tribal identity and one's relationship through the maternal line. Condren believes the cloak is an inclusive, ecumenical and non–gender-divisive symbol, and that "when you put your precious cloth on the ground, remember that you are doing so to collect the dew of mercy, to celebrate our common origins in the great womb of the earth, and to resist the sacrificial fires and theologies that abject women and our bodies."[21] I believe Brigid is still inspiring us all to wear her sacred mantle and stretch her sacred cloak to manifest our dreams and heal our world.

One year after presenting this paper at the 2018 Association for the Study of Women & Mythology conference, I moved to Ireland permanently where I continue to be delighted at the flourishing of Brigid's presence throughout the island. Rituals surrounding her February Feast Day are increasingly active in many communities, most notably the weaving of the Brigid Cross, and visits to her holy wells to ask for blessings, cures and protection for the coming year. I was delighted to be invited to join a group of local women to weave the crosses in spring 2019. Over an afternoon of lunch, tea, wine and chat, we wove nearly 100 crosses from a table piled high with freshly cut rushes from the surrounding fields. Our surpluses were placed in the back of the local church for others to freely take, and they were gone the first day.

I was surprised by the active use of the Brideog ritual at one of her shrines in Lahinch, County Clare, in which an effigy in made with wheat or straw and adorned with colorful fabrics, shells, buttons or ribbons by local schoolchildren and women in the community. Some were carried or attached to placards and processed to the local church and placed on the altar for a celebratory mass. A friend sent pictures of this event to me, and I was amazed to see the elaborate dedication and pride evident, along with a large plaited Crios Brighe placed in the center. My youngest son recently pointed out that Brigid's cross is displayed prominently on the sports jerseys of the men's hurling team from the county of Brigid's birthplace (Louth). The Solas Bhride community has grown from a small sanctuary to a large hermitage center with visitors from all over the world and year-long festivities, all done in Brigid's honor. I am thrilled to continue my research into Brigid's veneration while living in Ireland!

Saint Brigid of Ireland was a strong, powerful, and engaging female spiritual leader whose legacy continues to grow. Through the mists of time, her sustainable flame after 1,500 years continues to burn brighter than ever, and the healing waters of her holy wells flow deeper, as her legacy is experiencing an enormous revitalization. Perhaps this revitalization is occurring in response to the proliferation of hatred, injustice and despair experienced by so many in her world today. Brigid offers us a blueprint for embracing rich and poor; for unifying political, spiritual and cultural differences; for educational equality; and for creating a life overflowing with generosity, compassion and abundance for all. Brigid's legacy compels us to return to the wisdom of sacred divine female leadership now, in this present moment.

References

Barber, Elizabeth Wayland. *Women's Work, the First 20,000 Years: Women, Cloth and Society in Early Times*. New York: W.W. Norton, 1994.

Berger, Pamela. *The Goddess Obscured: Transformation of the Grain Protectress from Goddess to Saint*. Boston: Beacon Press, 1985.

Biaggi, Cristina. *Habitations of the Goddess*. Manchester, CT: Knowledge, Ideas & Trends, 1994.

Birnbaum, Lucia Chiavola. *Dark Mother: African Origins and Godmother*. Lincoln, NE: Authors Choice Press, 2001.

———. *The Future Has an Ancient Heart*. Bloomington, IN: iUniverse, 2012.

Callan, Barbara. "In Search of Crios Bride." In *Irish Spirit: Pagan, Celtic, Christian*, Global, edited by Patricia Monaghan, 134–40. Dublin: Wolfhound Press, 2001.

Condren, Mary. *The Serpent and the Goddess: Women, Religion and Power in Celtic Ireland*. Dublin: New Island Books, [1989] 2002.

Dames, Michael. *Mythic Ireland*. London: Thames and Hudson, 1992.

Gimbutas, Marija. *The Goddesses and Gods of Old Europe, 6500–3500 BC: Myths and Cult Images*. Berkeley: University of California Press, 1982.

———. *The Language of the Goddess*. San Francisco: Harper & Row, 1989.

Heaney, Seamus. *The Spirit Level*. New York: Farrar Straus Giroux, 1996.

McNally, Kenneth. *Standing Stones and Other Monuments of Early Ireland*. Belfast: Appletree Press, 1984.

Minehan, Rita. *Rekindling the Flame: A Pilgrimage in the Footsteps of Brigid of Kildare*. Kildare: Solas Bhride Community, 1999.

Monaghan, Patricia. *The Red-Haired Girl from the Bog: The Landscape of Celtic Myth and Spirit*. Novato, CA: New World Library, 2003.

O'Duinn, Sean. *The Rites of Brigid: Goddess and Saint*. Dublin: Columba Press, 2005.

Endnotes

1 Kenneth McNally, *Standing Stones and Other Monuments of Early Ireland* (Belfast: Appletree Press, 1984), 14.

2 Lucia Chiavola Birnbaum, *Dark Mother: African Origins and Godmother* (Lincoln, NE: Authors Choice Press, 2001).

3 Birnbaum, *The Future Has an Ancient Heart* (Bloomington, IN: iUniverse, 2012), 113.

4 Sean O'Duinn, *The Rites of Brigid: Goddess and Saint* (Dublin: Columba Press, 2005), 169–72.

5 Marija Gimbutas, *The Language of the Goddess* (San Francisco: Harper & Row, 1989), 51.

6 Ibid., 56.

7 Mary Condren, *The Serpent and the Goddess: Women, Religion and Power in Celtic Ireland* (Dublin: New Island Books, [1989] 2002), 58.

8 Gimbutas, *Language of the Goddess*, 154.

9 Cristina Biaggi, *Habitations of the Goddess* (Manchester, CT: Knowledge, Ideas & Trends, 1994).

10 Michael Dames, *Mythic Ireland* (London: Thames and Hudson, 1992), 228.

11 See Rita Minehan, *Rekindling the Flame: A Pilgrimage in the Footsteps of Brigid of Kildare* (Kildare: Solas Bhride Community, 1999).

12 Barbara Callan, "In Search of Crios Bride," in *Irish Spirit: Pagan, Celtic, Christian,* Global, ed. Patricia Monaghan, 134–40 (Dublin: Wolfhound Press, 2001).

13 Seamus Heaney, *The Spirit Level* (New York: Farrar Straus Giroux, 1996).

14 Elizabeth Wayland Barber, *Women's Work, the First 20,000 Years: Women, Cloth and Society in Early Times* (New York: W.W. Norton, 1994), 44.

15 Marija Gimbutas, *The Goddesses and Gods of Old Europe, 6500–3500 BC: Myths and Cult Images* (Berkeley: University of California Press, 1982), 44–56.

16 Gimbutas, *Language of the Goddess*, 67–68.

17 Pamela Berger, *The Goddess Obscured: Transformation of the Grain Protectress from Goddess to Saint* (Boston: Beacon Press, 1985), 71.

18 O'Duinn, *Rites of Brigid*, 136–44.

19   Patricia Monaghan, *The Red-Haired Girl from the Bog: The Landscape of Celtic Myth and Spirit* (Novato, CA: New World Library, 2003), 162.

20   Mara Lynn Keller, California Institute of Integral Studies, email message to author containing following posting on private Internet forum: Mary Condren, "Brigit's Dew Soaked Cloak of Mercy," 2015.

21   Ibid.

THE SYMBOLIC ROLE OF STRING

Kristen K. Calvert

String

*Long connective tissue
From a woman's celestial body.
Threading the needle through
and back out again
Into the future.
Tying, piercing into wholeness,
Almost formless, then long, supple and strong.
Length and expansion in forward body motion,
Connecting to tree, person . . . spirit.
Weaving thought into form,
Spinning the web ad infinitum
down the red thread matrix line.*

—Author's original poem

Spider Biomimicry and Creative Application

The invention of string is one of the most ancient and formative of technologies in shaping human culture. Try to imagine a world without string; it is almost impossible to do. It is all around us, inherent even in our own bodies, within our muscles and our DNA. The production of string and textiles allowed primitive humans to create their own portable shelters, protect their bodies from the elements, and produce baskets-bags-nets for the basic necessities of life. String technology produced a freedom that allowed humans to survive and thrive.

First, how was string possibly invented? It is difficult to estimate when exactly string was initially used because, as a fiber, it disintegrated over time. Evidence exists only as fossilized impressions, carvings and drawings of string, as well as tools used to create textiles such as needles. In nature, string is produced naturally as in animal sinew, plants are held together with long strings of interconnecting fibers and spiders produce string internally spinning it into webs. There were many factors, but from myths it is evident that women observed spiders spinning webs and called on their own ingenuity to imitate them. The art of spinning and weaving was created by humans observing nature. This is now known as biomimicry and is how many of our ancestresses learned about their environment.

In the examination of sacred myths, there are several references of women learning some of the textile arts from spiders. One of the best known in Native American mythology is how Spider Woman first taught her people how to weave. She was mythologized because she could create what the spider could.[1] The function and form of the spiders' webs could have even appeared as supernatural. Consider how magical a web can appear, especially after a misty rain—a gossamer, silver spiral glistening in the sun with mirror-like jewel raindrops. Even after the spider abandons its web, something it had created from its body continues on to inspire future observers. Learning from the spider, women also created something with their bodies to manipulate their environment for optimal survival, which was functional, tactile and beautiful—string.

String: The Birth of the String Skirt

Women in particular must have felt a kinship with the spider because its seat of power and creation is in the lower half of its body. This is true for women as well with regard to their capacity to give birth and access root wisdom. The concept of string not only comes from nature but women's bodies. Picture the umbilical cord which is in essence a long connective string uniting mother and baby. Elizabeth Barber speculates that string skirts were created to draw attention to women's private areas and suggest the woman was of childbearing age (see Fig. 16).[2] This concept is substantiated by the tradition that in some cultures the making of and giving of skirts marked specific biological functions in a woman's life such as menstruation. For example, a Kabyle (Berber tribe) mother would ceremoniously bestow a new red girdle upon her daughter's first menstruation.[3] The linking of menstruation with the string skirt is very significant. Judy Grahn's book *Blood, Bread and Roses* details how menstruation was instrumental in shaping culture. For example, Grahn claims that the passage of time was originally recognized and counted through a menstruating woman, as the cycle has a beginning, middle, end and re-beginning. This cyclical process is similar to the phases of the moon. "She marked a definitive, externally visible, unit of time, the month (*moon*th) as synchronized with the human body."[4] String, being highly connected to a woman's body and cycles, also took on this role as a practical time function. String, and textiles in general, are tactile pieces of information that could be shared. An example of this function of information transference located on string comes from the Incas of Peru. Knotted string or *khipu qiipu* was used to represent the passage of time, numbers and record complex coded messages.[5]

Fig. 16. Neolithic string skirt, drawing by Rita Hillman, 2019.

Functional and symbolic, the string skirt recalled a woman's capacity to create life, not only biological life, but also a technology to enhance and sustain life, and quoting Barber thus began the "the string revolution." The prestige that women gained from this association was enhanced by wearing the strings around her hips because this tied her to her biological capacity to create life for which the feminine was already revered. To visually connect these two aspects would have made a strong symbolic statement.

String Skirts: Death and Regeneration

String skirts were as significant and valued in the passage of death as they were in celebrating life. The evidence lies in the fact that women and men were sometimes buried in their string skirts. Even in Africa today among the Kuba culture, this acknowledgement of the capacity to create and transform life is symbolically represented on the body at death. When dressed for a burial, both men and women are covered with a red-dyed raffia skirt.[6]

Cloth in general plays a significant role in funerals and accessing spirits of the deceased. In the Sakalava culture in Madagascar, cloth wrapped around the lower half of the body is viewed as a gateway to the spirit world and the identifier in the afterlife of common ancestry. A shaman will wrap a person suffering a serious illness in a specific cloth of a royal ancestor to call upon that ancestor's assistance in healing. Through the textile the ancestor will recognize the person as a relative and be willing to offer assistance.[7]

This form of recognition from the spirit world through textiles is also prevalent among the Hmong (originally from Southeast Asia). Some of the Hmong believe the spirits identify the recently deceased through the "flower cloth" created by the Hmong women. The female ancestor, —such as the mother or grandmother who was already in the spirit world, —"upon seeing the recently deceased person in the spirit world wearing a textile she had sewn, would acknowledged the wearer as kin."[8] To better understand this relationship of string in concert with death and deceased ancestors, a Hmong string birthing ritual is described in the next section.

String, birth and ancestor regeneration

Death is partially interwoven with string because birth in some cultures signifies rebirth. Among the Hmong, when a child is born, the soul of an ancestor is reincarnated as well. String is representative of this role of regeneration, as well as evidenced by the Hmong birth and naming string rituals. String is used to mark both the birth of the new baby and the subsequent rebirth of an ancestor. According to Symonds, a newborn's umbilical cord is tied with two pieces of string and then a white cord and red cord are tied around the baby's neck. The white cord "ties in" the two souls now in the child's body. The red cord protects the child during the first three days of life, before the baby's naming ceremony in which the ancestor who has returned is recognized.[9] At the ceremony, the child, its family and attendants all have red threads secured on them, and the visitors bond with the baby by attaching red threads around the infant's wrist to welcome the baby and reclaim the returning ancestor.[10]

The additional responsibility of ancestor regeneration through birth makes a woman's role doubly significant but can also cause her birthing capacities and sexuality to be conceived of as something almost intimidating. Such a belief is evidenced by the significance placed on the wearing of a femaled *osev*, two apron-like pieces that hang from a girl's belt in front and in the back. Some traditional Hmong even hold the belief that it would be "dangerous for women to go without *sev*—dangerous for them and men, too.[11]

Although girls wear the *sev* to cover genitalia with additional protective material, *sev* are also on special occasions the most decorative piece of clothing worn to accentuate the lower extremities of the body. Similar to the string skirt, the *sev* is a matter of pride for Hmong women who take great care with its embroidery using infinitesimal detail. The *sev* serves as an outward expression of the woman's artistic self. A *sev* that is embroidered for special occasions can sometimes take up to a year to complete, and features an array of flower cloth designs.[12] It is a showpiece that demonstrates the creator's/wearer's prowess with textiles.

For Hmong woman, this display of the *sev* is another extension of the string skirt whence a woman's ingenuity, artistic talents and biology are symbolically linked. These associations are also present in another form of textile art, the art of weaving. The weaving process demonstrates how a woman's birthing capacities and the ability to form cloth are intertwined. Also, with weaving, it is evident how a woman's power to form life correlates with the life-giving forces of nature.

Weaving as Divine: Transformations with Nature

Women's weaving achieves mythic stature through divine inspiration from the environment. The generative, connective powers present

in nature are symbolically enacted by the weaver as the string is transformed; the weaver becomes the symbolic performer of nature's birthing
processes. For instance, some Mayan women weave on a backstrap (hip
tension) loom that is wrapped around the waist. Paola Gianturco, who
interviewed and photographed Mayan weavers, states that the women
"speak of cloth as being 'born on the loom.'"[13] According to modern
Mayan weaver Benita Yaqui, when she weaves, as in birthing, she is
physically creating from her womb center[14] Furthermore, Jules Cashford
argues that the synchronicity found among weaving, birth and the continuity of life is logical:

> The connection between the weaving on the loom, and the
> pattern, and the span of life may have one source—in the
> fact that spinning and weaving were the work of women
> who, as mothers, also spun the tissue of their children out
> of the loom of their bodies.[15]

This biological explanation could explain why a symbiotic relationship
between textile formation and women is prevalent in many cultures.

In some instances, weaving is tied not only to human birth but also
the creative forces of nature. Beverly Gordon noted that with some
backstrap weaving, women transform string through the assistance of
the local trees. In this form of weaving, the other end of the loom is
normally tied to a tree or an upright post.[16] With the trees supporting in
the physical birthing of the weavings, a woman's loom takes on a mythic
and ritualistic role, as she gives birth to her string creation through
nature's assistance. According to Gordon, the cord that attaches the
weaving from the women's waist to this "mother" tree is known as the
"umbilical cord."[17] The woman and a part of her natural environment
unite to give birth to the cloth.

Also, among the Kabyle the women treat the creation of a textile as
they do the birth of their own children. Makilam writes:

> [L]ike a child, the textile will be removed with cere-
> mony, then shaken in order to reveal its true appearance,
> hidden until now. All these gestures are similar to those
> that Kabyle women perform when they give birth, plac-
> ing a child on the earth. As in birth, the weaver must

say: "*May I continue living in order to begin again,*"
and then wish for its owner to be granted the resistance
of the earth.[18]

However, this "birthing process" extends beyond the scope of human
birth into the birth of the cosmos and the parallel solar forces of the sun
and moon. The rollers of a loom that a Kabyle woman weaves with are
known as the upper sun roller and the lower moon roller. While weaving,
the weaver is continually intertwining these cosmic bodies.[19] The weaving
takes on a cosmological association with the loom, becoming a simulacrum
for the heavens.

> In her lap, the Kabyle woman weaves the woof of the
> threads round the upper solar roller, unraveling it by pull-
> ing it towards her. She horizontally unites the strands of
> the vertical warp threads that link the sun to the moon by
> garnishing them with wool. Through this act of weaving,
> the moon and sun have magically descended from the sky
> into the terrestrial world in order to clothe humans.[20]

Composing in this manner, weaving and looms transform string by joining
heaven, earth, moon, sun, *ying* and *yang* together.

This idea of ritualistically weaving together the forces of nature is also
present in the Navajo, or Diné, tradition as the loom becomes a magical
instrument containing or uniting the natural elements. According to Diné
mythology, Spider Woman taught weaving as a sacred process of stringing
together the sky and the earth. Gary Witherspoon writes:

> [T]he loom of Spider Woman represents the Navajo uni-
> verse in microcosm and in metaphor. The act of weaving
> on Spider Woman's loom made of earth and sky cords, sun
> rays and halos of the sun, lightning in zigzags, flashes, and
> sheets, and rain steamers and precious jewels, the Navajo
> weaver unites the Sky Father with the Earth Mother, and
> this interwoven union brings together all the cosmic forces
> associated with fertility, fecundity, beauty, and power.[21]

With this mythic, symbolic stature of the loom the woman is like the spider recreating the web of life—threading together the strings or nature's cosmic umbilical cords into connective balance.

Birthing the Self: How the Process Shapes the Weaver

By connecting with Spider Woman, the weaver not only enacts nature's creation processes but also learns how to relate to the world. Spider Woman was also called "Thinking Woman" and was a principal in forming the world through her own thoughts.[22] From the Diné perspective, weaving with Spider Woman's teachings in mind helps to inform the weaver's life views. Contemporary Diné weaver Irene Clark says of weaving: "When you're doing your designing, the process makes you think, and it teaches you... Our designs are our thinking."[23]

Spider Woman has several symbols and instructions that can help shape the weaver's mind. For example, in weaving Spider Woman's cross, the weaver becomes more acutely aware of the four directions and "Spider Woman's hole," which sometimes remains in the center reminding the weaver of the significance of the void or space. This opening was originally left as a tribute to Spider Woman. According to Gerald Hausman's account of the Diné,

> [I]n acknowledgement of their debt to Spider Woman, one
> of the Holy People of Navajo mythology, Navajo weavers
> always left a hole in the center of each blanket, like that
> of a spider's web, until the traders in the early part of this
> century refused to buy such blankets.[24]

Then instead of leaving the "spirit hole," weavers began to leave a "spirit line"—a woven thread that created a pathway from the inner part of the weaving to the edge.[25]

> Thus, the spirit outlet usually took the form of a thin line
> made from the center of the blanket to the edge. It also
> served, as Navajo Dine weavers believed[,] as a prevention
> for "blanket sickness" or "cobwebs in the brain" as they
> thought that Spider Woman, to whom the tribute of a spider

hole has been denied, would spin webs in the head of the weaver if the spirit outlet is omitted.[26]

Contemporary Navajo weavers give us a glimpse into what these "cobwebs" may be. They say that the line reminds the weaver not to have strict borders or to get caught up in mind patterns, but instead to make a spirit line and opening for the next creation.[27] This act of the weaver demonstrates how the Dine acknowledge how closely connected the weavers' mentality was and is affected by not only the physical act of weaving but its inherent symbolism. The line today is still also intimately joined with the spiritual origins of weaving and can be emblematic of the weavers' outlook on life.

Weaver Irene Clark takes the sentiment of the spirit line to another level, stating that in some of her weavings instead of having a spirit line she opts for no borders. She equates the lack of borders in her weaving with the receptivity and expansiveness she feels in herself speaking about her creations and spirit being limitless: "The spirit line is what we are talking about—the way out... My weaving is borderless, it is all open. My spirits are open."[28] Even without the symbolic spirit line, the act of weaving can be a meditative process accessing the body's wisdom through a repetitive motion while relating with the Divine.

For indigenous Mayan Guatemalan women, weaving also takes on a spiritual status, partly because weaving is connected to the Divine in nature, and weaving is extended to nature/creation goddesses who in Mayan myths were weavers. In certain Mayan myths, the moon is said to be the creator of weaving.

> It used to be that yarn was made the same way as we make children now. The women made it themselves with the strength of their flesh. When the world began, they say the moon climbed a tree. There she was weaving and spinning, up there in the tree. You should weave, she told the first mothers. You should spin, she said. She taught them to weave from up there. That was the origin of weaving... The moon left us her *huipil* when she left. She left her loom and her machete.[29]

The significance of this indicates as how the moon is typically associated with women's cycles and menstruation, in particular. Comparing what research shows regarding the invention of weaving in conjunction with the moon cycles, there is a clear correlation between the female body and the conception of textiles. The natural functions of a woman's body along with nature served as an impetus for weaving. This connection with a woman's cycles was later transferred to goddesses associated with the moon, childbirth and weaving. For example, Ix Chel is the Mayan goddess of the moon, water, weaving, childbirth and destruction/rebirth; like Spider Woman, Ix Chel was also referred to as a mythical spider, Ix Kanleon, the spider's web that catches the dew.[30]

I created a painting several years ago depicting Ix Chel with her red thread flowing to the Virgin of Guadalupe. It is not a coincidence that the Virgin of Guadalupe mythically appeared on a *tilma* or woven cloak. This *tilma* speaks to the symbolic significance of cloth in connection with the Divine and was built on a long line of women and spirituality being associated with string in the rituals and mythologies of Mesoamerica.

Contemporary Mayan weaver Pedro Meza says that "the goddesses created weaving. They were the first teachers of the art. In dreams, they reveal our duties."[31] Some contemporary Christian weavers have extended this insight to the Virgin Mary and call upon her for inspiration. Similarly, the Chamula indigenous people view the Virgin of the Rosary and St. Rose as benefactors:

> They were the first ones to weave, and it was they who
> taught the craft to the Chamulas. The women often dream
> that either St. Rose or the Virgin is explaining how to
> embroider a special design.[32]

Thus, the designs for the weavings are believed to be channeled from the Feminine Divine. Furthermore, in some instances when wearing the textile one created (traditionally a woman would wear the *huipil* or tunic she had woven), one embodies this spiritual lineage. De Orellana cites Walter Morris, a leading authority on indigenous Chiapas Mayan clothing and custom:

> A *huipil* is a symbolic universe. When a Mayan woman puts
> her head through the neck hole, she emerges as the center
> of the world. The world's drawings radiate from her head
> and extend down the blouse's sleeves and across the bodice

to form an open cross with the woman at the center. This is
where the supernatural meets the ordinary. In the center of
a world woven from dreams and myths, the woman stands
between the sky-cosmos and the underworld.[33]

Using this allegory, the creation and wearing of the textile is analogous to
creating and wearing a symbolic conception of the universe. The representation is understandable because the mythological originators of the textile,
such as Spider Woman and Ix Chel, assisted in forming the world. Such a
mythological legacy is also present in the weavings, which connects the
creator/wearer to the Divine.

Embodying the Feminine Divine

In some instances, a woman could be said to embody a particular goddess's specific abilities by simply wearing similar iconography on her skirt.
In pre-Columbian times in the Americas and in other cultures women would
wear symbols or skirts that were analogous to images various goddesses
would wear. According to art historian Cecelia Klein, in the Aztec pantheon many goddesses were simply labeled by the skirts they wore. The
Goddess Citlalinicue's name is translated as Her Skirt Is Stars (Star-Her-
Skirt), which refers to Her connection to the Milky Way.[34] Furthermore,
when a woman was wearing Citlalinicue's skirt/apron, she was said to
embody some of the Goddess's powers. Klein states that "regardless of
who wore it, the back apron apparently referred to in 'shorthand' fashion,
Citlalinicue and her generative powers during the darkness of creation."[35]
Garbed in this fashion, Aztec women were essentially investing their body
with the power of the goddess.

This desire to embody the goddess through textiles could have dark
connotations when the symbol became more important than the flesh-
and-blood woman. A horrific example of such disregard for living women
was evident in an Aztec ritual. Once a year, they held a festival to honor
Xochiquetzal—Precious Feather Flower—one of the Aztec goddesses associated with weaving and childbirth. During this festival, a woman would
spin, embodying Xochiquetzal. Eventually, the spinner would be killed and
flayed so that an Aztec priest could wear the skin of the woman and "sit at
a loom to impersonate the Goddess."[36] Take a moment to really "feel" this
story in your body and touch your own skin. Feel the knowledge of not

only the killing, but having such a strong connection between a woman's body and spinning string that a supposed priest had to physically put on her skin to convey this symbolic connection. Even then, the "priest" could not fully embody her power because it was only skin deep. He could not possess the internal connections or the ancient symbolic ties; he could only mimic her identification with the divine. But the power that he hoped to claim is innate in all women.

All women are women of the web—interconnected because of their biological and symbolic history. These threads go back ancestress after ancestress to that first woman who looked at the spider weaving its web—weaving its destiny—and felt a kinship knowing she could do the same. These ancestresses' legacy must be remembered, and their indigenous wisdom that some contemporary textile artists use must be more fully acknowledged and brought into the mainstream. Ultimately, this knowledge will assist more women in accessing the collective, connective capacities and wisdom of their ancestresses—the connectors between life and death, weavers of the present and future, and conduits to the Divine. Through a deeper association with the symbolism inherent in string, women may gain a richer understanding of their bodies, their history and their synergetic relationship with nature. And with this deep-seated awareness, women may more fully access the inner spiritual spiral of their soul, their deep symbolic memory, their body memory and thus their very own DNA strands ("strings").

References

Arthurson, Wayne. *Spirit Animals: The Wisdom of Nature.* Alberta: Eschia Books, Inc., 2012.

Barber, Elizabeth Wayland. *Women's Work: The First 20,000 Years.* New York: W.W. Norton & Co., 1996.

Cashford, Jules. *The Moon: Myth and Image.* New York: Four Walls Eight Windows, 2002.

Darish, Patricia. "Dressing for the Next Life: Raffia Textile Production and Use among the Kuba of Zaire." In *Cloth and Human Experience*, edited by Annette Weiner and Jane Schneider, 117–40. Washington, DC: Smithsonian Institution Press, 1989.

Feeley-Harnik, Julian. "Cloth and the Creation of Ancestors in Madagascar." In *Cloth and Human Experience*, edited by Annette Weiner and Jane Schneider, 73–116. Washington, DC: Smithsonian Institution Press, 1989.

Gianturco, Paola, and Toby Tuttle. *In Her Hands: Craftswomen Changing the World*. Brooklyn: Power House Books, 2000.

Gibson, Clare. *Symbols of the Goddess*. Glasgow: Saraband Publishing, 2004.

Gordon, Beverly. *Textiles: The Whole Story*. London: Thames and Hudson, 2011.

Grahn, Judy. *Blood, Bread and Roses: How Menstruation Created the World*. Boston: Beacon Press, 1993.

Hausman, Gerald. *The Gift of the Gila Monster: Navajo Ceremonial Tales*. New York: Simon and Schuster, Touchstone Books, 1993.

Jimenez Lopez, Lexa. "How the Moon Taught Us to Weave." In *The Arts and Crafts of Mexico*, edited by Margarita de Orellana and Alberto Ruy-Sanchez. Washington, DC: Smithsonian Books, 2004.

Klein, Cecelia. "The Devil in the Skirt: An Iconographic Inquiry into the Pre-Hispanic Nature of the Tzitizimime." *Ancient Mesoamerica* 11, no. 1 (2000): 1–26.

Makilam. *Symbols and Magic in the Arts of Kabyle Women*. Translated by Elizabeth Corp. New York: Peter Lang Publishing, 2007.

McEwan, Colin. *Ancient American Art in Detail*. Cambridge: Harvard University Press, 2009.

McLerran, Jennifer, and Kennedy Museum of Art. *Weaving Is Life: Navajo Weavings from the Edwin L. and Ruth E. Kennedy Southwest Native American Collection*. Athens: Kennedy Museum of Art, Ohio University, 2006.

Symonds, Patricia. *Calling in the Soul: Gender and the Cycle of Life in a Hmong Village*. Seattle: University of Washington Press, 2002.

Witherspoon, Gary. "Cultural Motifs in Navajo Weaving." In *North American Indian Anthropology Essays on Society and Culture*, edited by Raymond J. Demallie and Alfonso Ortiz, 355–76. Norman: University of Oklahoma Press, 1994.

Endnotes

1   Wayne Arthurson, *Spirit Animals: The Wisdom of Nature* (Alberta: Eschia Books, Inc., 2012), 176.

2   Elizabeth Wayland Barber, *Women's Work: The First 20,000 Years* (New York: W.W. Norton & Co, 1996), 59, 60.

3   Makilam, *Symbols and Magic in the Arts of Kabyle Women*, trans. Elizabeth Corp (New York: Peter Lang Publishing, 2007), 99.

4   Judy Grahn, *Blood, Bread and Roses: How Menstruation Created the World* (Boston: Beacon Press, 1993), 155.

5 Colin McEwan, *Ancient American Art in Detail* (Cambridge, MA: Harvard University Press, 2009), 70.

6 Patricia Darish, "Dressing for the Next Life: Raffia Textile Production and Use among the Kuba of Zaire," in *Cloth and Human Experience*, ed. Annette Weiner and Jane Schneider (Washington, DC: Smithsonian Institution Press, 1989), 137.

7 Julian Feeley-Harnik, "Cloth and the Creation of Ancestors in Madagascar," in *Cloth and Human Experience*, ed. Annette Weiner and Jane Schneider (Washington, DC: Smithsonian Institution Press, 1989), 87–88.

8 Patricia Symonds, *Calling in the Soul: Gender and the Cycle of Life in a Hmong Village* (Seattle: University of Washington Press, 2002), 50.

9 Ibid., 79.

10 Ibid., 90–91.

11 Ibid., 51.

12 Ibid., 50.

13 Paola Gianturco and Toby Tuttle, *In Her Hands: Craftswomen Changing the World* (Brooklyn: Power House Books, 2000), 30.

14 Ibid., 38–39.

15 Jules Cashford, *The Moon: Myth and Image* (New York: Four Wall Eight Windows, 2002), 158.

16 Beverly Gordon, *Textiles: The Whole Story* (London: Thames and Hudson, 2011).

17 Ibid.

18 Makilam, *Symbols and Magic*, 37.

19 Ibid., 36.

20 Ibid.

21 Gary Witherspoon, "Cultural Motifs in Navajo Weaving," in *North American Indian Anthropology Essays on Society and Culture*, ed. Raymond J. Demallie and Alfonso Ortiz (Norman: University of Oklahoma, 1994), 356.

22 Ibid.

23 Jennifer McLerran and Kennedy Museum of Art, *Weaving Is Life: Navajo Weavings from the Edwin L. and Ruth E. Kennedy Southwest Native American Collection* (Athens: Kennedy Museum of Art, Ohio University, 2006), 9–10.

24 Gerald Hausman, *The Gift of the Gila Monster: Navajo Ceremonial Tales* (New York: Simon and Schuster, Touchstone Books, 1993), 32.

25 Ibid., 34.

26 Ibid.

27 Ibid.

28 McLerran and Kennedy Museum of Art, *Weaving Is Life*, 67.

29 Lexa Jimenez Lopez, "How the Moon Taught Us to Weave," in *Arts and Crafts of Mexico*, ed. Margarita de Orellana and Alberto Ruy-Sanchez (Washington, DC: Smithsonian Books, 2004), 192.

30 Cashford, *The Moon*, 115.

31 Jimenez Lopez, "How the Moon Taught Us to Weave," 209.

32 Ibid., 210.

33 Ibid., 59.

34 Cecelia F. Klein, "The Devil and the Skirt: An Iconographic Inquiry into the Pre-Hispanic Nature of the Tzitzimime," *Ancient Mesoamerica* 11, no. 1 (2000): 16.

35 Ibid.

36 Clare Gibson, *Symbols of the Goddess* (Glasgow: Saraband Publishing, 2004), 94.

WHAT'S PLACE GOT TO DO WITH IT? A NON-INDIGENOUS WOMAN'S SEARCH FOR PLACE WISDOM

BARBARA DAUGHTER

This paper considers whether non-Indigenous people can find a connection to a specific place or land, as it also reflects on how to honor the Indigenous peoples who originate from places that resonate with the Great Mystery, which non-native individuals may also experience. In the Dakota language, their connection to this planet is evidenced through their name for her: *Ina Makoce*, which denotes "Mother Earth, or the land that claims you, that speaks your language."[1] "The land that claims you" conveys a reciprocal relationship, even a sense of human beings belonging to the land, instead of the reverse.

In contrast, I cannot ever remember hearing a non-Indigenous US citizen refer to any local region as their "homeland." What ground, then, can non-Indigenous peoples consider their homeland? Whether or not we feel a relationship to the area we call "home," what happens when we, as non-Indigenous people, venture away from there and encounter a place that calls to us? For example, what are the implications when I, as a woman of white privilege, feel a deep, spiritual, personal connection with the Goddess Pele, when exploring land that Hawai'ians hold sacred? Is there a way to honor their *āina*, while not negating my bond?

In order for me to address ideas about place wisdom, I need to situate my sharing. I will do so within the context of the places from where I come, this place where I stand today, as well as where I feel a deep connection, a kind of belonging.

I would like to begin by describing the landscapes of my childhood, so you may have a perspective on where I come from, which certainly informs where I am currently situated. Although I do not remember it, I am told that as a toddler, climbing hills at Arnold Arboretum near my first home, I would pick up rocks along the way, stuffing my pockets to overflowing so that by the time I reached the top, my pants would be falling down. I have continued to pick up rocks and stones along the many paths I have traveled.

During my childhood years, I remember climbing the boulders behind my suburban home, before they were dynamited to build an interstate immediately behind our property line. Before that modern, six-lane divided highway severed this landscape, we gathered blueberries on steamy August afternoons, filling up brown paper grocery bag upon bag. Spring brought bright yellow forsythia blooms; summer lawns provided us with tasty discoveries like tart wild sorrel, bitter dandelion, and tough plantain with its flower spike we tried to strip of all of its seeds. In the fall, we pondered the edibility of acorns and the red berries on the ubiquitous yew bushes planted by earnest parents. Winter brought snow so wet that simply scooping it up in our mittened hands resulted in a snowball.

When we ventured outside this groomed, yet not entirely tamed, environ—bounded by a swampy pond edged with skunk[2] cabbage or a rocky pasture from which cows occasionally wandered into our backyards, causing us to wake our parents on a sleepy Saturday morning and nervously ask whether cows ate dogs—we were blessed with even more beauty. When camping, we splashed in a cool mountain stream in the shallow riffles, or during a day at the shore, we waded out, chest deep, where we bounced endlessly in cadence with the warm ocean's rolling waves, our bodies memorizing that rhythm so as we drifted off to sleep it caressed and carried us still.

On drives to visit my grandparents, I could always see the Great Blue Hills in the distance and we occasionally hiked them. These Blue Hills, outside of Boston, were home to the Native Americans calling themselves "Massachusett" or "people of the great hills," who had lived there for over 10,000 years before the Puritans' arrival.[3] The peoples indigenous to what we now call eastern Massachusetts had been decimated—their populations reduced by 75 percent—by what has been described as either yellow fever[4] or smallpox epidemics in 1617–1619 and again in 1633.[5] The Massachusett, the Neponset, the Shawmut, the Patuxet, and the Wampanoag people all suffered similarly.[6] In fact, in 1620, Plimoth Plantation was founded on the abandoned fields and lands of a Patuxet village.[7]

At the foot of the Blue Hills flows the Neponset River, whose head-waters are in my hometown of Foxborough, Massachusetts. Dammed in the 1840s to become the Neponset Reservoir, it provided a source of water for local industries.[8] The Neponset River was also named for a group from the Massachusett tribe, who used the river as a primary source of trans-port within this watershed all the way to the Boston Harbor. Now, years later, after over twenty years of pollution with cadmium and phosphates by The Foxborough Company, the Neponset Reservoir has been declared a Superfund Site.[9]

The native tribes were heavily proselytized by the English Puritans, who sought to Christianize them. Because the Neponset community was so fragmented and isolated as a result of the epidemics that left fewer than a thousand people alive, they sought to establish a "Praying Town."[10] In 1657, the Dorchester Company deeded to the Neponset lands known as Ponkapoag.[11] In winter, our favorite place to toboggan[12] nearby was the Ponkapoag Golf Course, named for those 6,000 acres deeded to the Neponset, a miniscule portion of their original habitat. Within decades of deeding the land to them, self-appointed guardians for the area known as Ponkapoag began selling the land, and within two centuries, it was entirely subsumed within the municipality of Canton, Massachusetts.[13] Both these facts and these people were hidden from my view as a child. Moreover, despite fond memories and connections to these places, none of these are my ancestral homelands. Is this land sacred?

What of *this* land then, this small parcel up a steep bank from a pond near the cranberry bogs, where my ancestors did celebrate, and mourn? Those tall pines stood watch as my great-great uncle, in his seventies, built that modest summer cottage, with a pump out back and a pot-bellied stove to heat the kettle and take the chill off the early mornings. Here his wife's sister's eight children, their grandchildren, great-grandchildren, and even great-great grandchildren have come to gather, eat, swim, argue, laugh, plant, share, pray, fish, celebrate, console, and play with each other and with ever-widening circles of friends. However, many, many generations before them, the Wampanoag peoples lived in this area—those who had not been decimated by introduced diseases since before the Mayflower's arrival. This is the closest to an ancestral home I will ever know, a place of my ancestors' memories as well as my own. Is this land sacred?

The Dakota peoples, before the influx of European settlers and colonists, inhabited the land I called my home for nearly 35 years, which today we call Minnesota. In tribute, the name "Minnesota" has its roots in three Dakota words, "*Mni*" and "*Sota*," which reference what is now called the Minnesota River, signifying "sky-tinted water,"[14] and "*Makoce*," referring to the land in this area. Other sources indicate the phrase *Mni Sota* meant that the river reflected whatever the sky looked like; thus "sky tinted" did not necessarily mean "sky blue."[15] Indeed, many place names throughout this state, and on this continent, have their roots in the panoply of Native American/First Nations languages' evocative descriptions.

In addition to the Dakota peoples who lived here, the Anishinaabe people, also called the Ojibwe, dwelled in this vicinity. The word "Mississippi," the river with its pristine headwaters farther north in this state, is derived from an Ojibwe name meaning "great river."[16] Today, these are the two largest groups of Indigenous peoples in Minnesota, and I acknowledge their ongoing presence and struggles against the dominant cultural ways from which I benefit.

In their traditional stories, the Anishinaabek recount their peoples' journeying from eastern areas of this continent, and guided by their prophecies, finding seven places to re-establish their communities. As seen in maps included in Edward Benton-Banai's *The Mishomis Book: The Voice of the Ojibway*,[17] the last of these places was Mooningwanekaaning-minis, or Madeline Island, in Lake Superior off the coast of Wisconsin.[18]

In the early 1990s, I was invited with other white women to sit in circle as part of a group ceremony on Madeline Island, where a channeler evoked past-life memories:

> I was in that circle, dozens and dozens of lifetimes ago—or in another manner of thinking about it—I am in that circle right now. The drone of the drumbeat entranced me, as my feet traced the steps 'round and 'round our sacred hoop. I dreamt this day—today—this time of our yearning and desperate need, this cry from our planet, our Mother Earth. I dreamt where I would stand, how I would feel, whom I would love. But not what I would do.

Is there a reverential way to experience sacred places to which I have no ancestral connection? Although I have no Greek ancestry, in 2012 I was drawn to join Carol Christ on her Goddess Pilgrimage to Crete. There, at one of the archaeological sites of Minoan Crete, I felt a sense of familiarity, almost as though I were at home, despite being in an unfamiliar land. Christ has written and spoken movingly about her experience many years before at Kato Zakros.[19] Although I would not describe my encounter as transcendent, as she did, I felt in my body (or imagined) the coziness of sleeping there, as though I could have easily spent the night under the stars there on a rock palette. Is this land sacred?

Near the end of the nineteenth century, my great-grandmother immigrated with her sister to the United States from Visby, Gotland, Sweden. One of the folk sayings passed down to me from my maternal grandmother, always spoken in English, but delivered with a sing-song lilt—and used to describe those circumstances when the item you'd been searching for was right in front of you—was "If it were a snake, it'd bite ya." Of all the expressions handed down from my mother's side of the family, this is the only one I can remember said in this way. Furthermore, it was not until I lived in Minnesota, and heard the Scandinavian-accented speech of some rural citizens that I recognized the source of the lilt in my family's phrase.

Traveling to my ancestral land, I explored the Baltic Sea island with its unfamiliar landscapes, finding on one side, fields of blueweed, which locals described as "blue fire." On the northern coast, I marveled at surreal paleo-sea-stacks or *raukurs*, which look like remnants from a prehistoric era. Included within Gotland's collection of over 400 picture stones, one of their oldest has an enigmatic figure—her pose seems an amalgam of the Snake Goddess of Crete and the Sheela-na-gigs of Ireland—she holds a snake in each of her outstretched hands. Was my great-grandmother's adage somehow embedded with a reference to these snakes, depicted over 1,500 years ago? I marveled at this image stone, about three feet tall, and searched further at the Gotlands Museum in Visby for traces of an ancestral culture that revered women. To my chagrin, none of the other stones focused on women exclusively, and most did not image them at all.

Delighted as I was to see this magnificent carving from one of my ancestor's homelands, I felt no urge to bond with the land, to commune with the energy there. Indeed, this island has been populated since the Stone Age, as early as 900 CE. The Goths, thought by some to have Scandinavian origins share their name's root with Gotland.[20] Later, this area was home to the Vikings, who were known to raid and pillage other island nations in the north Atlantic. The town of Visby, a UNESCO World Heritage Site, still boasts remains of the defensive twelfth-century ring wall (*ringmuren*) that for the most part still surrounds it. These people understood the need to defend their lands, as they were clearly familiar with invading those of others.

The first time I had the opportunity to visit Pele, on the island of Hawai'i, the clouds hung low in the sky, an enveloping mist, throughout Volcano National Park. We drove cautiously on the winding roads, seeing only a few feet ahead of us into the fog. Periodically, I would notice a spot to pull over, with a few parking spots and a plaque designating a particular geographic feature. As soon as we steered the car into the rest stop, ever so slightly, the mist would begin to lift. While I read the commemorative inscription or searched for a path into this alien landscape, increasingly, the haze evaporated, or was blown away by an unfelt wind, and before my eyes appeared deep crevasses, completely cloaked moments earlier. At every turn, it seemed, Pele revealed Herself to me. I prepared an offering, something valuable to me, as a thanksgiving and whispered prayers as I cast it into a chasm. At nightfall, we descended 13,000 feet to watch the lava flow just inches away and below our feet. Pele was there, in all her raw beauty and fierce destruction/re-creation.

Also, on the island of Hawai'i, I experienced powerful energies at the Place of Refuge—Puuhonua o Honaunau. Even before arriving, my body seemed aware of the sacredness of t his land, where in ancient times those who had broken *kapu*, or sacred laws, should they be able to reach this hallowed ground, would be absolved of their missteps and welcomed back into the community. Similarly, whenever I traveled to Mooningwanekaaning-minis, I could feel the power of this land; in both places my digestive system seemed to recognize the need to purge in order to be purified and made whole. Can I consider these lands sacred to me?

I believe we cannot know who we are without knowing where we come from, yet this is not enough. To know ourselves through the eyes of the land that raised us, as it were, or in the understanding of the Dakota people "that speaks our language," we need an appreciation for the lives that preceded ours, their cultures and our limitations. We need to learn to become allies, to accept what is offered from others' cultures and respect their boundaries on what cannot be known or shared outside their circle.

Postlude

For the past four years, I have had the privilege of living where the Suisun people are the first known to have called it home, in the north Bay Area of California. As I acclimate to my new home with its unique traits and reflect on the opportunity and privilege I have had to live in and travel to many locales with a diversity of flora and fauna, landscapes and climates, cultures, foods, clothes and spiritual beliefs, I accept all of these lands as sacred. Each place is home to histories and peoples, some of whom are recognized as Indigenous to a specific area. The Massachusett, the Neponset, the Wampanoag, the Ojibwe, the Dakota, the Hawai'ian, the Suisun peoples all experienced land where they lived as sacred. Even the Swedes and Greeks may regard their ancestral homelands as sacred and researching their ancient cultural ways may reveal traces of their own indigeneity.

Living in a region where one has ancestral connections, where one's language describes the landscapes and spirits who inhabit it, where one's family tree may be researched almost entirely at the local cemetery, may give those fortunate enough to experience it a love and reverence unknown to those of us whose ancestors are immigrants. Yet each of us can cultivate a deep connection with the lands on which we live if we acknowledge that every blade of grass, every drop of water belongs, as each of us does, to Mother Earth.

References

Addis, Cameron. "Pre-Columbian America." *History Hub: Textbook for American Surveys.* www.austincc.edu/caddis/nativeamerica (accessed April 2, 2013).

Armstrong, Jeanette C. "En'owkin: Decision-Making as If Sustainability Mattered." In *Ecological Literacy: Educating Our Children for a Sustainable World*, edited by Michael K. Stone and Zenobia Barlow, 11–17. San Francisco: Sierra Club Books, 2005.

———. "Indigenization." TEDx Okanagan College, TEDx Talks video, 17:54. November 1, 2011. www.youtube.com/watch?v=jLOfXsFlb18.

Callahan, Kevin L. "The Ojibway Migration Story." *An Introduction to Ojibway Culture and History.* Accessed April 5, 2013. www.tc.umn.edu/~call0031/ ojibwa.html.

Earth Island Institute. *In the Light of Reverence.* DVD. Directed by Christopher McLeod. Berkeley, CA: Sacred Land Film Project, 2001.

Ehrlich, Gretel. *Islands, the Universe, Home.* New York: Penguin, 1991.

Heath, Richard. "The Converging Cultures of the Neponset River Estuary." *Dorchester Atheneum*, September 25, 2009. Accessed April 16, 2013. www.dorchesteratheneum.org/page.php?id=679.

Intellectual Reserve, Inc. "Indians of Minnesota." *Family Search*, February 7, 2013. Accessed April 1, 2013. familysearch.org/learn/wiki/en/Indians_of_Minnesota.

Lastrealindians and International Native American Memorial. "500 Years Since Ponce de Leon Landed on an Already Civilized Continent." YouTube video, 5:22. April 2, 2013. Accessed April 5, 2013. www.youtube.com/watch?v=C2tztLYi3yQ.

Mashpee Wampanoag Tribe. "Timeline," 2013. Accessed April 15, 2013. mwtribe.exstream.tv/timeline.

Neponset Reservoir Reclamation Committee. "History of the Neponset Reservoir." Neponset Reservoir Foxboro. Accessed April 16, 2013. www.neponsetreservoir.org/index.php/history-of-the-neponset-reservoir.

Neponsett/Ponkapoag Tribe. "History of Tribe." Accessed April 17, 2013. www.neponsett.org/#top.

Ogden Publications. "Using Your Phone to Connect with Urban Nature." *Utne Reader.* March 25, 2013. Accessed April 3, 2013. www.utne.com/arts-culture/using-your-phone-connect-with-urban-nature.aspx.

Rheingold, Howard. *They Have a Word for It: A Lighthearted Lexicon of Untranslatable Words and Phrases.* Louisville, KY: Sarabande Books, 2000.

Roscoe, Will. *Living the Spirit: A Gay American Indian Anthology.* New York: St. Martin's Press, 1988.

Sams, Jamie, and Twylah Nitsch. *Other Council Fires Were Here Before Ours: A Classic Native American Creation Story as Retold by a Seneca Elder and Her Granddaughter.* New York: HarperCollins, 1991.

Tennant, Emma. *A House in Corfu: A Family's Sojourn in Greece.* New York: Henry Holt & Co., 2002.

Endnotes

1 Unsettling Minnesota Collective, "Unsettling Ourselves: Reflections and Resources for Deconstructing Colonial Mentality," Unsettling America, September 2009, accessed April 6, 2013, unsettlingminnesota.files.wordpress. com/2009/11/um_sourcebook_jan10_revision.pdf.

2 In my narrative, I have deliberately included a few of the dozens of words with Indigenous language origins, of which many of us from the dominant culture are completely unaware. "Skunk" is from a Massachusett word for "to urinate" and "fox." Wikipedia Foundation, Inc., "List of English Words from Indigenous Languages of the Americas," *Wikipedia*, April 6, 2013, accessed April 6, 2013, en.wikipedia.org/wiki/ List_of_English_words_from_indigenous_languages_of_the_Americas.

3 Wikipedia Foundation, Inc., "Blue Hills Reservation," *Wikipedia*, March 15, 2013, accessed April 16, 2013, en.wikipedia.org/wiki/Blue_Hills_Reservation.

4 Mashpee Wampanoag Tribe, "Timeline," 2013, accessed April 15, 2013, mwtribe.exstream.tv/timeline.

5 Richard Heath, "The Converging Cultures of the Neponset River Estuary," *Dorchester Atheneum*, September 25, 2009, accessed April 16, 2013, www. dorchesteratheneum.org/page.php?id=679.

6 Ibid.

7 Ibid.

8 Neponset Reservoir Reclamation Committee, "History of the Neponset Reservoir," Neponset Reservoir Foxboro, accessed April 17, 2013, www.neponsetreservoir.org/index.php/history-of-the-neponset-reservoir.

9 Ibid.

10 Heath, "The Converging Cultures."

11 Neponsett/Ponkapoag Tribe, "History of Tribe," accessed April 17, 2013, www.neponsett.org/#top.

12 Wikipedia Foundation, Inc., "List of English Words from Indigenous Languages of the Americas," Toboggan, *Wikipedia*, April 6, 2013, accessed April 16, 2013, en.wikipedia.org/wiki/ List_of_English_words_from_indigenous_languages_of_the_Americas.

13 Neponsett/Ponkapoag Tribe, "History of Tribe."

14 Intellectual Reserve, Inc., "Indians of Minnesota," *Family Search*, February 7, 2013, accessed April 1, 2013, https://familysearch.org/learn/wiki/en/ Indians_of_Minnesota.

15   Wikipedia Foundation, Inc., "Minnesota," *Wikipedia*, March 29, 2013, April 5, 2013, en.wikipedia.org/wiki/Minnesota.

16   Greg Breining, "A Sense of Place: The Legacy of Names," Minnesota Department of Natural Resources, January 2001, accessed April 6, 2013, www. dnr.state.mn.us/volunteer/janfeb01/legacyofnames_sop.html.

17   See maps included in Edward Benton-Banai, *The Mishomis Book: The Voice of the Ojibway*, 2nd ed. (Minneapolis: University of Minnesota Press, 2010), 53.

18   Kevin L. Callahan, "The Ojibway Migration Story," *An Introduction to Ojibway Culture and History*, accessed April 5, 2013, www.tc.umn.edu/~-call0031/ojibwa.html.

19   Carol P. Christ, *Odyssey with the Goddess: A Spiritual Quest in Crete* (New York: Continuum, 1995), 125–28.

20   Wikipedia Foundation, Inc., "Gotland," *Wikipedia*, April 5, 2013, accessed April 5, 2013, en.wikipedia.org/wiki/Gotland.

WILD WOMEN ON THE MOVE: UNDERSTANDING AN ETHIC OF EARTH CARE THROUGH AN ARTEMIS LENS

DENISE MITTEN

W omen have been a part of nature since human speciation. We have lived and journeyed in many different outdoor environments throughout the ages. Even since the incursion of patriarchy many women have continued a rich intertwined relationship with nature that includes travel and adventure. Though in Western cultures, women have not been and are not socially conditioned to be in the wilderness or outdoors, and their presence there is often ignored or questioned. However, many women are drawn to travel, play and adventure in the outdoors.[1] In this paper parallels are drawn between Artemis and these women. Data were obtained through biographies and autobiographies about women who explored and traveled in outdoor environments, research about women's outdoor trips, and over 20 years of the author's observations while leading trips and directing a women's adventure travel organization, Woodswomen, Inc.[2] It could be that women with Artemis traits are drawn to being with nature and/or it could be that time with more-than-human worlds can help women develop Artemis characteristics and the healthy relationship with nature that Artemis lived and embodied. The evidence presented in this paper show that both are probably true.

Women Outdoor Travelers Resonate with Artemis Energies

In the last 200 years there are many contemporary examples of women, such as Isabella Bird Bishop (1831–1904, adventurer, world traveler and writer), Annie Peck (1850–1935, mountaineer, adventurer, world traveler and suffragette), Fanny Bullock Workman (1859–1925, mountaineer, adventurer, world traveler and suffragette), Mina Benson Hubbard (1870–1956, grieving widow, geographer and writer), Georgie Clark White (1910–1992, grieving mother, bicyclist, operator of the first commercial rafting company in the Colorado Canyon), and Gwen Moffat (1925, Army driver, climbing guide, first British woman certified-mountain guide and novelist), who enthusiastically traveled, lived and/or worked in the outdoors. These and many other outdoor women lived embodying some of the archetypal energies of the goddess Artemis summed up by Jean Shinoda Bolen[3] as the indomitable spirit in every woman. These women were their authentic selves when they traveled and interacted with the more-than-human worlds and often developed or understood more about their authenticity through their journeys and interactions. Each of these adventuring women gained and displayed tenacity, competency and courage; they could focus on goals—traits often attributed to the Greek goddess of the hunt, Artemis.

The archetypal energies of the goddess Artemis resonate with women adventurers, who are often curious, self-reliant and in deep relationship with the wilderness or more-than-human worlds. In tune with outer cycles of seasons and inner cycles of dreams, these moon goddess aspects of Artemis are displayed by women living closely with the more-than-human worlds. In writings by women adventurers it seems that they probably thought of the Earth and place as dynamic co-adventurers. They did not seem to seek power over or have a conquering mentality toward the land or local residents of that land. These personal explorations were spiritual as well as physical. Many began their adventures as a way to work with their grief and found the natural environment engaged in co-healing with them. Like Artemis these women ended up with a reverence for nature and more-than-human worlds and showed their passion for being with nature.

As an example, Mina Benson Hubbard, a Canadian, traveled in July 1905 to finish her husband's work in Labrador. Laddie Hubbard had died the year before while on an extended trip to map the George River. Mina primarily wanted to see where he had been, finish his work and complete her grieving process. What she did not expect was to fall in love with the tundra and be enlivened by her experiences with the Naskapi people. One passage in her book, "What do I care of mosquitoes when I am free," illustrates the incredible aliveness and joy she felt during her extended trip in Labrador[4] and the release of her indomitable spirit. At

Ungava Bay, the end of her journey in November 1905, Mina was sad to be leaving the vast outdoors and the peace and freedom she found there. In contrast, Dillon Wallace, the second in command during the trip on which Laddie died of starvation, also mounted a trip to finish Laddie's work. In his book about that second trip through his picture captions (e.g., "Our lonely perilous journey into the dismal wastes . . . was begun"), his deprecating attitude toward the people of the area whom he labeled as "Labrador type[s]" and demonstrated adversarial bond with the land in his writing, he illustrated a typical power over or patriarchal perspective toward the local people and the land.

As another example, in 1953 during the first recorded Western all-women's mountaineering trip in Nepal, Monica Jackson, Betty Stark and Evelyn Camrass, in opposition to the norms of the time, worked hard not to interface with the press and gain notoriety for their endeavor. They traveled in an area not yet mapped by Westerners because the more popular mountaineering areas were off-limits to them as women. Their expedition was charged with mapping the area. Contrary to standard European procedures, they did not name mountains or areas after themselves or white men. They named places after the Sherpa people with them, including a 22,000-foot peak they climbed, naming it Gyalgen Peak after their head Sherpa. They reported that they splurged and named one glacier the "Ladies' Glacier."[5] These women concerned themselves with caring relationships among themselves, with their Sherpas and with the land. They appreciated the land and did not engage in the conqueror language and behavior typical of the colonizing explorers of the time. These seemingly small differences such as understating their accomplishments and not attempting to conquer the land, come about from women "being with" the more-than-human world and other humans without having any notion of taming or controlling them. Artemis is thought of as a wanderer in the forest and protector of wild animals, especially pregnant and newborn ones. Artemis was in caring relationships with the land and living beings; she did not engage in "power over," although she firmly held her own power.

Some mythology scholars say that Artemis represents the spirit of dangerous, untamed femininity common in ancient cultures. Women on all-women's trips sometimes are thought of as dangerous and unfeminine. Some people may call these women "lesbians" in hopes of scaring them into remaining docile and staying home.[6] In my experience leading women's trips many women on the trips identified as lesbians and many did not. However, rarely did women on trips care who identified as what. The sisterhood and feeling of acceptance and belonging were stronger than a pull to honor a patriarchal method to keep women in line. It is a patriarchal misinterpretation, or an intentional overlay of patriarchal values, to equate untamed with dangerous. The untamed wilderness and untamed women are not dangerous; they are strong, confident and have opinions.

Women Adventurers and Artemis Explore Uncharted Territory

Artemis went into the wilderness, uncharted territory. Monica, Betty and Evelyn during their Himalayan climb were physically in uncharted territory, as was Georgie Clark White in 1945, the first time she and her comrade jumped into the Colorado River in the Grand Canyon with nothing but lifejackets and small packs and swam over 70 miles through large rapids. These women are not slaying dragons or conquering the land, each other or even their fears. They are learning about themselves, expanding their spirituality and discovering different ways to be strong. They were exploring their inner wilderness, while in the physical wilderness, and they often found and experienced restoration. Georgie Clarke White was so taken with her Grand Canyon swim that she dedicated her life to bringing people down the Canyon in rafts, especially encouraging women and children to participate. Like a mother bear, and like Artemis, Georgie Clark White protected her clients while she taught them the skills to thrive in the environment.

Why Do Women Participate in All-Women's Outdoor Trips?

Hornibrook et al.'s[7] research summarized three primary reasons as to why women participate in all-women outdoor adventure programs. Women want to (1) be with all-women participants, (2) be in and with nature and (3) be in an inclusive environment. Additionally, women feel that they have better opportunities to learn and practice skills, feel empowered, relax, have fun, gain a sense of renewal, network and find spiritual healing in nature as part of all-women's outdoor groups.[8] In my observations, women having fun, being playful and laughing are major parts of women's trips.

Like Artemis, these women feel at home in more-than-human worlds— some as soon as they arrive and others after an initial get-to-know-you period. One woman said, "Nature is so healing, I can't help but feel good and powerful out here." Another indicated that the outdoors was a powerful place for her by stating, "I can't control, so I don't. And because I don't I have to take care of it or control it, I have time to focus on myself."[9] Many women have life-changing and positive experiences while participating in outdoor adventures. Many women return to the town or city more centered and feeling more capable. Women report increases in empowerment, self-esteem, personal control, self-efficacy, physical strength, body image and self-care. They return from their journeys more able to bring their Artemis selves fully to their lives.

Several studies have surveyed women who participated in outdoor activities and discovered that many active outdoorswomen are satisfied with their physical attractiveness and their body's physical effectiveness,[10] which is in contrast with the norm in the US of women being dissatisfied with their bodies. The aim of a recent study about body image was to help researchers and outdoor practitioners better understand connections between participation in outdoor activities, including the impact of time spent in the natural world on women's body image.[11] The findings indicated that women who spend more than three hours a week engaging in outdoor activities had a significantly higher (more positive) body image than their less-active counterparts. Additionally, as women experience greater duration of concurrent overnights outdoors, number of overnight trips and total number of overnights outdoors their body image is more positive. Further, in this study body image is lowest for people who have never experienced an overnight outdoors and increases with the experience of one to three nights outdoors and with the experience of four or more concurrent nights outdoors.

These active outdoorswomen seem to rebuff cultural and stereotypical definitions of beauty and, as a result, maintain a more positive body image. Women reported that as their level of participation in outdoor activity increased, the more important it was for them to be physically effective and the less they worried about culturally prescribed physical attractiveness. Specifically, as their level of participation increased, the more important it was for these study participants to be physically effective. The participants defined physical effectiveness as having intrinsic motivation and physical capability. The qualitative results substantiated a connection between participation in outdoor adventure activities and positive body image. Participants indicated that for them, attractiveness and effectiveness are interconnected. Participants reported that being physically attractive means one possesses a combination of physical ability, inner confidence, expressed self-assuredness and physical proportion; this broader definition counteracts the current Western societal norm of preferring an ultra-thin body and objectifying the physical body. Through outdoor activity, self-concept may increase, beliefs about attractiveness change and psychosocial variables about the ideal body may be mitigated. This means that the external influence of the socially or culturally preferred body type had less influence on this population of women than their internalized desire for engaging in outdoor activities and their self-determined need for physical effectiveness to do so. Like Artemis they live what they know to be true. Through experiencing themselves as active women in natural environments they learned more about their true nature—that it feels good to be active and that they are physically competent.

An Artemis-Inspired Organization

Woodswomen, Inc., a women's adventure travel organization (1975–1998), offered a variety of trips (e.g., hiking, canoeing, kayaking, backpacking, rock climbing, mountaineering, SCUBA) in about 10 different countries. It was one of a number of women's outdoor tripping organizations formed in the 1970s in the US, specifically living Artemis values, including (a) coming home to nature, (b) being in a trip environment that feels emotionally, spiritually and physically nurturing, (c) traveling in natural environments for their own sake, not using them as a means to an end, to create situations to take risk or prove competency and (d) seeing women's strengths as assets to trips.[12] According to travel writer Arthur Frommer,[13] by the 1980s there were over 50 companies in the US that offered trips in the outdoors that were "openly feminist in their orientation, and limit their clients and leadership to women only" (p. 56). Many women wanted to lead trips and be on trips that reflected these Artemis-inspired values and living the Artemis mindset of comfort and strong ties with other women.

Seeing Women's Strengths as Assets to Trips, as Artemis Would

Leaders having an attitude that participants do not need to be changed or taught in order to be good enough to be in the outdoors helps create an inclusive and welcoming trip atmosphere. This includes the belief that women and women's strengths are assets to outdoor trips. From a study that included 36 outdoor leaders (split close to 50–50 men and women), with more than about 20 years of experience each,[14] researchers found that in adventure education programming there is a valuing of physical and technical skills over interpersonal skills. Both women and men can be highly skilled in technical activities; however, there are strong under-current assumptions about the roles of women and men on outdoor trips. The leaders surveyed agreed that women are expected to use interpersonal skills more than men, and men are expected to engage more in physical and technical skills than women. Therefore, in co-ed and mainstream outdoor programming, women's strengths are often undervalued (e.g., relational skills) or overlooked (e.g., technical and activity skills).

Because of our collective experience as women, as well as our experience in Western culture as mothers, daughters and sisters, women generally come on trips understanding the importance of nurturing, compassion and connections. The *way* women are is not something that should be diminished; these traits are our strengths and assets, not our weakness. These attributes for some indicate a gendered morality present through the ages and named as an ethic of care.[15]

While women's outdoor programs generally do not intentionally use the outdoors as a testing or proving ground, there are challenges and maybe even hardships during outdoor trips. During challenges or hardships, women typically show caring and nurturing behavior toward each other including another woman having a hard time. This behavior has been described as tending and befriending, and is in contrast to the more publicized fight-or-flight reaction to hardship and stress.[16] During hardships, women tend to build alliances and work as a group to conserve and share resources or develop solutions. This attachment to and compassion for other group members and women's tendency to nurture and care in the face of hardship is a positive attribute.

Coming Home to Nature

The women leaders at Woodswomen were chosen in large part based on their comfort in the outdoors, their ability to be with nature. These outdoor leaders or *guides*, as they were called at Woodswomen, truly seemed to belong in the outdoors. Nature had become a way of life for them. Many participants came on trips with the perception that traveling in the outdoors was the idealized world and that when the trip ended they had to return to the *real* world. Gently, guides reinforced that the outdoor world *is* the real world and that this reality can stay with them when they return to the city. Being with nature is a lifestyle or a way of being in relationship that can be adopted and lived wherever one is.

Today many humans are able to live entire lifetimes seemingly without having to encounter nature. Exceptions to this isolation often occur only in the midst of natural disasters: earthquakes, fires, tornadoes, hurricanes, flooding, mudslides and tidal waves. To consider the impact such encounters imprint on those who experience them, it makes sense that many women's reaction is pervasive fear and mistrust of the natural world. Many women adventure leaders consider the cultural and societal relationship to nature and provide tangible tools to participants in order to provide an experience that offers a renewed, integrated, and healthy relationship to the natural or more-than-human worlds.

Contemporary writers often say modern humans are disconnected from nature, but this notion is not accurate.[17] We are part of a living system where we are nature, and nature is us—whether it is the biomes of bacteria and other organisms in our body that outnumber our own cells or that we need the trees and other plants for the oxygen on which we depend for life. Rather than disconnected, humans likely have an estranged relationship with nature or a disordered attachment with nature. Children without a secure attachment to a caregiver may have an attachment disorder, signs of which generally include a lack of impulse control, violence, and a tendency toward addictions. Many humans may have an attachment disorder with nature, and certain cultures, including the US, exhibit symptoms of attachment disorder, such as the violence and addiction problems. Similar to children needing a nurturing and safe-feeling environment with an attentive caregiver to develop secure attachments, humans need nurturing and safe-feeling time in natural environments to grow a secure attachment to more-than-human worlds. Time in nature with guides encouraging healthy relationships, as Artemis had with the more-than-human worlds help create secure healthy attachment. Research results indicate that emotional and psychological health can improve with a healthy relationship to nature.[18]

While it is true that many women have started out uncertain or even afraid of being outdoors, like Mina Hubbard, many found that after camping and traveling outdoors they truly feel at home there. Healthy experiences with nature can help women heal and engage in healthy relationships with nature. During a Grand Canyon rafting trip, one participant stated, "It was so amazing. My friend convinced me to go on the Grand Canyon rafting trip; I didn't really want to go. I hadn't slept through the night in years. On this trip I slept through the night every night."[19] Many women are able to engage and fully come home in nature.

Creating a Nurturing Environment

Women's programs placed high value on inclusivity and acceptance and tended to operate using an ethic of care.[20] The women leaders care about each other and care about the environment; relationships are based on the ethic of care. Artemis is the archetype of the sister, which is played out in the way women form a sisterhood during trips. Women support each other in taking care of their needs while achieving trip goals as well as individual goals. One common Western leadership assumption is that of "equal weight," meaning that each individual must be able to walk equal distance with equal ease, while carrying equal weight. The feminist or compassionate approach shifts the concept of equality to acknowledge that noticing the way the light plays on the canyon may be as important as building a fire. Or that group members singing through a downpour of biblical proportions may be as important as being able to carry fifty pounds. Typically, when offered support and space, participants equalize the necessary tasks including community-building actions. Often a result is that with resourcefulness and cooperation, many tasks can be accomplished and that the physically strongest people are not singled out as heroes.

While leaders or guides cannot guarantee safety in the outdoors one hundred percent of the time, by using the ethic of care to set a tone of inclusivity, acceptance and reflection, safety (physical, social, emotional and spiritual) and the perception of safety is increased. These ethical values are fundamental because they provide participants with a culture of openness and awareness to both the individual and the collective whole within the context of an outdoor trip or wilderness experience. Inherent in traveling outdoors are the risks of unplanned hardship, difficulty, and even pain. This means that in the face of challenging situations, leaders or guides have the ability to remain optimistic and realistic, coping with patience and resourcefulness, which models working with the natural environment or the Earth as a co-adventurer rather than something to be fought or feared.

The environment on an emotionally and spiritually nurturing trip is non-threatening in a social sense, and participants often feel *included*, but do not necessarily feel like they have to *belong* to the group. Cohesion is based on healthy relationships, shared goals, and shared experiences, rather than reactive relationships or bonding based on a common dislike. Humor is laughing with, not at others, and problems are solved without blaming or fault-finding. Emotionally nurturing trips create spaces where people can try new relationship skills or new behaviors (and maybe choose to keep or not to keep them), and get support for their efforts as they practice skills or behaviors even if they feel or are awkward. While the guides help provide a nurturing environment, women are encouraged to exercise choice in defining their own level of emotional and spiritual safety.

One might say that Nel Noddings' ethic of care is extended to include an Artemis lens of Earth care. Many women's outdoor adventure education programs in the US have emphasized a respect for life and a deep relationship with nature, as well as emotional ties and identification with the landscape. Meaningful aspects of trips that contribute to spiritual well-being include the environmental characteristics of the setting, including wildlife, being in a wilderness area, seeing geological formations and so on. Like Artemis, when in the natural environment, seeing and experiencing oneself as being with nature and in community with the more-than-human worlds serves as an action metaphor for human relationships. Being in the outdoors and feeling connected to nature combined with an understanding that natural environments are grounded in mutualism helps promote community in a larger sense. In other words, being in nature imparts an understanding of community that reaches beyond the group members in the program and human communities—it promotes being with and in the land or place and with more-than-human worlds. Extending the ethic of care to more-than-human worlds includes a sense of this larger community. When guides act ethically and with sensitivity to the biosphere, including using state-of-the-art, low-trace traveling and camping techniques, they help participants to understand, thrive in and enhance our world community and the natural environment. Most women value relationships and connections and this helps shape the way they view nature, and can inspire a spiritual way of being within the natural world that encourages authenticity and impacts the ways in which women lead. The purpose is not to teach or even impose a certain set of beliefs or preordained responses and reaction to or about nature but to allow nature to be the space with which spiritual connections can be revealed.

Vocabulary is an important component of emotional safety within feminist outdoor leadership for both participants and the environment. Avoiding using "survival mode" conversation, which can imply a win/lose or conflict situation, as well as words that connote domination, such as "attack the trail," "conquer the summit," "assault the mountain" or "hit the water," encourages healthy bonding and community. Using adapting or coping language complements an atmosphere of leading with, not over.

Mainstream Western culture has treated women and nature similarly, subjugating both to a lesser status than men. Françoise d'Eaubonne,[21] a French activist, recognized that by externalizing and treating the environment in ways that were violent, uncaring and destructive, humans actually hurt themselves. She coined the term ecofeminism to describe her activism, which was to help people see the links between relationships and to change the patterns of violence. Ecofeminism, based on care and mutualism, fosters a sense of belonging with, rather than being in control of, the community of life. This sense of belonging is why in women's programming it has been important not to use the wilderness as a means to an end, but rather be in the wilderness or with the more-than-human worlds for their own sake. Some mainstream adventure education groups use the outdoors as a proving ground and way to achieve accomplishments. This is often done through taking risks and completing challenges. Taking risks can help one feel powerful and also can help one feel superior. In the case of outdoor adventure education, risk-taking without intention can occur at the expense of the environment and one's spiritual health and it ultimately belittles the environment and humans.

The feminine approach to leadership tends to be inclusive and shared. In a sense, many group members, if not everyone, perform leadership functions at some time. The more this shared leadership is recognized, the more likely that all trip participants will share in the power and responsibility for the trip. If guides are explicit about leadership functions as well as trip details, then engaging in leadership is more accessible. For example, all participants can help in the psychological functions of leadership such as morale building using encouragement, recognition, companionship and support, conflict resolution and helping people express their feelings. Participants can share in effective leadership realms including giving information and opinions, asking for information and opinions, initiating action (such as starting a meal or loading the canoes), and problem solving.

A spiritually nurturing environment is one that opens the way for individuals to find space and time within their own experiences to be attentive to their spiritual needs. It means having time and the conscience to be in awe of nature and relax in its beauty. It may mean offering open time for individuals to meditate, pray, journal, practice yoga or simply be silent. It may also mean having a variety of spiritual practices available for people if they want them. Nature often offers an opening for spirituality to flourish.

Feminist leaders create a programmatic environment that offer their participants choice—choice that encourages and empowers women to claim their own voice and power within their outdoor adventure experiences.[22] Additional stress can be caused when individuals feel they have a lack of choice within adventure experiences. Authentic choice within adventure experiences provides participants with opportunities to claim their own unique experiences—their indomitable spirit. It offers participants space to encounter the natural environment in a non-threatening way, and encourages a spiritual bond with nature.

Concluding Thoughts

Women's programs, especially those based on ecofeminist values, encourage women to live Artemis traits and values. They tend to place high value on inclusivity and acceptance and tend to operate using an ethic of care. "Equality" does not mean that everyone carries the same number of pounds, but rather women contribute to the well-being of the group in various ways that feel safe and work for them. Each woman brings her own particular unique gifts, fears, needs and offerings to outdoor trips. Feminist leadership brings to light some of the assumptions that can exist without awareness of the impact those assumptions have. For example, community organizers and ecologists share an understanding that diversity can strengthen communities and is often a sign of healthy communities. Embracing diversity helps communities be sustainable. Leaders modeling diversity awareness and pluralism help participants learn from differences and help participants understand the importance of protecting biodiversity as well as accepting many expressions of spirituality.

An epic struggle for many women has been in response to many of the deeply held views of women depicted in both current literature and in ancient and mythological references as the princess (maiden), the witch, the temptress, and the all-sacrificing mother and wife archetypes. My experience has been that during outdoor trips women compare their collective thoughts about society's categories for them. In part because of the nurturing natural environment and the strength that comes from being with the more-than-human worlds, women can find their own identities including the caring and responsible mother, the wise and strong crone, the fierce mother protector (mother lion or mother bear), the loving life-giving spirit and others. And women can don different identities every day. By honoring the feminine in each of us we can, by extension, offer women opportunities to understand their own needs and to value those needs. Time with nature with an Artemis lens reinforces women's strengths and helps the indomitable spirit in every woman flourish. Like Artemis, women are one with themselves in meadows, woods, deserts, mountains, lakes, rivers, seas…

References

Bolen, Jean Shinoda. *Artemis: The Indomitable Spirit in Everywoman*. San Francisco: Conari Press, 2014.

Cosgriff, Marg, Donna E. Little, and Erica Wilson. "The Nature of Nature: How New Zealand Women in Middle to Later Life Experience Nature-Based Leisure." *Leisure Sciences* 32, no. 1 (2009): 15–32.

D'Amore, C., and D. Mitten. "Relationship between Outdoor Experience and Body Image in Female College Students." Paper presented at Coalition for Education in the Outdoors Twelfth Biennial Research Symposium, January 2014, 38–40. www2.cortland.edu/dotAsset/d447c0c5-0bb4-4f4c-a1e7-47a7c4247043.pdf.

D'Eaubonne, Françoise. "Feminism or Death." In *New French Feminisms: An Anthology*. Françoise d'Eaubonne, "Feminism or Death," *New French Feminisms: An Anthology*, 64–67. New York: Schocken Books, 1974.

Ewert, Alan W., Denise S. Mitten, and Jillisa R. Overholt. *Natural Environments and Human Health*. CAB International, 2014.

Fredrickson, Laura Marie. "Exploring Spiritual Benefits of Person–Nature Interactions through an Ecosystem Management Approach." PhD diss., University of Minnesota, 1996.

Frommer, Arthur. *The New World of Travel*. New York: Prentice Hall Press, 1988.

Gilligan, Carol. *In a Different Voice: Psychological Theory and Women's Development*. Cambridge, MA: Harvard University Press, 1982.

Gray, Tonia, and Denise Mitten, eds. *The Palgrave International Handbook of Women and Outdoor Learning*. London: Palgrave MacMillan, 2018.

Hornibrook, Taflyn, Elaine Brinkert, Diana Parry, Renita Seimens, Denise Mitten, and Simon Priest. "The Benefits and Motivations of All-Women Outdoor Programs." *The Journal of Experiential Education* 20, no. 3 (1997): 152–58.

Hubbard, Mina Benson. *A Woman's Way through Unknown Labrador*. 1908. Reprint, Newfoundland: Breakwater Books, 1982.

Jackson, Monica, and Elizabeth Stark. *Tents in the Clouds: The First Women's Himalayan Expedition*. London: Collins, 1956.

Mitten, Denise. "A Philosophical Basis for a Women's Outdoor Adventure Program." *Journal of Experiential Education* 8, no. 2 (1985): 20–24.

———. "Empowering Girls and Women in the Outdoors." *Journal of Physical Education, Recreation & Dance* 63, no. 2 (1992): 56–60.

———. "Connections, Compassion, and Co-healing: The Ecology of Relationship." In *Reimagining Sustainability in Precarious Times*, edited by K. Malone, S. Truong, and T. Gray, 173–86. London: Springer, 2017.

———. "Let's Meet at the Picnic Table at Midnight." In *The Palgrave International Handbook of Women and Outdoor Learning*, edited by T. Gray and D. Mitten, 19–34. London: Palgrave Macmillan, 2018.

Noddings, Nel. *Caring: A Feminine Approach to Ethics and Moral Education*. Berkeley, CA: University of California Press, 1984.

Taylor, Shelley E. *The Tending Instinct: Women, Men, and the Biology of Relationships*. Macmillan, 2003.

Tyson, Laura, and Katie Asmus. "Deepening the Paradigm of Choice: Exploring Choice and Power in Experiential Education." In *Theory and Practice of Experiential Education*, edited by K. Warren, D. Mitten, and T.A. Loeffler, 262–81. Boulder, CO: Association for Experiential Education, 2008.

Warren, Karen, Denise Mitten, Chiara D'Amore, and Erin Lotz. "The Gendered Hidden Curriculum of Adventure Education." *Journal of Experiential Education* 42, no. 2 (2019): 140–54.

West-Smith, Lisa. "Body Image Perceptions of Active Outdoorswomen: Toward a New Definition of Physical Attractiveness." PhD diss., University of Michigan, 1998.

Yerkes, R., and Miranda, W. "Outdoor Adventure Courses for Women: Implications for New Programming." *Journal of Health, Physical Education, and Dance* 53, no. 4 (1982): 82–85.

Endnotes

1 Tonia Gray and Denise Mitten, eds., *The Palgrave International Handbook of Women and Outdoor Learning* (London: Palgrave MacMillan, 2018).

2 Woodswomen, Inc., *Wikipedia*, last edited August 9, 2018, en.wikipedia.org/wiki/Woodswomen,_Inc.

3 Jean Shinoda Bolen, *Artemis: The Indomitable Spirit in Everywoman* (San Francisco: Conari Press, 2014).

4 Mina Benson Hubbard, *A Woman's Way through Unknown Labrador* (1908; repr., Newfoundland: Breakwater Books, 1982).

5 Monica Jackson and Elizabeth Stark, *Tents in the Clouds: The First Women's Himalayan Expedition* (London: Collins, 1956).

6 Denise Mitten, "Let's Meet at the Picnic Table at Midnight," in *The Palgrave International Handbook of Women and Outdoor Learning*, ed. Tonia Gray and Denise Mitten, 19–34 (London: Palgrave Macmillan, 2018).

7 Taflyn Hornibrook, Elaine Brinkert, Diana Parry, Renita Seimens, Denise Mitten, and Simon Priest, "The Benefits and Motivations of All-Women Outdoor Programs," *The Journal of Experiential Education* 20, no. 3 (1997): 152–58.

8 Marg Cosgriff, Donna E. Little, and Erica Wilson, "The Nature of Nature: How New Zealand Women in Middle to Later Life Experience Nature-Based Leisure," *Leisure Sciences* 32, no. 1 (2009): 15–32; Laura Marie Fredrickson, "Exploring Spiritual Benefits of Person–Nature Interactions through an Ecosystem Management Approach" (PhD diss., University of Minnesota, 1996); R. Yerkes and W. Miranda, "Outdoor Adventure Courses for Women: Implications for New Programming," *Journal of Health, Physical Education, and Dance* 53, no. 4 (1982): 82–85.

9 Denise Mitten, "Empowering Girls and Women in the Outdoors," *Journal of Physical Education, Recreation & Dance* 63, no. 2 (1992): 56–60.

10 Lisa West-Smith, "Body Image Perceptions of Active Outdoorswomen: Toward a New Definition of Physical Attractiveness" (PhD diss., University of Michigan, 1998).

11   C. D'Amore and D. Mitten, "Relationship between Outdoor Experience and Body Image in Female College Students," paper presented at Coalition for Education in the Outdoors Twelfth Biennial Research Symposium, January 2014, 38–40. www2.cortland.edu/dotAsset/d447c0c5-0bb4-4f4c-a1e7-47a7c4247043.pdf.

12   Denise Mitten, "A Philosophical Basis for a Women's Outdoor Adventure Program," *Journal of Experiential Education* 8, no. 2 (1985): 20–24.

13   Arthur Frommer, *The New World of Travel* (New York: Prentice Hall, 1988), 56.

14   Karen Warren, Denise Mitten, Chiara D'Amore, and Erin Lotz, "The Gendered Hidden Curriculum of Adventure Education," *Journal of Experiential Education* 42, no. 2 (2019): 140–54.

15   Carol Gilligan, *In a Different Voice: Psychological Theory and Women's Development* (Cambridge, MA: Harvard University Press, 1982); Nel Noddings, *Caring: A Feminine Approach to Ethics and Moral Education* (Berkeley: University of California Press, 1984).

16   Shelley E. Taylor, *The Tending Instinct: Women, Men, and the Biology of Relationships* (Macmillan, 2003).

17   D. Mitten, "Connections, Compassion, and Co-healing: The Ecology of Relationship," in *Reimagining Sustainability in Precarious Times*, ed. K. Malone, S. Truong, and T. Gray, 173–86 (London: Springer, 2017).

18   Alan W. Ewert, Denise S. Mitten, and Jillisa R. Overholt, *Natural Environments and Human Health* (CAB International, 2014).

19   Mitten, "Empowering Girls and Women in the Outdoors," 56.

20   Denise Mitten, "A Philosophical Basis for a Women's Outdoor Adventure Program," *Journal of Experiential Education* 8, no. 2 (1985): 20–24.

21   Françoise d'Eaubonne, "Feminism or Death," *New French Feminisms: An Anthology*, 64–67 (New York: Schocken Books, 1974).

22   Mitten, "A Philosophical Basis"; Laura Tyson and Katie Asmus, "Deepening the Paradigm of Choice: Exploring Choice and Power in Experiential Education," in *Theory and Practice of Experiential Education*, ed. K. Warren, D. Mitten, and T.A. Loeffler, 262–81 (Boulder, CO: Association for Experiential Education, 2008).

CRONES OF GAIA: AN ECOCENTRIC PERSPECTIVE OF BEING ON THE LAND

NOËL COX CANIGLIA

*I reach across generations to stand with many others in
reclaiming the accolade of crone. I celebrate the nurtured
and oftentimes hard-earned wisdom of our elder sisters. I
see the Goddess hidden within our everyday lives. I think
and feel, to the depths of my being, the oneness that we
share with place, with the regeneration of Gaia.*[1]

My research has explored the perceptions of elder women ranchers
in the US Southwest. It is a cultural study of the ranchers' social
and ecological sense of place[2] embedded in Gaia. The research illuminated the role these elders played as informal ecojustice[3] educators in the
conveyance of local expert knowledge, cultural values, and pathways of
wisdom to future generations. I chose these ranchers, aged from 69 to 88,
because of their long-lived experience as ranchers (minimum of 25 years
living and working as cattle ranchers) and because these elders' voices
were important to hear. The research indicated that their self-identifica-
tion emerged through their inter- and intra-relationships with the land[4] and
their ranching backgrounds in land-based cultures. Although these ranchers expressed ecofeminist ideals in the rich and simple stories they told
about their everyday lives, they would not recognize nor self-identify with
the scholarly term, ecofeminism.[5] My research has honored what might
mistakenly be seem as an unresolved dichotomy: It highlights both the
indomitable strength of ranchers and simultaneously their stalwart aversion
to being associated in any way as a feminist—"I'm not [a] women libber."[6]
I argue that these entangled and apparently contradictory ideals are merely

examples of feminist new materialism tenets of complexity. While there are notable exceptions to the exclusion of female voices, the dominant paradigm in the literature is based on cow*boys* and male ranchers. Because of this dominated position, women ranchers have been excluded from traditional knowledge production. Ergo, in this chapter, the term *rancher* refers to women who ranch desert bioregions of the US Southwest. If references to male ranchers are made, the gender will be noted. This will avoid otherwise pejorative assumptions that men are ranchers and women can only be termed ranch wives. Such a patriarchal assumption that a rancher is male, tends to covertly relegate a woman's role in ranching to a footnote in the description of this iconic way of life.

As a feminist ethnographer, I viewed my research through differentiated and entangled lenses, as modeled by feminist researchers who preceded me.[7] I selected rancher-participants for two reasons related to my own positionality. First, I have been intimately connected to a ranching culture for close to forty years. Although I still live and labor on a working cattle ranch in Arizona, my full-time (as opposed to part-time) work on ranches accounted for only fifteen of those years—living in hardscrabble conditions while punching cows and raising a family. I identify my *insider* position as a rancher based on those first years of living from hand to mouth on the ranch and knowing only the practical beauty and exhaustion of a working rancher's life—seven days a week, 360 days a year. For the last 26 years, however, I have split my time between ranching and teaching graduate and doctoral students at Prescott College. I identify my *outsider* position because of the privilege I have experienced as a scholar and academic. This privilege has afforded me a broader scope of knowing through both primary and secondary knowledge research. While I can still personally identify with overarching concepts and daily details that are reflected in the ranching world, my privilege has distanced me from a lifestyle that I dearly love. Because of my positionality on and off of the ranch, I have a profound interest in this culture and its ecological interrelationships with Gaia. The practical and unwavering commitment to a social and ecological place that women in the ranching community share inspired me to explore ways to better understand their interactions and entanglements with the more-than-human natural world. The second determinant for this research was that I became aware of increasing challenges for the aging female population in the United States. The tidal wave of aging adults will expand to an unprecedented level in the decades to come. Arguably, there is often a certain amount of dependence that occurs because of deterioration in the aging process. This may be problematic in a society that values and idealizes autonomy and independence. The stress on the country's economy, health system, and social structure will be significant. Senior populations, then, are often viewed as a liability and are therefore treated as problems. These issues are amplified for women.

For many women, this is compounded by the trend that part of the aging process includes an increasing and well-documented disempowerment[8] surpassing that of their male counterparts. The marginalization of women currently practiced within much of society will be magnified when women lose their culturally defined physical allure and no longer contribute to society's economic bottom line. From a feminist perspective, these aging women are in danger of becoming disenfranchised from the larger community. The elder ranchers I have observed were strong, engaged and vibrant women. Therefore, offering these women a voice in explaining their way of life is beneficial for them and others who may read this study.

Oftentimes the messages communicated in writing by ranchers in the Western United States were concealed in prose or poetry and described their lives in terms of work,[9] their relationship to the land,[10] their sense of freedom,[11] their sometimes-ironic view of gender roles,[12] or, occasionally, their understanding of the preeminence of other, older cultures.[13] Within the extensive review of literature completed for this research, I sampled stories spanning the last two hundred years and found that the most common theme was the ranchers' relationship to the land.

The literature suggested several other themes. Although these tended to be anthropocentric[14] in nature, they are worth sharing to provide some context for my ongoing research. First, ranchers' relationship with the land has grown from one that might have, at one time, only identified human and other-than-human separateness, to one that acknowledges an important relationship between humans and other species. Second, human independence was as much a part of this relationship with the land as was human community interdependence. Third, the ranchers who wrote about their lives almost exclusively came from either educationally or economically privileged backgrounds. Fourth, gender roles were also assumed and based on a Victorian image of women. More recently, issues of inequality and the marginalization of ranchers have emerged in the literature. Finally, tangential themes in wisdom theory, informal education, place-based learning theory and sense of place support the idea that ranchers may act as ecojustice educators who promote sustainability.[15] They do this by making use of an informal system of teaching and learning that is based on their sense of place (self in association with *other*). When employing these culturally embedded methods, they arguably act as a vehicle through which local expert knowledge, cultural ways of knowing and pathways to wisdom are transmitted to subsequent generations.

In my research I attempted to give voice to the voiceless. I listened to ranchers whose life experiences flowed, like strong subterranean rivers, from generation to generation. My commitment to giving voice to these women, who may not have otherwise had the opportunity to be heard, grew from my position as a feminist and scholar. For example, one recent addition to this academic dialogue on voice has been particularly important to my research. Alecia Youngblood Jackson[16] expanded upon the idea of the feminist voice in research in her description of the coined concept, *rhizovocality*. The term is based on a combination of words: rhizome and vocality. A rhizome[17] is a horizontal root-like stem of a plant that is usually found underground and often sends out roots and shoots from its apex. Vocality refers to the participants' and researchers' authentic voices within the research process. Rhizovocality is based on the acceptance of conflicting and evolving ideas of voice. The feminist voice, like the voice of Gaia, is not unified; rather it is what Jackson described as "circular interconnected and territorializing."[18] In congruence with this idea of rhizovocality, the ranchers that I interviewed had that same type of complex and contradictory voice, both individually and as a group.

It may be argued that the ranchers teetered on the cusp of Western paradigms toward the more-than-human natural environment. *Backgrounding*[19] and *radical exclusion*[20] may have originally framed their dominant cultural beliefs; however, they also practiced a way of knowing based on place sensitivity and place-based spirituality. Certainly, living within the emergent essence of Nature,[21] a natural environment provided ranchers with the opportunity to recognize similar survival patterns of other species. When I asked what one participant thought was important to learn from Nature, she just patiently shook her head:

Everything. . . . [Laughing] Oh, dear. I don't know, you just lived with what you had and were glad to have it. Yeah, all kids learn what it's like to get thirsty; how fun it is to swim in a stock tank. [Laughing] Oh boy, it is! Many [are the] ones I've swum in but they've been fun, you know, it's been refreshing because those hot summer days are pretty hot sometimes. There's swimmin' with the horses, too, if you have a decent tank. What do we learn? You learn chores are to be done and that's life. You do your chores and take care of yourself. You take on jobs that you know you can do, or at least try to do or do part of. But you have to have a realism of how long the day is and can you be out that long or do you need to be in before dark or you don't get in. Or, I don't know, you just learn to limit yourself . . . by the day. You learn to take care of your ranges; you learn to take care of your horses; you become part of your horse practically. It's funny—when I had kids, well you had horses, too, and every once in a while you call a kid by the horse's name. [Laughing] It's kind of weird. You try to teach your kids the things that you thought were important growing up and to pinpoint those things.[22]

Interestingly, the lessons learned from the ecosystem appeared in three stages of learning[23] throughout all the ranchers' stories: *awareness*, *acceptance* and *actualization*. The first stage, *awareness*, was one earned through long hours, days and years of working and living in an isolated and pristine setting.

To me, that's . . . appreciating nature, not only just the grasses and country, just the animals and everything that's in 'em. It is that you learn to love it all. Even with coyotes, you know they have a purpose and you hate their guts sometimes, especially on heifers. It's just a different type of life, it really is. You have to be able to either love it or hate it because there's no in-between, I don't think. You have to love it to the point that you hate to leave it.[24]

251

The second stage, *acceptance*, was one in which the ranchers were humbled by the power, vastness and complexity of their ecosystem.

> You're out there and you just see this stuff happening all the time and it's just a part of your environment. Because you're out there all the time, you learn what grasses are gonna help your cows, you learn what's poisonous out there because you're out there all the time. And so you learn from just being out there. You know, . . . if you're totally into ranching, it's a part of your everyday life. It's a part of you. You're not separated from it. You're part of that land, you're part of that tree, you're part of that stuff because you're there. It's just a part of you.[25]

The final state, *actualization*, grew as the ranchers learned to live as an integral constituent of their ecosystem. Often decisions made relating to managing the business side of ranching grew from the lessons learned from the dynamism of Nature. For example, after many hours of an informal, in-depth interview, one of the ranchers struggled to help me understand her deep love of the place that she shared with all other living beings:

> Well, one of my favorite spots when I was growing up was Granite Creek. There's a big canyon that goes through there. My dad used to work the trail up there. There's a big waterhole up in one end of it and he'd work that trail so the cows could go up there to water. That was a beautiful place. You could ride up that canyon and there'd be little hummingbird nests hanging from the bushes. You'd be down in there and you'd have walls on each side of you that went up and some of these bigger planes went over and you could almost feel the walls shake—the vibration from those airplanes. The only place you could look was straight up. There wudn't [*sic*] anything to see. It was cool and the cows would go up in there and lay down in the shade. There were places where it was a lot of silt and soft ground. The main channel, of course, was rocky, but on each side, there would be grass. They'd go up in there and stay two or three days. Didn't bother to come out.[26]

After spending long periods of time appreciating the beauty and complexity of the living systems in which they live and work, ranchers have grown to accept Gaia on her own terms, rather than from an anthropocentric vantage point. This paradigm shift naturally grew from the consistent interrelationships between rancher and Nature.

Partially due to the ranchers' dependence on ecosystem health and their observation of and participation with the community of living beings, they discovered that the human animal and other animals were very much alike. An implication of this ecocentric perspective might be that human and other-than-human animals share a similar sense of being. One of the ranchers saw the interrelationships in the ecosystem (including humans) to be one characterized by honesty and truth.

> Well to be honest or truthful [is] what you see in nature, that's what there is, and to accept [the] good or bad of it. And it's to be respected, that's the whole thing. It's being respectful of the country. Of appreciating it, to respect it for what it is. Respect your country. That's the whole thing, . . . to be respectful of it and not damage it. Whatever it is . . . , whether you got cattle on it or whatever it is you're doin' with it.[27]

I have been honored and humbled to be a conduit for these ranchers' voices. Their simple, beautiful and heart-warming stories illustrated their deep identification with Gaia, not as a separate and secondary lens of their personal being, but as their primary and initial sense of an organic whole. This flies in the face of what I have been taught in formal education: the primary lens through which humans view the world begins with self and expands in concentric circles to include others. The ranchers' unconscious[28] and conscious knowing, on the other hand, harkens back to a time when being *of* Gaia was an obvious part of all life. For me, this was a revolutionary idea of becoming—of seeing and being Gaia from within. This discovery, ironically, emerged from the fabric of what I would normally consider a conservative way of life—cattle ranching. The ranchers displayed a shift in perspective from one that is "I-centered" to one that is centered within the complexity and entanglement of Gaia.

Arguably, the ranchers' more planetary perspective privileged the dynamic and emerging interrelationships of Gaia over an anthropocentric or egocentric point of reference. This shift in our original frame of reference may point toward ways for humans to reduce their negative impact on the biosphere by reframing their human exceptionalism and moving toward a more inclusive Gaia-centered vantage point. Although ranchers' ecocentric perspective is one that has been noted in other, less-industrialized cultures,[29] it has not been previously recognized among ranchers. In fact, negative stereotypes of ranchers as abusers of the land still abound (Russell, 2001).[30] I was humbled by the voices of the ranchers who shared countless hours of their stories with me and I feel honored to be able to give voice to their life-long commitment to the land.

My hope is that my ongoing research into the everyday lives of land-based women will spark others to explore the unheard voices of women that are *of* the Earth—whether they be foresters, farmers, fisher people, factory workers or homeless. I believe this type of a deep feminist ethnographic study—or, even better, one that relies on a diffractive methodology—has the potential to shed new light on the power of Gaia to shape the way humans think and become. Please join me in this research. I invite readers to take just one step toward "giving voice to the voiceless" by the simple act of recording stories from other women and/or other species (see Haraway, 2003, 2007, 2016a, 2016b) and then sharing these with the rest of the world.

References

Ardelt, Monika. "Wisdom as Expert Knowledge System: A Critical Review of a Contemporary Operationalization of an Ancient Concept." *Human Development* 47, no. 5 (2004): 257–85.

———. "Where Can Wisdom Be Found? A Reply to the Commentaries by Baltes and Kunzmann, Sternberg, and Achenbaum." *Human Development* 47, no. 5 (2004b): 304–307.

Auker, Amy Hale. *Rightful Place*. Lubbock: Texas Tech University Press, 2011.

———. With foreword by Linda Hasselstrom. *Rightful Place (Voice in the American West)*. Lubbock: Texas Tech University Press, 2014.

Austin, Mary. *The Land of Little Rain*. Random House LLC, 2010.

Barad, Karen. *Meeting the Universe Halfway*. Durham, NC: Duke University Press, 2007.

Barnes, Kim, and Mary Clearman Blew, eds. *Circle of Women: An Anthology of Contemporary Western Women Writers*. University of Oklahoma Press, 2001.

Behar, Ruth. *The Vulnerable Observer: Anthropology That Breaks Your Heart*. Beacon Press, 1996.

———. *Adio Kerida/Good Bye Dear Love: A Cuban Sephardic Journey*. Documentary film (VHS). New York: Women Make Movies, 2002.

———. *Translated Woman: Crossing the Border with Esperanza's Story*. Beacon Press, 2003.

Biggs, Simon. "Age, Gender, Narratives, and Masquerades." *Journal of Aging Studies* 18, no. 1 (2004): 45–58.

Blunt, Judy. *Breaking Clean*. Random House LLC, 2003.

Bourne, Eulalia. *Woman in Levi's*. University of Arizona Press, 1967.

Bowers, Chet A. "Toward an Eco-Justice Pedagogy." *Environmental Education Research* 8, no. 1 (2002): 21–34. doi: 10.1080/13504620120109628

———, Joseph Progler, and Thomas Nelson. *Eco-Justice: Essays on Theory and Practice*. Torrance, CA: Eco-Justice Press, 2016.

Butala, Sharon. *The Perfection of the Morning: An Apprenticeship in Nature*. Toronto, ON: HarperCollins, 1994.

Calasanti, Toni M., and Kathleen F. Slevin, eds. *Age Matters: Realigning Feminist Thinking*. Taylor & Francis, 2006.

Cleaveland, Agnes Morley. *No Life for a Lady*. Lincoln: University of Nebraska Press, 1977.

Coole, Diana, and Samantha Frost, eds. *New Materialisms: Ontology, Agency, and Politics*. Durham, NC: Duke Univerrsity Press, 2010.

D'Eaubonne, Françoise. *Le Féminisme ou la mort*. Paris: Pierre Horay, 1974.

Gilligan, Carol. *In a Different Voice*. Harvard University Press, 1982.

Haraway, Donna. *The Companion Species Manifesto: Dogs, People, and Significant Otherness*. Chicago: Prickly Paradigm Press, 2003.

———. *When Species Meet*. Minneapolis: University of Minnesota Press, 2007.

———. *Manifestly Haraway*. Minneapolis: University of Minnesota Press, 2016a.

———. *Staying with the Trouble: Making Kin in the Chthulucene*. Durham, NC: Duke University Press, 2016b.

Hasselstrom, Linda M. *Windbreak: A Woman Rancher on the Northern Plains*. Barn Owl Books, 1987.

———. *Land Circle: Writings Collected from the Land*. Golden, CO: Fulcrum Publishing, 2008.

Healey, Shevy. "Growing to be an Old Woman: Aging and Ageism." *Women and Aging* (1986): 58–62.

Heilbrun, Carolyn G. *Women's Lives: The View from the Threshold*. University of Toronto Press, 1999.

Henderson, Alice Corbin. *Red Earth: Poems of New Mexico*. RF Seymour, 1920.

Jackson, Alecia Youngblood. "Rhizovocality." *Qualitative Studies in Education* 16, no. 5 (2003): 693–710.

Merchant, Carolyn. *The Death of Nature: Women, Ecology, and the Scientific Revolution*. New York: HarperCollins, 1992.

Plumwood, Valerie. *Feminism and the Mastery of Nature*. London: Routledge, 1993.

Rak, Mary Kidder. *Cowman's Wife*. Texas State Historical Association, 1993.

Reinharz, Shulamit, and Lynn Davidman. *Feminist Methods in Social Research*. Oxford University Press, 1992.

Richardson, Laurel. "Writing: A Method of Inquiry." In *Handbook of Qualitative Research*, edited by Norman K. Denzin and Yvonna S. Lincoln, 923–48. Thousand Oaks, CA: Sage Publications, 1994.

———, and Elizabeth Adams St. Pierre. "A Method of Inquiry." In *Collecting and Interpreting Qualitative Materials*, 3rd ed., edited by Norman K. Denzin and Yvonna S. Lincoln, 473–500. Thousand Oaks, CA: Sage Publications, 2008.

Rudnick, Lois. "Re-Naming the Land: Anglo Expatriate Women in the Southwest." *The Desert Is No Lady: Southwestern Landscapes in Women's Writing and Art*, edited by Vera Norwood and Janice Monk, 10–26. University of Arizona Press, 1987.

Russell, Sharman Apt. *Kill the Cowboy: A Battle of Mythology in the New West*. University of Nebraska Press, 1993.

Shiva, Vandana. *Staying Alive: Women, Ecology and Development*. Zed Books, 1988.

————. *Earth Democracy: Justice, Sustainability and Peace*. Zed Books, 2006.

————. "Soil Not Oil: Environmental Justice in an Age of Climate Crisis."
Alternatives Journal 35, no. 3 (2009): 19–23.

Endnotes

1 N.C. Caniglia, "Elder Wisdom and Land Wisdom" (unpublished manuscript, 2019).

2 The concept of a *social and ecological sense of place* refers to an individual's identification through experience and knowledge with a geographical area and community. It is a region's cultural and ecological heritage. A sense of place emerges through such things as knowledge of and experience with the local history, geography, climate and geology of an area, as well as its biota and legends. It represents an emotional, intellectual, physical and spiritual attachment and engagement that develops over time. It is difficult to trace the origin of the concept of a sense of place because it has been an inherent part of nature writing for centuries.

3 The term "ecojustice" has been most recently associated with the work of C.A. Bowers: "[E]cojustice provides the larger moral and conceptual framework for understanding how to achieve the goals of social justice." It is based on "revitalizing the commons in order to: Achieve a healthier balance between market and non-market aspects of community life; Ensure that the prospects of future generations are not diminished by the hubris and ideology that drives the globalization of the West's industrial culture; Reduce the threat to what Vandana Shiva refers to as Earth Democracy—that is, the right of natural systems to reproduce themselves rather than to have their existence contingent upon the demands of humans."
See Bowers, "Toward an Eco-Justice Pedagogy," *Environmental Education Research* 8, no. 1 (2002): 21–34. doi: 10.1080/13504620120109628; Bowers, Joseph Progler, and Thomas Nelson, *Eco-Justice: Essays on Theory and Practice* (Torrance, CA: Eco-Justice Press, 2016).

4 The term "land" is used in this paper to represent a larger social and ecological context that includes components of both more-than-human and human environments in a natural setting.

5 The concept of *ecofeminism* can refer to a social and political movement, mostly grassroots, which integrates deep ecology with feminism; ecofeminists maintain that there is a strong relationship between the oppression of women and the degradation of the more-than-human natural environment. In her book, *Le féminisme ou la Mort*, French writer Francoise d'Eaubonne (1974) challenged "women to lead an ecological revolution to save the planet." Answering

this challenge would mean nothing less than an ecological revolution; it would require new relationships to be established between women and men as well as between humans and nature (Merchant, 1992: 184). Ecofeminists often explore the relationship between the how women are dominated and exploited in a parallel way that the environment is dominated and exploited. It is worth noting that Vandana Shiva (2003, 2005) noted that women in subsistence economies sometimes demonstrate an intimate connection to the environment because of their unique relationship to it.

6 Rosalie, personal communication, November 14, 2008.

7 Karen Barad, *Meeting the Universe Halfway* (Duke University Press, 2007); Ruth Behar, *The Vulnerable Observer: Anthropology That Breaks Your Heart* (Beacon Press, 1996); Ruth Behar, *Adio Kerida/Good Bye Dear Love. A Cuban Sephardic Journey*, documentary (New York: Women Make Movies, 2002); Ruth Behar, *Translated Woman: Crossing the Border with Esperanza's Story* (Beacon Press, 2003); Laurel Richardson and Elizabeth Adams St. Pierre, "A Method of Inquiry," in *Collecting and Interpreting Qualitative Materials*, 3rd ed., Norman K. Denzin and Yvonna S. Lincoln, eds., 473–500 (Thousand Oaks, CA: Sage Publications, 2008); Shulamit Reinharz and Lynn Davidman, *Feminist Methods in Social Research* (Oxford University Press, 1992).

8 Simon Biggs, "Age, Gender, Narratives, and Masquerades," *Journal of Aging Studies* 18, no. 1 (2004): 45–58; Toni M. Calasanti and Kathleen F. Slevin, eds., *Age Matters: Realigning Feminist Thinking* (Taylor & Francis, 2006); Shevy Healey, "Growing to Be an Old Woman: Aging and Ageism," *Women and Aging* (1986): 58–62; Carolyn G. Heilbrun, *Women's Lives: The View from the Threshold* (University of Toronto Press, 1999); Carol Gilligan, *In a Different Voice* (Harvard University Press, 1982); Laurel Richardson, "Writing: A Method of Inquiry," in *Handbook of Qualitative Research*, eds. Norman K. Denzin and Yvonna S. Lincoln, 923–48 (Thousand Oaks, CA: Sage Publications, 1994).

9 Amy Hale Auker, with foreword by Linda Hasselstrom. *Rightful Place (Voice in the American West)* (Lubbock: Texas Tech University Press, 2014); Mary Austin, *The Land of Little Rain* (Random House LLC, 2010); Kim Barnes and Mary Clearman Blew, eds., *Circle of Women: An Anthology of Contemporary Western Women Writers* (University of Oklahoma Press, 2001); Alice Corbin Henderson, *Red Earth: Poems of New Mexico* (RF Seymour, 1920).

10 Amy Hale Auker, *Rightful Place* (Lubbock: Texas Tech University Press, 2011); Eulalia Bourne, *Woman in Levi's* (University of Arizona Press, 1967); Sharon Butala, *The Perfection of the Morning: An Apprenticeship in Nature* (Toronto: HarperCollins, 1994); Mary Kidder Rak, *Cowman's Wife* (Texas State Historical Association, 1993).

11 Linda M. Hasselstrom, *Windbreak: A Woman Rancher on the Northern Plains* (Barn Owl Books, 1987); Linda M. Hasselstrom, *Land Circle: Writings Collected from the Land* (Golden, CO: Fulcrum Publishing, 2008).

12 Judy Blunt, *Breaking Clean* (Random House LLC, 2003); Agnes Morley Cleaveland, *No Life for a Lady* (University of Nebraska Press, 1977).

13 Lois Rudnick, "Re-Naming the Land: Anglo Expatriate Women in the Southwest," *The Desert Is No Lady: Southwestern Landscapes in Women's Writing and Art* (1987): 10–26.

14 The term "anthropocentrism" represents a way of thinking that privileges humans above other species and assumes the other-than-human natural world to be an exploitable resource for human use. Until recently an anthropocentric view also assumed that the fate of the environment was unconnected to the fate of humans, and that while humans were rational (superior), the other-than-human natural environment was something wild that needed to be conquered or subjugated to that rational will.

15 From a human species standpoint, the term "sustainability" refers to the capacity to maintain and continue to enhance the systems that nourish us. However, from a larger perspective, sustainability must presume that human and ecosystem well-being are inexorably interdependent; in order to meet current human needs, they must be maintained without compromising ecosystems or future generations. This concept of survival has environmental, social, political, economic, cultural, and spiritual dimensions. Sustainability, as applied to the larger field of education, alludes to a holistic, eco-judicial, and culturally relevant approach to teaching and learning that is intergenerational, self-renewing, and built on a model of healthy interrelationships within the community of all beings.

16 Alecia Youngblood Jackson, "Rhizovocality," *Qualitative Studies in Education* 16, no. 5 (2003): 693–710.

17 As an Arizona native, rancher, and avid gardener, I am reminded of *rhizome* examples such as the tenacious and apparent omnipresence of aspen, Bermuda grass, mint, or iris.

18 Jackson, "Rhizovocality," 693.

19 Val Plumwood (1993) used the term *backgrounding* to refer to the denial of the *other* not merely as different but as inferior. Within the context of this dissertation, *backgrounding* refers to the relegation of nature and/or the natural environment as the *other*. By separating human identity from the identity of the "natural environment," patterns of human domination are reinforced.

20 Based on the concept of backgrounding, the term "radical exclusion" refers to the practice of focusing on only the hierarchical differences of the dominant and domineering identity (humans) and the inferior *other* (the other than human natural environment). The perceived separation between these two (dominant humans and inferior natural environment) are extreme.

21 I often use the generic term Nature in place of Gaia, because the ranchers identified with that term.

22 Emma, personal communication, October 9, 2008.

23 Interestingly, these stages of learning foreshadowed what Ardelt (2004a, 2004b) asserted as the three necessary dimensions of wise people: cognition (truth-seeking), reflection (self-examination and ability to view phenomena from different points of view) and affective (both a sympathetic and empathetic love for others).

24 Bonnie, personal communication, November 12, 2008.

25 Rosalie, personal communication, November 14, 2008.

26 Grace, personal communication, January 6, 2009.

27 Bonnie, personal communication, November 12, 2008.

28 From an academic perspective, the idea of *unconscious knowing* is a facet of *new materialism* (Barad, 2007; Coole and Frost, 2010) because what the world is and what we know about different things in the world are fluid and constantly shaping one another. I contend that ranchers know this without having the theoretical constructs or words to explain it.

29 Vandana Shiva, *Staying Alive: Women, Ecology and Development* (Zed Books, 1988); Vandana Shiva, *Earth Democracy: Justice, Sustainability and Peace* (Zed Books, 2006); Vandana Shiva, "Soil Not Oil," *Alternatives Journal* 35, no. 3 (2009): 19.

30 Sharman Apt Russell, *Kill the Cowboy: A Battle of Mythology in the New West* (University of Nebraska Press, 1993).

AN ANCIENT FESTIVAL EMBRACES
A MODERN MIRACLE

VICKI NOBLE

The Feast of Santa Gemma of Goriano Sicoli takes place in early May in the Italian region of Abruzzo near the Adriatic Sea. This annual spring festival celebrates the return of a daughter to her mother, very much in keeping with the rites of Demeter and Persephone so pervasive in the Mediterranean region during ancient and classical times. For this contemporary festival, each year the women of the village come together in a special house ("the house of Santa Gemma") to spend an entire night collectively baking bread, which is then blessed by the priests and distributed to everyone in town by the young maidens of the village. When I was shown an old book of black-and-white photos depicting this pagan "festival of the bread," I saw obvious connections with the work of Marija Gimbutas and the motifs of Old Europe (Europe before patriarchy).[1] One has only to think of the numerous models of ancient temples and shrines where bread ovens, some in the shape of a pregnant womb, were unearthed from the temple courtyards, along with evidence of ritually baked bread. Using the interdisciplinary work of Gimbutas as a model, I will use an archaeomythology process to track the long continuity of several motifs central to Old Europe in the Neolithic period (and even earlier), and extending all the way to the present day.

After I had made arrangements to attend this and other nearby festivals in early May of 2009, a destructive earthquake hit the region of Abruzzo in April. The epicenter was L'Aquila, the capital city, where buildings collapsed, people died and thousands of refugees fled the rubble. Nearby villages were also affected and several of the annual festivals were canceled; others were significantly modified, including the one in Goriano

Sicoli, on which this paper is based. I flew to Italy on May 1, the pagan holy day of Beltane or May Day, and I went to the festival knowing that the bread-baking part of the ritual, sadly, had been canceled—surely a big disappointment for the young women who, dressed in festive costumes, would normally have been called into service distributing the homemade bread to festival-goers. That particular year, the bread was instead baked industrially, because the "house of Santa Gemma" where the women do the baking had been seriously damaged by the earthquake, as well as the Church of Santa Gemma, where the saint's body was ordinarily kept during the year (more on that later).

When I arrived in the village on the festival morning of May 11, 2009, my host for the week, Luciana Percovich, introduced me to her friend Christina, the local village expert on the annual celebration, who claimed to have in her possession a loaf of festival bread from 1926, which, she said, is preserved—that is, it does not "corrupt," but remains the same over time—one of many miracles attributed to the patron saint for whom the festival is named—Saint Gemma.

Gemma, so the story goes, was born in the fourteenth century into a poor but devout family living in the town of San Sebastian, who then moved to nearby Goriano, where the festival is held. Their twelve-year-old Gemma looked after a small flock of sheep belonging to her parents. She was an especially beautiful girl and a powerful nobleman tried to seduce her. She was jailed for resisting his advances and died in jail 56 years later. But an Internet version of this story makes her eight years old at the time and says she reproached the count so forcefully that he was shamed and made it up to her by building a hermitage for her, where she lived the rest of her life. Another story says he built for her the Church of San Giovanni in town, where she requested a room with a small window from which she could see the altar. Christina told me the villagers went to the window of her prison (or alternately the church) to give Gemma bread that she then gave to the poor—surely a modern rationale for the bread-baking ritual and communal distribution.

One can see, however, in the works of Gimbutas and other investigators, an abundance of evidence for much more ancient rituals "associating grain, flour, and baking with the goddess, performed in order to assure abundant bread."[2] Gimbutas noted that even during the Paleolithic period, before the Pregnant Goddess was "mother to the domestic grains, she was mother to the wild grasses," pointing to the famous Venus of Laussel, whose figure graced the overhang of an entrance into the cave by that name in France.[3] Speaking of the later Neolithic period, she wrote that,

> special altars were built for [the Pregnant Goddess] next to the bread baking ovens, and she was worshiped wherever grain was ground and bread was being prepared and baked.[4]

In my own research, I found that these practices are documented from as far back as 9500 BCE. In my book, *Shakti Woman*, I wrote about the ten thousand tiny *bladelets* found at the end of the Ice Age (or Magdalenian period) in the French Pyrenees (Basque country), where archaeologists discovered, along with "ocher crayons and pierced teeth,"[5] the "charred remains of fire, mortars and pestles for grinding grain, and the remains of bread having been baked in the primitive ovens."[6] Microscopic research revealed grass resins on the *bladelets*, suggesting they had been attached to wood or bone handles and used for cutting wild grasses to make "some kind of bread, porridge, or cake" 12,000 years ago.[7] Although this seems very early to us, archaeologists have found similar artifacts at a cave in South Africa called Pinnacle Point, where early humans worked red ocher and utilized tiny bladelets—164,000 years ago![8]

At the beginning of the Neolithic period, when people began domesticating grains in Anatolia and Old Europe,

> this already ancient deity was transformed into an agricultural goddess, the progenitor and protectress of all fruits of the harvest, but especially grain and bread.[9]

Throughout the Neolithic, she was "worshiped at bread ovens in courtyards or in houses as bread giver."[10] In fact, according to Gimbutas, "The bread oven was the principal feature of Old European shrines."[11] We can see from archaeological finds in temples, as well as miniature temple models from the Neolithic period, that bread baking was often performed as a collective women's ritual—just as it is still done for the contemporary feast of Santa Gemma.

Terracotta figurines of Bird and Snake Goddesses were installed in house shrines, from several to as many as fifteen, using grinding stones and bread ovens.[12] In one such shrine model found in Thessaly from the fifth millennium BCE, several female figurines surround a bread oven, as though preparing the sacred bread. Gimbutas reported that,

> Excavators came upon this model under the floor of a building, perhaps deposited there to honor the bird goddess upon construction of her temple.[13]

This ancient building antedates by seven thousand years the House of Gemma, where the women of Goriano stayed up all night to bake their annual feast bread in the twenty-first century CE.

On an earlier trip in June 2004, I traveled to Bulgaria and Serbia with a tour group of archaeologists and scholars organized by Joan Marler. The Mesolithic site of Lepinski Vir had been built on the Serbian bank of the Danube River, located at a place called the Iron Gates, where there was once an enormous whirlpool before the gorge was flooded in 1971. Archaeologists had to move the ancient site and reconstruct it farther up on the banks, before the waters rose. During our visit, we were outside on the lawn listening to archaeologists explaining and showing us the latest finds from the site, when an old man from the village appeared with an elaborately decorated round loaf of bread (Fig. 17). To my shock, I found myself looking at a set of motifs on a loaf of bread from this rural site in Europe that reminded me of the shape of a Tibetan *mandala* with four gates in the cardinal directions, and four secondary points in between. A few years later I was given a new book published by the National Museum in Belgrade showing that the original site of Lepinski Vir was laid out as a solar-lunar calendar with the requisite eight points: the four cardinal directions and the cross-quarter points in between.[14] The old man described the bread as having to do with "death rites."

Gimbutas noted that likewise in her native Lithuania, "offerings of bread to [the fertility goddess] Zemyna continued through the early twentieth century.[15] Zemyna, in traditional Great Mother style, "creates life out of herself, performing the miracle of renewal."[16] Furthermore, the Basque goddess Mari is invoked by her

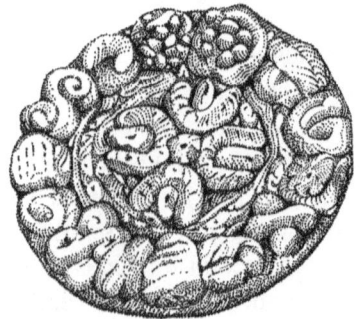

Fig. 17. Ritual bread, Lepinski Vir. Drawing by Andrew Fearnside, 2019.

devotees at the entrances to caves that "shelter a fire and bread oven, since she bakes bread on Friday."[17] Gimbutas called Basques the "living Old Europeans whose traditions descend directly from Neolithic times," who speak "the only indigenous language to survive the Indo-European invasions and cult influences of the last 3000 years," and still have "goddess religion, the lunar calendar, matrilineal inheritance laws, and agricultural work performed by women."[18]

> In later antiquity, bread and cakes for ritual purposes were baked in various shapes—loaf, snake, bird, animal, flower—or had an impressed design.[19]

Neolithic clay models of such loaves have been found—precursors to the one we were shown at Lepinski Vir in 2004.

The Return of the Maiden to the Mother

During the main pageant of Santa Gemma's feast day, spring renewal is re-enacted each year in the ritualized return of a daughter to her mother. Gimbutas reported that the Neolithic Pregnant Goddess was sometimes represented in "dual form, very likely depicting mother–daughter pairs, the spring-summer and fall-winter aspects of the goddess."[20] At the start of the festival day's events, the villagers walked out of the village of Goriano and processed down a steep hill to a place where the road curves around and becomes the road to Gemma's birthplace, the nearby town of San Sebastian. At the crossroads was a small shrine built to house an image of Santa Gemma. This is the formal meeting place where the crowd gathered and waited for the ritualized return of the maiden (Gemma) to her mother A continuous crowd of people streamed from the village of Goriano and down the hill to the meeting place. Another almost equally large crowd approached from the direction of San Sebastian. A poised young woman walked in front of that procession, representing the maiden returning to her mother, accompanied by attendants, civil leaders and Catholic priests (Fig. 18).

As the procession came closer, we could see the ones in front carrying a banner depicting the saint. Christina told us about the song they were singing—a "sad song" because they had to leave the girl in Goriano now. But afterward a woman named Adele who

Fig. 18. Maiden and attendant with scroll. Drawing by Rita Hillman, 2019.

joined us for lunch told about an earlier song that they used to sing when she was a child participating in the festival. She sang for us the words she could recall of the devotional, "Le Devo Cantare," which included references to the hands of Saint Gemma, requests for her protection, and the singing of "[*I*]*o le adoro* . . . *Le adoro, le adoro* ("I adore you"). Now, she told us, they have changed it to a church song (the "sad song" Christina had mentioned), showing how in recent generations, the archaic pagan elements, which had previously been joyful, have been compromised. As the people from Goriano came down the long hill en masse from the village, the marching band played a "glad song," a deliberate contrast, to celebrate that they were now receiving the young woman (Saint Gemma) back into their fold. A young girl kissed *la Tocchia*, the state papers and manuscripts carried by the maiden, demonstrating the importance of her role in blessing the community at this festival.

After the formal welcomes from governing officials and various townspeople, each giving her kisses on both cheeks, the whole procession went back up the hill in anticipation of the much-awaited culminating event—the dramatized meeting of the *kore* (young woman) and *la comare* (the older woman). A marching band played and priests milled about. By the time the maiden met up with the mother and they embraced, both women, along with many of the village women around me, were seriously crying.

Behind these strong emotions lie the many miracles attributed to the "cult of Saint Gemma." For example, during World War II, when the Germans tried to enter the church with tanks, the tanks would not fit through the door. A soldier took munitions into the church, but he fled because a young woman appeared and said, "Go away, this is my house." She was, of course, Santa Gemma. Another time, the front lines were expected to trek through the village, which would have been very destructive, and instead two meters of snow fell, saving the town. Again the people gave credit to Gemma. So it wasn't surprising to learn, at the end of the festival in 2009, that the villagers believed Santa Gemma had performed yet another miracle during the earthquake. The fact that the Church of Santa Gemma and her feast house suffered the most damage was considered to be evidence that the saint took the catastrophe onto herself and spared the village. No wonder the villagers had shown such strong feelings!

One cannot help but wonder if the general emotional atmosphere of the festival is also connected with ancestral memory and the long continuity of Goddess worship that still exists today under a veneer of Christianity. The spring rites of Greek Demeter and Persephone, or Roman Ceres and Proserpina, go back to the late Bronze Age in Greece—if not long before that. Cristina Biaggi suggested, in her book on the stone structures of Malta,[21] that the red designs painted on the ceiling of the underground hypogeum (3500 BCE) might represent pomegranates. The underground rituals practiced there appear to have been precursors to the Eleusinian Mysteries later performed in Greece for more than a thousand years. The return of the maiden to the mother in the spring is at least as old as these rituals.

Santa Gemma's Supernatural Qualities

The central miracle connected with Santa Gemma and her feast day is the story of events around her death in 1426. After her death but before the funeral, according to Christina, a high priest arrived from Rome. Gemma had been laid out with two crosses in her hands and he took one of them from the corpse. As he tried to leave the village, lightning struck him. The priest had to return and replace the cross in Gemma's funeral box. In later years, another priest arrived and opened the box of her burial to find her corpse "uncorrupted." (This bears some resemblance to similar stories of Buddhist and Taoist monks, whose bodies also do not decay but remain in pristine condition after death.) Naturally, after this incident, a great veneration for her arose among the populace and she has been celebrated since then. The current tradition of a meeting between the two villages has taken place since the eighteenth century, with Gemma arriving as a maiden from the other village only since the nineteenth century.

The festivities on that day in 2009 ended in a rather remarkable fashion. Together the townspeople returned to the area across the street from Gemma's damaged church, where a temporary tent had been set up for services. We all entered the tent sanctuary where, lo and behold, the body of Saint Gemma herself was on display in front of the makeshift church. She looked like Sleeping Beauty in her precious display case, her face paint enhanced by a special team of people trained for that purpose (I was told). There were images of Gemma everywhere in the temporary church, including the two oil paintings that had been carried in the procession, embroideries on the table cloth covering the altar, more textiles wrapped around the central tent pole near where the priests said mass, and a large iconic statue at the front of the church showing Gemma holding the cross she used to reproach the nobleman who tried to rape her.

Other Archaic Festivals in Abruzzo

In Italy a festival like the Feast of Santa Gemma is anything but unusual or anachronistic. Seasonal festivals take place in tiny mountain towns all over the country and throughout the entire calendar year. According to Gimbutas,

> Farmers throughout prehistory recognized cyclical time,
> since they knew the annual cycles of planting, growth, and
> harvest. They observed festivals and rituals at appropriate
> times during the cycle.[22]

These old fertility or calendar rituals have been attached to various Catholic saints and incorporated into Christianity to some extent, but obvious relics from pagan times remain resolutely in the foreground.

During the same week of early May, I attended a famous "snake festival" in a nearby village where girls and boys, men and women, freely handled snakes and a contest was held to determine which ones were the biggest and the best. Snakes gathered at Spring Equinox and kept for the festival in early May were draped over the statue of a male saint and paraded through town. The snakes were then released back into the forest afterwards, having no doubt re-established some ancient state of balance and renewal. I was told that the Catholic Church tried to ban this festival, but the people would not allow it, and so the festival was reinstated.

In another village, I was able to attend the annual "festival of the Virgins" where little girls (as well as bigger ones), were sewn into ancient costumes and adorned with gold jewelry by their mothers, aunts, and grandmothers. The girls led a procession through the streets, in which priests and townsmen carried a statue of the patron saint from the newer church up the hill, all the way through the town, and down to the old church that villagers believe belongs to *her*. These contemporary Italian festivals go back to ancient times and confirm the continuity of extremely archaic practices and beliefs stemming from the Neolithic civilization documented so thoroughly by Marija Gimbutas in her archaeomythological work on Old Europe. Gimbutas demonstrated that although the Goddess religion went underground after patriarchal invasions, many of "the old traditions, particularly those connected with birth and death, and earth fertility rituals, have continued to this day without much change in some regions."[23] Certainly such continuity holds true in remote mountain villages of Italy.

The "Madonna" in the old church is the central icon in the village, featured at the front of the cathedral-like church overseeing the mass and depicted in sanctified paintings. I found it quite wondrous to know that there, in the mountains of Abruzzo, only hours away from Rome and the watchful eye of the Vatican, the Goddess appears to be very much alive and well. Like an ancient underground stream, she continuously bubbles to the surface in these festivals that refuse to forget her, so powerful in their capacity to reawaken even the most jaded among us.

References

Babović, Ljubinka. *The Mystery of Lepenski Vir: The Image of the Sun Deity* (from 7th millennium BCE). Belgrade: National Museum, 2008.

Biaggi, Cristina. *Habitations of the Great Goddess*. Manchester, CT: Knowledge, Ideas & Trends Inc., 1994.

Edgar, Blake. "Home of the Modern Mind: Did Culture Begin with the Color Red and a Stone Age Clambake?" *Archaeology Magazine* 61, 2 (2008): 59–65.

Hadingham, Evan. *Secrets of the Ice Age: The World of the Cave Artists*. New York: Walker & Company, 1979.

Gimbutas, Marija. *The Goddesses and Gods of Old Europe: Myths and Cult Images*, new and updated edition. Berkeley: University of California Press, 1982.

Gimbutas, Marija. *The Language of the Goddess*, foreword by Joseph Campbell. New York: Harper & Row, 1989.

Gimbutas, Marija. *The Civilization of the Goddess: The World of Old Europe*. HarperSanFrancisco, 1991.

Gimbutas, Marija. *The Living Goddesses*, edited and supplemented by Miriam Robbins Dexter. Berkeley: University of California Press, 1999.

Noble, Vicki. *Shakti Woman: Feeling Our Fire, Healing Our World—The New Female Shamanism*. HarperSanFrancisco, 1991.

Endnotes

1 Marija Gimbutas, *The Goddesses and Gods of Old Europe: Myths and Cult Images*, new and updated edition (Berkeley: University of California Press, 1982); Gimbutas, *The Language of the Goddess*, foreword by Joseph Campbell (New York: Harper & Row, 1989); *The Civilization of the Goddess: The World of Old Europe* (HarperSanFrancisco, 1991); Gimbutas, *The Living Goddesses*, edited and supplemented by Miriam Robbins Dexter (Oakland: University of California Press, 1999).

2 Gimbutas, *The Living Goddesses*, 16.

3 Gimbutas, *The Civilization of the Goddess*, 228.

4 Gimbutas, *The Civilization of the Goddess*, 228.

5 Evan Hadingham, *Secrets of the Ice Age: The World of the Cave Artists* (New York: Walker & Company, 1979), 84.

6 Vicki Noble, *Shakti Woman: Feeling Our Fire, Healing Our World—The New Female Shamanism* (HarperSanFrancisco, 1991), 24.

7 Hadingham, *Secrets of the Ice Age*, 84.

8   Blake Edgar, "Home of the Modern Mind: Did Culture Begin with the Color Red and a Stone Age Clambake?" *Archaeology Magazine* 61, 2 (2008): 59–65.

9   Gimbutas, *The Civilization of the Goddess*, 228.

10   Gimbutas, *The Civilization of the Goddess*, 342.

11   Gimbutas, *The Language of the Goddess*, 147.

12   Gimbutas, *The Language of the Goddess*, 132–33.

13   Gimbutas, *The Living Goddesses*, 86.

14   Ljubinka Babović, *The Mystery of Lepenski Vir: The Image of the Sun Deity* (from 7th millennium BC) (Belgrade: National Museum, 2008).

15   Gimbutas, *The Living Goddesses*, 209.

16   Gimbutas, *The Living Goddesses*, 208.

17   Gimbutas, *The Living Goddesses*, 173.

18   Gimbutas, *The Living Goddesses*, 172.

19   Gimbutas, *The Language of the Goddess*, 147.

20   Gimbutas, *The Living Goddesses*, 16.

21   Cristina Biaggi, *Habitations of the Great Goddess* (Manchester, CT: Knowledge, Ideas & Trends Inc., 1994).

22   Gimbutas, *The Living Goddesses*, 16.

23   Gimbutas, *The Language of the Goddess*, 318.

SERPENT, EARTH, HEALING, INITIATION

MONICA MODY

Introduction

The worship of serpents evokes older ways of revering earth energies that can be found in mythological and cosmological systems of many ancient cultures. In South Asia, ancient Hindu and Buddhist texts depict the complex and shifting position of serpent deities as the Vedic culture began to spread into, incorporate, appropriate and/or demonize presences and motifs found in pre-Vedic and non-Vedic cultures.

In 2016, serpents slipped into my life of their own accord. An encounter with Nagadevi drew me irresistibly toward nagas and sacralized or deified serpents in other civilizations. Through this engagement, I have come to see that reconnecting with and decolonizing the earth/snake energies is one way in which the borderlands feminine can heal her pasts, presents and futures.

Serpent Tongue

Her startled black tongue, enigma
I entered the cave large as her tongue
Red dripping from her doorway
She who is of passion & might combined
Arose from her red-waisted leisure
They all fled
What was left was my tongue's desire to call out her name
Parrots whispered secrets to each other
Like lovers, their heads bent to each other
I chose to be bold & speak
The secrets
Of silence

273

Nagadevi's Call

When I encountered Nagadevi in 2016 in Bangalore in a small temple inside the perimeter of the residential complex where my family lives, she captivated me. I wanted to know who she was. It was a deep, instinctual calling. I felt directed to go to Mannarsala in Kerala, which has a serpent temple.

The Mannarsala temple is presided over by Nagaraja—king of serpents. Also in the temple complex are shrines for Nagaraja's two consorts, Sarpayakshi and Nagayakshi. The temple had an additional draw for me: it is rare in that even though it is maintained by a Brahmin lineage, its chief priestess heading the rituals is a woman.

At Nagadevi's small temple, I had felt an invitation—and spaciousness—to freely embody my own priestess self, without being weighed down by extrinsic rules or any fear of judgment. I could appear before her in the fullness of my intuition: I could receive her from that same fullness. Often, she would be a living presence to me, granting me direct experiencing and esoteric knowledge. No intermediaries—no male priests—were needed between us. My call was sufficient to bring her into living, faintly vibrating, presence. In meditations with her, for the first time I began experiencing living archetypal energies at the root of deities in the ancient Hindu pantheon. I journeyed to the cosmological time of their forming that antedated the appropriation of these energies by a repressive patriarchal Brahmanical order.

At Mannarsala, on the other hand, I ran into the androcentric Brahmanic culture and administration. Brahmin men were everywhere on the temple grounds, managing the flow of visitors, conducting rituals, carrying out the multifarious responsibilities of an active house of worship in India. It appeared to my outsider eye that the movements of the head priestess (Amma) herself were directed and regulated by male Brahmins. This was not a woman's world. Its standards and norms were determined and enforced by Brahmin men. As a woman who has grown up in a man's world, I know when I am in a context when men walk with the sureness of privilege, and women are given eggshells to walk on. In this temple, it was clear that men were the custodians, even if Amma herself is named as the chief priestess. I had received spirit guidance for a personal ritual I needed to do at the temple. In the milieu I found myself in, I felt furtive as I did the ritual one sleepy afternoon, lest one of the temple men see me.

Within a patriarchal and hierarchical Brahmanical order, I often experience double disability as a woman and as a non-Brahmin. There is minimal room for me to have unfiltered, unmediated access to the sacred, or to my own sacred self. Hindu patriarchies have sought to regulate and impose external and internal conditions under which I may relate to the sacred. They have shamed and derogated the parts of me that expand upon coming in contact with sacred mysteries.

With Nagadevi, I had the sense that she began to know me as much as I began to know her. That at her shrine, I could have a direct relationship with Nagadevi was partly my will; partly, it may have been hers. There was tremendous healing in this.

Yet, at the Mannarsala temple, the patriarchal androcentric Brahmanical culture perpetuated gender and caste hierarchies, and belied the emancipatory promise held out to me by virtue of its retaining a woman as spiritual head. The dominance of the Brahmin male was left undisturbed at this serpent temple.

Upon encountering the legend of the founding of the temple, I experienced a further cognitive dissonance at the absence of the feminine. Neither Sarpayakshi nor Nagayakshi play a role of any significance in the temple legends that are told today among Mannarsala's Namboodiri Brahmins.[1] I felt betrayed by yet another narration assuming "the 'common-sense' character of patriarchal reality."[2] My own sense was that the narrative lacunae surrounding Sarpayakshi and Nagayakshi could be associated with the discourse of Brahminical patriarchy in which the feminine is marginalized or subordinated.

Despite everything, the fact remained that in going to Mannarsala, I had let myself trust an impulse my rational mind did not fully understand. Appropriately enough, Dianne Jenett calls this process of trusting the chthonic, "following the snake."[3] This itself constituted a moment of transformation—an interstitial moment, when I transcended my fistful of knowns and summoned my voice, vitality and authority into serpent movement.[4] As Anzaldúa puts it, "La mestiza has gone from being the sacrificial goat to becoming the officiating priestess at the crossroads."[5]

Serpent

Which coiled rope will you pick up
&
unravel?
Whose syllable seeded itself into your mouth &
washed incoming sounds
with breath of oneness?
Is there a story?
That vanished under earth
Was swallowed by earth
A burning maze spins under surface
Spinning fire under surface gathers momentum
waiting to emerge at an eligible moment
We who live under belly of time often wondered
how cosmos would turn out
Womb-tree of mother grew
Time in its anxiety buzzing around above our heads
White tail shedding fear
We learnt to dive into mother's ocean whenever time came near
We offered ourselves to mother, whole
Beloved's eyes are creased with age
She is all ages at once
O fragrant one
I begin lifting fibrils of her skin one at a time and lick
My tongue swells with the need to tell a story
Bodies begin dancing above my head
In the beginning
There was one clan, not two
Bird that broke free from belly of snake
Snake that wiggled its way out of bird's beak
Keepers, both
of ancient waters of life
Every struggle later, blood & skin collected under their fingernails
To recover, I go into past
where I'd forgotten my bags & trunks

Three silver-haired women are waiting with my baggage
Salt in their hair gleams with something beyond wisdom
I lick the salt & remember
She whose sharp-jutted call lived among trees
She whose cheeks wind scratched from too long a proximity
I wore her skin painted around my waist
I singed to her feathers, slowly
I wriggled down tree of life and curled around its trunk
in sinuous mass, not much but sinecure
This long sleep woke up giants
This sleep rumbled under earth and crept into cracks
I lifted strands of time one after the other,
looking for my parts
Timeline in which I was change
I spanned seven oceans, seven worlds, with each step
Something moved under my dream
In dream-bed, I cavorted, one amongst a million snakes
Millennia we spun swiftly off into a horizon
finding newness of possibility
Flinging ourselves into infinity, riding waves, we met
ourselves
They spoke from behind the sun
(Sun was a distant relative who sometimes crossed sky to meet them)
Animal that came down from stars looked nothing like you or me
Its tail was close to the ground
They spoke
They vanished then, crawled into different dimensions of cosmos
She who was sovereign unto herself
split into two
They placed half of her skin in a museum & called it temple
Deep white land of sleep is oblivious to anything happening
White sleep of oblivion that stretches into your eyes
You have to get through trees to find & bring back what got lost there
It is appropriate
Jewel that lives in the belly of snake is nothing but life
Life matters

A New Vision

Patriarchy deems certain figures as marginal or less relevant, perhaps even ostracizes them. Yet, we might still experience an instinctive, insistent pull toward them, even deeper than the ocean. We can give these energies a respectable garb, and even put on a sari around them (e.g., see Nagadevi's image in Fig. 19). The fact remains that they come from a part of us/the world that is wild and untamable.

Fig. 19. Nagadevi. Drawing by Rita Hillman, 2019.

It is not necessary here that I make a cognitive-intellectual accounting of serpents—or explicate upon their mythic, historical and cultural significance in South Asia or elsewhere—to avow my draw towards them. In Mannarsala, Brahmin male priests have grabbed control of the wild, primordial energy of serpents by subjugating the sacred relationships through which—I am intuiting—the priestesses of old tended serpent energies. At least, this has been attempted. Priestesses' access to the borderlands itself is controlled and patrolled by the patriarchal authority.

Yet, primordial energies—and those who are conduits for them—are never entirely tamable. Surely, embers lie asleep in the folds of the earth where the ancients are born as energies. It takes but a wind to spark an ember into fire. With its vast distribution of microconsciousnesses, India is yet poised to birth a new vision for the future.

Snake, Woman

Secret terrain where oneness resides
one-seeing
Snake looks at woman
It is not distance
Terroir of oneness
through which they move together
snake, woman
Energies folding out of me
Energies folding out of you
Inner the mystery:
Enter
What comes across like rivers undammed
arose through thrill of tale
In deep time, they live still
as one

The Serpent Movement

Subsequent to my visit to Mannarsala, I have had other encounters with serpent deities as well as with living serpents. Snakes are not merely symbols or mythic-sacral constructs: they are our co-dwellers in an ecological real. The animistic expression of the Nagas depends on their co-evolving on this Earth in their form as animals. As beings of nature, they need a biosphere in which to thrive.

I have found that one answer for the healing of post-patriarchal possibilities for the body, intimacy, and futurities in the remantling of serpent energies.

Many of us have found ourselves activated into both hope and trauma by the repeated evidencing of patriarchy's utter disregard for the well-being of women. In the face of this experience, one of the questions I have found myself asking is this: How may we make ourselves more available to an imagination that orients us better to becoming denizens of dawning post-patriarchal moments?

Patriarchy does not exist singly. The social system of exclusion is constructed as a set of interlocking structures of oppression, domination and subjugation: kyriarchy as a system is multiplicative.[6]

Centuries of living within social systems of domination has left our bodies, nervous systems, and wills with accumulated trauma that, we have found, acts as a limitation upon—or wars upon—the arc of the possible. It wars upon our promise to ourselves, and our promise to each other. This trauma must not only be discharged to make us more available to ourselves, our promise and each other: it must be transformed in a way that the energy released contributes to the liberation of all life. It is my hypothesis that the medicine of serpents holds one key for our safer embodied being, relationships and resilience.

In *Borderlands*,[7] Gloria Anzaldúa uses the term "spiritual mestizaje" to describe the ways in which spirituality informs every aspect of the work of evolution—and revolution—entailed in bringing two cultures together. Giving rise to new subjectivities, epistemologies and healing from the ashes of the old—transforming the old—asks from us a critical mobility—the ability to live *as* "the opus, the great alchemical work."[8] Then, Anzaldúa writes, "We have become the quickening serpent movement."[9]

To birth the possibilities that will come together from the clash of patriarchy and what will arise from the healing of it, we invoke within ourselves the serpent—a process that continually allows us to shed old identities, agreements and codes, a process that allows us to renew ourselves into wholeness. We get to know the serpent, and come into relation with it.

Naga Gnosis

Shortly after Christine Blasey's testimony and the eruption of the #MeToo in India, one afternoon I made offerings at a eucalyptus tree in San Francisco's Golden Gate Park, and asked to make contact with the ancient tree in the temple compound of Mannarsala. I asked the Nagas what they had to say about the traumas ensuing in the collective from the somatic and lived experience of being in patriarchy. I asked them about the healing of the feminine and the masculine. This is the serpent gnosis I received as I sat with my back against the tree.

A caveat is to remember that serpents—whether we know them as ecological beings or through ritual texts, traditions and myths—by their very nature resist both control and exclusivity of narrative as well as interpretation. Any gnosis, revelation or knowing that arises through our relationship as humans to their realms must of necessity allow for a multitude of layers.

> The phenomenon of serpents is sensed within our own somatic awareness, first of all, through how differently they move. They undulate.

> Serpent reminds us, even if part of us wants to stay stagnant, that the only way out is moving through it. Serpents are sacred because they embody the movement of living life. The movement of the serpent is against perfection.

> Within our bodies, the nervous system is a counterpart of the serpent. The nervous system cannot be controlled. It will have its own reactions. In that way, its responses are primitive—they are reptilian.

> The response of the nervous system comes from the deep core of our being. It is that pure. This means that we can chart our journeys to sovereignty through the divining rod of our nervous systems. Bringing awareness to the subtle responses in our nervous systems allows us to begin to see the patterns we hold within. It allows us to see the whole of our relationship with coherence and flow.

Relationships are what have been affected in societies of domination. This started out with that cutting out of that first, most central of relationships: with the Mother.

The mother is also an aspect of ourselves. By disallowing this relationship in its fullness—and the consistent experience of nurture, seeing, knowing, allowing and attunement with the mother—we were rendered insecure. The deep attachment traumas many of us carry within us come from within this source wound.

They diminish our autonomy. They diminish our ability to trust ourselves. They render us easily porous to the energies that want us to experience scarcity. They make us more preoccupied with being safe, and less willing to take risks. They keep us loyal to the old paradigm, and less willing to transform it.

By making our relationship to ourselves unsafe, it is our ability to respond to the collective crisis—and our will to participate in creating alternatives to oppressive systems—that patriarchy diminishes.

In patriarchy, many priestesses and priests of ancient serpent traditions also lost their autonomy. Many of us have experienced the pain of being born amidst traditions that are merely distorted refractions of the primordial truths they were born to witness.

With the pervasive experience of disconnection and alienation, not only do we feel unsafe, but our very bodies have developed a defensive physiology.

The spine is an alive band of circuitry. Spinal practitioners tell us that our spine shows what kind of pressures we have had in life. All unintegrated emotional traumas leave an energetic and structural imprint on it. The spine shows what our experiences have shaped us into. It carries the traces of our individual, collective, cultural and ancestral memories.

The shape and alignment of the spine determines the clarity and creativity with which our nervous system functions.

The stress that we live amidst gets stored within our bodies, spine, and nervous system—the stress within our spine and our nervous system speaks to our disconnection from the serpent energies.

$$\oint$$

By invoking the serpent, we are invoking our capacity to be in sovereign connection with the Earth, with ourselves and with our will.

From ancient sources in diverse cultures, we have learned about the different ways in which we may come into contact with serpent energies. In many traditions, dance is one way in which people come into contact with them. These energies are sinuous; they are wave-like. They are not stiff or static. Serpents do not move in blocks or chunks of energy, but in waves. Theirs is a fluid energy. They embody the fluidity that makes up *being*—not just our own, but ours-beyond-duality.

There is a reason the serpent has a strong connection to water in ancient lore, why the Nagas are said to "haunt lakes, ponds and the sources of rivers, [be] beneficial givers of rain"[10]; why they are said to be guardians of the waters. Theirs were the first bodies that could survive in the watery realms of creation.

And, even more: the movement of the serpent evokes the living vital fluidity of the Earth.

We remantle serpent energies, then, by changing the liquid energetic core within ourselves. To become intimate with the serpent, we need to lose our fear of the deep electric within. We need to figure out how to sit with the serpent when the serpent is in front of us, looking at us. This encounter must be approached through non-rational faculties, in ways that go animal—beyond the rational. It must be approached at a level more-than-human, at the level of instinct.

We must regain our instincts—our trust in our perceptions, our discernment and our bodies.

$$\oint$$

The serpent is very much an other. I do know this, as someone who has danced with serpents in ceremony, and remembered being an oracle with them in another time.

When I've danced with serpents, I've felt an at-oneness with them.

If the serpent is also within us—as our spine, connected to our nervous system—we can only imagine with what tenderness we need to tend this other.

Can you imagine a traumatized serpent within you? A serpent that has lost its instinct to know when to strike, when to retreat? A serpent that responds in fight or flight or freeze patterns because it is stuck in those traumatic patterns?

When snakes in mythology are spoken of as malevolent, they are not being seen through the lenses of an animal that is frightened or hurt—an animal whose instinct has been messed with—but are ascribed intentionality that is "evil." It is possible that these mythic serpents had not been stripped of goodness—rather, on them were foisted qualities that are human. It is possible that speaking of serpents as evil comes from a loss of discrimination and sight that is part of the narrative of patriarchy.

This is different than recuperating the frightened, angry serpent asking to be soothed.

The serpent's connection to caves and darkness indicates the capacity to be with our fears. This is not fearlessness, but a kind of courage that is more: it is a recognition of the fears and the darkness itself as one that is deeply of the Self, something that allows you to find treasures by letting you momentarily close your ego-eye and shut out the ego-light.

These are all things that have been demonized: serpent, darkness, water, instinct, intuition, the feminine. They were demonized because they are outside the realm of control and rationality—they frighten patriarchy and colonialism. The serpent will just not be put into a grid—neither will darkness, water, instinct, intuition, the feminine. Their inner movement—inner technology—grants them the grace and capacity of subversion. Each of these energies—by the very way in which they can move—can surpass the grids of reality and create new zones and habitats of possibility.

The serpent comes out of the darkness. It is inextricably of the underworld, showing us how mysterious and inseparable the relationship between the void and light is.

Are we willing to sit with the chthonic, to let the chthonic come to us? To dwell in the Serpent is to give up our innocence. It is to give up the belief that it is possible to go back to what was, and to let ourselves be bathed by the deepest innocence that comes from Source.

⚕

Trauma is the response that gets stuck in the body until we can repair what is torn. The good thing about trauma is that it points to where and how we are disconnected in our energetic system.

Attachment patterns are one way in which this disconnection in our energetic system shows up. Are we living in reality, or are we living in fantasy? If there is a disconnection in the energetic system, it is very hard for the brain to give up even an illusion of attachment. Attachment is the bloom that sustains our yearning for the divine—our capacity to connect with the divine—the deep affect the divine generates in this human realm when it arrives here to play.

How our attachment patterns are replaying can be a good test for trauma, then. If what our instincts are taking us toward feels good, life-giving and life-enhancing, then we know we have reclaimed our sovereignty. If we find ourselves moving within patterns that keep us in a loop, instead of in a motion of liberation, then we know there is a call to change the way in which we move. This is a call for us to see the trauma, and to bring it liberation and more connection.

Trauma is not a block, but a reaction. It perverts our tendencies to *relax* into the moment, to be present in the moment, to see another person, to witness someone from a place of compassion, to not create stories about them.

But our bodies arrived into this world with all the codes necessary for us to thrive. This means that we can invoke

286

and call in our healing. We can invoke and call in the serpent to assist with that healing.

To remantle the serpent is to see them as our partners, not as objects. To invite the serpent in is not about adding them to our collections.

Mythology, lore and history point to the deep significance of serpent worship; they have something real to say to us about how nature wants us to move—not just our bodies, but our minds, souls and spirits.

Everything we have learned about consciousness, spirit, nature and our place in nature will be found by us in nature. We are of nature, we are not outside it.

In nature, then, these are the places I would tell you to go to, to connect with and honor the serpents: caves, waters, trees. I would tell you to dance. I would tell you to shed the veil of the rational and to slither on the edge that you can barely see with your rational mind, so that you may, from that vantage, call forth viable alternatives to the oh-so-rational reality that strangles what is most vital to us.

The serpent speaks to what has been persecuted: a kind of vital energy, a vital pulse. We need this today. That it has been persecuted does not mean it is not here for us to call forth, bring forth and re-member within ourselves.

The work is not something the serpents can do by themselves either. It has to be done by them in partnership, with humans.

Another deep practice would be to connect with and heal our pelvic region. The pelvic floor is the cave of the mother. Recuperating the spiraling threads of our stories, voices and motherlines is no further than the serpent that rises from our own sacral energies—the root of our creativity.

Remembering as Initiation

Remembering helps us endure. Remembering is an initiation too. Le'ema Kathleen Graham tells a beautiful story of how the serpent came through her as she danced after her own snakebite initiation.[11] She writes, about ancient priestesses: "What the serpent chose to teach, the priestess learned to offer to others."[12] Being initiated by serpents come with its own responsibility to dance the full dance. It comes with the responsibility to change the movements of energy and earth in our own lives, and to share our lives with others.

Neuroscience Research and Remembering

What we remember changes the pasts, the present and the futures available to us. This has now been corroborated by neuroscience research. According to interpersonal neurobiologist Daniel Siegel, "memory is the way past events affect future function."[13] What is encoded in the brain as memory—our experience of the world—constructs the future we anticipate.

From the work of Siegel and other neuroscientists, it appears that the memory that gets stored (as what is called an "engram") changes when it is retrieved.[14] Conceptualizing the engram not as static, unchanging content stored in the brain, but as an interconnected—and therefore malleable—patterning of energy flow and information, changes the picture of how we understand the pasts and futures. Honoring the serpent energy of memory allows us to use memory as a resource for the liberation of our experience in the present, in our pasts and in anticipated futures.

Neuronal activity is responsive—and the set of neurons that gets activated and fires in particular patterns (called "neural net profiles"), are never identical with profiles activated in the past, though they may resemble them.[15] Siegel writes, "remembering is not merely the reactivation of an old engram; it is the construction of a new neural net profile with features of the old engram and elements of memory from older experiences, as well as influences from the present state of mind."[16] To me, this suggests that we can change memory itself by what and how we remember. Remembering itself can become a way to trigger a different enough neural net profile that will change the possibilities for the future encoded in the nervous system.

As feminists at the borderlands, we can use this serpentine quality of memory to recover our motherlines. We can connect more deeply with our ancestresses, some of whom were perhaps the snake priestesses lost in modernity.

The serpent, remembered, is nothing less than a conceptual-sensual reclaiming of heterogenous temporality. The serpent initiates us into our embodied belonging to Earth. As we traverse our own vast underworlds, we grieve. Wave-like, pushing off of the bumps encountered, we heal and change the future(s) available to us. We remember that we are the ones who have come before; we are the ones who are coming.

References

"About the Temple—History." Mannarsala Sree Nagaraja Temple, 2010. www.mannarasala.org/dynamic.php?page=mannarasalaHistory.

Anzaldúa, Gloria. *Borderlands: The New Mestiza = La Frontera*. San Francisco: Spinsters/Aunt Lute, 1987.

Graham, Le'ema Kathleen. "Holy Bite." In *Stepping into Ourselves: An Anthology of Writings on Priestesses*, edited by Anne Key and Candace Kant, 273–75. Lanham: Goddess Ink, 2015.

Jenett, Dianne Elkins. "Red Rice for Bhagavati/Cooking for Kannaki: An Ethnographic Inquiry of the Pongala Ritual at Attukal Temple, Kerala, South India." PhD diss., California Institute of Integral Studies, 1999.

Schüssler Fiorenza, Elisabeth. "Method in Women's Studies in Religion: A Critical Feminist Hermeneutics." In *Methodology in Religious Studies: The Interface with Women's Studies*, edited by Arvind Sharma, 207–41. Albany: State University of New York Press, 2002.

———. *But She Said: Feminist Practices of Biblical Interpretation*. Boston: Beacon Press, 2005.

Siegel, Daniel. *The Developing Mind: How Relationships and the Brain Interact to Shape Who We Are*. 2nd ed. New York: Guilford Press, 2012.

Vogel, J. Ph. *Indian Serpent-Lore, or, The Nagas in Hindu Legend and Art*. Whitefish, MT: Kessinger, 2011.

Endnotes

1 The legends told by the Brahmin family that manages the temple center on Nagaraja's appearance before their forebears. Nagaraja, they say, appeared before a childless couple after the couple had nursed back to health numerous

serpents burned in a forest fire. Nagaraja blessed them and agreed to be born as their son. He has stayed on in the temple cellar, in samadhi, to bless the devotees. See "About the Temple—History," Mannarasala Sree Nagaraja Temple, 2010.

2 Elisabeth Schüssler Fiorenza, *But She Said: Feminist Practices of Biblical Interpretation* (Boston: Beacon Press, 2005), 53.

3 Dianne Elkins Jenett, "Red Rice for Bhagavati/Cooking for Kannaki: An Ethnographic Inquiry of the Pongala Ritual at Attukal Temple, Kerala, South India" (PhD diss., California Institute of Integral Studies, 1999), 53.

4 Gloria Anzaldúa, *Borderlands: The New Mestiza = La Frontera* (San Francisco: Spinsters/Aunt Lute, 1987), 81.

5 Ibid., 80.

6 Elisabeth Schüssler Fiorenza, "Method in Women's Studies in Religion: A Critical Feminist Hermeneutics," in *Methodology in Religious Studies: The Interface with Women's Studies*, ed. Arvind Sharma (Albany: State University of New York Press, 2002), 210.

7 Anzaldúa, *Borderlands*, 81.

8 Ibid., 81.

9 Ibid.

10 J. Ph Vogel, *Indian Serpent-Lore, or, The Nagas in Hindu Legend and Art* (Whitefish, MT: Kessinger, 2011), 4.

11 Le'ema Kathleen Graham, "Holy Bite," in *Stepping into Ourselves: An Anthology of Writings on Priestesses*, ed. Anne Key and Candace Kant (Lanham: Goddess Ink, 2015), 273.

12 Ibid., 274.

13 Daniel Siegel, *The Developing Mind: How Relationships and the Brain Interact to Shape Who We Are*, 2nd ed. (New York: Guilford Press, 2012), 46.

14 Ibid., 50.

15 Ibid., 47–48.

16 Ibid., 51.

GODDESS IS ALIVE!
BUT HOW DO WE KNOW?

JUDY GRAHN

M any of us have personal relationships with what we in the mainstream women's spirituality movement might broadly call "the
goddess"—but that can also be called by a particular name, and is a creatrix, a spirit, or an ancestor, or is called "Mother" or "Grandmother" or
"Sister." Many of us have experiences we would call paranormal, intuitive, psychic, visionary; some of us have experienced visitations, delivery
of information, ecstatic states and/or special relationships with creatures,
plants, the wind or other elements of nature.*

But how do we know when we are in contact? Sometimes the dream
is a pre-cog dream, sometimes the phone call *is* from the person you were
just thinking about; sometimes someone tells you that a dove is following
her and the dove really shows up.

Sometimes we romanticize and see synchronicities in everything,
which makes us seem silly, even to ourselves.

Science, especially the science of the paranormal, of remote viewing,
and so on, has been able to show that human beings have extrasensory
perception capacities that have successfully been the subject of double-
and triple-blind studies. Some of the research indicates that the time–space
continuum bends in such a way that sometimes we can perceive or sense the
future. There is nothing inherently "spiritual" about such abilities, scientists
have argued; they are simply functions of the human brain that have been
untested until now.

However, many of us who live our lives making use of such capacities
understand them as non-repeatable, and as relational rather than random
and take them as some sort of "message" whether from one's own psychic

capacity or from a human or a nonhuman being—because of their timing, because of our feeling states when they are happening and because something is different afterwards.

So yes, heat from a mechanical source under controlled circumstances can cause a pendulum to swing, but does this same mechanically induced movement answer yes and no questions? The answer is no. Answering of questions is a relational interactive process. And, the skeptical scientist is right, this can be a very messy, inaccurate process. It matters enormously that the diviner/asker is aware of the necessity to take care with the instrument—double and triple check, use testing to gauge probability of accuracy; do not ask emotionally risky life or death questions about oneself or loved ones. Diviners are using archaic and ancestral scientific methods.

What about those synchronicities? What kinds of confirmation do we need to be sure they are real and not our minds' romantic wish fulfillments that someone out there loves us and is watching us?

For example, a few years ago I had a student, a very sensitive artistic student, who kept getting involved with tough contentious people—boyfriends and also roommates. One day she came to my office for an advising session; it was late in the day and late in the week. I was tired, and initially her overly excited manner just irritated me. She was talking rapidly, something about birds, and synchronicities, and Jung. I half listened. She waited, then told her story again—something about seeing doves around her all morning, and then later in the afternoon coming down the steps at City Hall and a woman, a stranger, with a basket inexplicably stopping her, telling her to look inside the container, and there were doves.

"They are following me," she said, "everywhere I go for the past several days."

I half awoke. "Student getting paranoid" warning signs flashing in my directorial, professorial mind.

"Who is following you?"

"Doves."

"Doves? What doves?"

"Like *that*." She turned to the narrow window behind her, where a dove—not a pigeon but a little brown speckled dove—was in midair trying to get through the glass as though to reach her.

"Oh!" A *real* dove.

We both rushed to the window to witness the bird, who soon left and presumably went about its own business.

So we talked about why doves might be following her.

And soon after that, she changed her life—moved away from the angry roommates, and took a boyfriend who was sweet, loving, adoring of her in every way.

I could say, from this sequence of events, that the doves got her attention and brought her messages of peace.

But why, what could be a reason, that doves in San Francisco would be moved to go out of their way to bring to the student and me, a message that evidently enabled her to improve her life? Find real love in her life? Materialist science has been adamant in describing creatures as 100-percent self-absorbed in their own "survival"—postulating all behavior in terms of "biological economy." Eco-spiritual and eco-feminist interpretations and intersections with nature tell a far different story.

I too have had a number of inexplicable and seemingly significant encounters with birds. Just as one example, the year I wrote about crow dykes in *The Queen of Swords*, I came upon 35 crow feathers, one at a time, in California, Oregon, Nebraska and New England. I wasn't looking for them, they were just on my path. That year, and no other year.

Yet I remain skeptical because how is this very different from the novice who imagines the goddess is talking to her because an iris flower in her garden bloomed the very day she decided to attend a certain camp named "Iris"? Our minds draw our attention to what we are thinking about. And we can sound pretty silly when we claim synchronicities and guidance on every side—not so many steps different from the folks who say that Katrina ravaged New Orleans because of the sexual sins of the citizens or that gay people cause earthquakes.

And I don't want to be split from science, which has given us so much— so much free time, for one thing; so much capacity to travel and learn.

Yes, yes I know—the world is collapsing and science is to blame.

Francis Bacon, the father of scientific method—with his 16th-century understandings—made a mistake. He thought that science would be morally regulated by religion.

Some would say everything about him was a mistake, but I want to concentrate on one big mistake the founder of the scientific method made: he knew that his method—of setting aside our "idolatries"—by which he meant our assumptions and internalized mythologies, our prejudices—would enable us to open our eyes to realities and to open Nature's secrets, which he said should only be done with her permission. (He said other things about Nature but he also said this.) He knew that the science field would be successful and therefore subject to corruption by commerce, by the state with its armies and so on. But, he said, the Church would hold science in check, the Church would morally regulate science and hold it responsible.

Instead, as we know, the Church polarized science and religion by punishing and denying science, which forced a split between increasingly archaic old texts and increasing new knowledge, and between the heart and the mind. So science, which has made so much possible, also drifted quickly into misuse by the military, commercial and political sectors.

Instead of holding science responsible and keeping it a sacred calling, religion took an oppositional stance to some of the best insights that science had to offer, and science began to scorn the best that the Church has to offer, which includes community, personal responsibility and connection, as well as the aesthetics of mystery—mysteries that were once female. And science, together with religion, downplayed or denied the roles of women and the sacred feminine in creating culture and holding the human world together.

Science tied itself to the military industrial complex and allowed itself to become a competitive game, desecrated by commercial and political interests that have appropriated its language and pseudo versions of its methods, such as distorted and silly use of statistics to "prove" all kinds of vested interests.

For its part, religious authority has steadfastly abandoned scientific knowledge and prophecy, instead protecting encrusted busybodies using misogyny and meddling sexual regulation to cover up extremely serious sexual transgressions against women and children. Far from harnessing science toward the interests of peace, church leaders mindlessly bless military escapades and horrors; religious leaders tie themselves to the leaders of empire, are silent in the face of oppressions and silent for the most part on domestic violence, global warming, nuclear dangers, forced overpopulation. There are exceptions of course, but we all know what the critique of patriarchal religions has been. We all know why we are here today.

And, as feminists, women have been at the forefront of critiquing science as well as religious establishments, but at the price of rejection, the price of turning away from power in order to stay pure. The price of not being holistic about this is that we too have repeatedly abandoned the achievements of science. To be clear, we *have* contributed to the field of psychology by adding to mythology, with its power of healing psychic wounds. But there is a danger that we have sentimentalized or will sentimentalize the goddess, and keep her solely in a psychological arena, and make her irrelevant to international human affairs and human current-crisis–level needs. That her full philosophical power will not be realized.

This has not historically been the way of the goddess. At the risk of offending all my friends who have told me not to say this, let me say, in answer to Donna Haraway's challenge from the 1980s that she would rather be a cyborg than a goddess,[1] that the goddesses have always been cyborgs.

They have tools and special powers, they have geometry and the little machines we humans have developed to express our inventiveness—earrings the shape of light, or a ring through the lip to indicate "invention of sewing." Goddesses and gods hold spears, bows and arrows, a noose, a loom, a basket, a musical instrument, a measuring rod and line—machines of past time but just as important to human evolution as any machines today.

Goddesses of current indigenous and past historic cultures have been iconized and storied as a conflation of human characteristics and natural characteristics that reflected the people's psychology and also their most up-to-date science.

The ancient Mesopotamian pantheon shows us the development of human consciousness about the natural world, personified as deities: the separation of ocean waters (Nammu) from sweet river waters (Enki) and of the surface of the earth (Ninhursaga) from the world underneath this crust (Ereshkigal). Inanna, in the third generation of the cadre of deities, is the planet Venus, and a child of the Moon Couple. Because her literature and imagery was so rich, we still live in the era of the stars, with goddess icons to reflect this in Isis, Inanna-Ishtar-Astarte—and Aphrodite. Goddesses may begin as a particular element, like a named river, and go on for a long and vivid life even after the people have left that river area; Sarasvati's river dried up long ago, but India will never give up its goddess of wisdom, beauty, creativity and learning.

Currently in the women's spirituality movement, Goddess is mythologically and psychologically rich, but scientifically—not so much.

Yes, I know, she comes to get us, we do not "construct" her. And yet we do. We construct her by what we allow her descriptors to be, and what we disallow. By whether we imagine her as a sole creatrix or whether she is part of a collaboration. By whether we imagine her only in archaic "natural" terms or whether the goddess who enabled automobiles and highways also gets to play. How does the goddess intersect with transgender people? Much as I cherish that she is "Mother," as mothers have been so left out of the patriarchal world and worldview, I also think that if the goddess is singular and "gave birth" to the cosmos, where does this leave men, and childless women? How is the metaphor of "giving birth" to the universe a process that describes evolutionary processes of infinite varieties of life forms interacting with each other?

By saying "but the goddess has always been a cyborg," I mean that deity is a construction of how we comprehend the universe around us, combined with our psychological needs for a mother, a father, a whole family of elements, who help us to see ourselves in relationship with nature. Goddesses are dripping with machines: cloth, metal rings, sandals, jugs. Our inventions are part of how we imagine deity; as we are able to perceive nature's greatness, god becomes greater. Grandmother Spider of Plains and Southwestern First Nations people is not just a little being spinning a web—she also carries a basket, lined with pitch, filled with hot coals—so she brings fire to human beings—a tribute to ancestral females who created a technology—weaving—and a machine—a basket—and reinforced its heat resistance with pitch—to carry coals—a major and time-saving human achievement. Grandmother Spider, Thinking Woman, is much more than this, including being creator of the world, being the Milky Way galaxy, and being grandmother to male twins identified with the north and south poles.

Deities and creation parents of the distant past, including the snake and bird goddesses of Old Europe identified by Marija Gimbutas,[2] are indicative of expanding human awareness and capacity to encompass the largeness around us. The great pantheons of the river valleys of West and North Africa, of Mesopotamia, of the Yellow and Yangtze and the Indus river-valley peoples, as well as the pantheons of the Mayan peoples of Mexico and Central America and the Incan peoples of South America, show clearly that deity and the major elements of nature have long been merged. This allowed peoples to identify with and interact very personally with wind and water, fire and mountain and lights in the sky. Religion and science are married in these ancient systems. Gender is also balanced, at least in female and male if not also in more transgendered ways, within these pantheons of creation as these three-to-twelve thousand-year-old river-valley horticultural cultures understood it.

Peoples of the ancient traditions were and are in contact with the *minds* of the elements they personified and deified; they spoke/speak and played with the wind and rain, inducing it, placating it. They interact psychically with creatures. They prayed to sun goddesses and sun gods; they formed intimate relationships with trees and plants, especially those that now turn out our grains, fruits and vegetables. Those relationships and ritual practices were and are the creative horticultural sciences of ancestral peoples.

Goddess has always been in part a cyborg, by which I mean while she has emotional intelligence, she also has always incorporated the sciences of her times—she and her pantheons have embodied the full ranges of human knowledge; she has been the keeper of our machine inventions *and* our comprehensions of nature. This is why she holds tools or is mythologized as a stellar body; her descent journeys and cycles can be equated with the movements of the lights in the sky. Her temples have replicated the known dimensions of the human-understood world—as pillars that imitate groves of trees, as ziggurats that imitate mountains where mountains are understood as holding the world together; as sanctum sanctorums that replicate seclusion sites as the centers or wombs of the known world.

Mainstream patriarchal religion with its fixed, increasingly archaic texts, has struggled and largely failed to keep up with the developments in science—to say nothing of child welfare—for four hundred years. Hence, the entrenched resistance to evidence of human-impacted climate crises.

How is goddess faring in this dialectical struggle between tradition and invention, and the changing consciousness of humanity? What new directions in goddess studies are implied by wanting the sacred feminine to be congruent with modern times rather than complacent with the archaic and sentimental?

Science and religion have drifted apart since Bacon's pre-cogging of the Christian world of mass science–led culture, a drift that began with the ending of medieval times. Scientific explorations expanded; religious explorations did not. Now with the revisionary resurgence of goddess practices, iconography and stories, it seems to me it is urgent for the goddess movement and its scholars to re-appropriate science. This has to be done appropriately and mindfully.

We have the opportunity to unite scientific knowledge and methods with spirituality, tying the sacred feminine and her many-gendered pantheons once again to the best of the human mind, for the purpose of benefiting both. Spirituality enables people to identify with beings that are otherwise terrifying or alienating in their strangeness, their largeness, their mysteriousness. By calling Earth "the mother" we relate to the vastness of the forces with less terror; we relax knowing someone bigger than us is in charge. If studying what nature is actually like enables us to expand our creation stories to be more inclusive—perhaps "mother" isn't the only term for earth's living matrix.

For example, in *Biological Exuberance: Animal Homosexuality and Natural Diversity,* Bruce Bagemihl shows that nature is far more androgynous and versatile with respect to sex, bonding and reproduction than anyone admitted publicly prior to his 1999 book.[3] Over five hundred species have been identified who engage in homosexual sex, pair bonding, or both. This includes some birds, those sterling models of heterosexual monogamy. Layson albatrosses, held up as prime examples of the Adam and Eve story, were revealed through close observations to consist of 30-percent lesbian parenting couples. Male parenting couples are also more common than might have been supposed, and a surprising percentage of male goats have no interest in females at all.

The variety of genders in all kinds of species is beyond our imagining. Bagemihl's findings support the view that reproduction is not the only "purpose" of life, and that sexuality is used for a variety of purposes, including collaboration and social cohesion. In this (suppressed until recently) view of life on Earth, animals two by two into the ark would not have made the evolutionary cut—creature life is far more diverse than that.

Studies of microbiota are revealing another example: Lynn Margulis and Dorian Sagan in *What Is Life?*[4] describe microbes as tiny life beings who discovered how to trap time and space within cell walls, using the chemistry of metabolism to keep the past alive into the present, passing it on through reproduction and DNA communication among cells. They are our most faithful historians.

Lynn Margulis's hypothesis is that life is a matrix of microbiota who developed cellular walls and metabolism using sun and water, and who appear to have developed larger organisms—organ by organ—that ultimately led to plants, animals and us. Their metabolic processes developed the atmosphere and the rich earth floor that supports all of us. We live in their world, and they permeate us. They are our ancestors.

Unfortunately we first met them as conveyers of disease, needing to be killed and controlled, washed away, to protect "us" from "them." They invade, we said with our binary mind-set, they attack and give us bad stuff. Now microbiologists are telling us to adopt a different understanding.

A better idea is that *we live in the world of microbes*, rather than that they live in or "invade" us. And they certainly do live in us—for each one of our cells we contain ten microbes. There is no "us" without "them." They *are* us. And they are ancestral to us. They are the elemental forms of life, and they created the terms and substances of our life: photosynthesis and oxygen, plants and soil. Their metabolic processes are credited with the forms of over a hundred minerals, including iron and gold. The soil that grows plants, as well as the plant forms, are their creation. Hemoglobin precedes animals, and is their creation.

They form communities, they communicate across distances; they live in every extreme of hot and cold, in boiling thermal springs, in ice cores of glaciers; and their fossils have been found in the oldest rocks of earth's earliest formations. They live in cloud formations and other atmospheric places, and are suspected of precipitating raindrops.

Inside our bodies they are associated with our glandular functions, meaning they congregate near the chakras; they regulate our hormones, our diseases, our emotional health, and our deaths. They make choices, they communicate with each other and with our nervous systems. What part of goddess is left out of this picture?

Microbes are an interconnected, continually evolving matrix of life on earth. As I understand "goddess," this fills the bill. I call her *Microbia*, and understand her as multi-gendered and multiple in purpose and function.

Can we take another step now, with what science has achieved in the last three hundred years, and form some new conscious relationships? Microbia may be a place to start that addresses some current crises in human health, obesity and diabetes among them. Medical researchers think that antibiotics have eliminated some of the regulatory bacteria from our systems, triggering dietary problems. Many people currently ingest bacteria as probiotics, and eat what feeds them.

The microbes in our gut communicate with our brains. Microbia regulate levels of depression that lead to addiction. They produce neurotransmitters: serotonins, including oxytocin. Microbia regulate appetite and feelings of happiness and well-being—one might say, of "love."

Microbia regulate our gardens. Microbia may induce rain in the atmosphere. Loving, feeding, thinking about, making contact with, the microbiota that regulate our bodies—might we not develop some methods of communication, some very realistic prayers and offerings to some very real beings? Might we not enhance our meaningful relationships with nature?

Might Microbia be a reason people have believed in "eternal life" and reincarnation? Perhaps some of them coalesce following our deaths to form visible ghosts and ancestral voices—our cells die but the microbial family that knew us so well for decades, they go on reproducing, traveling, communicating. After the cellular structure called "Judy" has deteriorated back into minerals and moisture, the Microbia that kept her functioning will continue. Did she help them in ways she cannot even imagine? Do they remember her as a structure of their past? They are perhaps "eternal life" on earth.

As Margulis and her poet son Dorion Sagan described so beautifully, microbes are life; they have the essentials of life—metabolism, reproduction and bounded walls. They have DNA, which they exchange with each other, causing them to mutate rapidly; they travel across distances on moving bodies and on the winds and waters. They move toward what they like and away from what they dislike. They produce neurotransmitters that convey feelings of love. Is it too early and too great a leap to ask whether they have consciousness?

I think it may be psychologically irresponsible to construct deities of creation who are not inclusive—it triggers off a reactive response rather than a proactive response, from those who are excluded from the creative process.

Feminism and women's spirituality have often set their faces against science, especially "the" scientific method, but is this to the detriment of society and of our genuine capacity to lead the world out of its binary dilemmas? The world needs the sacred feminine, but not at her most frivolous nor at her dreamiest. The world needs her grounded and in the present, taking on real issues and willing to do the hard-headed methodologies that lead to real knowledge rather than wishful thinking.

Knowledge is power; relationship is how power functions.

I propose that we re-appropriate science in the interest of helping ourselves as well as other people connect and identify with difficult facts and with new ideas about the nature of reality. The material cosmos is larger than we can imagine or feel at home in; the matrix of life on earth is smaller, more numerous, and more varied than we can easily consider accessible or charming. If she is mistress of the animals, isn't she mistress of the bacteria as well? And if she is life, aren't they her as well?

Hey! Is that a bird trying to come in that window?

I had two possible encounters with Microbia recently. Soon after I first thought about them as living in my cells and basically engineering me, I was lying down in a still frame of mind. For several minutes, I heard singing, very high pitched and all over my body. This singing was like exceptionally tiny voices, and very joyful; hearing the sound made me happy. I had the sense that my own microbes were singing and that I was hearing them. This experience was quite distinctive and happened only once.

Then, just a couple of weeks ago, after I had read *What Is Life?* I was excited about the idea that I could possibly learn to communicate with some group(s) of Microbia. I had been taking probiotic capsules for digestion, and one evening I put one of the capsules of living organisms on my altar. My altar at that time was extremely cluttered, covered with various small objects my students and friends had given me—it was just a mess. To create a space, I put a tiny spoon inside a bracelet lying on the outside edge of the altar and placed a round probiotic capsule in the bowl of the spoon.

I had turned to stand beside my altar when all of a sudden my left arm moved about ten times faster than I could possibly move it consciously. The movement was like a spasm. My arm lifted and my hand swept over the objects of the altar. Only one of the many objects moved, and that was the capsule, which was swept up in the air, landing on my bed about a yard away. Shocked, and wondering if the gesture meant that I had somehow offended someone, I asked my pendulum, in whom I have gained a great deal of confidence over the years, if the event signaled that I should *not* put microbes on my altar. The pendulum answered that yes, the gesture had been a message, one that signaled approval by the microbiota who are part of "me," approval that I was trying to communicate with them. I await further insights or instructions.

References

Bagemihl, Bruce. *Biological Exuberance: Animal Homosexuality and Natural Diversity.* New York: St. Martin's, 1999.

Gimbutas, Marija. *Language of the Goddess*. San Francisco: Harper San Francisco, 1989.

Haraway, Donna. *Simians, Cyborgs, and Women: The Reinvention of Nature.* New York: Routledge, 1991.

Margulis, Lynn, and Dorion Sagan. *What Is Life?* Berkeley: University of California Press, 2000.

Endnotes

* This essay was presented as a keynote address on May 12, 2014, for the Association for the Study of Women and Mythology Conference, San Francisco.

1 Donna Haraway, "A Cyborg Manifesto: Science, Technology, and Socialist-Feminism in the Late Twentieth Century," In *Simians, Cyborgs, and Women: The Reinvention of Nature*, 149–81 (New York: Routledge, 1991)..

2 Marija Gimbutas, *Language of the Goddess* (HarperSanFrancisco, 1989).

3 Bruce Bagemihl, *Biological Exuberance: Animal Homosexuality and Natural Diversity* (New York: St. Martin's, 1999).

4 Lynn Margulis and Dorion Sagan, *What Is Life?* (Berkeley: University of California Press, 2000).

ABOUT THE CONTRIBUTORS

Idoia Arana-Beobide is an *Euskalduna* (Basque), living in Ottawa, Canada. She was raised with strong Basque traditional values that included the learning of ancient Basque belief systems and Catholicism. Idoia has always had a passion for understanding the nature and threat that the power of the feminine produces in society. Currently living with her Anishinaabe husband, she is furthering her studies regarding the principles of matriarchy in the Basque Country, and how it fits in the reemergence of indigenous feminine power values in the twenty-first century.

Arieahn Matamonasa-Bennett, PhD, is a healer, teacher, artist and writer. She is an assistant professor at DePaul University in Chicago and a licensed psychologist in private practice. Her specialties in clinical practice include connecting to nature and animals (equine-assisted psychotherapy) for healing, growth and change. She has explored issues in the psychology of women including feminist approaches to methodology considering historical, political, and religious contexts of interpersonal violence; the intersectionality of gender ethnicity, race and class; and ecofeminism—the relationship between societal attitudes towards women, animals and nature. She has spoken internationally and nationally, and published in these areas over the last decade.

Kristen Calvert has an MA in art history (San Jose State University) and an MA in women's spirituality (Institute of Transpersonal Psychology). She has worked/volunteered at various museums and galleries, most notably working six years at the San Jose Museum of Quilts and Textiles. She is a certified activities director, and has co-led workshops emphasizing nature, creative expression, the divine feminine and attuning to one's body. She is currently a practitioner-in-training of Rosen Method bodywork. She also creates under the name BlueGreenHorizons, specializing in nature photography, music, mixed media art, flower/feather pendants and Transformational Goddess Flower Cards.

Noël Cox Caniglia is a longtime teacher and adviser of graduate and doctoral students at Prescott College in Arizona. Her recent scholarly interests embrace post-qualitative research methodologies and methods honoring feminist new materialism and post-humanism. She considers her academic work to be secondary to her passion for living/working within a regenerative ecosystem as a sustainable Arizona cattle rancher—a calling that has been her primary focus for close to forty years. Her research weaves informal, place-based learning with ecologically sound agrarian practices. She studies transformational learning and culturally relevant approaches to teaching/learning that are multi-generational, self-renewing and grown from emergent, entangled models within the more than human world.

Barbara C. Daughter is an author, artist, Intentional Creativity™ teacher, independent scholar and a senior community-living expert serving seniors and their families in Solano County, California. She brings her passions for our Mother Earth, and women's lived, mythical and imagined experiences to the page and canvas, intending to transform herself and her audience. Barbara earned her MA in philosophy and religion with a concentration in women's spirituality from the California Institute of Integral Studies in San Francisco. She has had a lifelong interest in exploring often-hidden beliefs, while seeking to re-establish and dis-cover human's innate connection to the Divine.

Judy Grahn is an internationally known poet, author and social theorist. She has published fourteen books with two in process. She was an early gay activist and founder of Gay Women's Liberation and the Women's Press Collective. Her subjects include LGBT history and mythology, feminist critiques of current crises, new origin theories of inclusion, taking racism personally, stories of how to engage with creature-minds, and spirit and poetry of the goddess Inanna. She received The Fred Cody Lifetime Achievement Award for Literature and Social Service from the Northern California Book Reviewers in 2017, and she was inducted into the Tennessee Williams' Festival Saints and Sinners Hall of Fame in 2019.

Marna Hauk, PhD, teaches graduate students at Prescott and Champlain Colleges and directs the Institute for Earth Regenerative Studies (www. earthregenerative.org), at the convergence of eco-restoration, creativity and the living wisdom traditions. Dr Hauk actively researches, with over ninety peer-reviewed publications and presentations in climate justice, sustainability education, regenerative biomimicry, ecofeminism and research. A fellow of North American Association for Environmental Education, Marna co-edited *Community Climate Change Education: A Mosaic of Approaches* (2017). She serves on ASWM board of directors and co-edited the 2018 Women and Myth volume, *Vibrant Voices: Women, Myth, and the Arts*. Her work inquires: How is the planetary system learning and researching?

Candace C. Kant, PhD, is emeritus professor of history at the College of Southern Nevada. Her dissertation, *Zane Grey's Arizona*, was published by Northland Press. Her second book, *Letters from a Marriage: Dolly and Zane Grey*, was published by the University of Nevada Press. She also co-edited *Heart of the Sun: An Anthology in Exaltation of Sekhmet* and *Stepping into Ourselves: An Anthology of Writings on Priestesses,* both published by Goddess Ink. She is a devotee of Sekhmet and a priestess at the Temple of Goddess Spirituality dedicated to Sekhmet.

Mara Lynn Keller is professor of philosophy, religion and women's spirituality at the California Institute of Integral Studies, where she directed women's spirituality graduate studies from 1998 to 2008. Research centers on Goddess cultures of Old Europe, Crete, and Greece; and women's visionary culture in poetry, fiction and film. Articles include "Eleusinian Mysteries of Demeter and Persephone," "Ritual Path of Initiation into the Eleusinian Mysteries," "Ancient Crete of the Earth Mother Goddess," "Goddesses around the World" and "Women's Spirituality and Higher Education." She taught philosophy and women's studies at the University of California, Riverside, and San Francisco State University, where she co-founded Global Peace Studies.

Award-winning writer **Anne Key,** PhD, is the author of two memoirs: *Desert Priestess*, detailing the years she spent as priestess of the Temple of Goddess Spirituality Dedicated to Sekhmet, and *Burlesque, Yoga, Sex and Love: A Memoir of Life under the Albuquerque Sun*. She is the co-founder of the independent press Goddess Ink, co-editor of *Heart of the Sun: An Anthology in Exaltation to Sekhmet* and *Stepping into Ourselves: An Anthology of Writing on Priestesses,* and the author of several articles. She and Veronica Iglesias created the Jade Oracle deck and co-founded Sacred Tours of Mexico.

Margaret Lynn Mitchell is a mother of three sons, acupuncturist, educator, global explorer and scholar devoted to excavating the lineages and wisdom of sacred female divinity. In 2015, she completed her doctoral dissertation, a feminist cultural history of the abiding legacy of Saint Brigid of Ireland and graduated from the California Institute of Integral Studies with a PhD in philosophy and religion with a concentration in women's spirituality. In 2017, she moved to Ireland where she continues to search for evidence of Brigid's ongoing veneration and glimmers of other European and Mediterranean women's wisdom traditions.

Since the Girl Scouts in the 1960s, **Denise Mitten**, PhD, has explored the outdoors/more-than-human worlds with other women. Trained in forest ecology, she combines the ethics of care with expert outdoor skills from SCUBA to mountaineering and ecofeminism to help women learn outdoor living and traveling skills as well as experience the healing power of nature. Denise has worked with thousands of women including women felons, nuns in recovery, and women survivors, encouraging them to develop healthy relationships with more-than-human worlds. She co-authored *Natural Environments and Human Health* (2014) and co-edited the *Palgrave International Handbook of Women and Outdoor Learning* (2019).

Monica Mody holds a PhD in East West Psychology from the California Institute of Integral Studies, where her dissertation was entitled "Claiming Voice, Vitality, and Authority in Post-secular South Asian Borderlands: A Critical Hermeneutics and Autohistoria/teoría for Decolonial Feminist Consciousness." Excerpts from her dissertation have appeared in *Integral*

Review, and she has been awarded the Cultural Integration Fellowship Scholarship. Monica is also a poet and dancer. Her book of cross-genre poetry, *Kala Pani,* is out from 1913 Press.

Scholar and poet **Patricia Monaghan**, co-founder of the Association for the Study of Women and Mythology, passed away in 2012. In addition to many volumes of poetry and edited collections, Patricia's contributions to the fields of goddess studies and women's spirituality include *The Encyclopedia of Goddesses and Heroines, The Encyclopedia of Celtic Myth and Folklore, O Mother Sun, The Goddess Companion, The Red-Haired Girl from the Bog: The Landscape of Celtic Myth and Spirit* and *Wild Girls: The Path of the Young Goddess.* The last years of her life were devoted to ASWM, the Black Earth Institute and Irish folklore study.

Mary Beth Moser holds a PhD in philosophy and religion with a specialty in women's spirituality from the California Institute of Integral Studies. Mary Beth's dissertation, "The Everyday Spirituality of Women in the Italian Alps" (ProQuest, 2013), reflects her passion for her ancestral homeland. Mary Beth resides in the Northwest on the island in the Salish Sea, where she lives in close contact with Nature.

Susan Moulton earned a PhD in art history and languages at Stanford University and is professor emerita of art and art history at Sonoma State University in northern California where she received the Distinguished University Teaching Award. She has worked with a diverse range of rescued feral and domestic animals for forty-five years at her farm in Sebastopol, California, and studies the behavior of feral animals within the context of indigenous spirituality.

Vicki Noble is a feminist healer and wisdom teacher, co-creator of Motherpeace and author of numerous books including *Motherpeace, Shakti Woman* and *The Double Goddess.* For decades she has traveled, giving workshops and lectures in the US and Europe. Her books are translated and published in various languages. At home in Santa Cruz, California, she facilitates private intensives with clients and students from around the world who come to study Motherpeace Tarot or to learn the Tibetan Buddhist Dakini practices she adapts and creates especially for them. In 2017, Christian Dior licensed the round feminist Motherpeace images for a special "cruise line" of clothing.

After cross-cultural teaching in New Mexico, **Mary Louise Stone** lived twelve years in communities around Lake Titiqaqa in Peru and Bolivia. She consulted on community-run tourism with villages and universities, including Duke University. After completing her doctorate in religion and philosophy and winning the Kore Award for Best Dissertation Honorable Mention from ASWM in 2016, she works as an independent scholar in New Mexico and in La Paz, Bolivia, with the "Qamasa Weaving Insights Community." Her research interests include Pachamama, landscape sites, inclusive and gender-balanced Andean communities and mother-centered societies today and in archaeological remains.

Dawn Work-MaKinne is an independent scholar of Germanic goddess traditions. She received her PhD in women's studies in religion from The Union Institute in 2010. Her dissertation titled, "Deity in Sisterhood: The Collective Sacred Female in Germanic Europe," won both the Union Institute Sussman Award and the Association for the Study of Women and Mythology Kore Award. Dawn continues to research, write and teach, and is currently writing her first book. Dawn is on the faculty of the Women's Thealogical Institute and makes her home in Des Moines, Iowa.

www.ingramcontent.com/pod-product-compliance
Lightning Source LLC
Chambersburg PA
CBHW022004080426
42733CB00007B/467